CHEERS ~ FOR FORTY SIX YEARS OF FUN!

GW00370545

The GAMBOLS

BOOK Nº 46

by Barry Appleby and Roger Mahoney.

Published by
Pedigree
The Old Rectory
Matford Lane , Exeter
Devon EX2 4PS
under licence fromExpress Newspapers plc
Printed in Italy.

£6.99

(GA46)

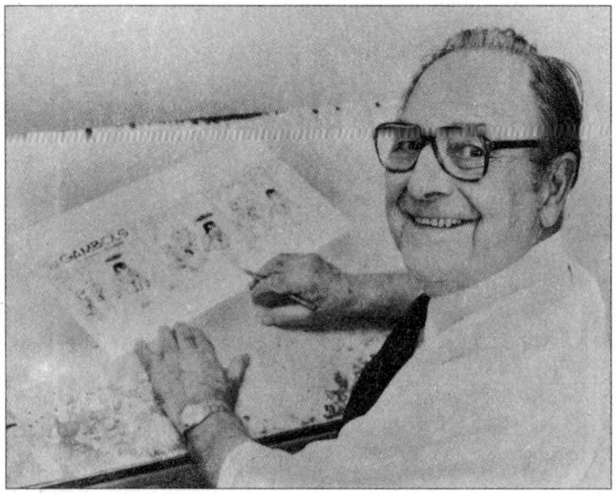

All cartoons on pages 3 - 48 are copyright of Barry Appleby, 1997.

For almost a half a century the Gambols strip has been supported by Express News papers. From its creation in 1947, when Barry Appleby and his wife Dobs jointly produced their observations on postwar married life, it has captured perfectly our domestic relationships.

With Barry's death last year the strip was continued by his great friend and fan, Roger Mahoney. Roger's strips appear from page fifty of this collection bringing George and Gaye, Flivver and Miggy right into the 1990's (Yes, there is even a computer game!).

None of the charm is lost in Roger's delightful characterisations which remain as ever wry observations on home life.

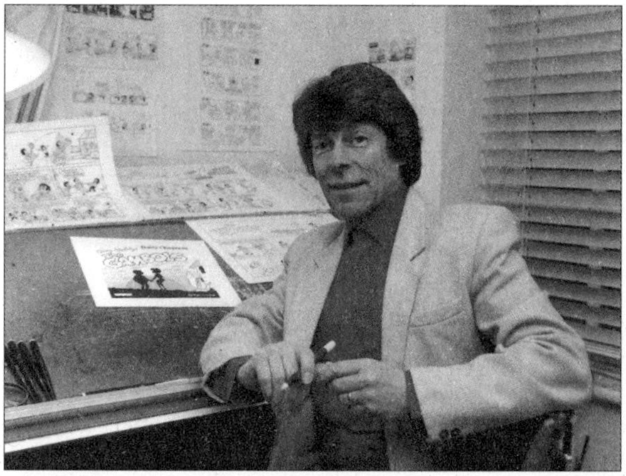

All cartoons on pages 49 - 112 are copyright Barry Appleby & Express Newspapers plc.

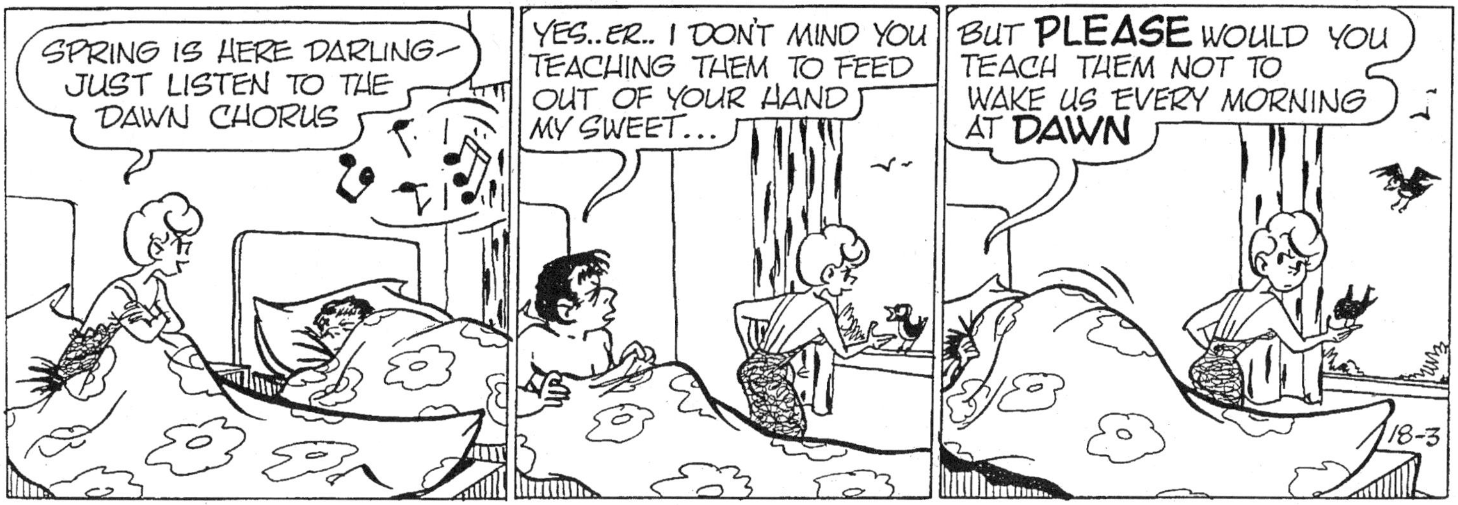
SPRING IS HERE DARLING- JUST LISTEN TO THE DAWN CHORUS
YES..ER.. I DON'T MIND YOU TEACHING THEM TO FEED OUT OF YOUR HAND MY SWEET...
BUT **PLEASE** WOULD YOU TEACH THEM NOT TO WAKE US EVERY MORNING AT **DAWN**
18-3

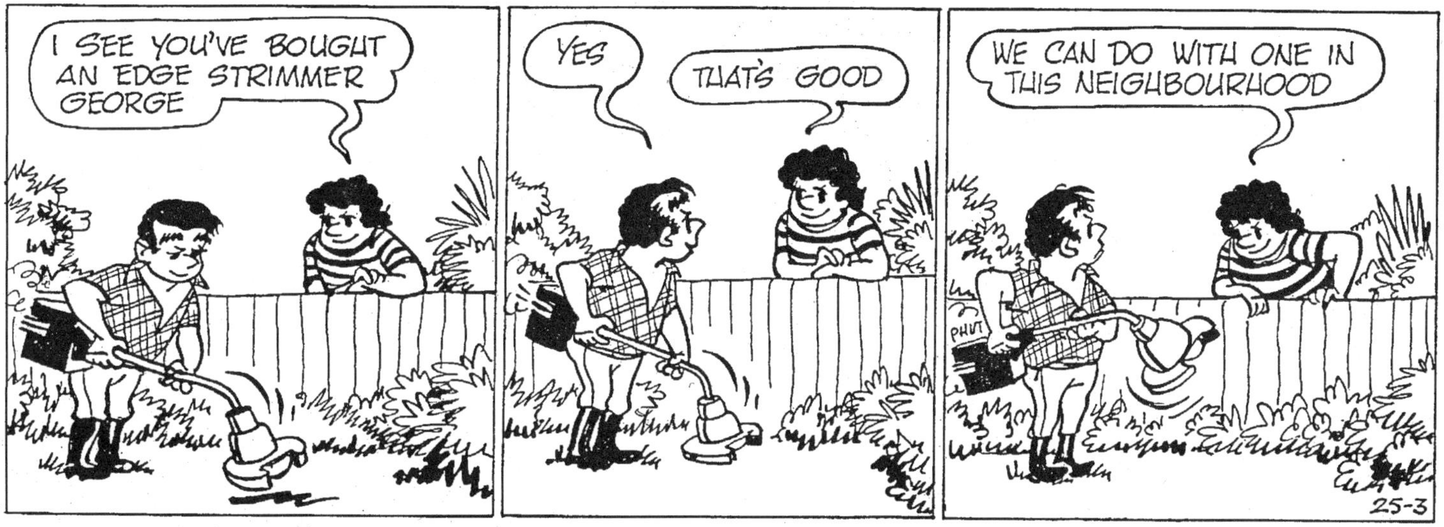
I SEE YOU'VE BOUGHT AN EDGE STRIMMER GEORGE
YES
THAT'S GOOD
WE CAN DO WITH ONE IN THIS NEIGHBOURHOOD
PHUT
25-3

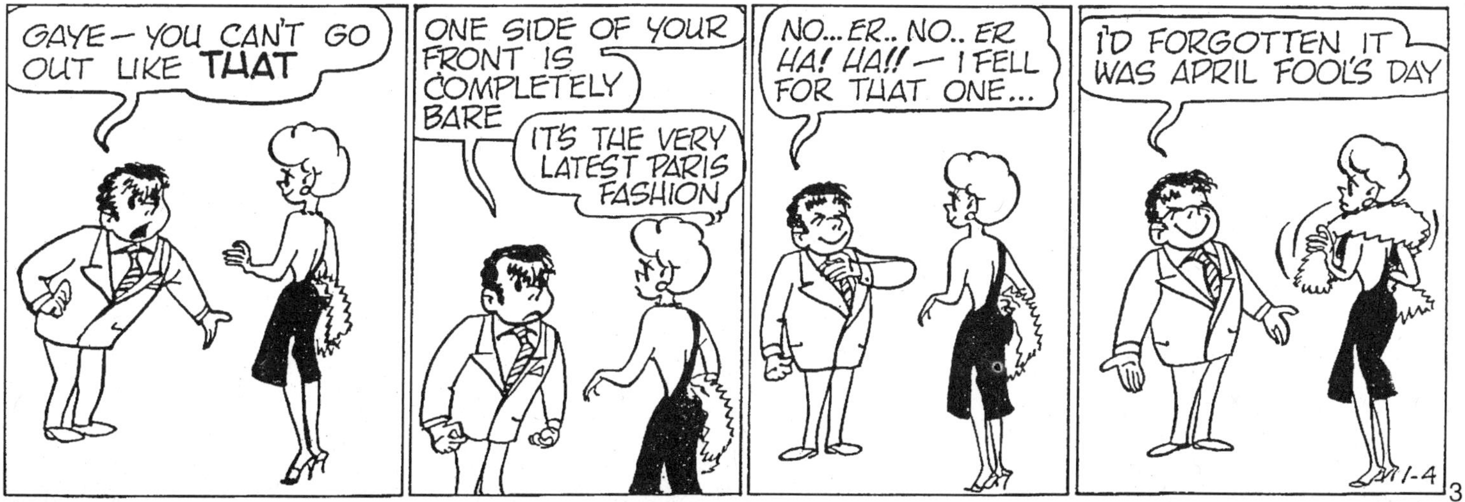
GAYE- YOU CAN'T GO OUT LIKE **THAT**
ONE SIDE OF YOUR FRONT IS COMPLETELY BARE
IT'S THE VERY LATEST PARIS FASHION
NO...ER.. NO.. ER HA! HA!! - I FELL FOR THAT ONE...
I'D FORGOTTEN IT WAS APRIL FOOL'S DAY
1-4

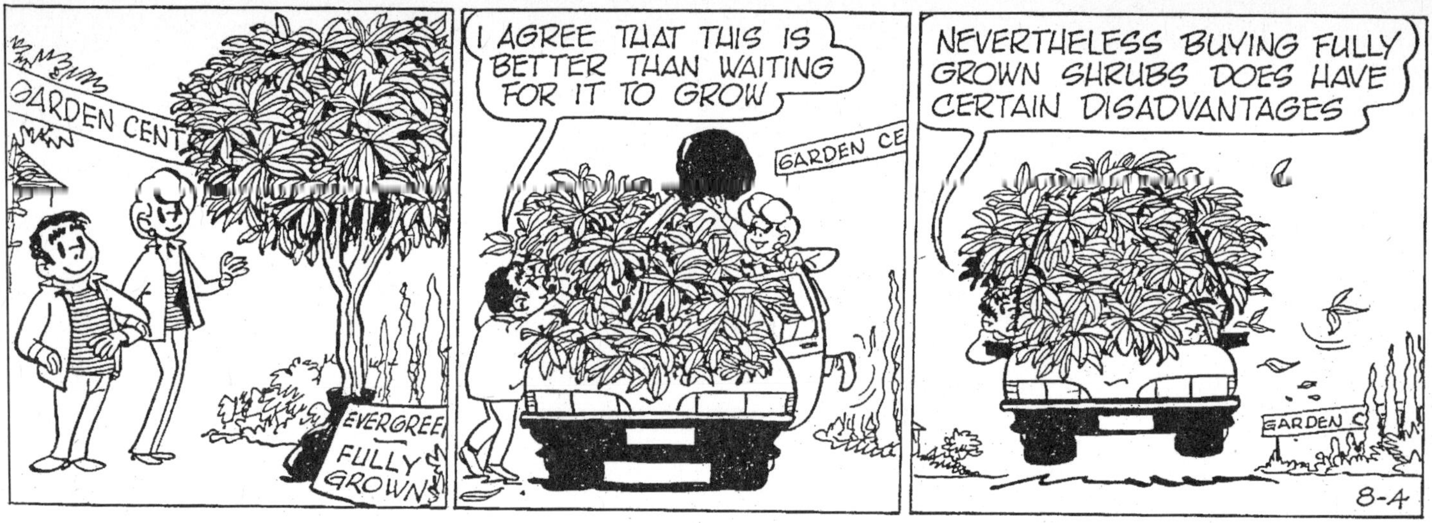
GARDEN CENT
EVERGREE
FULLY GROWN
I AGREE THAT THIS IS BETTER THAN WAITING FOR IT TO GROW
GARDEN CE
NEVERTHELESS BUYING FULLY GROWN SHRUBS DOES HAVE CERTAIN DISADVANTAGES
GARDEN C
8-4

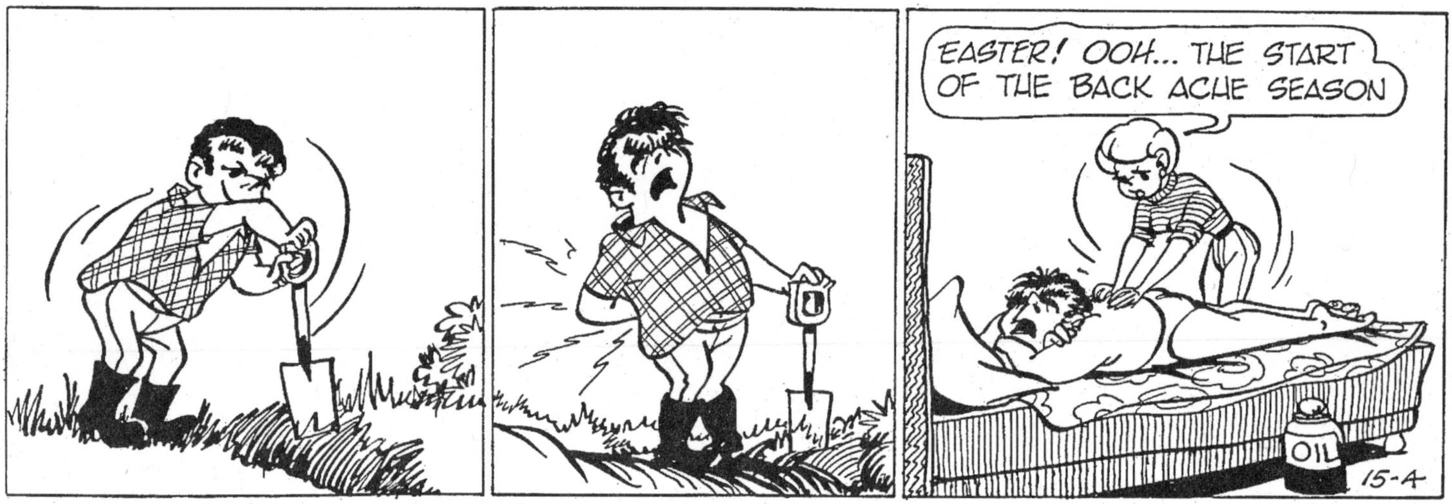
EASTER! OOH... THE START OF THE BACK ACHE SEASON
OIL
15-4

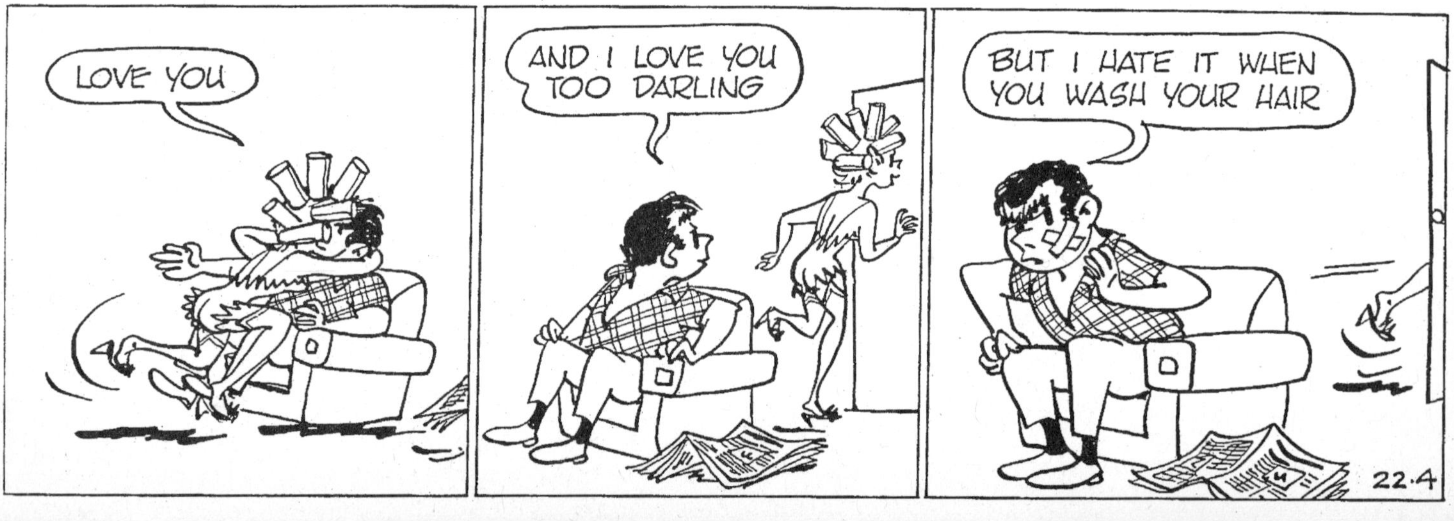
LOVE YOU
AND I LOVE YOU TOO DARLING
BUT I HATE IT WHEN YOU WASH YOUR HAIR
22·4

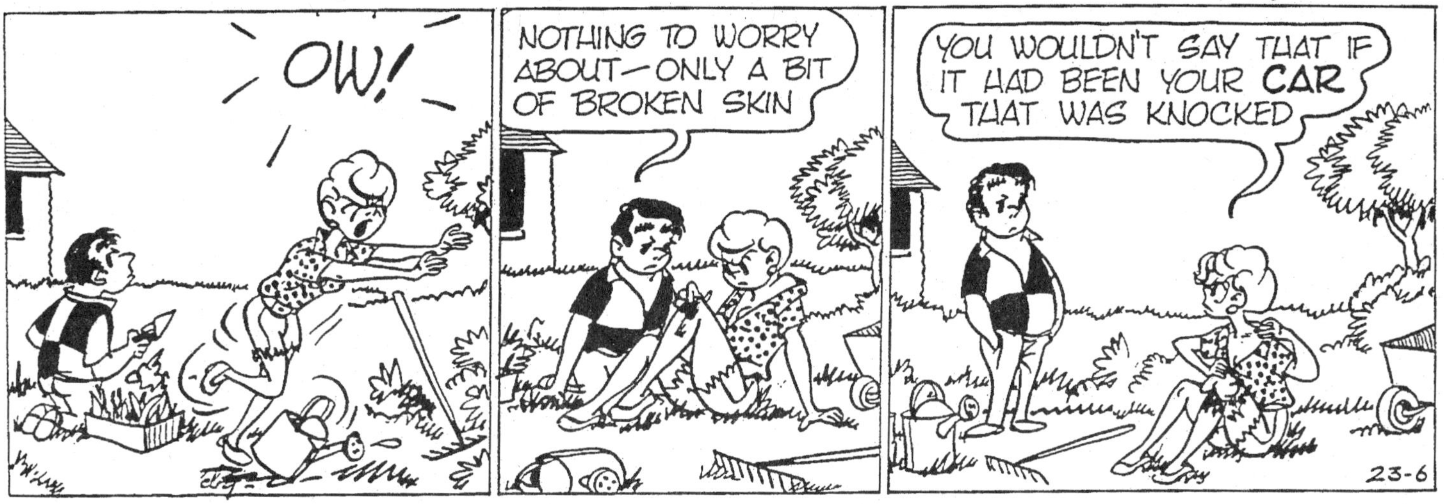
OW!
NOTHING TO WORRY ABOUT—ONLY A BIT OF BROKEN SKIN
YOU WOULDN'T SAY THAT IF IT HAD BEEN YOUR CAR THAT WAS KNOCKED
23-6

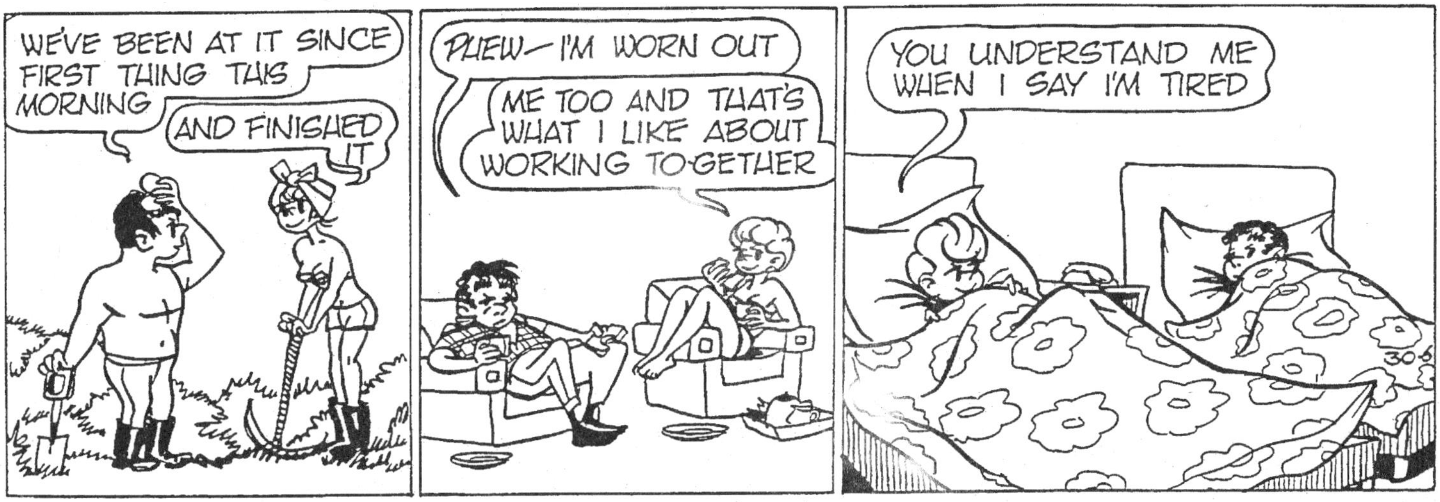
WE'VE BEEN AT IT SINCE FIRST THING THIS MORNING
AND FINISHED IT
PHEW—I'M WORN OUT
ME TOO AND THAT'S WHAT I LIKE ABOUT WORKING TO-GETHER
YOU UNDERSTAND ME WHEN I SAY I'M TIRED
30-6

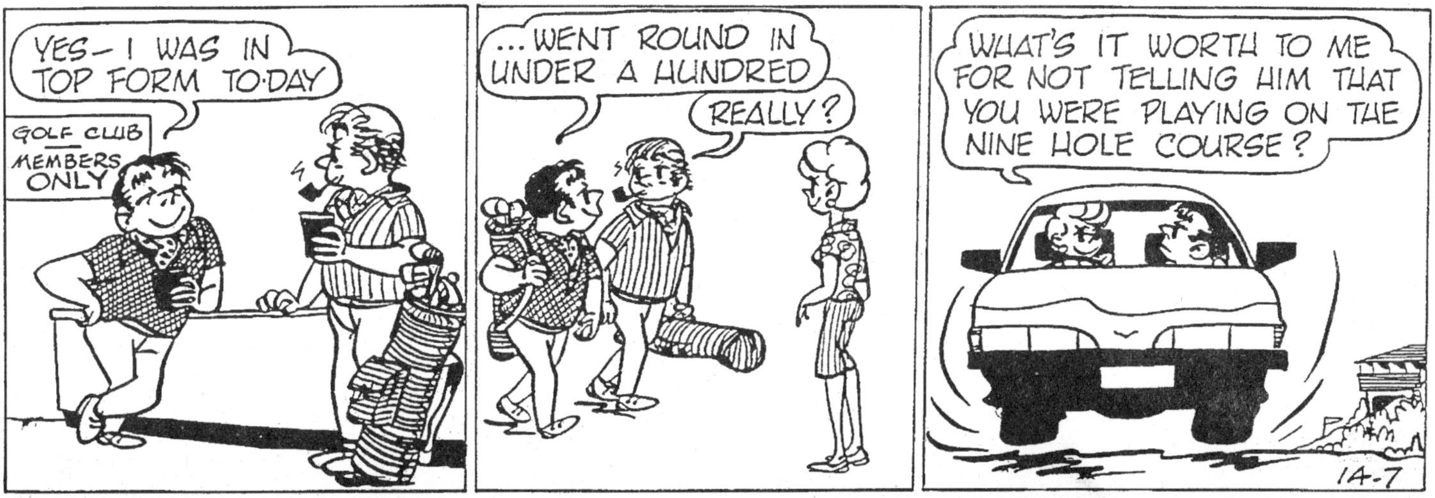
YES—I WAS IN TOP FORM TO-DAY
GOLF CLUB MEMBERS ONLY
...WENT ROUND IN UNDER A HUNDRED
REALLY?
WHAT'S IT WORTH TO ME FOR NOT TELLING HIM THAT YOU WERE PLAYING ON THE NINE HOLE COURSE?
14-7

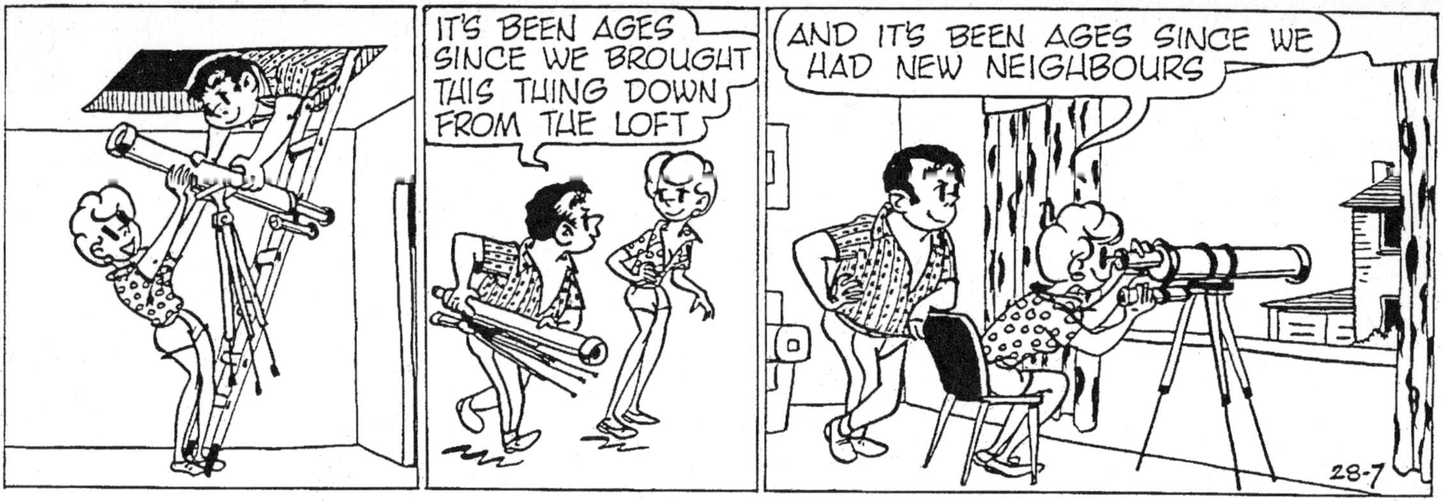
IT'S BEEN AGES SINCE WE BROUGHT THIS THING DOWN FROM THE LOFT
AND IT'S BEEN AGES SINCE WE HAD NEW NEIGHBOURS
28-7

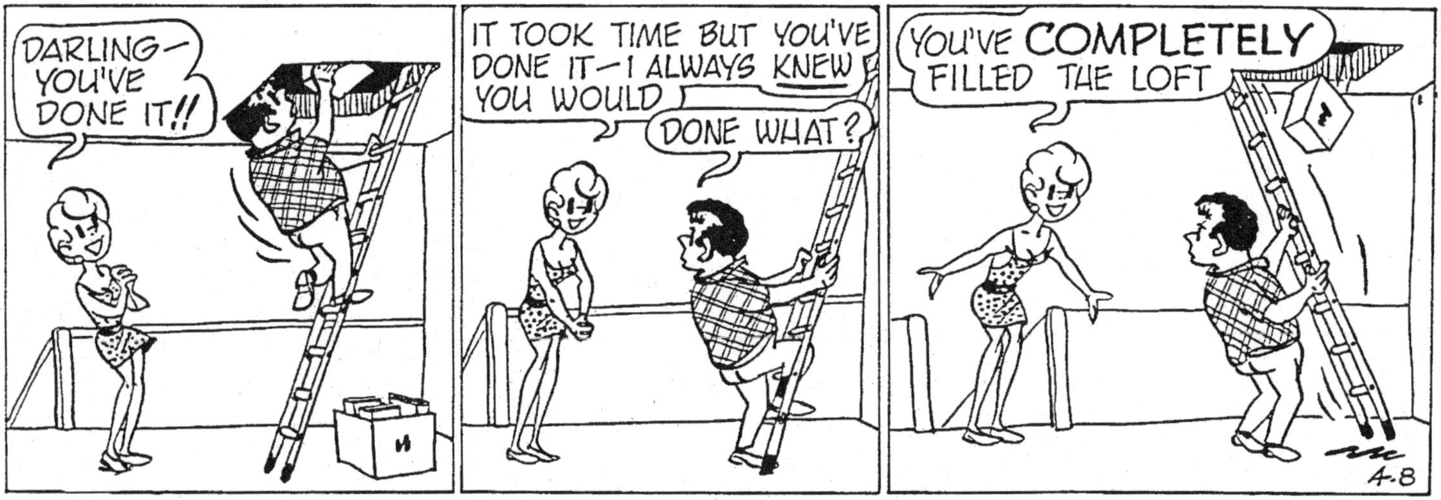
DARLING— YOU'VE DONE IT!!
IT TOOK TIME BUT YOU'VE DONE IT—I ALWAYS KNEW YOU WOULD
DONE WHAT?
YOU'VE COMPLETELY FILLED THE LOFT
4-8

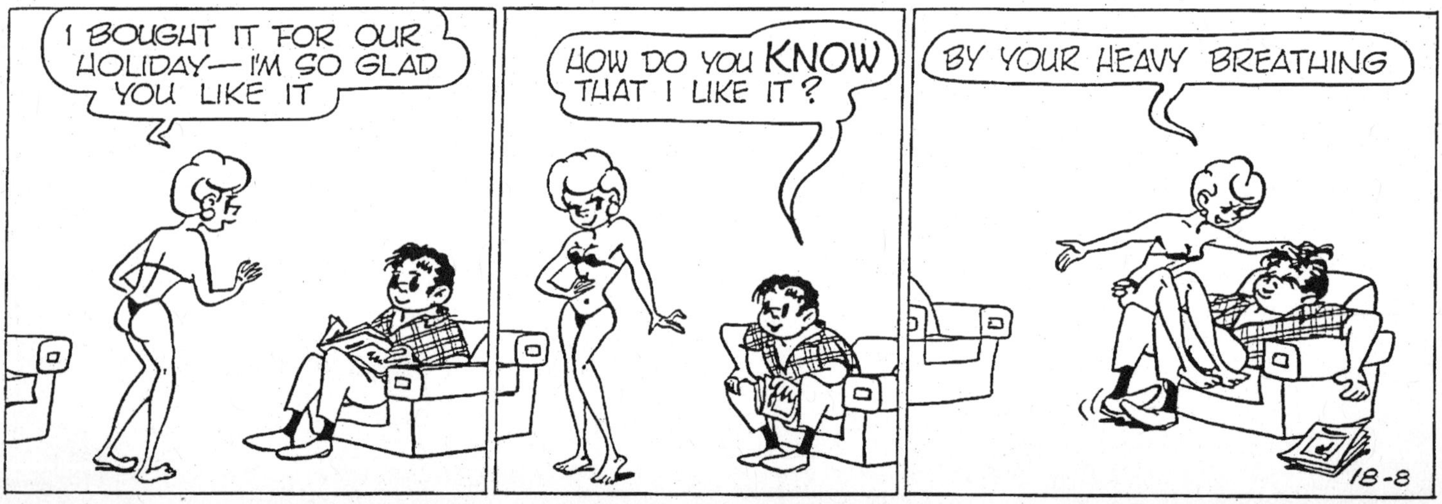
I BOUGHT IT FOR OUR HOLIDAY— I'M SO GLAD YOU LIKE IT
HOW DO YOU KNOW THAT I LIKE IT?
BY YOUR HEAVY BREATHING
18-8

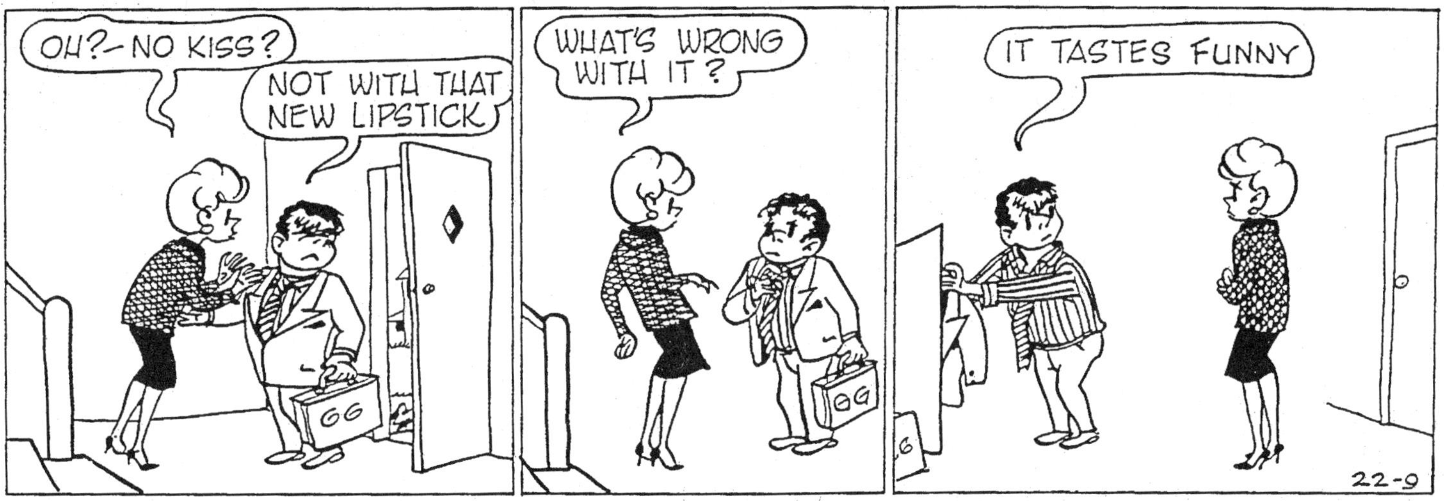
OH?– NO KISS?
NOT WITH THAT NEW LIPSTICK
WHAT'S WRONG WITH IT?
IT TASTES FUNNY
22-9

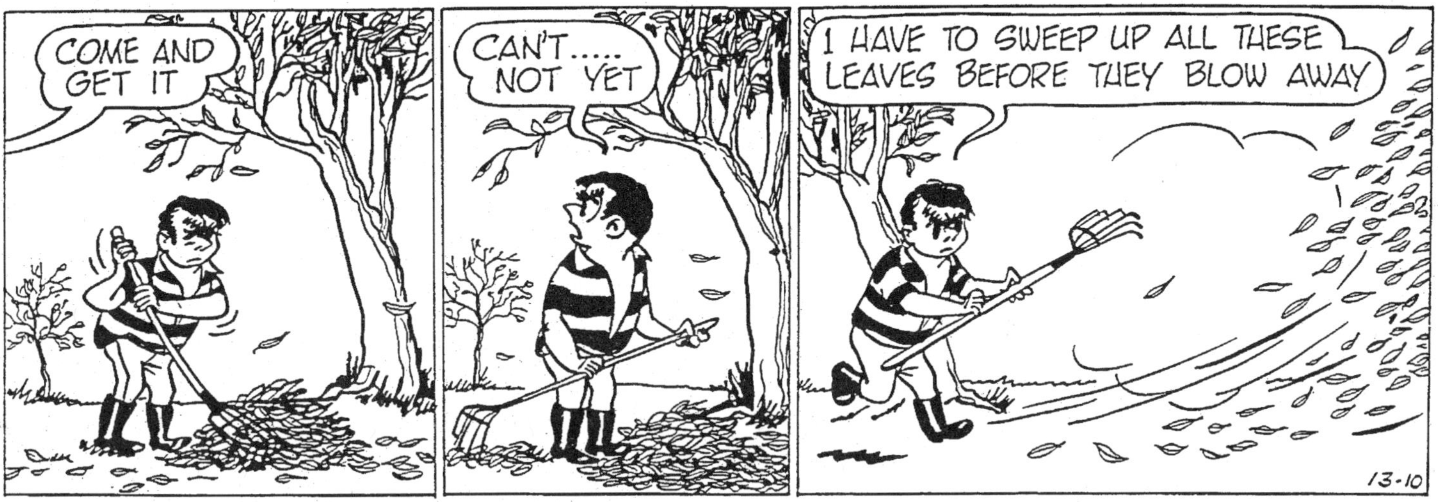
COME AND GET IT
CAN'T..... NOT YET
I HAVE TO SWEEP UP ALL THESE LEAVES BEFORE THEY BLOW AWAY
13-10

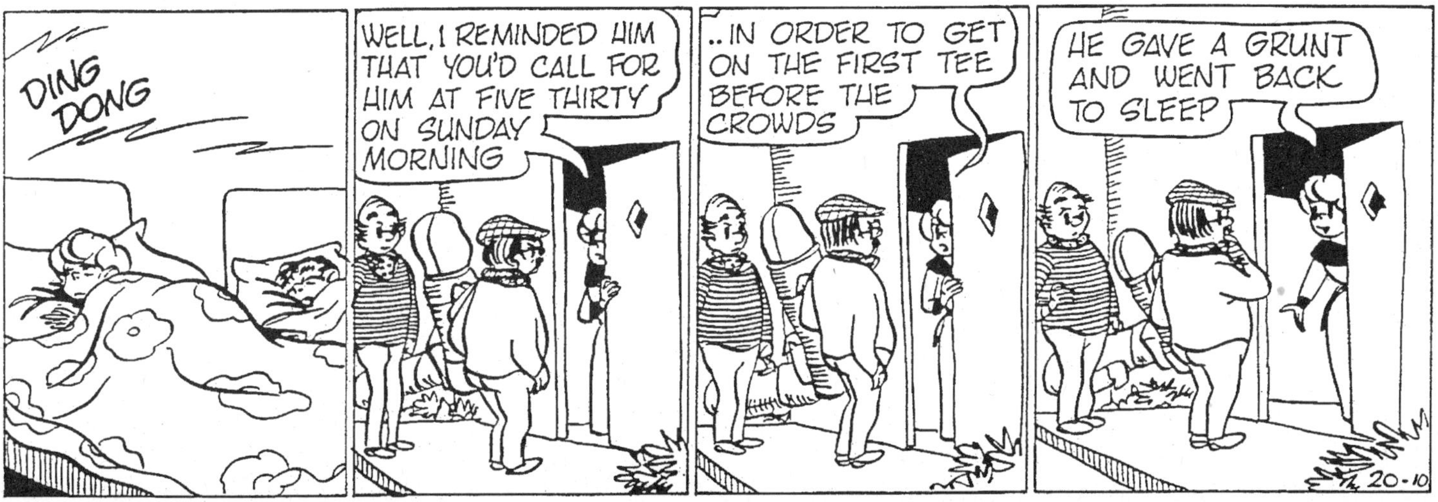
DING DONG
WELL, I REMINDED HIM THAT YOU'D CALL FOR HIM AT FIVE THIRTY ON SUNDAY MORNING
..IN ORDER TO GET ON THE FIRST TEE BEFORE THE CROWDS
HE GAVE A GRUNT AND WENT BACK TO SLEEP
20-10

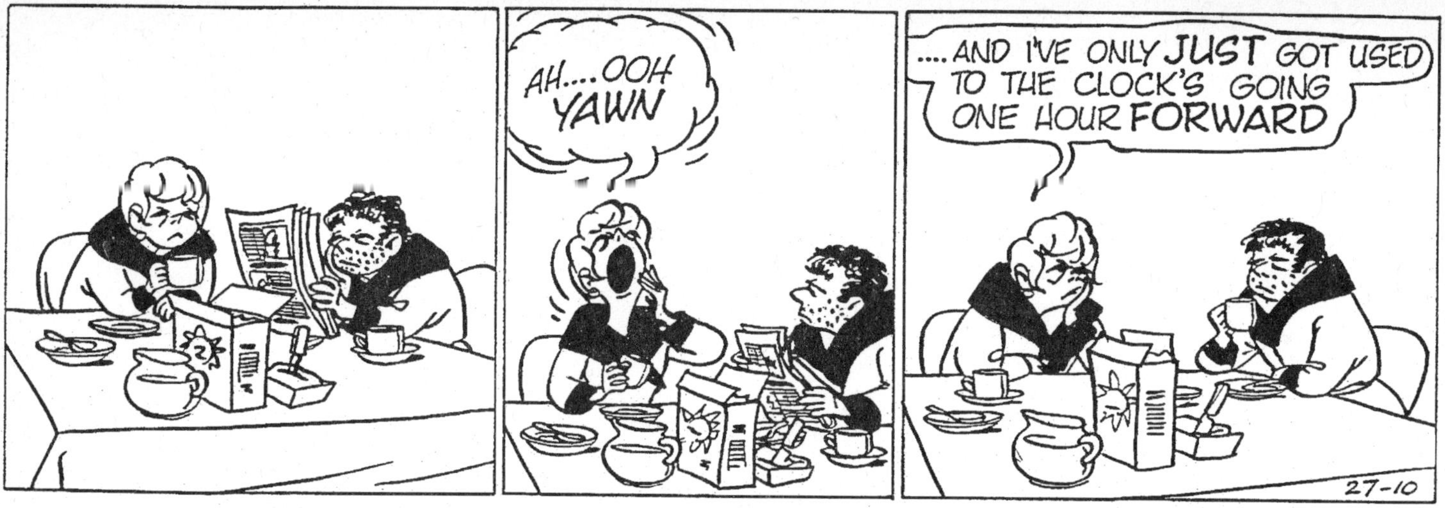
AH....OOH YAWN
....AND I'VE ONLY JUST GOT USED TO THE CLOCK'S GOING ONE HOUR FORWARD
27-10

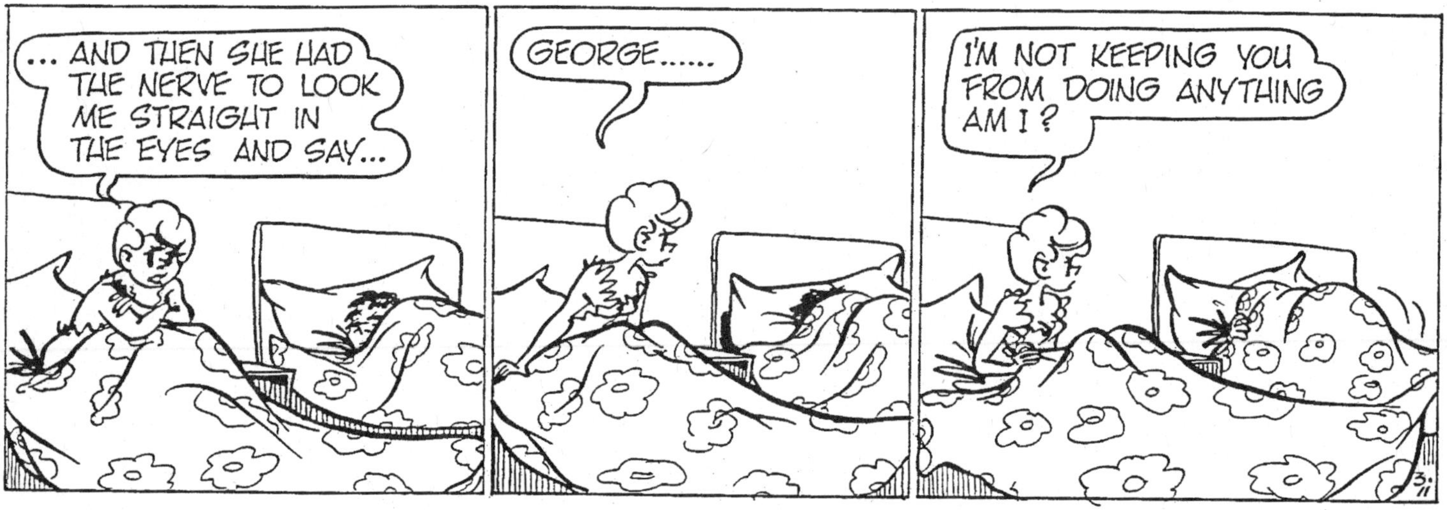
... AND THEN SHE HAD THE NERVE TO LOOK ME STRAIGHT IN THE EYES AND SAY...
GEORGE......
I'M NOT KEEPING YOU FROM DOING ANYTHING AM I?
3-11

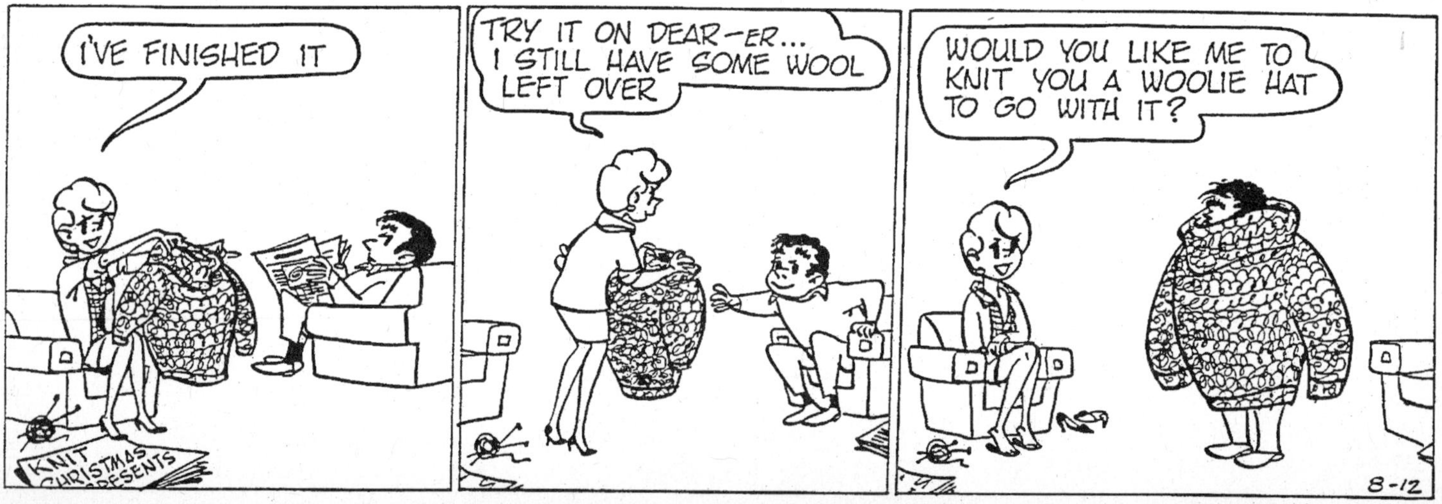
I'VE FINISHED IT
KNIT CHRISTMAS PRESENTS
TRY IT ON DEAR—ER... I STILL HAVE SOME WOOL LEFT OVER
WOULD YOU LIKE ME TO KNIT YOU A WOOLIE HAT TO GO WITH IT?
8-12

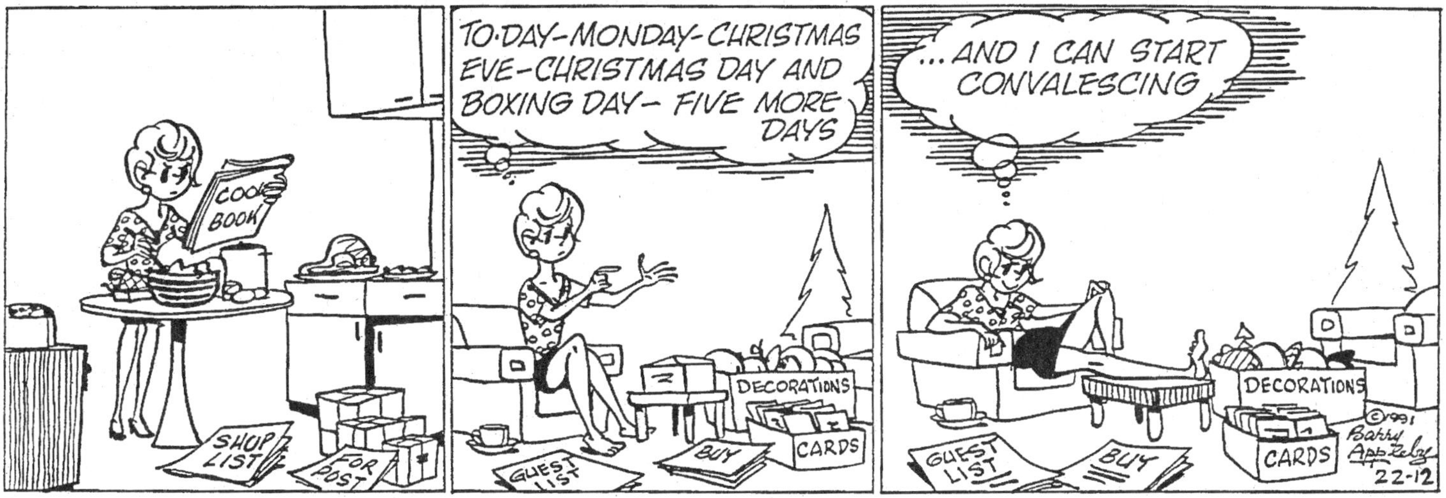
COOK BOOK
SHOP LIST
FOR POST
TO-DAY-MONDAY-CHRISTMAS EVE-CHRISTMAS DAY AND BOXING DAY- FIVE MORE DAYS
DECORATIONS
GUEST LIST
BUY
CARDS
...AND I CAN START CONVALESCING
DECORATIONS
CARDS
GUEST LIST
BUY
©1991 Barry Appleby
22-12

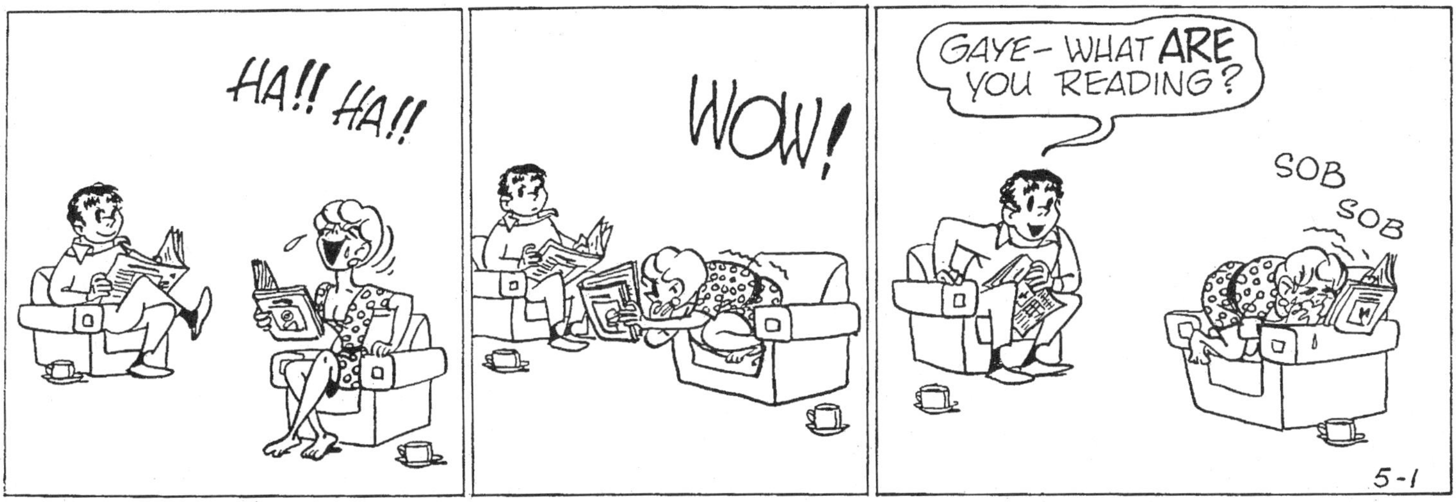
HA!! HA!!
WOW!
GAYE- WHAT **ARE** YOU READING?
SOB SOB
5-1

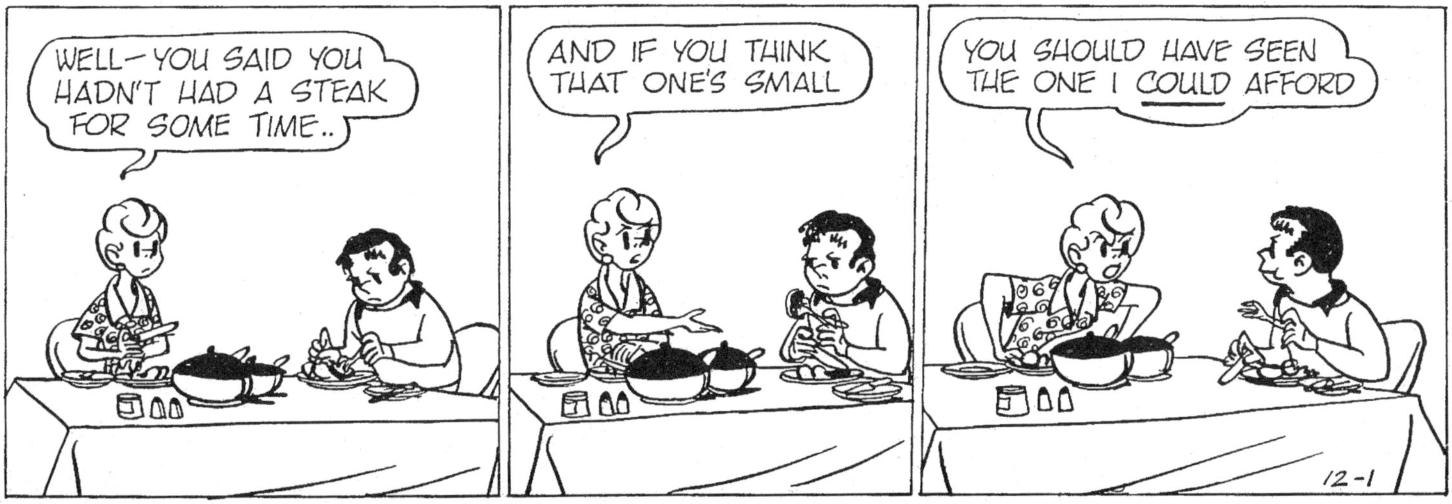
WELL- YOU SAID YOU HADN'T HAD A STEAK FOR SOME TIME..
AND IF YOU THINK THAT ONE'S SMALL
YOU SHOULD HAVE SEEN THE ONE I COULD AFFORD
12-1

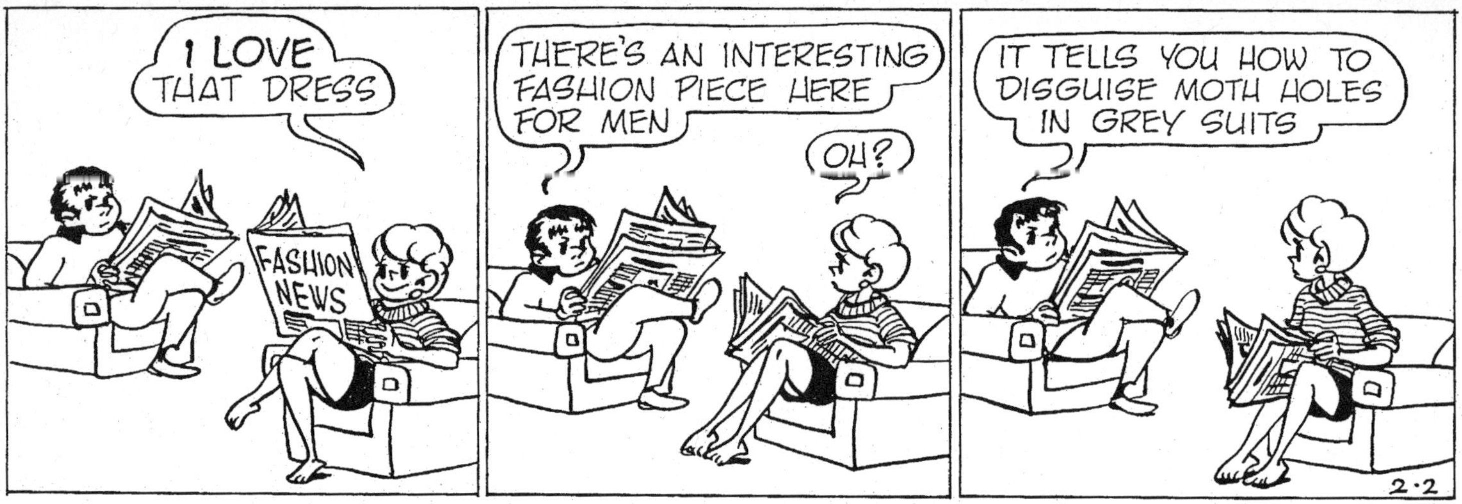
I LOVE THAT DRESS
FASHION NEWS
THERE'S AN INTERESTING FASHION PIECE HERE FOR MEN
OH?
IT TELLS YOU HOW TO DISGUISE MOTH HOLES IN GREY SUITS
2·2

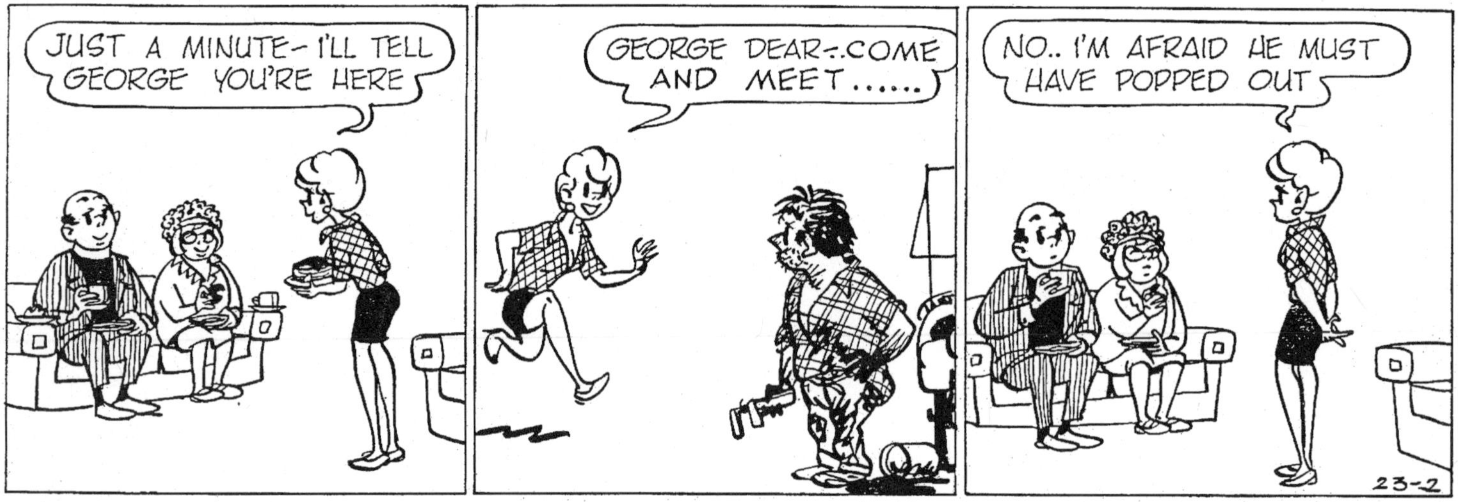
JUST A MINUTE- I'LL TELL GEORGE YOU'RE HERE
GEORGE DEAR-.COME AND MEET......
NO.. I'M AFRAID HE MUST HAVE POPPED OUT
23-2

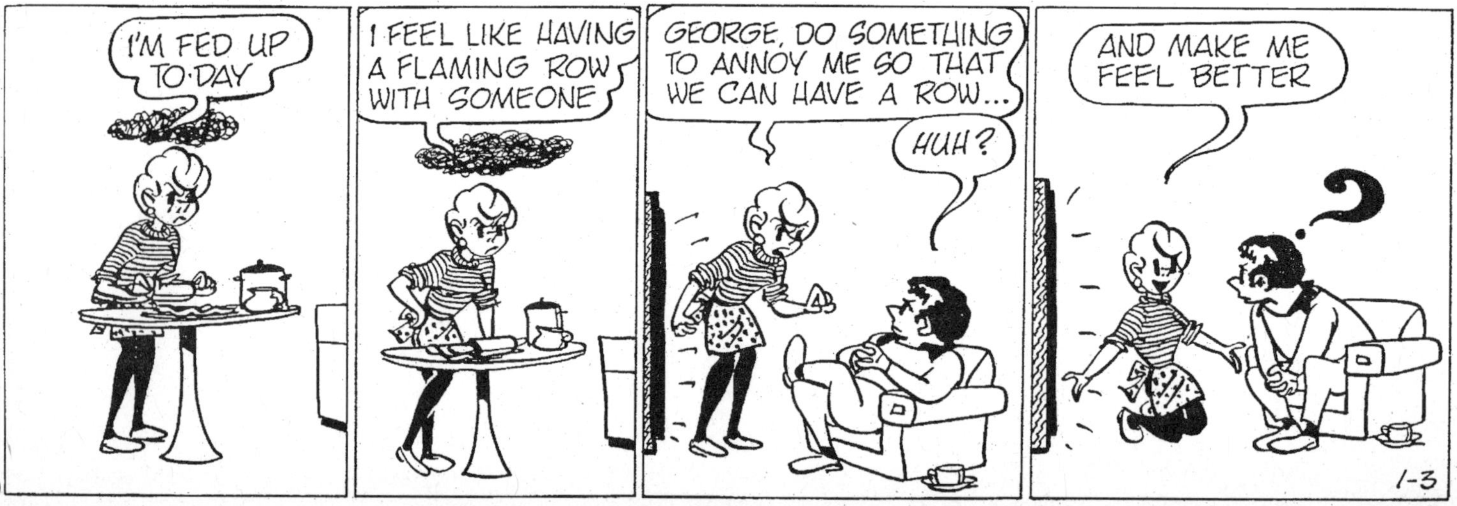
I'M FED UP TO·DAY
I FEEL LIKE HAVING A FLAMING ROW WITH SOMEONE
GEORGE, DO SOMETHING TO ANNOY ME SO THAT WE CAN HAVE A ROW...
HUH?
AND MAKE ME FEEL BETTER
1-3

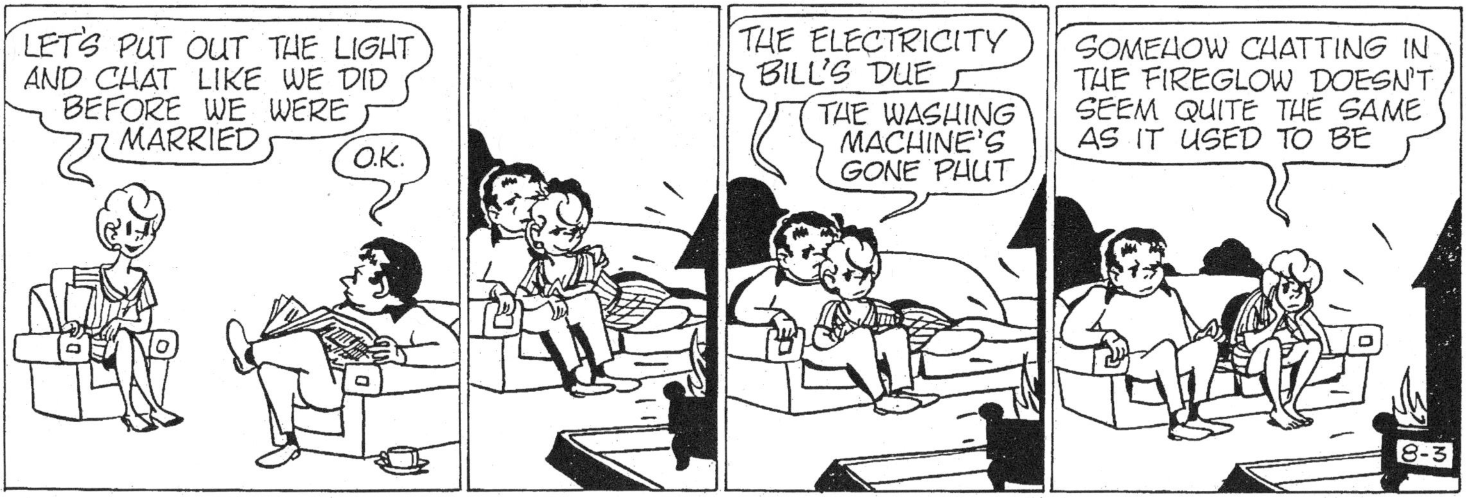
LET'S PUT OUT THE LIGHT AND CHAT LIKE WE DID BEFORE WE WERE MARRIED
O.K.
THE ELECTRICITY BILL'S DUE
THE WASHING MACHINE'S GONE PHUT
SOMEHOW CHATTING IN THE FIREGLOW DOESN'T SEEM QUITE THE SAME AS IT USED TO BE
8-3

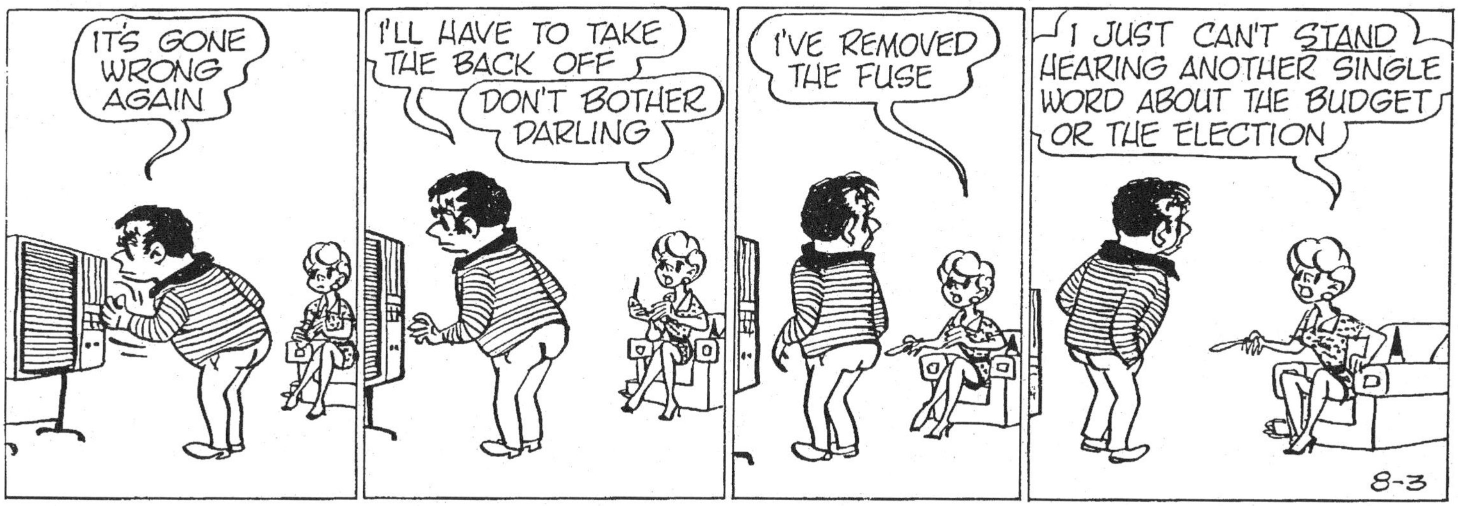
IT'S GONE WRONG AGAIN
I'LL HAVE TO TAKE THE BACK OFF
DON'T BOTHER DARLING
I'VE REMOVED THE FUSE
I JUST CAN'T STAND HEARING ANOTHER SINGLE WORD ABOUT THE BUDGET OR THE ELECTION
8-3

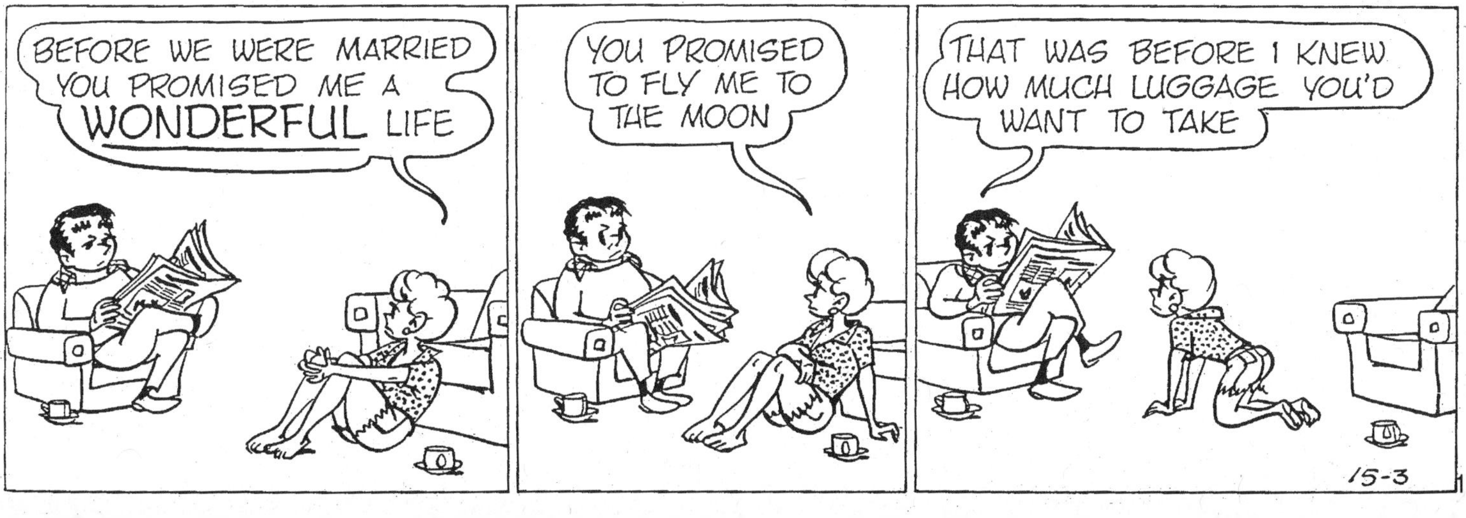
BEFORE WE WERE MARRIED YOU PROMISED ME A WONDERFUL LIFE
YOU PROMISED TO FLY ME TO THE MOON
THAT WAS BEFORE I KNEW HOW MUCH LUGGAGE YOU'D WANT TO TAKE
15-3

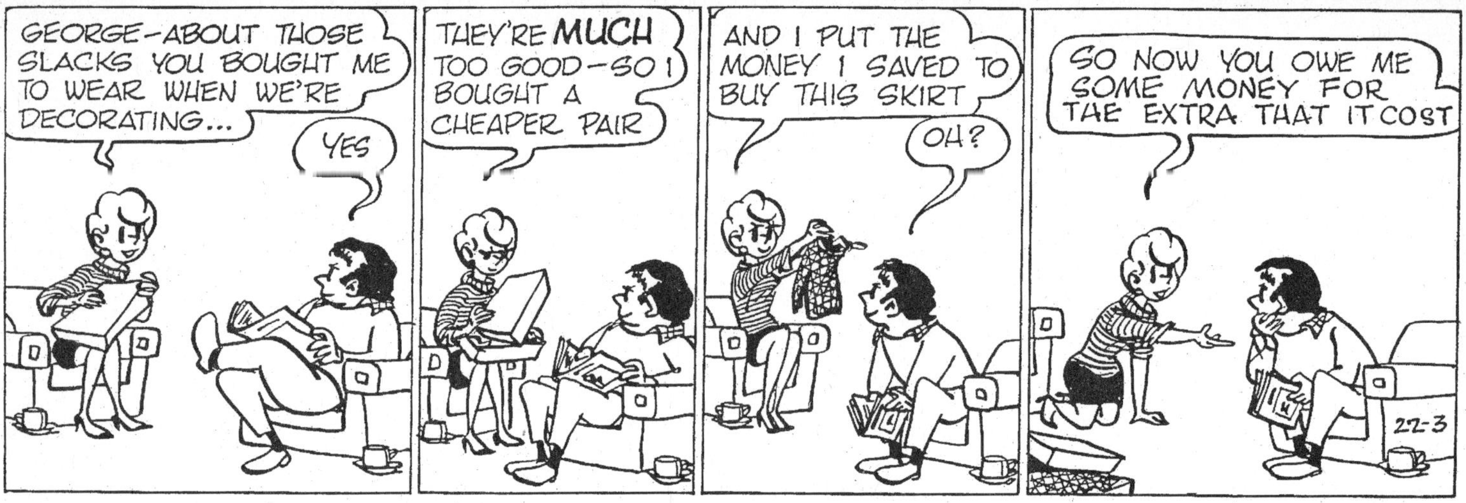
GEORGE–ABOUT THOSE SLACKS YOU BOUGHT ME TO WEAR WHEN WE'RE DECORATING...
YES
THEY'RE **MUCH** TOO GOOD–SO I BOUGHT A CHEAPER PAIR
AND I PUT THE MONEY I SAVED TO BUY THIS SKIRT
OH?
SO NOW YOU OWE ME SOME MONEY FOR THE EXTRA THAT IT COST
22-3

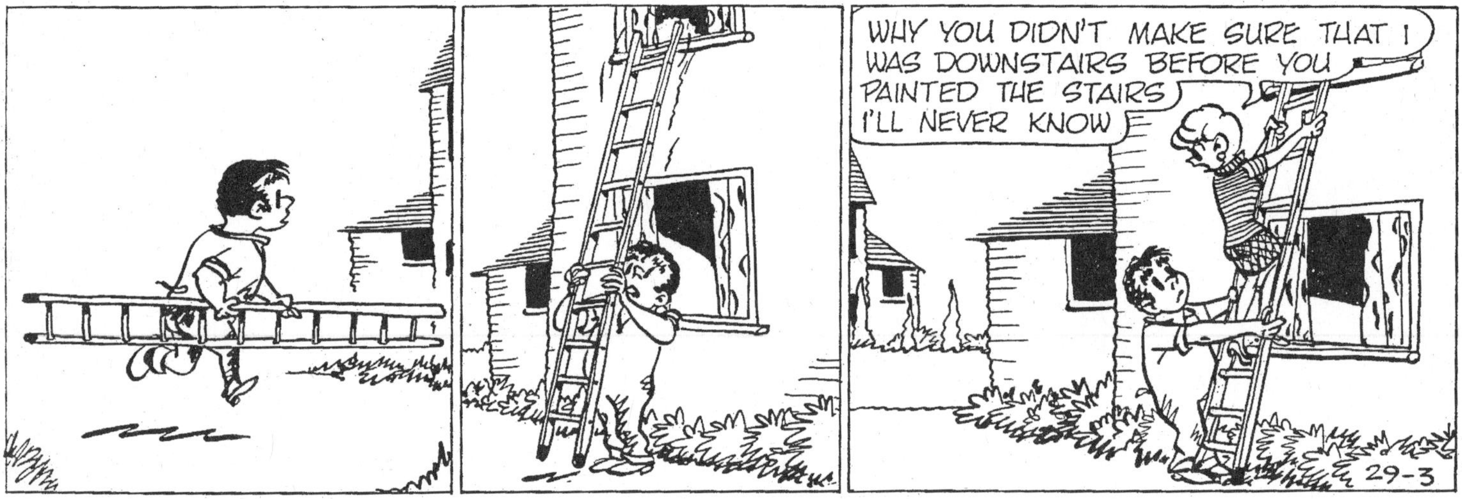
WHY YOU DIDN'T MAKE SURE THAT I WAS DOWNSTAIRS BEFORE YOU PAINTED THE STAIRS I'LL NEVER KNOW
29-3

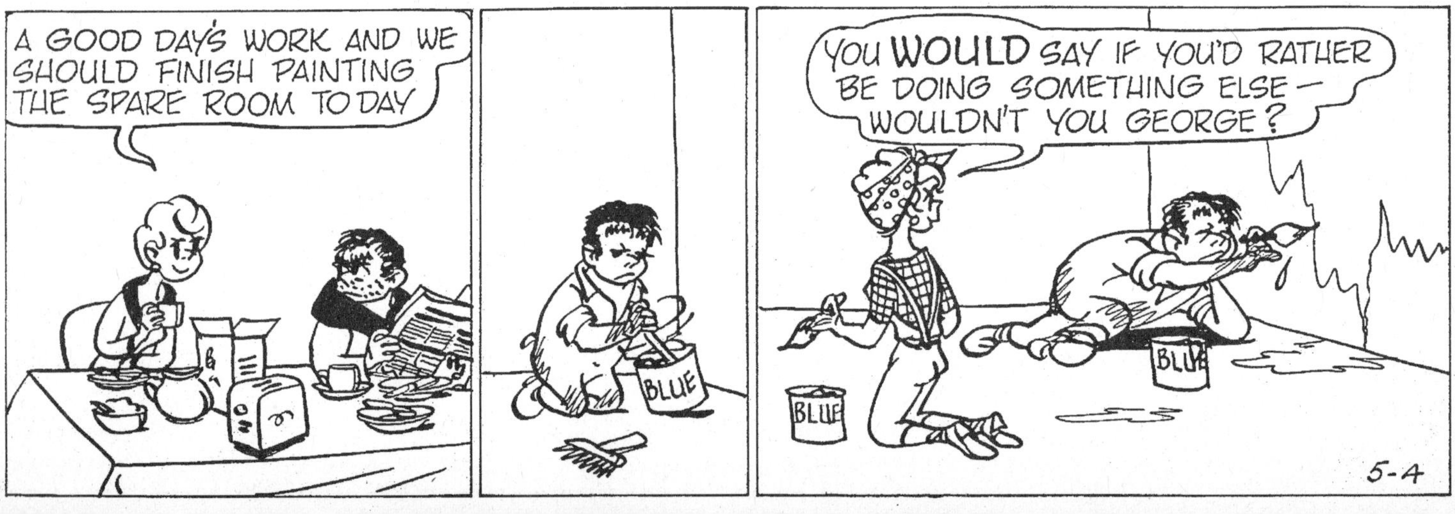
A GOOD DAY'S WORK AND WE SHOULD FINISH PAINTING THE SPARE ROOM TODAY
BLUE
YOU **WOULD** SAY IF YOU'D RATHER BE DOING SOMETHING ELSE–WOULDN'T YOU GEORGE?
BLUE
BLUE
5-4

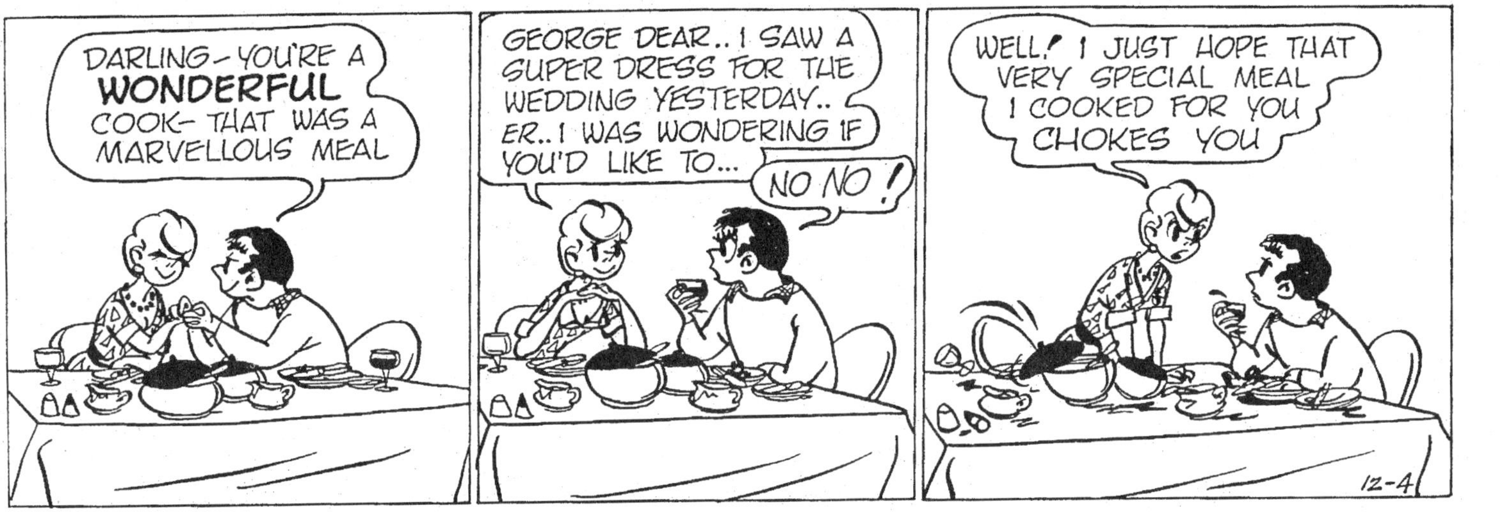
DARLING - YOU'RE A WONDERFUL COOK - THAT WAS A MARVELLOUS MEAL
GEORGE DEAR.. I SAW A SUPER DRESS FOR THE WEDDING YESTERDAY.. ER.. I WAS WONDERING IF YOU'D LIKE TO...
NO NO!
WELL! I JUST HOPE THAT VERY SPECIAL MEAL I COOKED FOR YOU CHOKES YOU
12-4

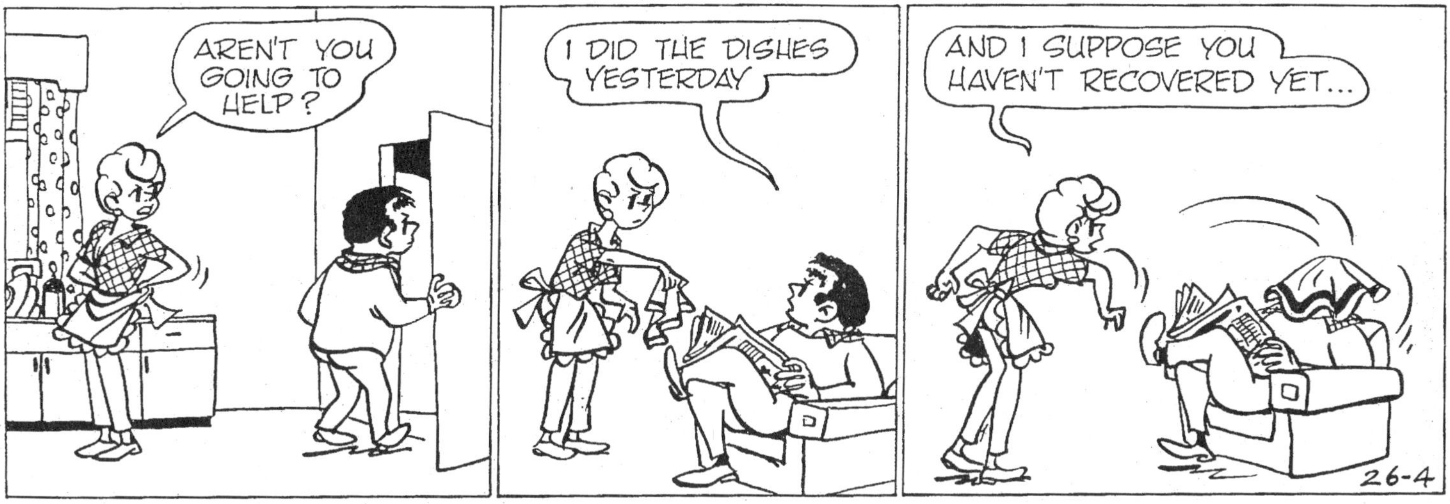
AREN'T YOU GOING TO HELP?
I DID THE DISHES YESTERDAY
AND I SUPPOSE YOU HAVEN'T RECOVERED YET...
26-4

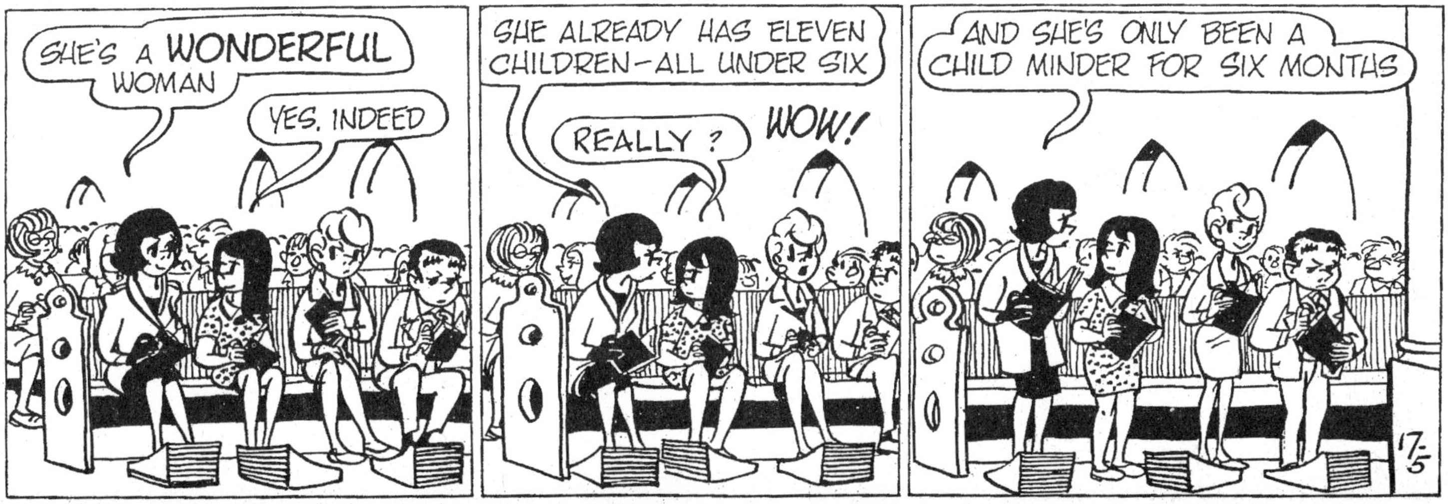
SHE'S A WONDERFUL WOMAN
YES, INDEED
SHE ALREADY HAS ELEVEN CHILDREN - ALL UNDER SIX
REALLY?
WOW!
AND SHE'S ONLY BEEN A CHILD MINDER FOR SIX MONTHS
17-5

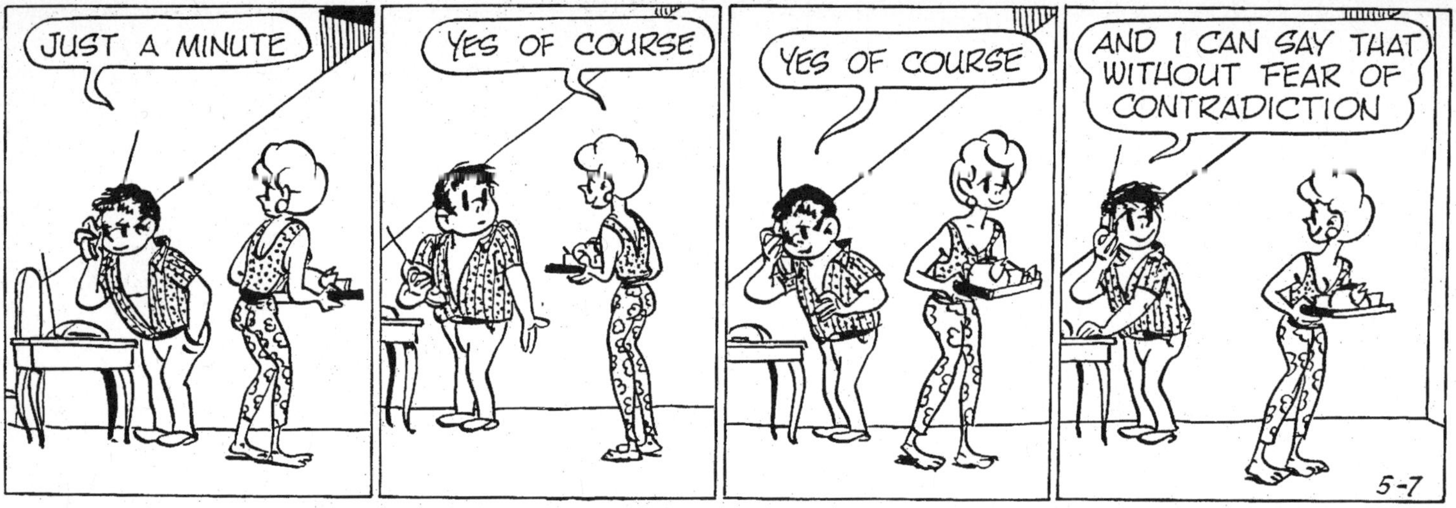
JUST A MINUTE
YES OF COURSE
YES OF COURSE
AND I CAN SAY THAT WITHOUT FEAR OF CONTRADICTION
5-7

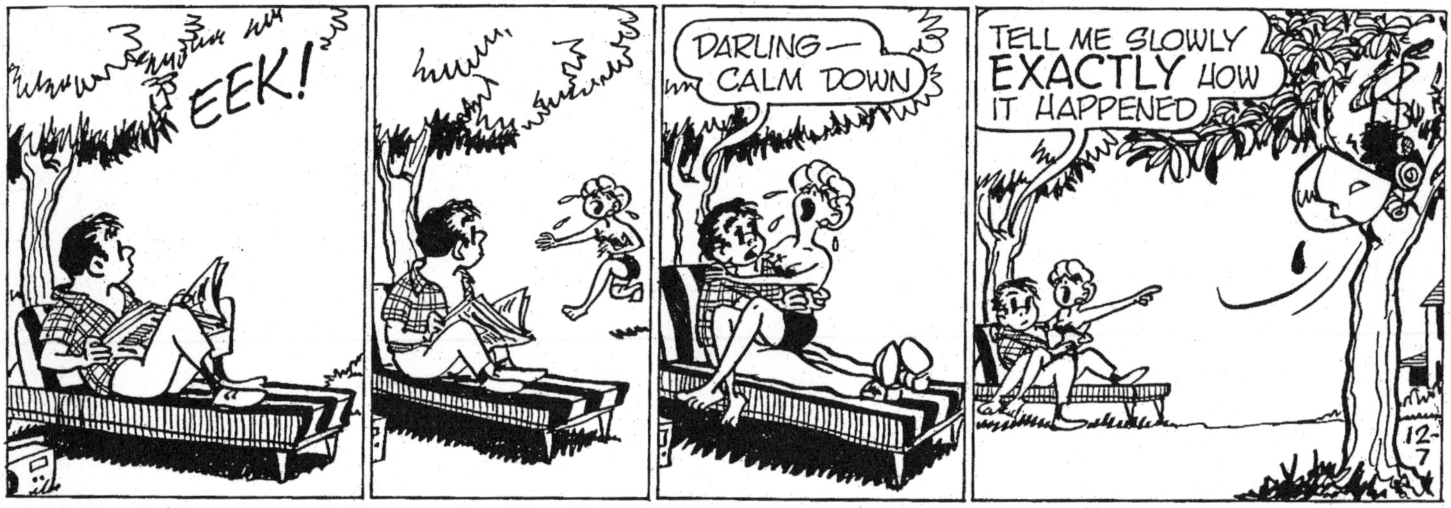
EEK!
DARLING— CALM DOWN
TELL ME SLOWLY EXACTLY HOW IT HAPPENED
12-7

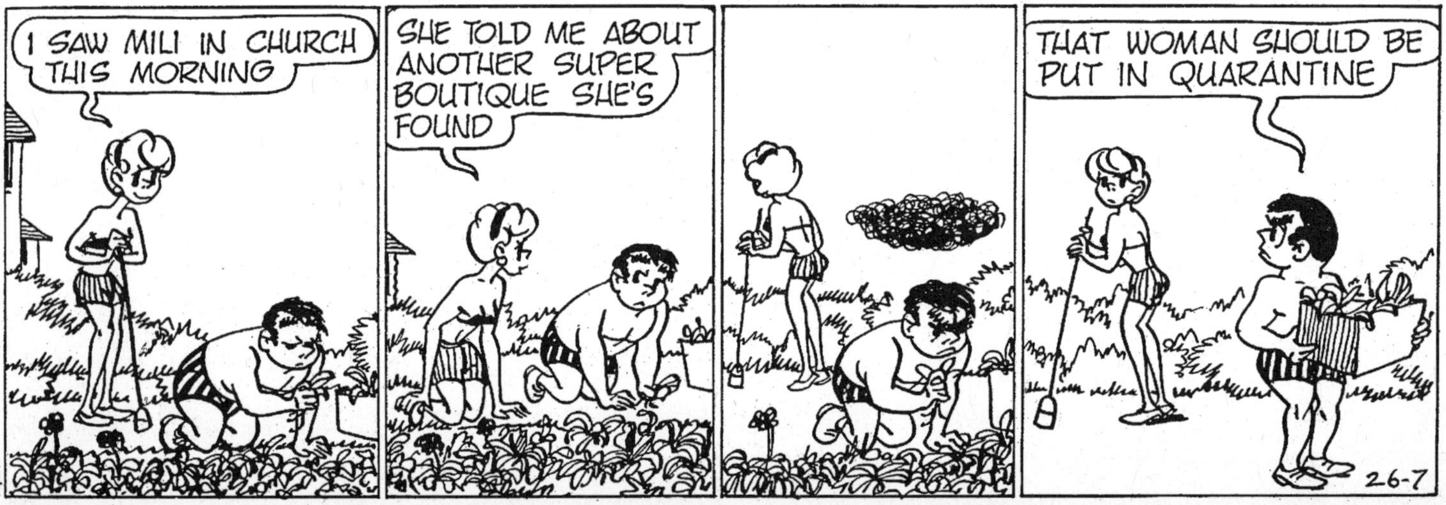
I SAW MILI IN CHURCH THIS MORNING
SHE TOLD ME ABOUT ANOTHER SUPER BOUTIQUE SHE'S FOUND
THAT WOMAN SHOULD BE PUT IN QUARANTINE
26-7

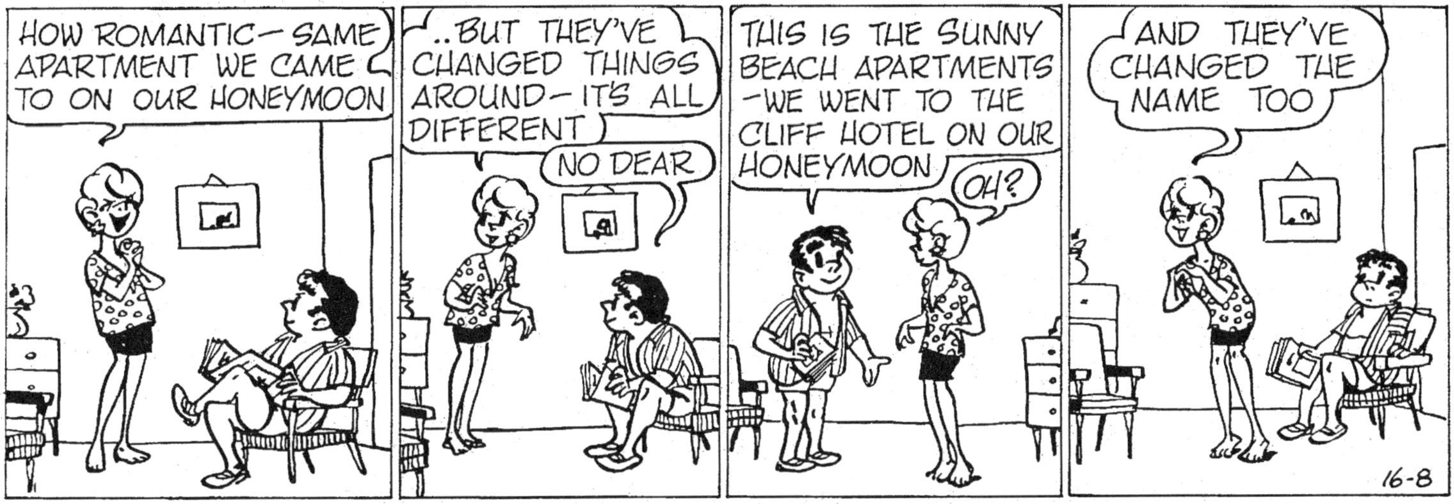
HOW ROMANTIC— SAME APARTMENT WE CAME TO ON OUR HONEYMOON
..BUT THEY'VE CHANGED THINGS AROUND— IT'S ALL DIFFERENT
NO DEAR
THIS IS THE SUNNY BEACH APARTMENTS —WE WENT TO THE CLIFF HOTEL ON OUR HONEYMOON
OH?
AND THEY'VE CHANGED THE NAME TOO
16-8

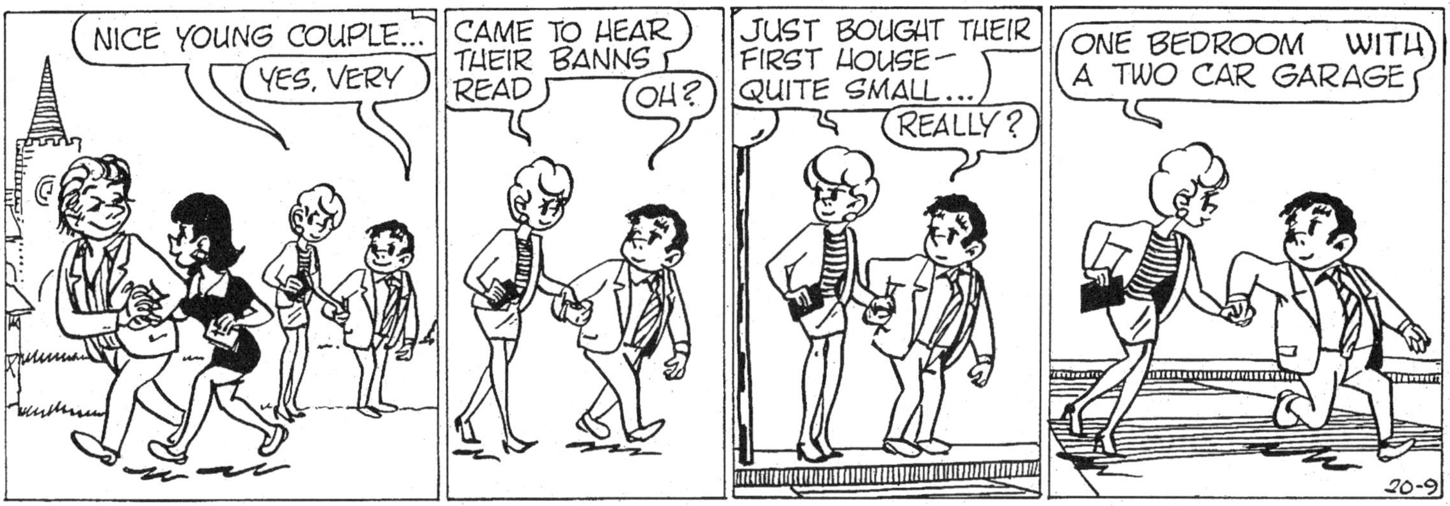
NICE YOUNG COUPLE...
YES, VERY
CAME TO HEAR THEIR BANNS READ
OH?
JUST BOUGHT THEIR FIRST HOUSE— QUITE SMALL...
REALLY?
ONE BEDROOM WITH A TWO CAR GARAGE
20-9

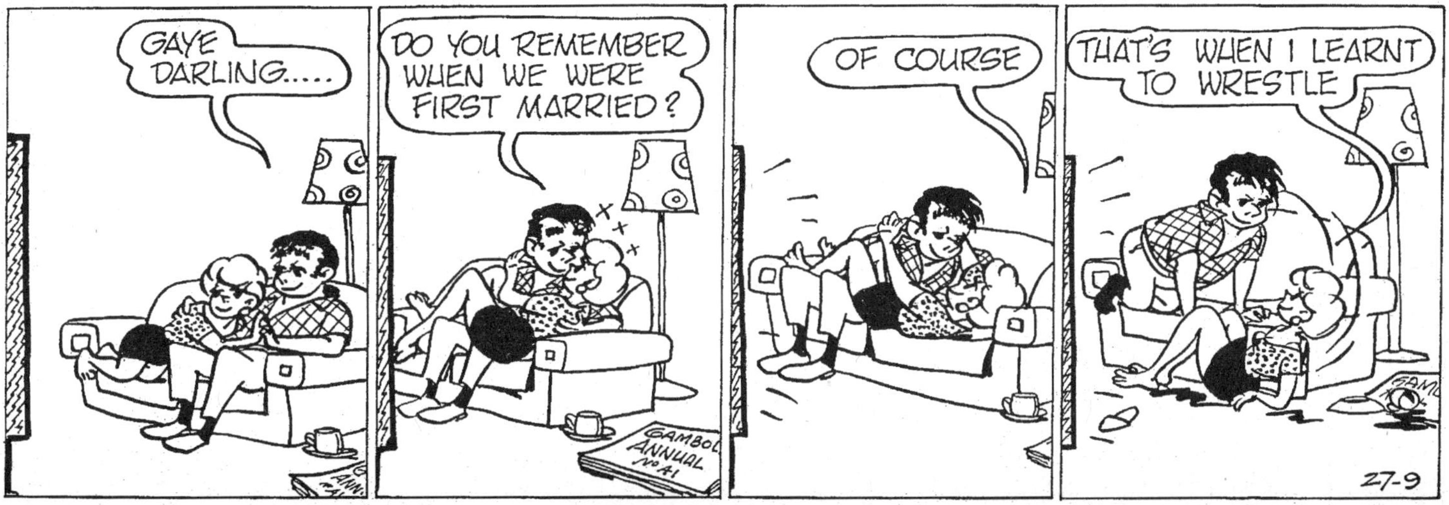
GAYE DARLING.....
DO YOU REMEMBER WHEN WE WERE FIRST MARRIED?
GAMBOL ANNUAL No 41
OF COURSE
THAT'S WHEN I LEARNT TO WRESTLE
27-9

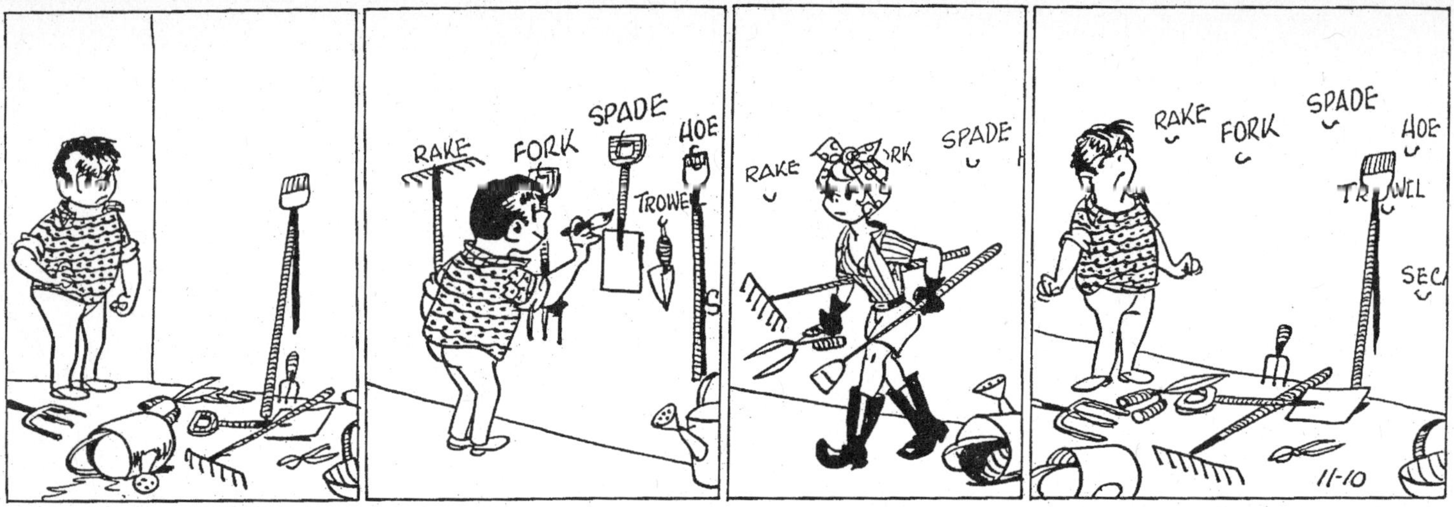
RAKE
FORK
SPADE
HOE
TROWEL
RAKE
SPADE
RAKE
FORK
SPADE
HOE
11-10

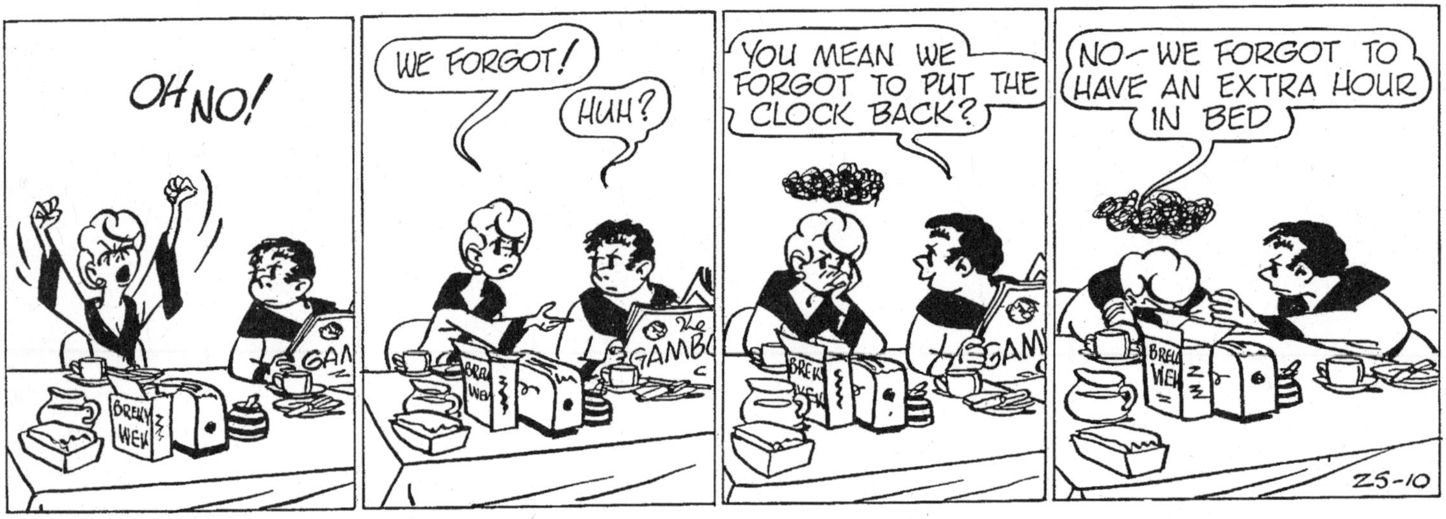
OH NO!
WE FORGOT!
HUH?
YOU MEAN WE FORGOT TO PUT THE CLOCK BACK?
NO— WE FORGOT TO HAVE AN EXTRA HOUR IN BED
25-10

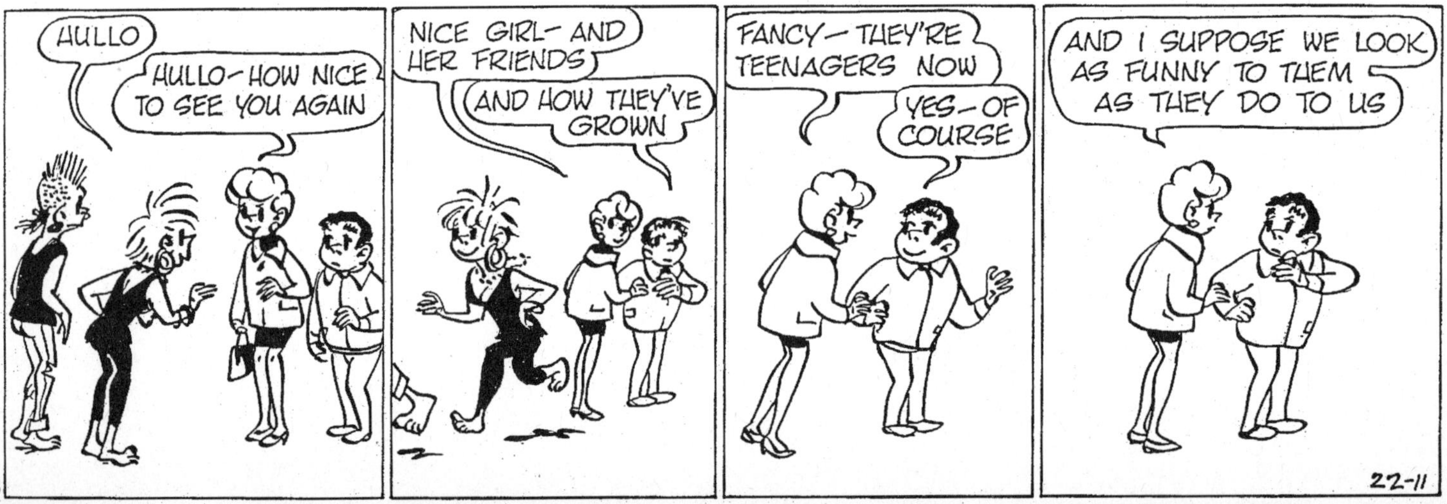
HULLO
HULLO— HOW NICE TO SEE YOU AGAIN
NICE GIRL— AND HER FRIENDS
AND HOW THEY'VE GROWN
FANCY— THEY'RE TEENAGERS NOW
YES— OF COURSE
AND I SUPPOSE WE LOOK AS FUNNY TO THEM AS THEY DO TO US
22-11

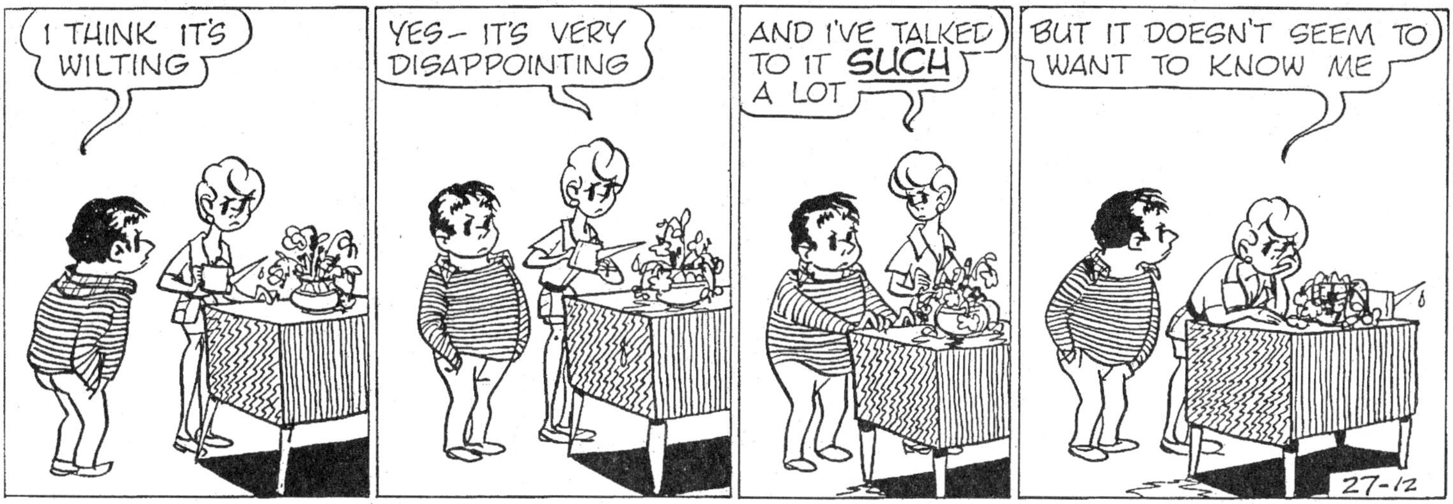
I THINK IT'S WILTING
YES– IT'S VERY DISAPPOINTING
AND I'VE TALKED TO IT SUCH A LOT
BUT IT DOESN'T SEEM TO WANT TO KNOW ME
27-12

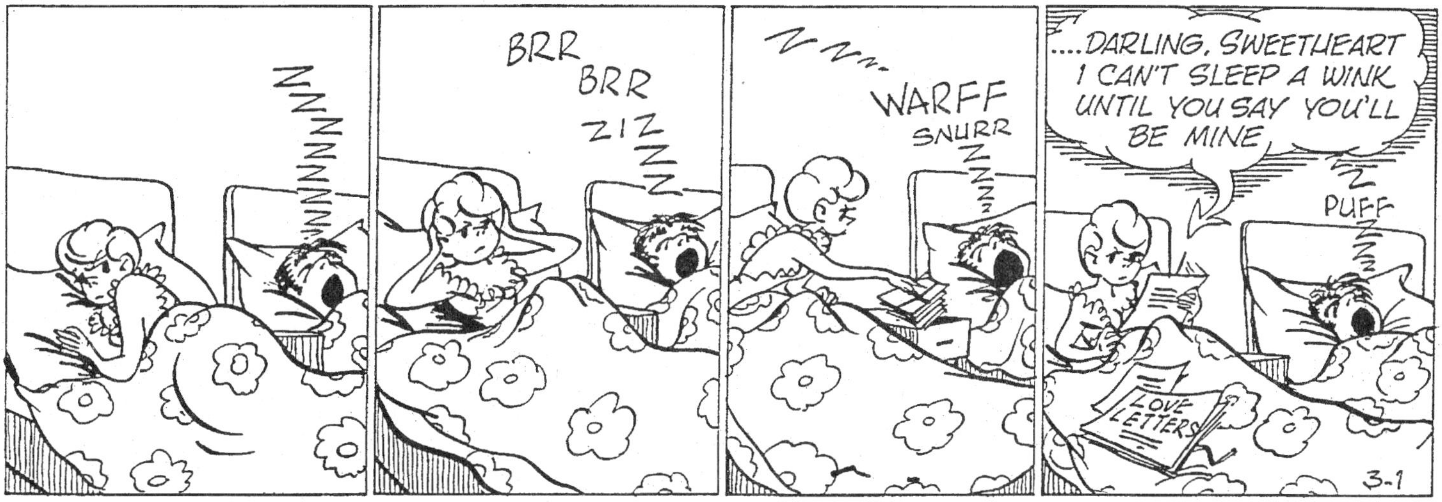
ZZZZZZZZ
BRR BRR ZIZ ZZ
ZZZ..
WARFF
SNURR
....DARLING, SWEETHEART I CAN'T SLEEP A WINK UNTIL YOU SAY YOU'LL BE MINE
PUFF
LOVE LETTERS
3-1

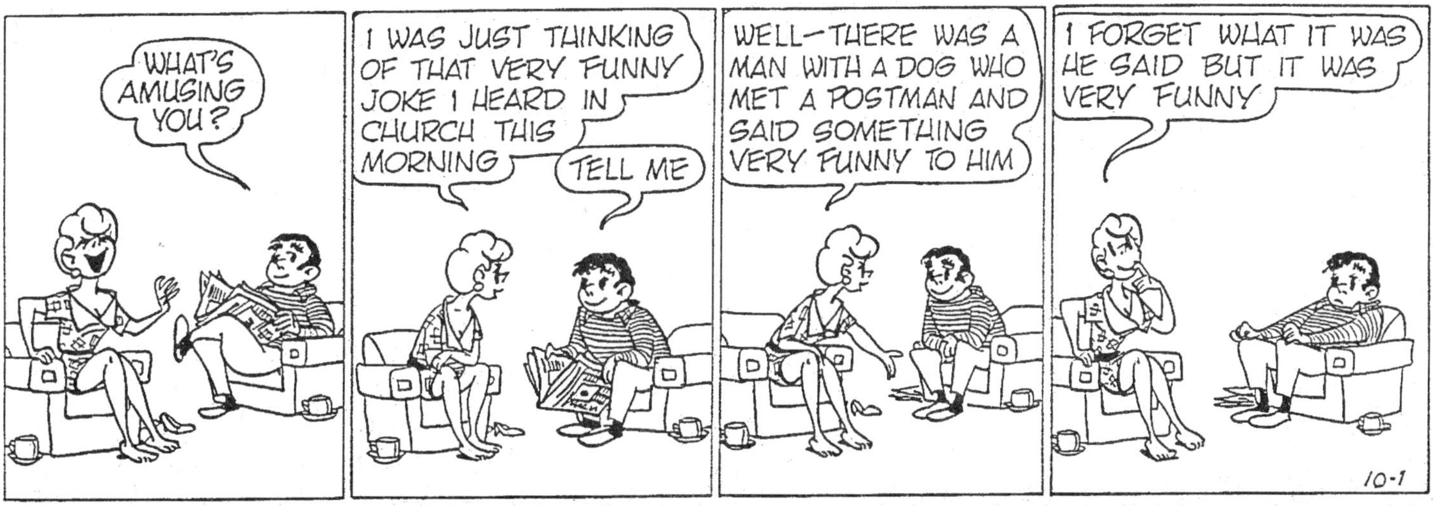
WHAT'S AMUSING YOU?
I WAS JUST THINKING OF THAT VERY FUNNY JOKE I HEARD IN CHURCH THIS MORNING
TELL ME
WELL–THERE WAS A MAN WITH A DOG WHO MET A POSTMAN AND SAID SOMETHING VERY FUNNY TO HIM
I FORGET WHAT IT WAS HE SAID BUT IT WAS VERY FUNNY
10-1

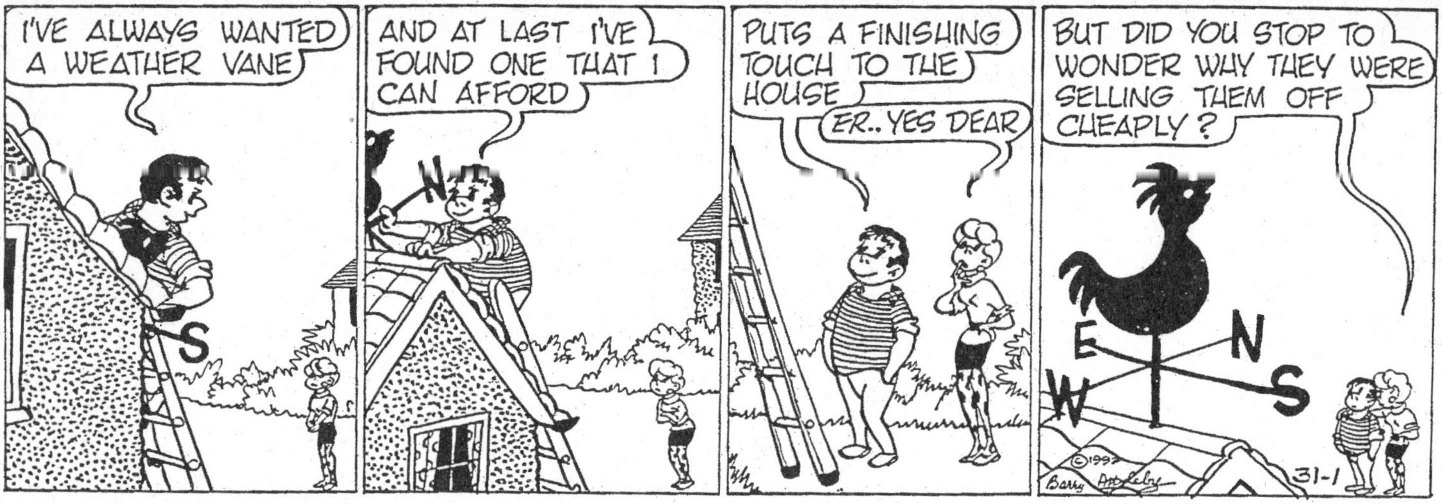
I'VE ALWAYS WANTED A WEATHER VANE
AND AT LAST I'VE FOUND ONE THAT I CAN AFFORD
N
S
PUTS A FINISHING TOUCH TO THE HOUSE
ER.. YES DEAR
BUT DID YOU STOP TO WONDER WHY THEY WERE SELLING THEM OFF CHEAPLY ?
E
N
W
S
31-1

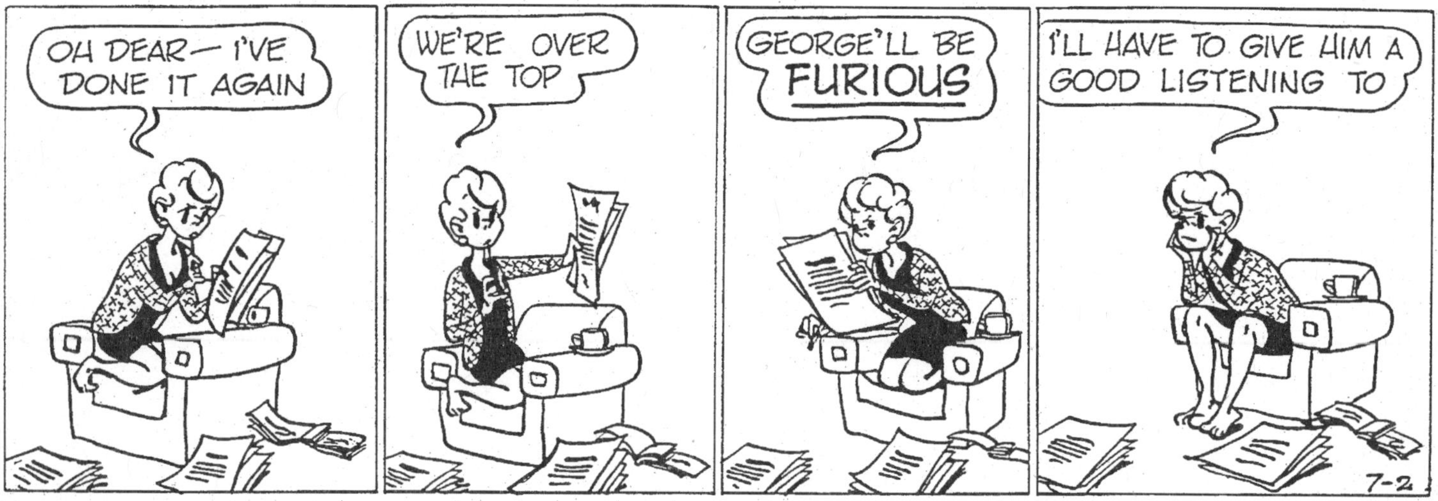
OH DEAR— I'VE DONE IT AGAIN
WE'RE OVER THE TOP
GEORGE'LL BE FURIOUS
I'LL HAVE TO GIVE HIM A GOOD LISTENING TO
7-2

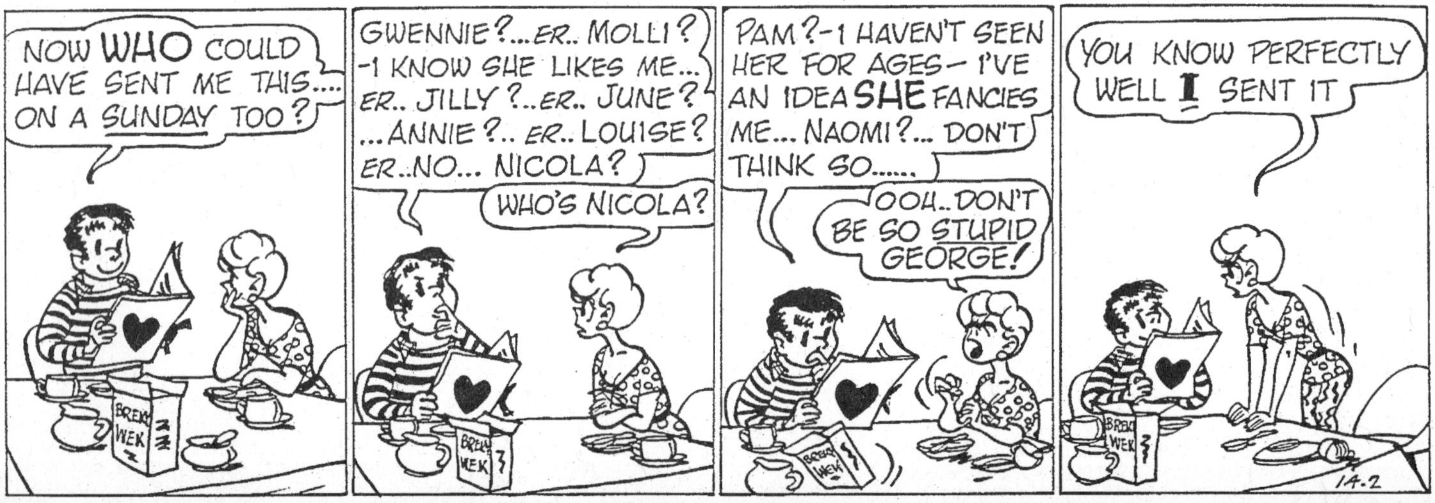
NOW WHO COULD HAVE SENT ME THIS.... ON A SUNDAY TOO ?
GWENNIE ?...ER.. MOLLI ? -I KNOW SHE LIKES ME... ER.. JILLY ?..ER.. JUNE ? ...ANNIE ?.. ER.. LOUISE ? ER..NO... NICOLA ?
WHO'S NICOLA ?
PAM ?-I HAVEN'T SEEN HER FOR AGES- I'VE AN IDEA SHE FANCIES ME... NAOMI ?... DON'T THINK SO......
OOH.. DON'T BE SO STUPID GEORGE!
YOU KNOW PERFECTLY WELL I SENT IT
14.2

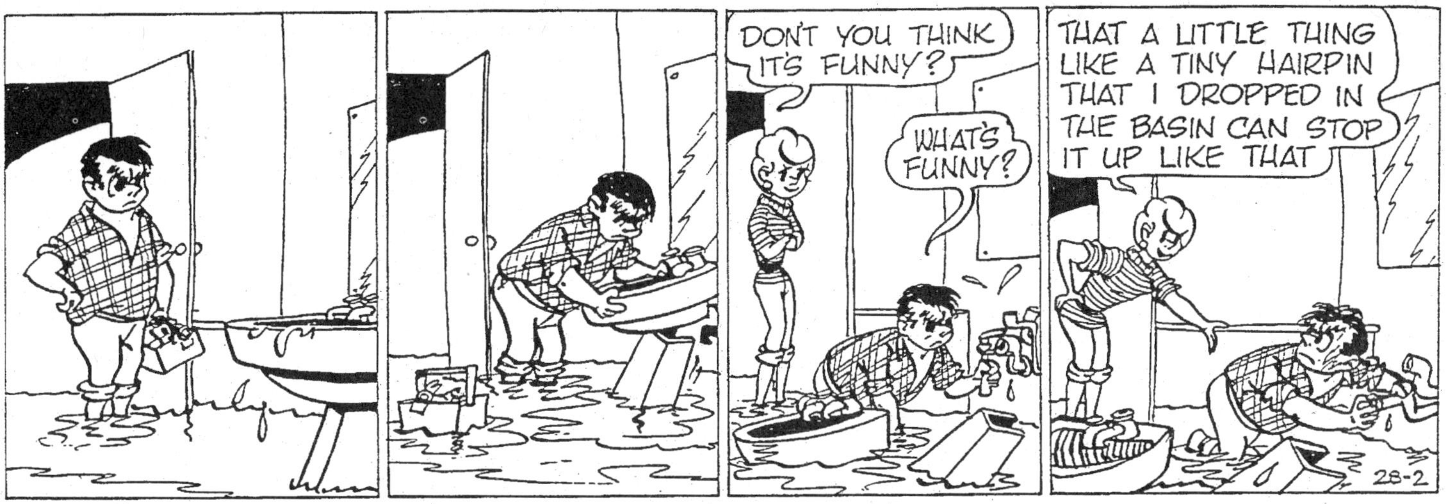
DON'T YOU THINK IT'S FUNNY?
WHAT'S FUNNY?
THAT A LITTLE THING LIKE A TINY HAIRPIN THAT I DROPPED IN THE BASIN CAN STOP IT UP LIKE THAT
28-2

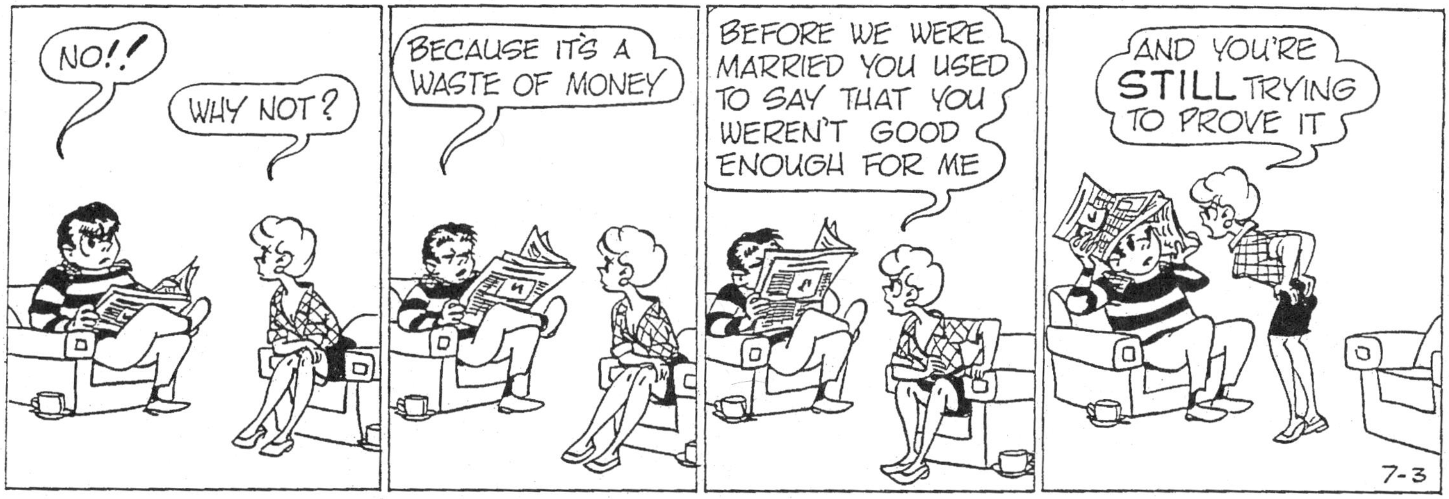
NO!!
WHY NOT?
BECAUSE IT'S A WASTE OF MONEY
BEFORE WE WERE MARRIED YOU USED TO SAY THAT YOU WEREN'T GOOD ENOUGH FOR ME
AND YOU'RE STILL TRYING TO PROVE IT
7-3

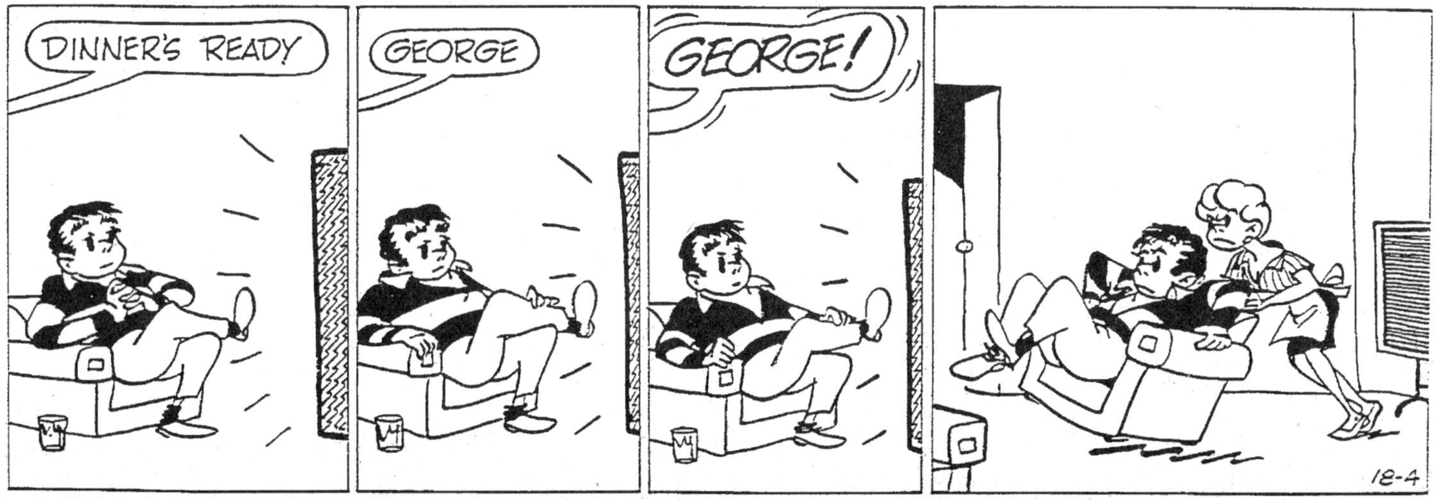
DINNER'S READY
GEORGE
GEORGE!
18-4

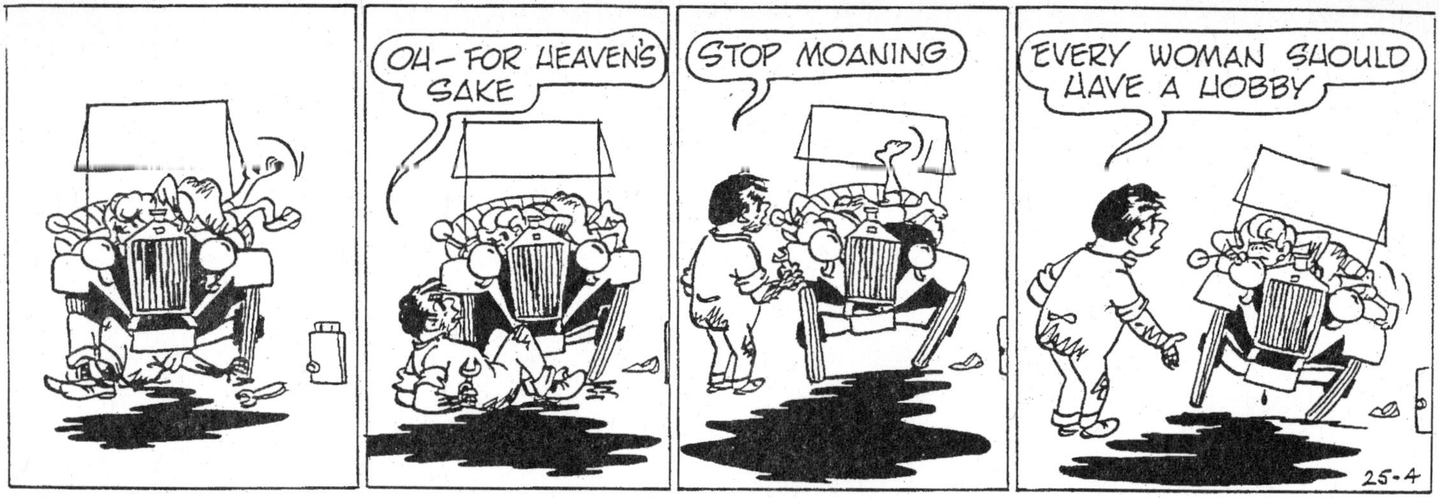
OH- FOR HEAVEN'S SAKE
STOP MOANING
EVERY WOMAN SHOULD HAVE A HOBBY
25-4

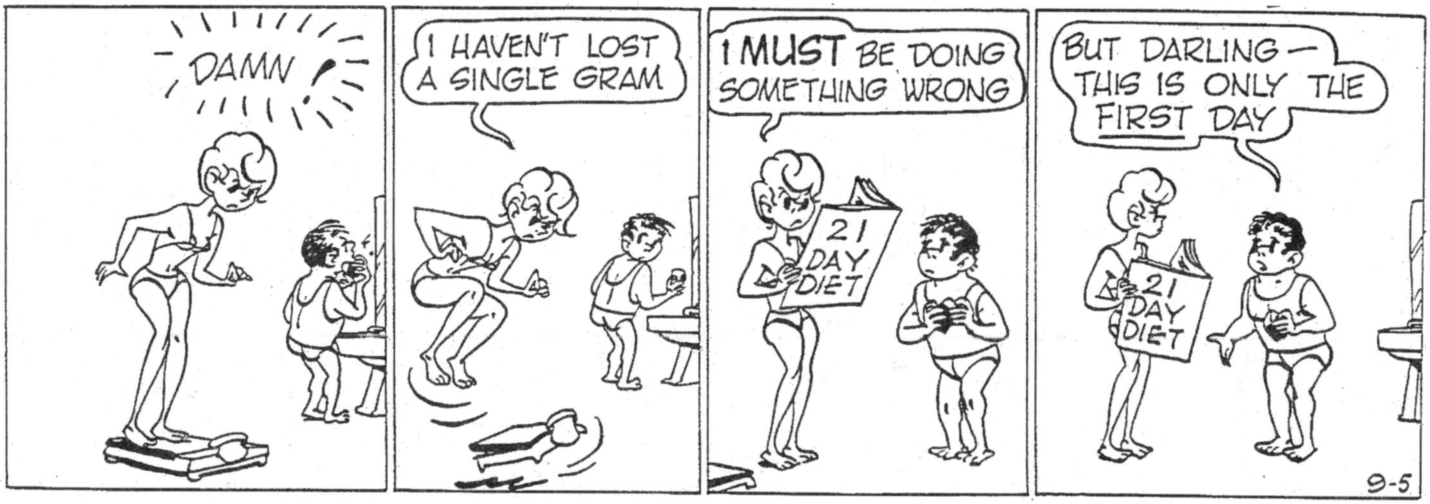
DAMN!
I HAVEN'T LOST A SINGLE GRAM
I MUST BE DOING SOMETHING WRONG
21 DAY DIET
BUT DARLING— THIS IS ONLY THE FIRST DAY
21 DAY DIET
9-5

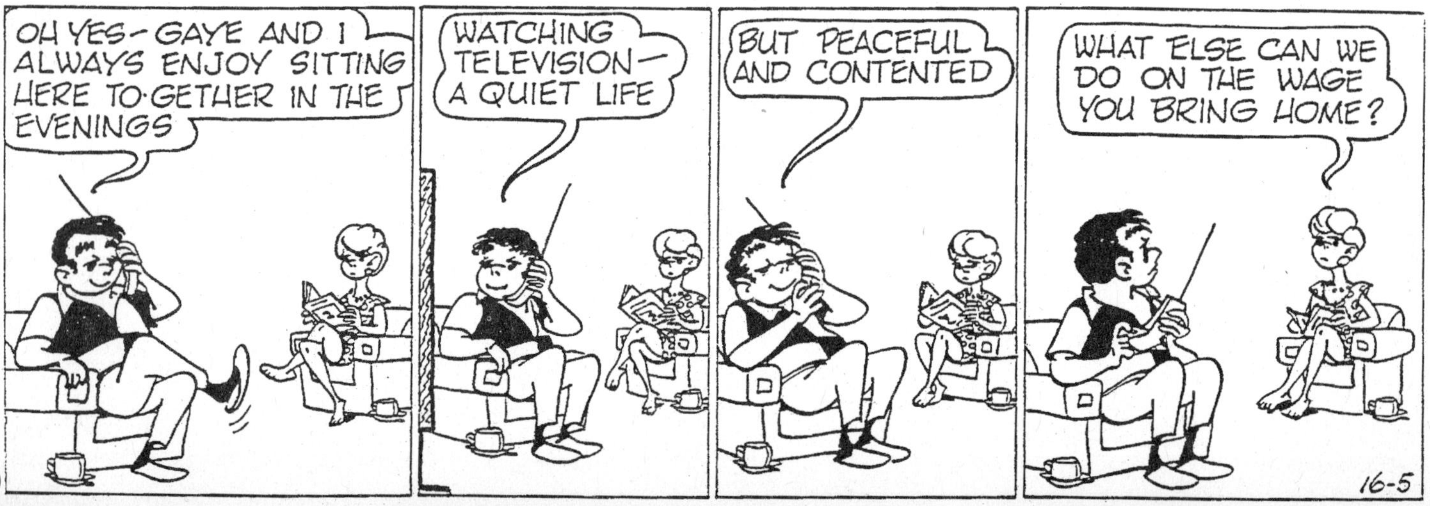
OH YES- GAYE AND I ALWAYS ENJOY SITTING HERE TO·GETHER IN THE EVENINGS
WATCHING TELEVISION— A QUIET LIFE
BUT PEACEFUL AND CONTENTED
WHAT ELSE CAN WE DO ON THE WAGE YOU BRING HOME?
16-5

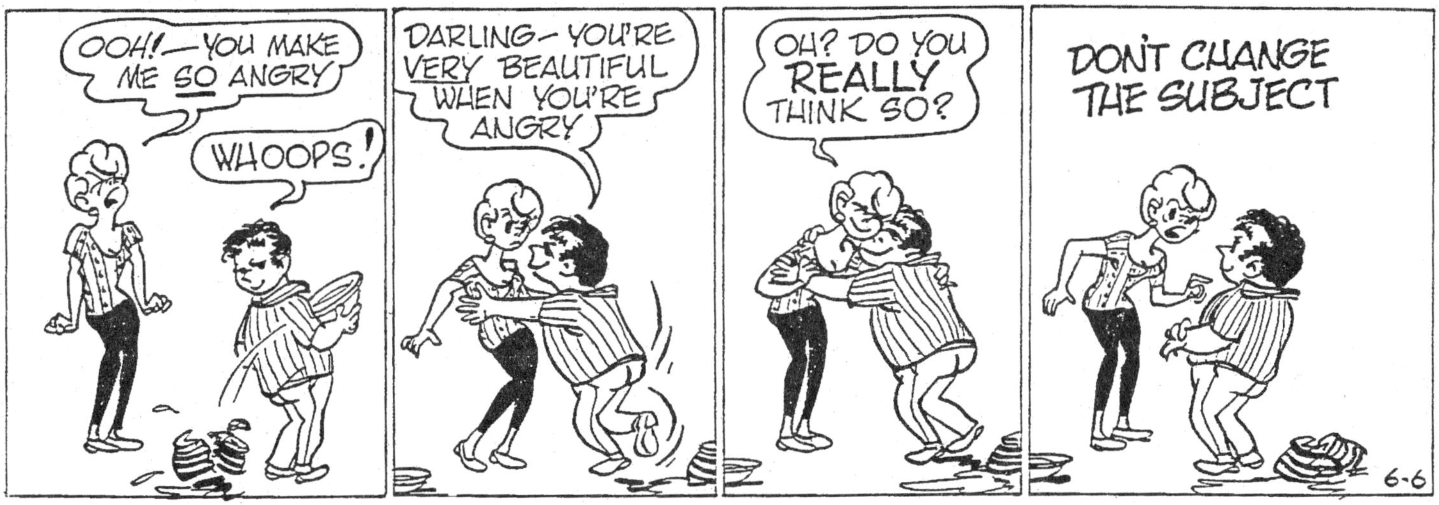
OOH!—YOU MAKE ME SO ANGRY
WHOOPS!
DARLING—YOU'RE VERY BEAUTIFUL WHEN YOU'RE ANGRY
OH? DO YOU REALLY THINK SO?
DON'T CHANGE THE SUBJECT
6-6

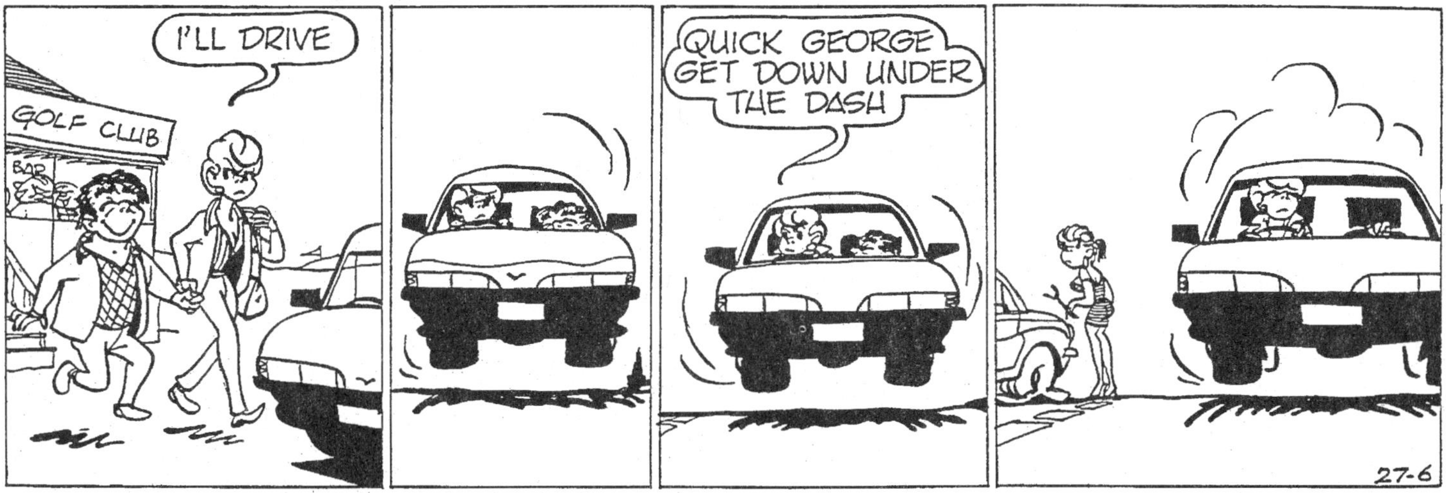
I'LL DRIVE
GOLF CLUB
BAR
QUICK GEORGE GET DOWN UNDER THE DASH
27-6

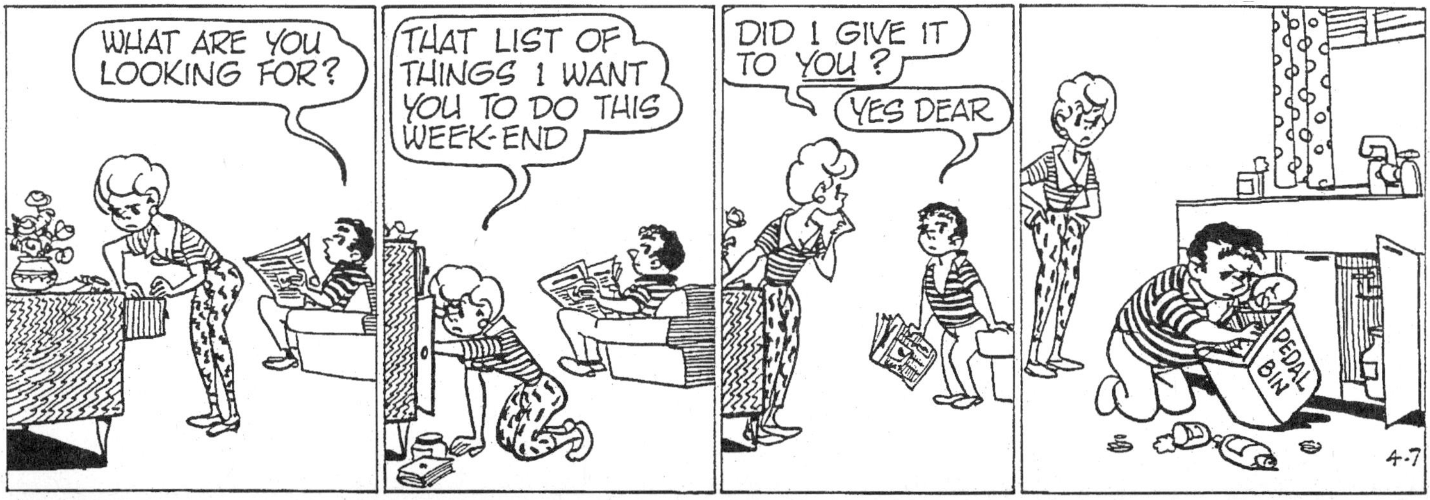
WHAT ARE YOU LOOKING FOR?
THAT LIST OF THINGS I WANT YOU TO DO THIS WEEK-END
DID I GIVE IT TO YOU?
YES DEAR
PEDAL BIN
4-7

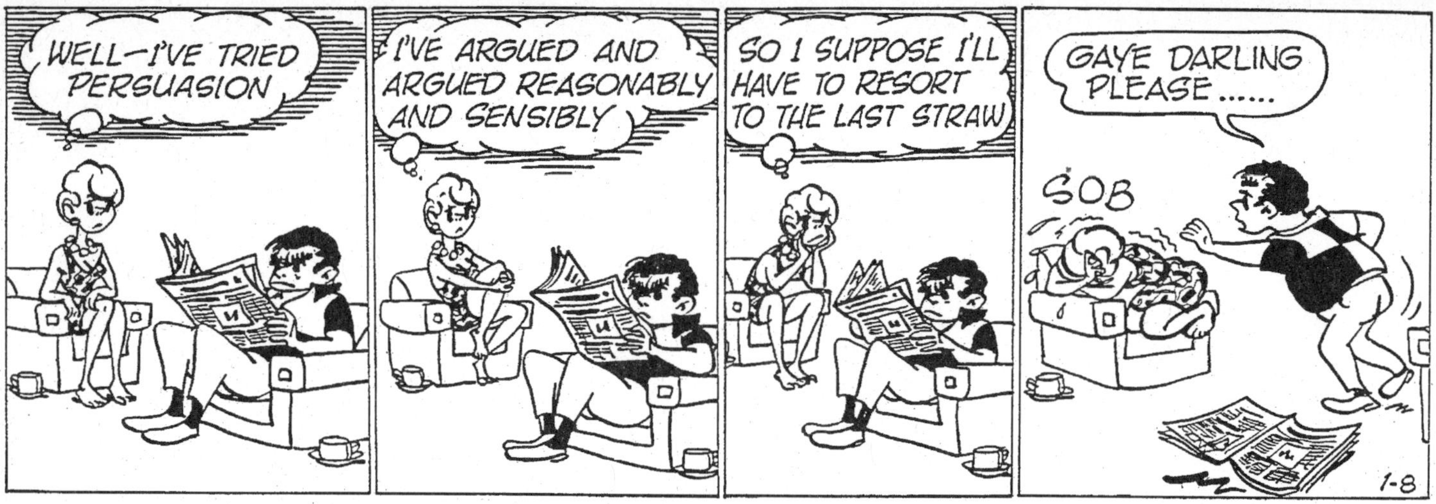
WELL—I'VE TRIED PERSUASION
I'VE ARGUED AND ARGUED REASONABLY AND SENSIBLY
SO I SUPPOSE I'LL HAVE TO RESORT TO THE LAST STRAW
SOB
GAYE DARLING PLEASE......
1-8

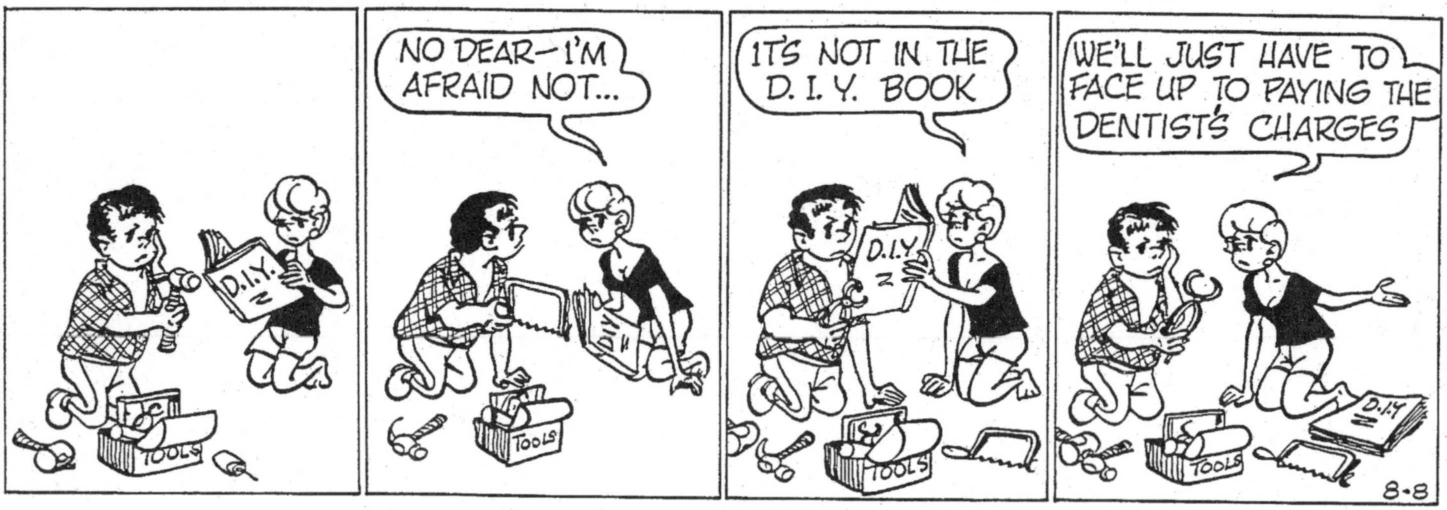
NO DEAR—I'M AFRAID NOT...
IT'S NOT IN THE D. I. Y. BOOK
WE'LL JUST HAVE TO FACE UP TO PAYING THE DENTIST'S CHARGES
8-8

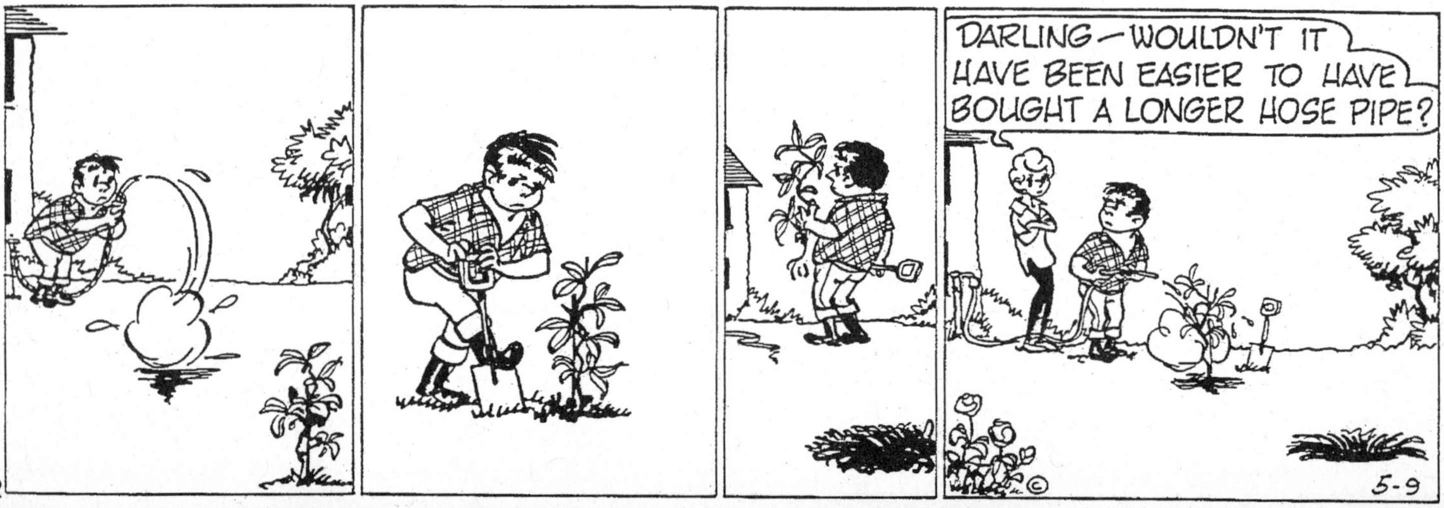
DARLING—WOULDN'T IT HAVE BEEN EASIER TO HAVE BOUGHT A LONGER HOSE PIPE?
©
5-9

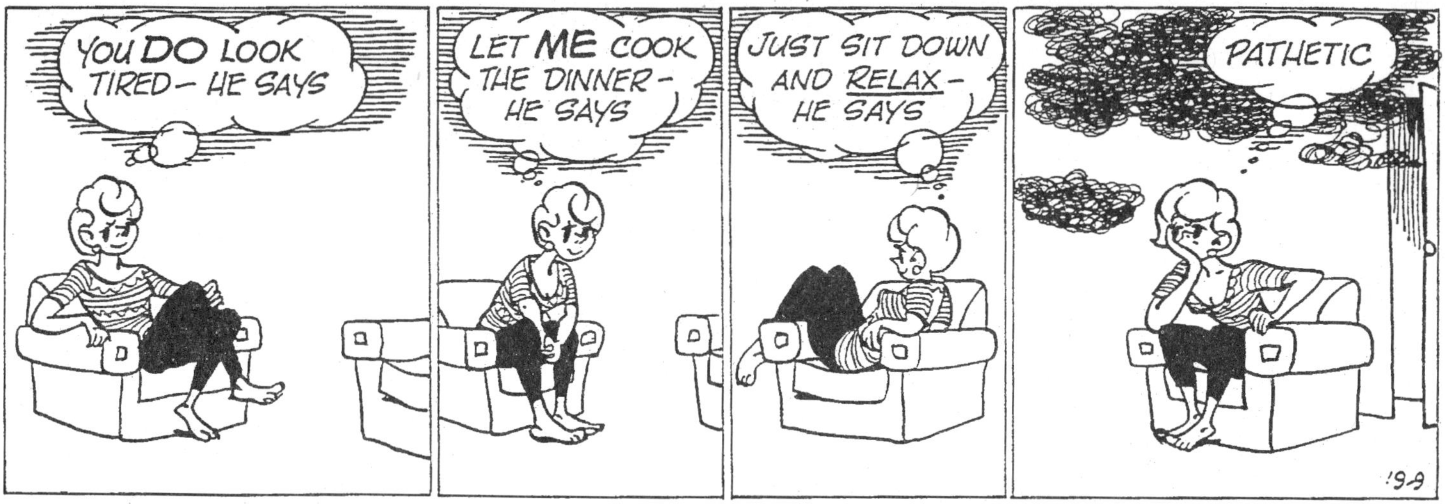
YOU DO LOOK TIRED– HE SAYS
LET ME COOK THE DINNER– HE SAYS
JUST SIT DOWN AND RELAX– HE SAYS
PATHETIC
19-9

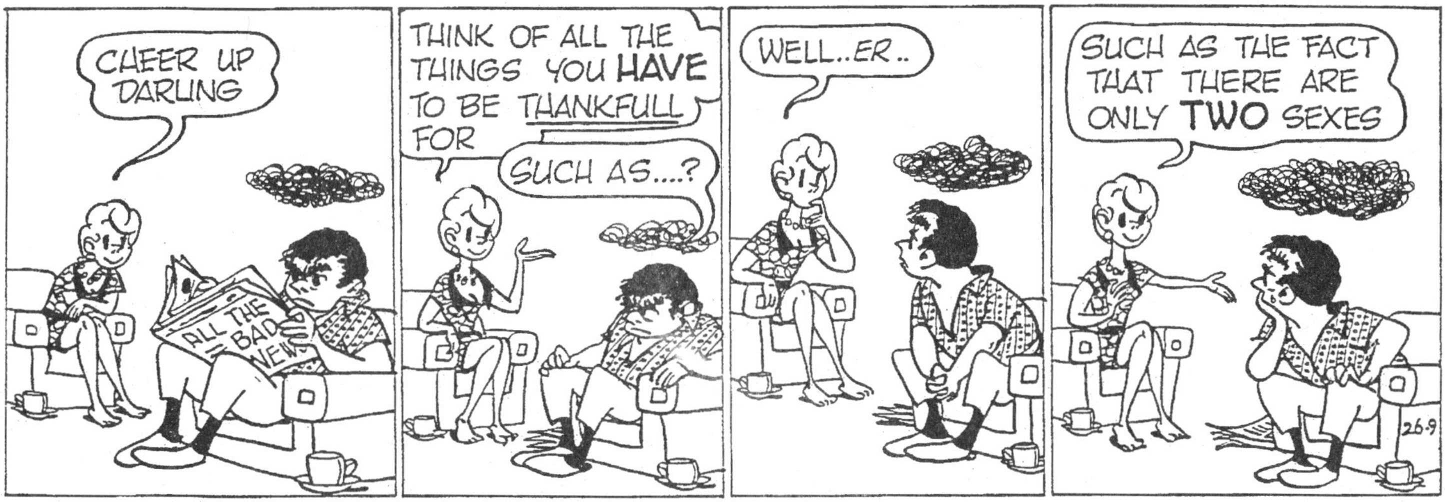
CHEER UP DARLING
ALL THE BAD NEWS
THINK OF ALL THE THINGS YOU HAVE TO BE THANKFULL FOR
SUCH AS....?
WELL..ER..
SUCH AS THE FACT THAT THERE ARE ONLY TWO SEXES
26-9

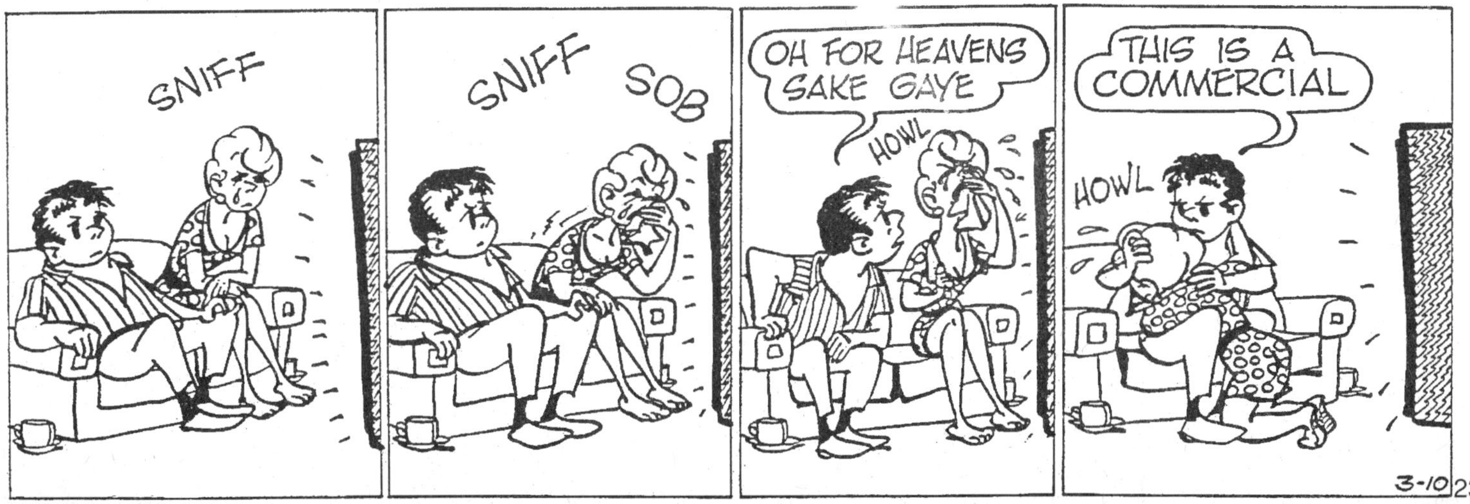
SNIFF
SNIFF
SOB
OH FOR HEAVENS SAKE GAYE
HOWL
THIS IS A COMMERCIAL
HOWL
3-10

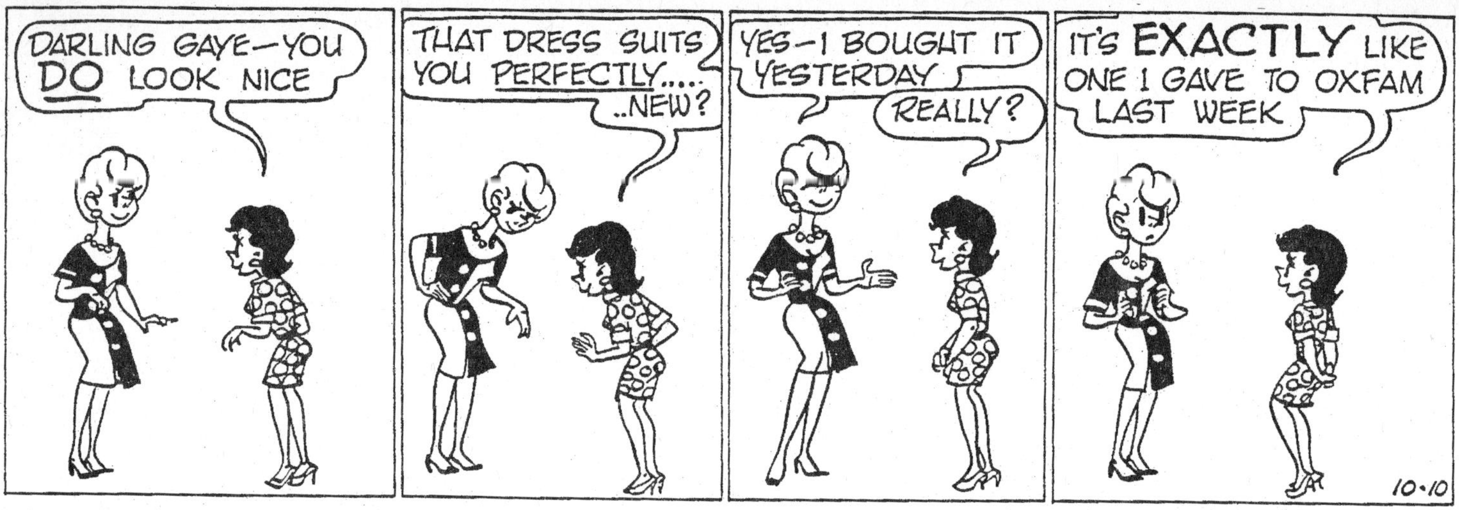
DARLING GAYE—YOU DO LOOK NICE
THAT DRESS SUITS YOU PERFECTLY..... ..NEW?
YES—I BOUGHT IT YESTERDAY
REALLY?
IT'S EXACTLY LIKE ONE I GAVE TO OXFAM LAST WEEK
10•10

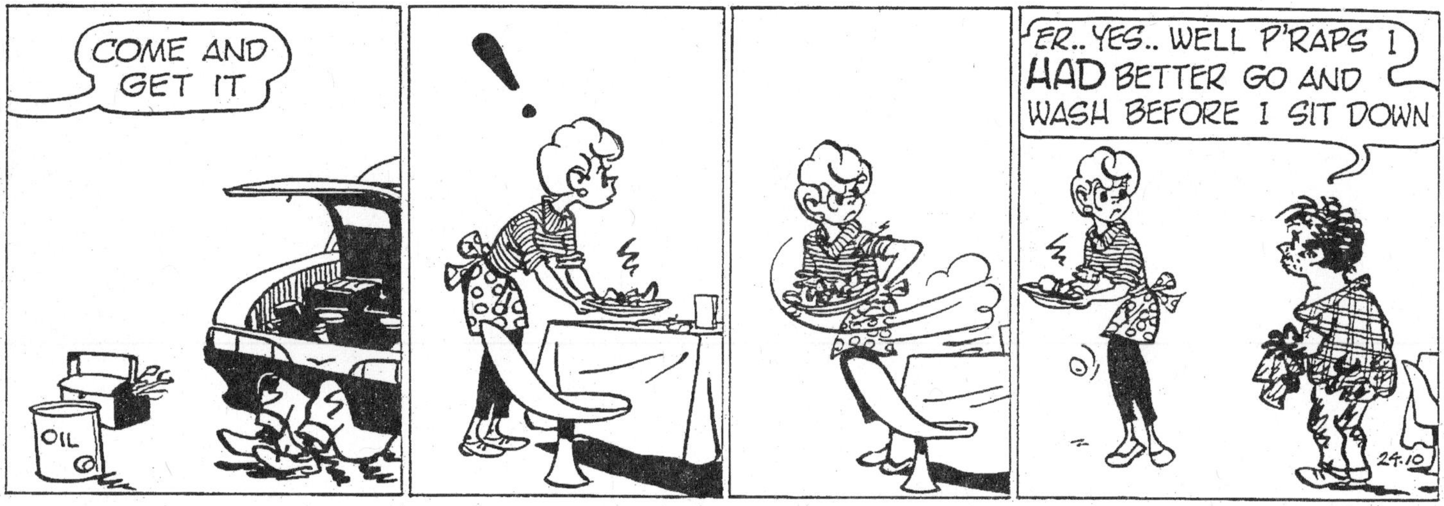
COME AND GET IT
OIL
!
ER.. YES.. WELL P'RAPS I HAD BETTER GO AND WASH BEFORE I SIT DOWN
24.10

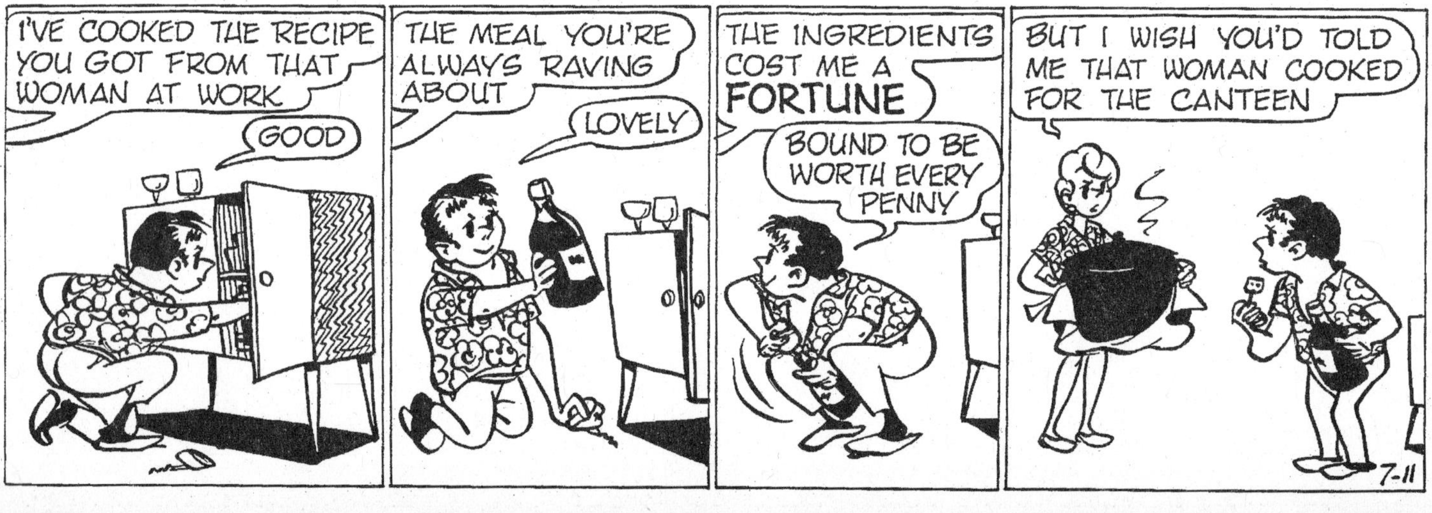
I'VE COOKED THE RECIPE YOU GOT FROM THAT WOMAN AT WORK
GOOD
THE MEAL YOU'RE ALWAYS RAVING ABOUT
LOVELY
THE INGREDIENTS COST ME A FORTUNE
BOUND TO BE WORTH EVERY PENNY
BUT I WISH YOU'D TOLD ME THAT WOMAN COOKED FOR THE CANTEEN
7-11

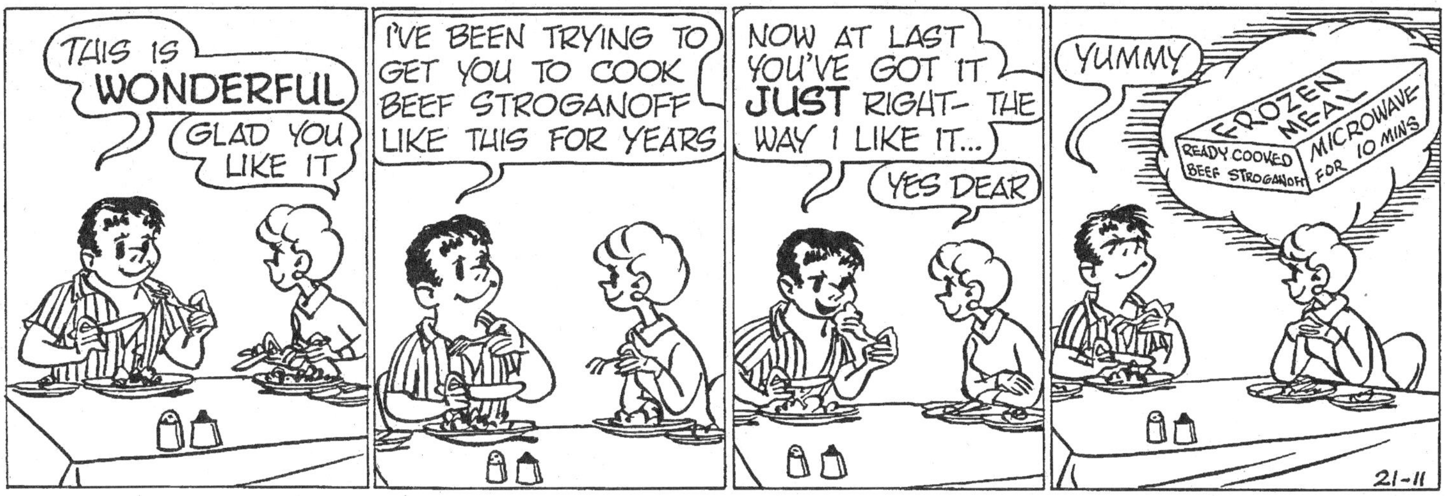
THIS IS WONDERFUL
GLAD YOU LIKE IT
I'VE BEEN TRYING TO GET YOU TO COOK BEEF STROGANOFF LIKE THIS FOR YEARS
NOW AT LAST YOU'VE GOT IT JUST RIGHT- THE WAY I LIKE IT...
YES DEAR
YUMMY
FROZEN MEAL
READY COOKED BEEF STROGANOFF
MICROWAVE FOR 10 MINS
21-11

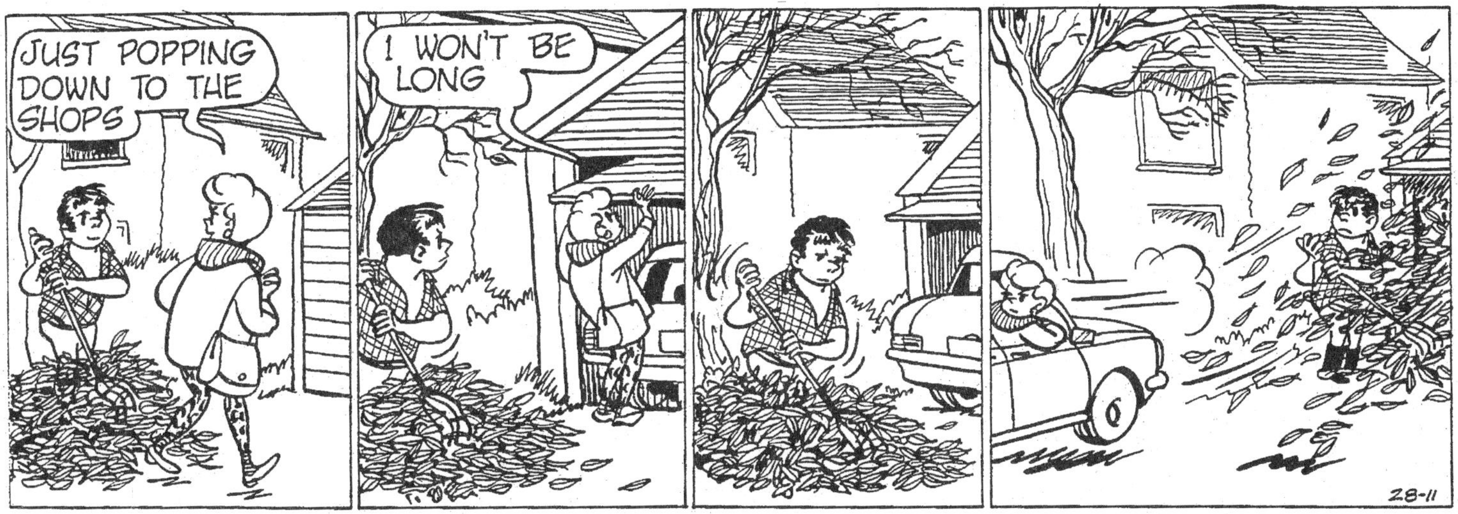
JUST POPPING DOWN TO THE SHOPS
I WON'T BE LONG
28-11

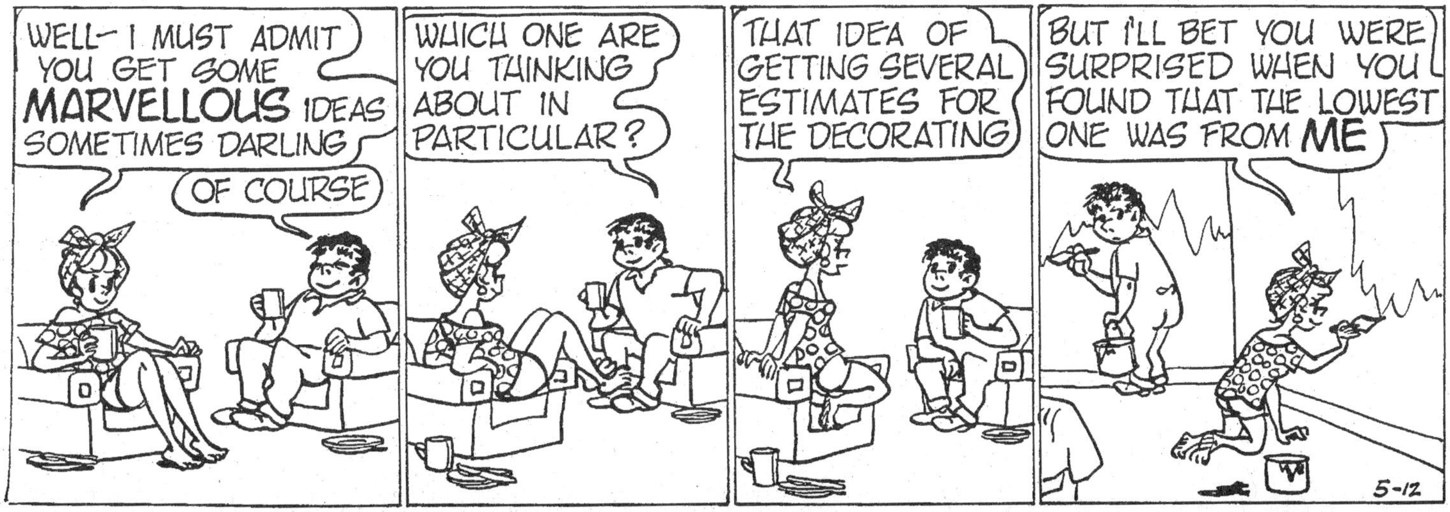
WELL- I MUST ADMIT YOU GET SOME MARVELLOUS IDEAS SOMETIMES DARLING
OF COURSE
WHICH ONE ARE YOU THINKING ABOUT IN PARTICULAR?
THAT IDEA OF GETTING SEVERAL ESTIMATES FOR THE DECORATING
BUT I'LL BET YOU WERE SURPRISED WHEN YOU FOUND THAT THE LOWEST ONE WAS FROM ME
5-12

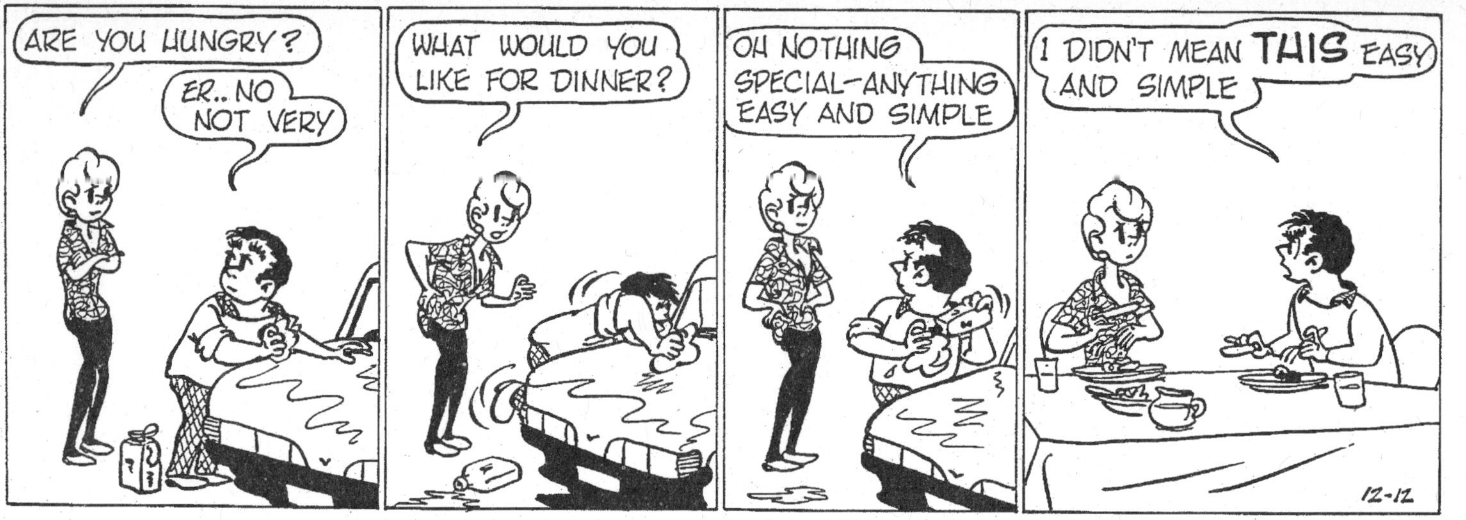
ARE YOU HUNGRY?
ER.. NO NOT VERY
WHAT WOULD YOU LIKE FOR DINNER?
OH NOTHING SPECIAL—ANYTHING EASY AND SIMPLE
I DIDN'T MEAN THIS EASY AND SIMPLE
12-12

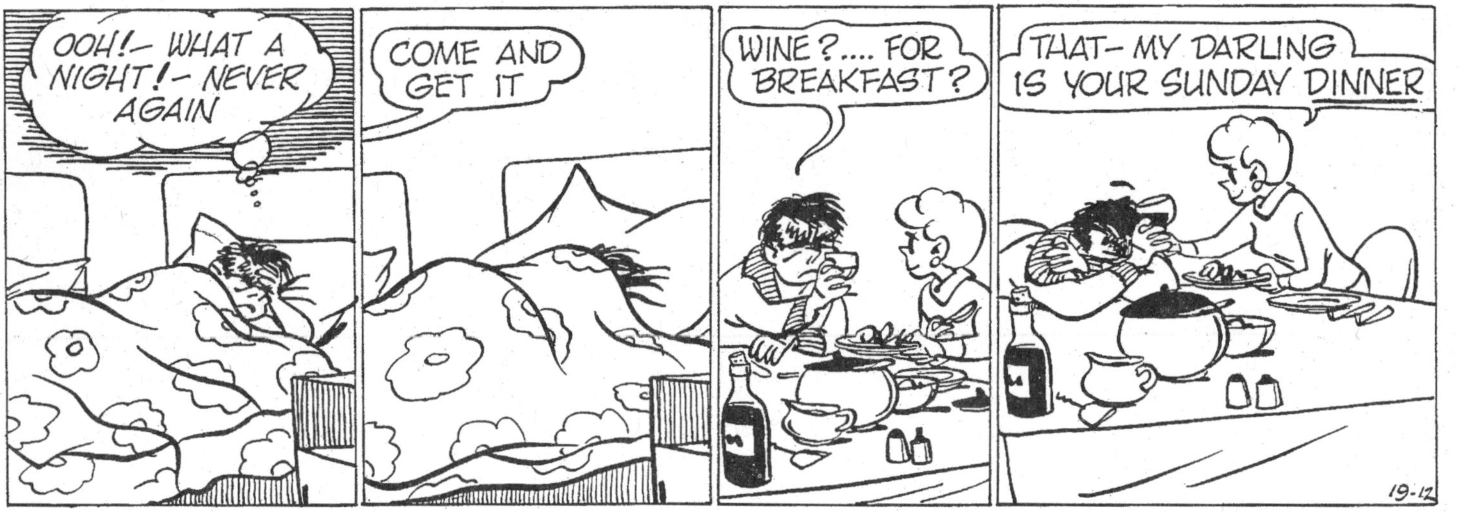
OOH!— WHAT A NIGHT!— NEVER AGAIN
COME AND GET IT
WINE?.... FOR BREAKFAST?
THAT— MY DARLING IS YOUR SUNDAY DINNER
19-12

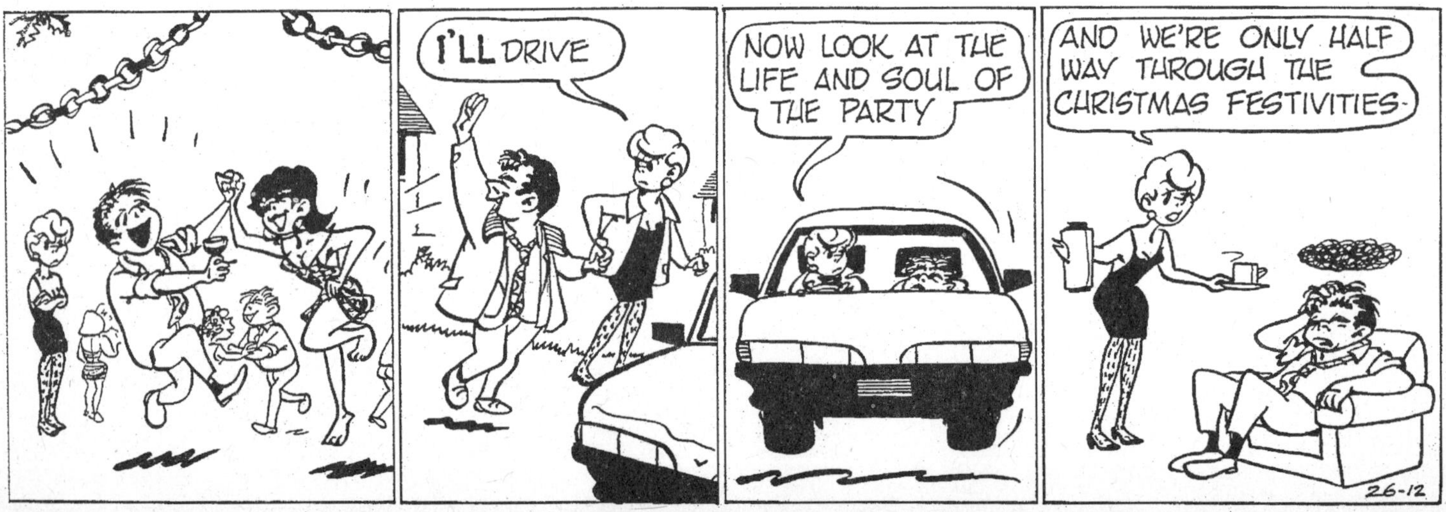
I'LL DRIVE
NOW LOOK AT THE LIFE AND SOUL OF THE PARTY
AND WE'RE ONLY HALF WAY THROUGH THE CHRISTMAS FESTIVITIES-
26-12

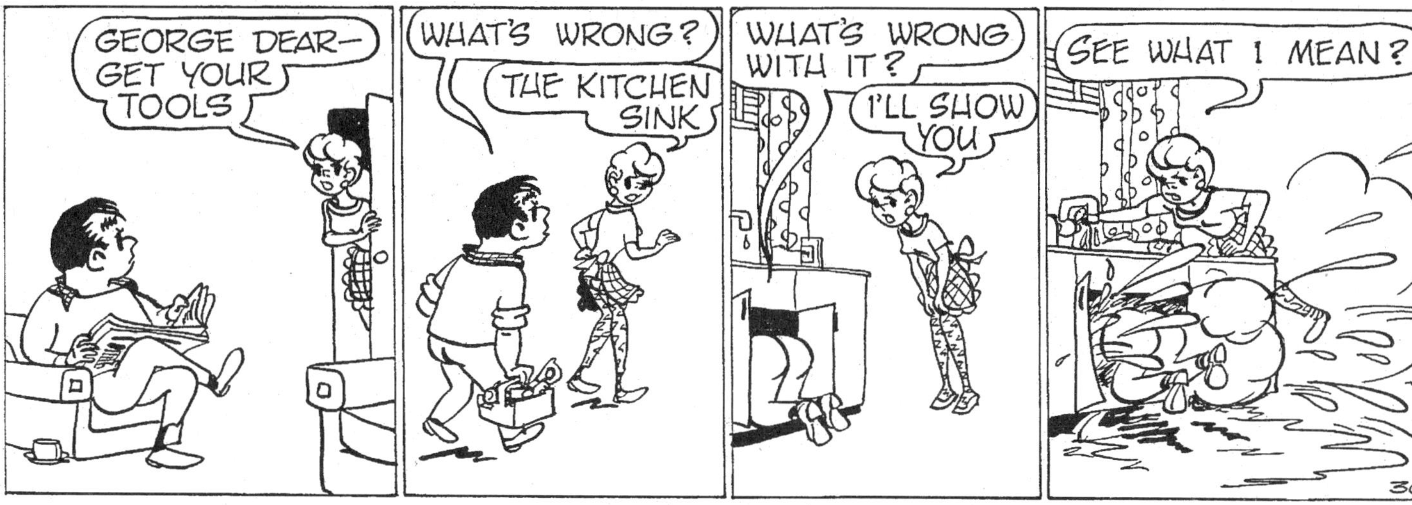
GEORGE DEAR— GET YOUR TOOLS
WHAT'S WRONG?
THE KITCHEN SINK
WHAT'S WRONG WITH IT?
I'LL SHOW YOU
SEE WHAT I MEAN?
30.1

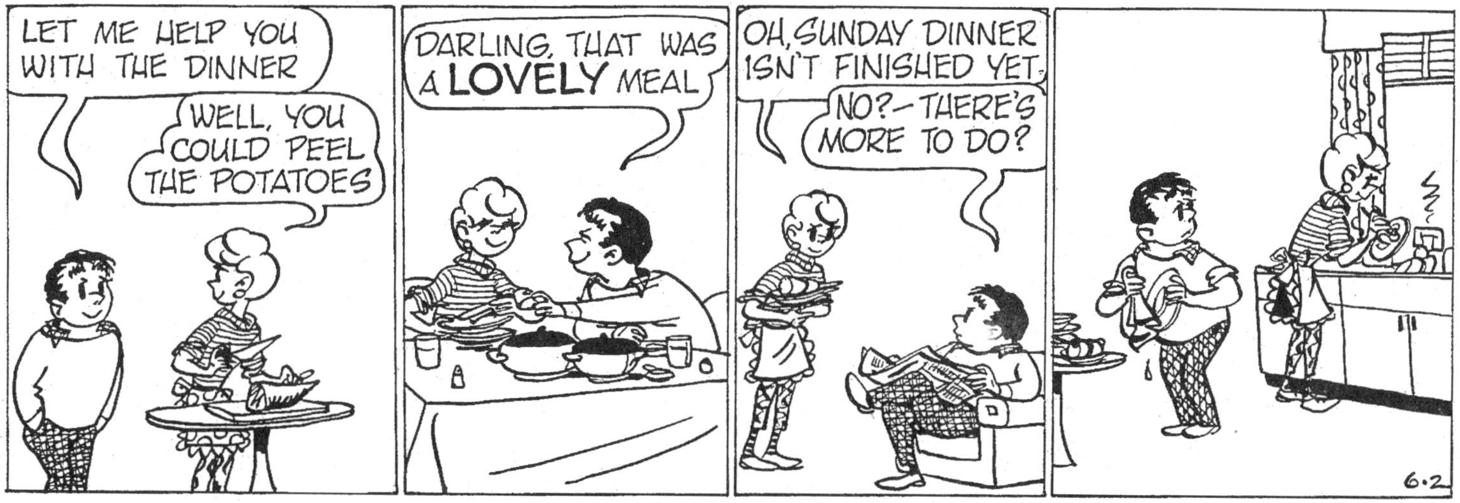
LET ME HELP YOU WITH THE DINNER
WELL, YOU COULD PEEL THE POTATOES
DARLING, THAT WAS A LOVELY MEAL
OH, SUNDAY DINNER ISN'T FINISHED YET
NO?— THERE'S MORE TO DO?
6.2

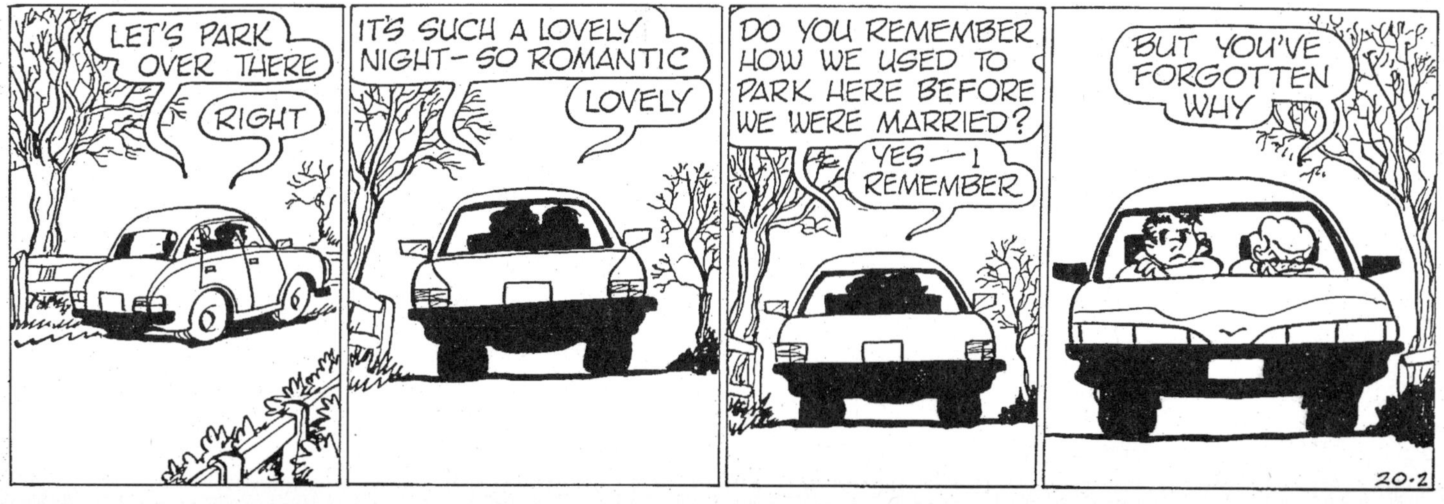
LET'S PARK OVER THERE
RIGHT
IT'S SUCH A LOVELY NIGHT— SO ROMANTIC
LOVELY
DO YOU REMEMBER HOW WE USED TO PARK HERE BEFORE WE WERE MARRIED?
YES— I REMEMBER
BUT YOU'VE FORGOTTEN WHY
20.2

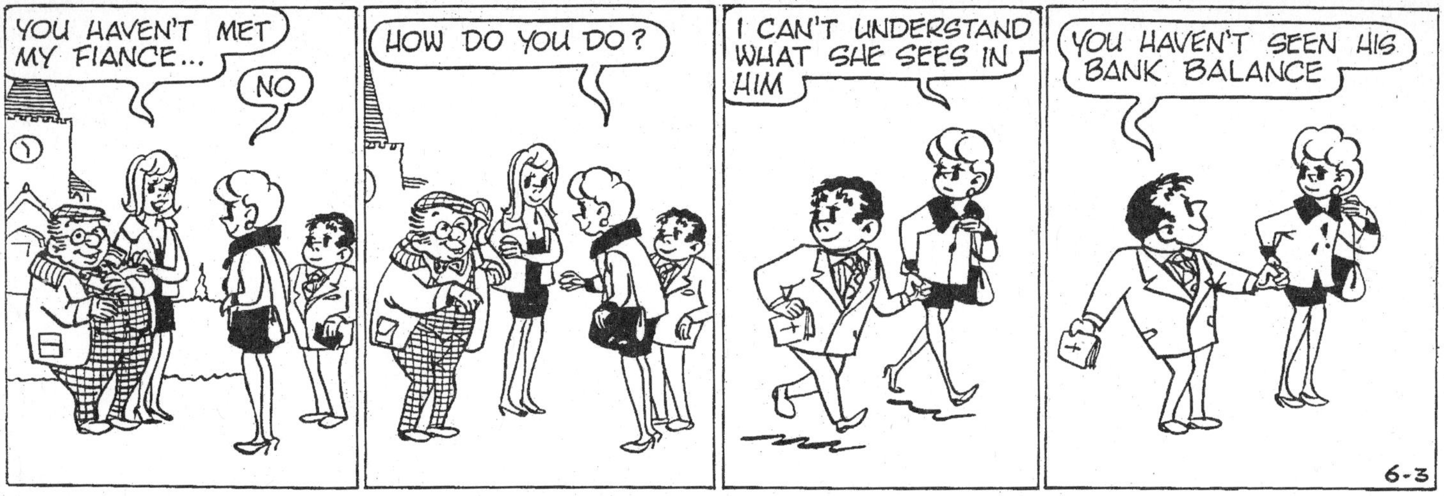
YOU HAVEN'T MET MY FIANCE...
NO
HOW DO YOU DO?
I CAN'T UNDERSTAND WHAT SHE SEES IN HIM
YOU HAVEN'T SEEN HIS BANK BALANCE
6-3

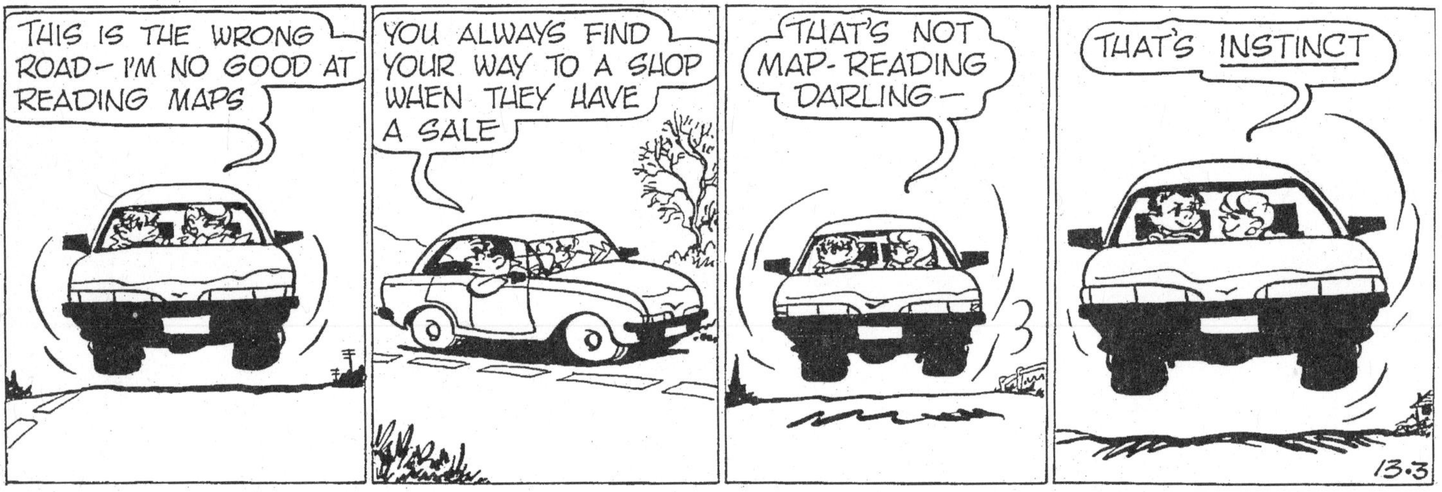
THIS IS THE WRONG ROAD— I'M NO GOOD AT READING MAPS
YOU ALWAYS FIND YOUR WAY TO A SHOP WHEN THEY HAVE A SALE
THAT'S NOT MAP-READING DARLING—
THAT'S INSTINCT
13-3

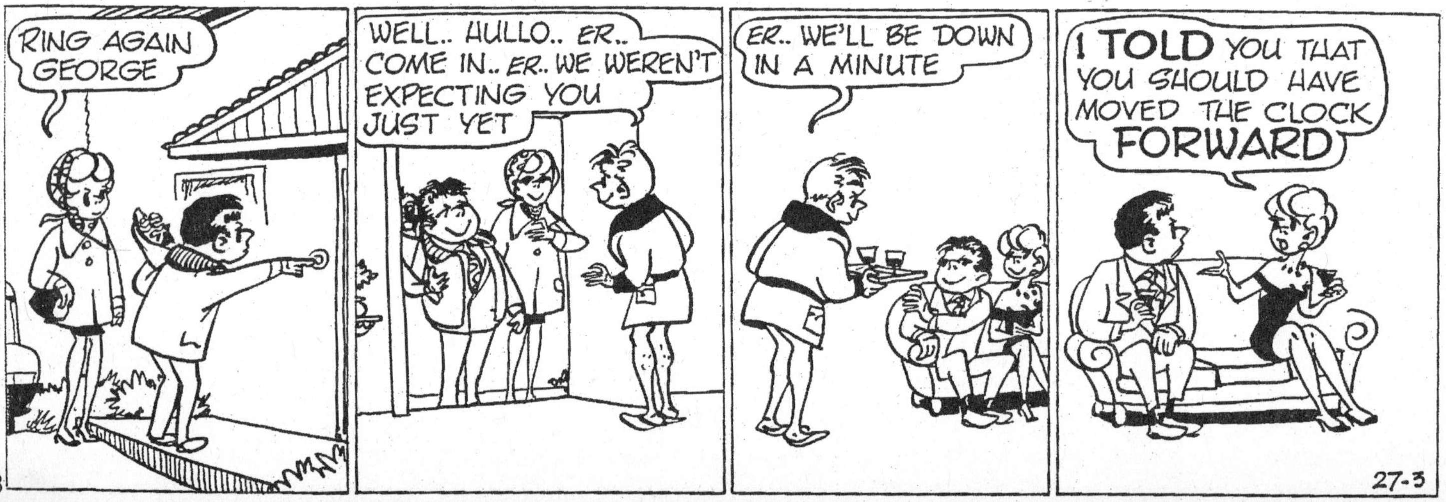
RING AGAIN GEORGE
WELL.. HULLO.. ER.. COME IN.. ER.. WE WEREN'T EXPECTING YOU JUST YET
ER.. WE'LL BE DOWN IN A MINUTE
I TOLD YOU THAT YOU SHOULD HAVE MOVED THE CLOCK FORWARD
27-3

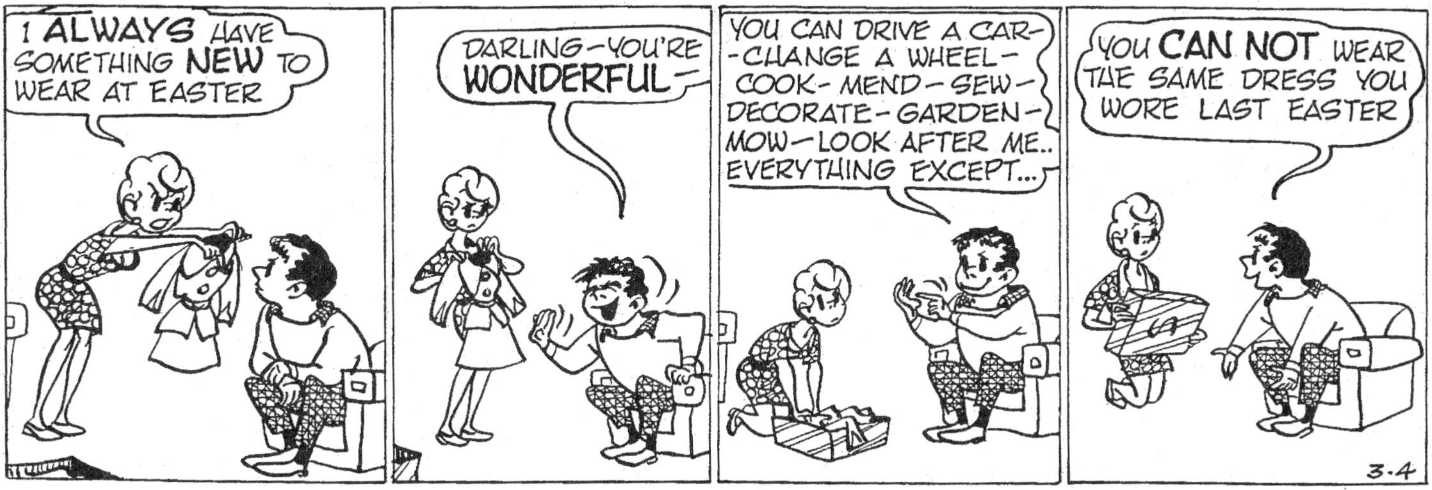
I ALWAYS HAVE SOMETHING NEW TO WEAR AT EASTER
DARLING—YOU'RE WONDERFUL—
YOU CAN DRIVE A CAR- -CHANGE A WHEEL- COOK- MEND- SEW- DECORATE- GARDEN- MOW—LOOK AFTER ME.. EVERYTHING EXCEPT...
YOU CAN NOT WEAR THE SAME DRESS YOU WORE LAST EASTER
3.4

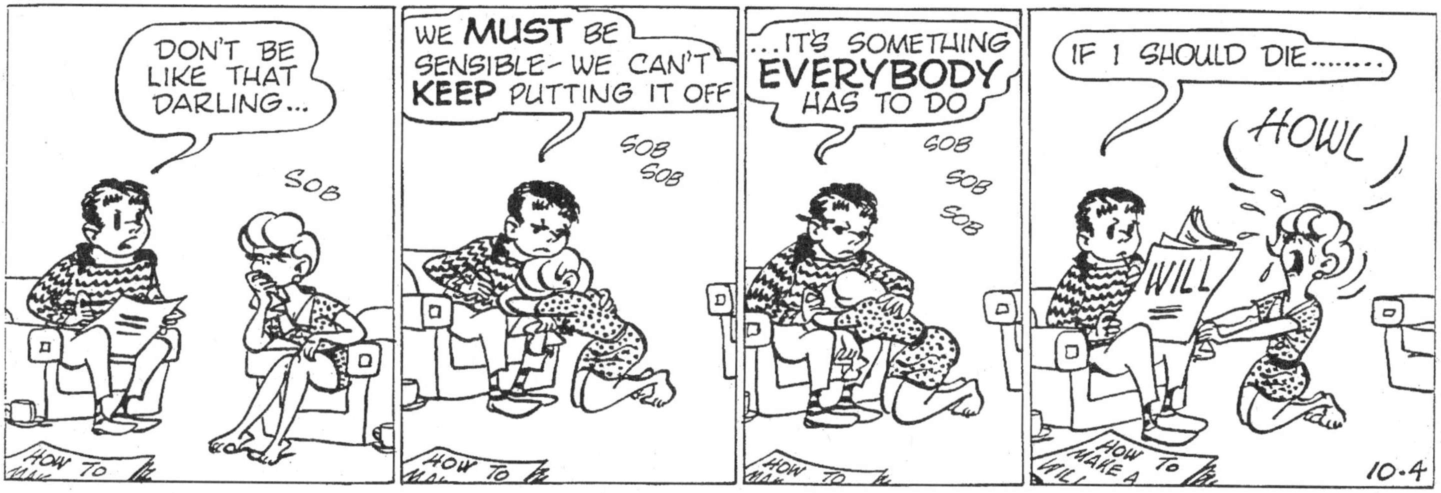
DON'T BE LIKE THAT DARLING...
SOB
WE MUST BE SENSIBLE- WE CAN'T KEEP PUTTING IT OFF
SOB SOB
...IT'S SOMETHING EVERYBODY HAS TO DO
SOB SOB SOB
IF I SHOULD DIE........
HOWL
WILL
HOW TO MAKE A WILL
10.4

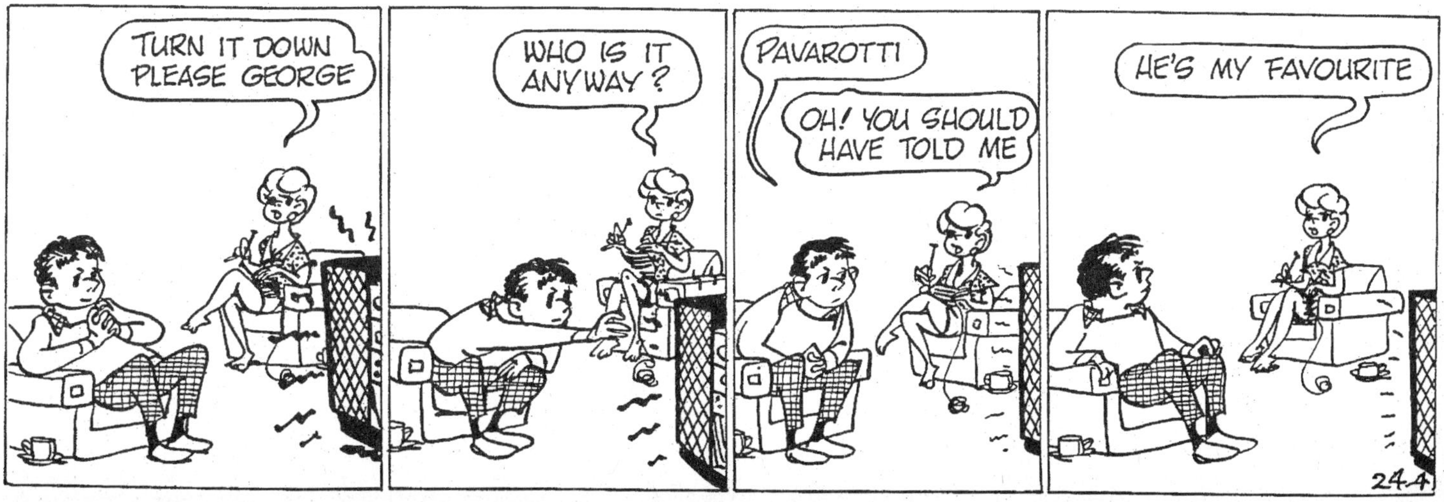
TURN IT DOWN PLEASE GEORGE
WHO IS IT ANYWAY?
PAVAROTTI
OH! YOU SHOULD HAVE TOLD ME
HE'S MY FAVOURITE
24.4

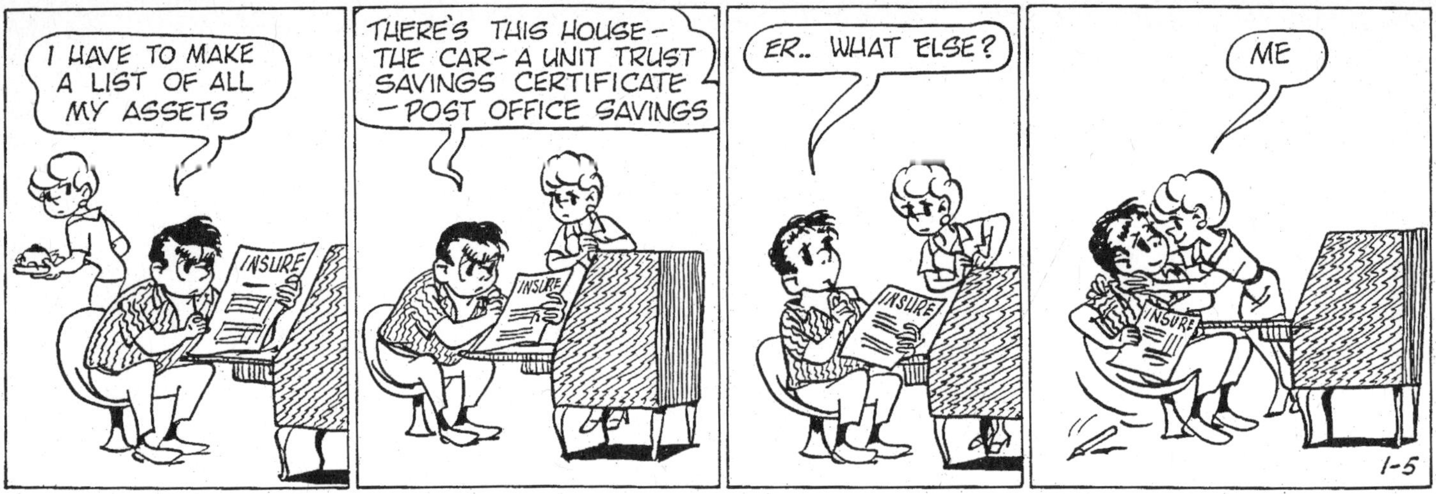
I HAVE TO MAKE A LIST OF ALL MY ASSETS
INSURE
THERE'S THIS HOUSE- THE CAR- A UNIT TRUST SAVINGS CERTIFICATE -POST OFFICE SAVINGS
INSURE
ER.. WHAT ELSE?
INSURE
ME
INSURE
1-5

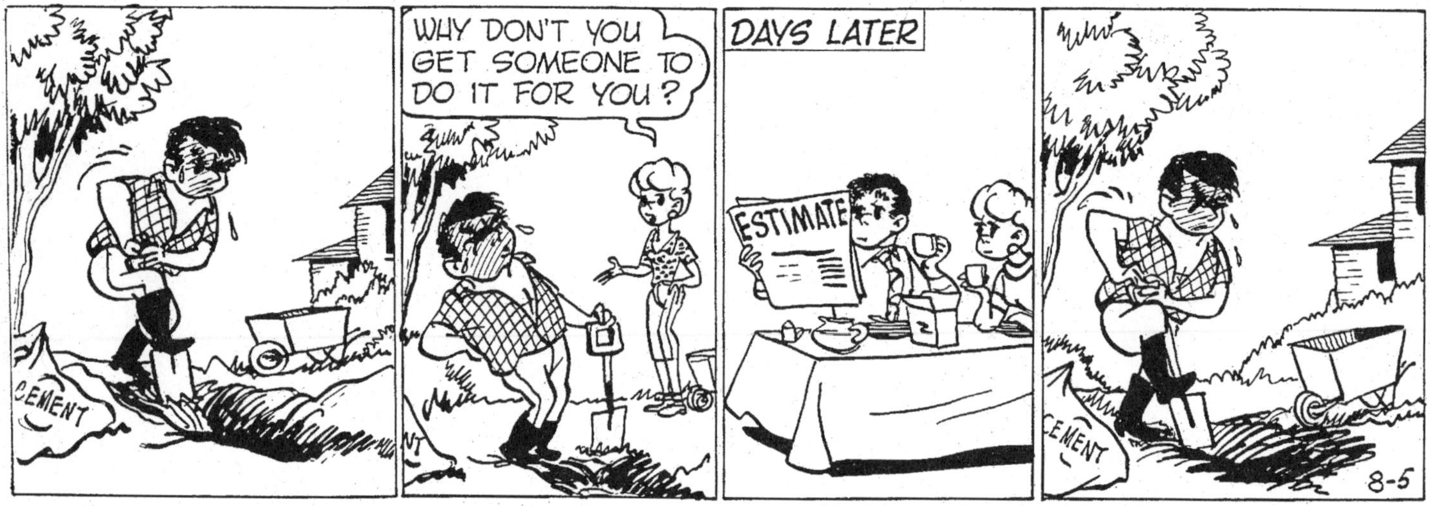
CEMENT
WHY DON'T YOU GET SOMEONE TO DO IT FOR YOU?
DAYS LATER
ESTIMATE
CEMENT
8-5

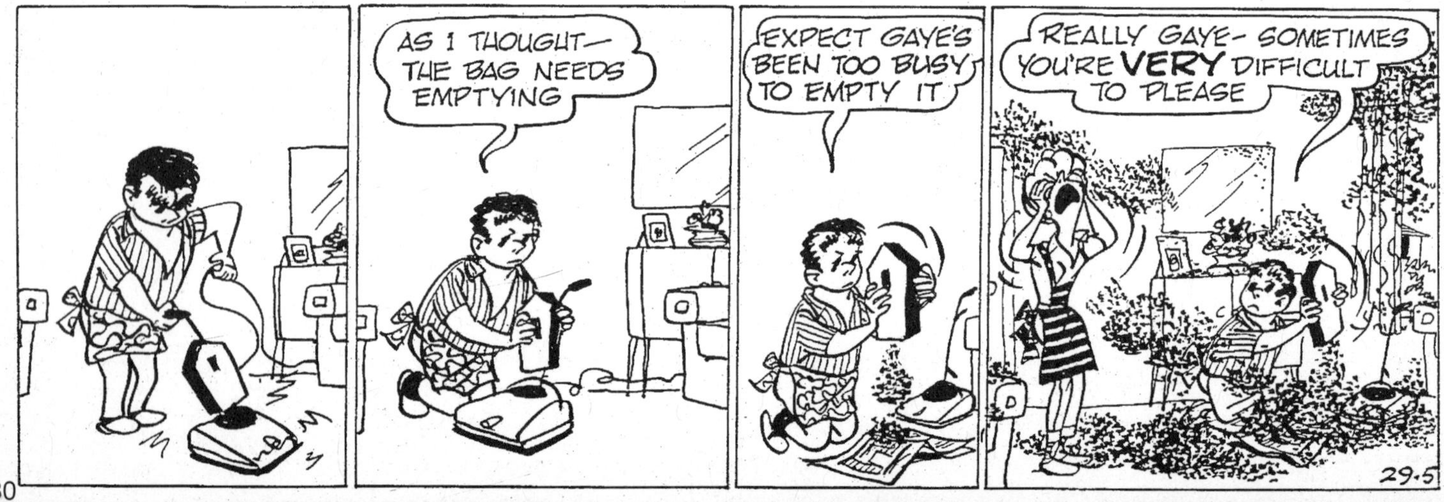
AS I THOUGHT— THE BAG NEEDS EMPTYING
EXPECT GAYE'S BEEN TOO BUSY TO EMPTY IT
REALLY GAYE- SOMETIMES YOU'RE **VERY** DIFFICULT TO PLEASE
29-5

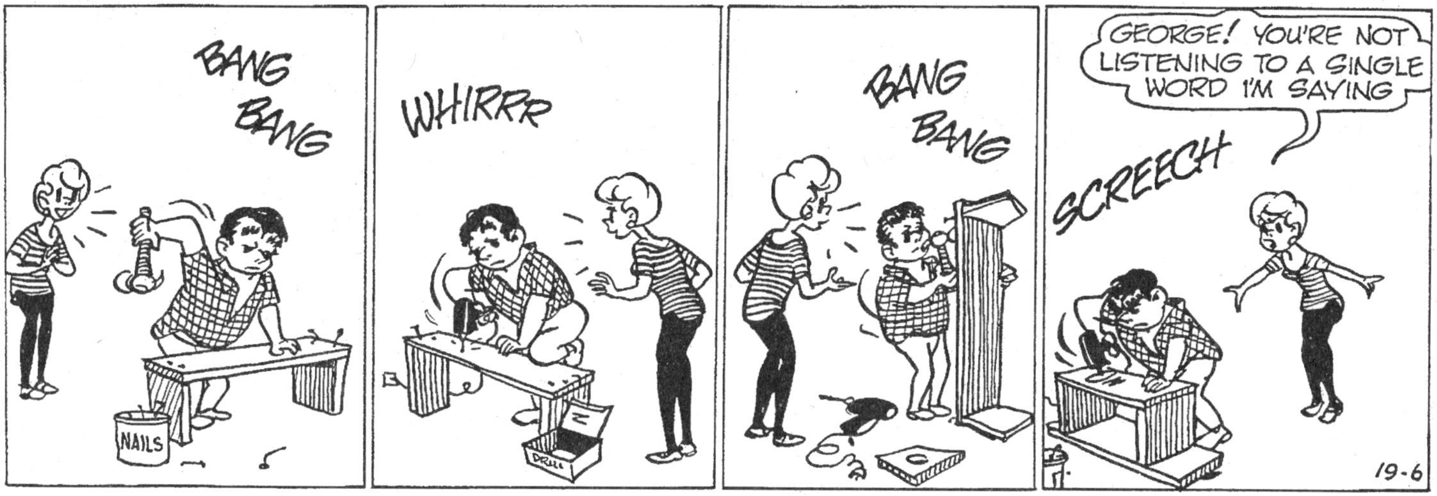
BANG BANG
WHIRRR
BANG BANG
SCREECH
GEORGE! YOU'RE NOT LISTENING TO A SINGLE WORD I'M SAYING
19-6

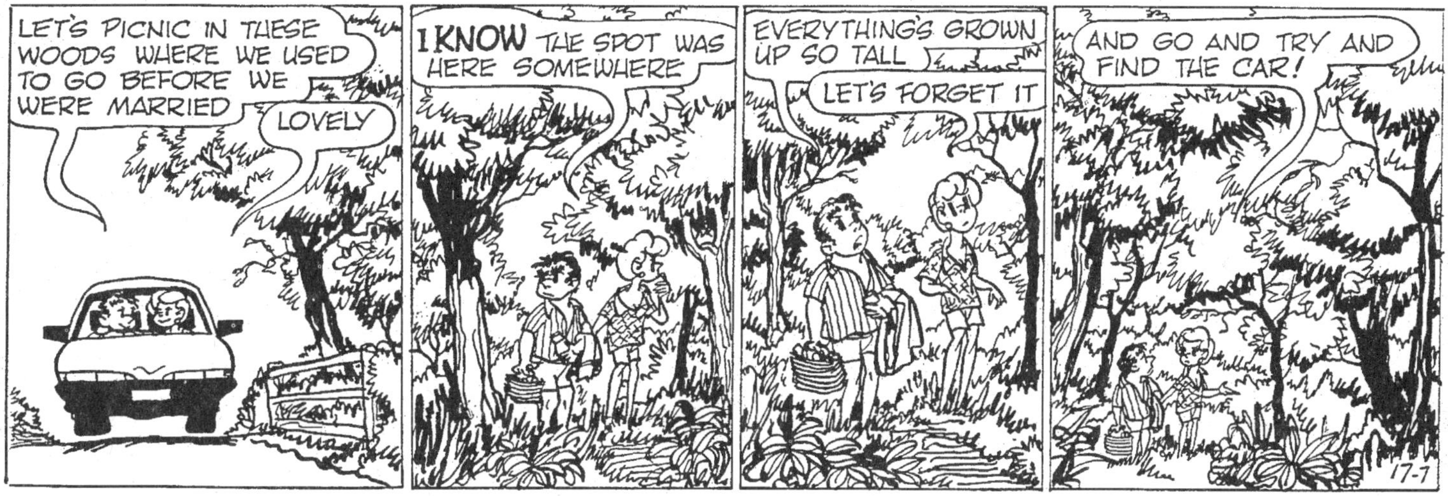
LET'S PICNIC IN THESE WOODS WHERE WE USED TO GO BEFORE WE WERE MARRIED
LOVELY
I KNOW THE SPOT WAS HERE SOMEWHERE
EVERYTHING'S GROWN UP SO TALL
LET'S FORGET IT
AND GO AND TRY AND FIND THE CAR!
17-7

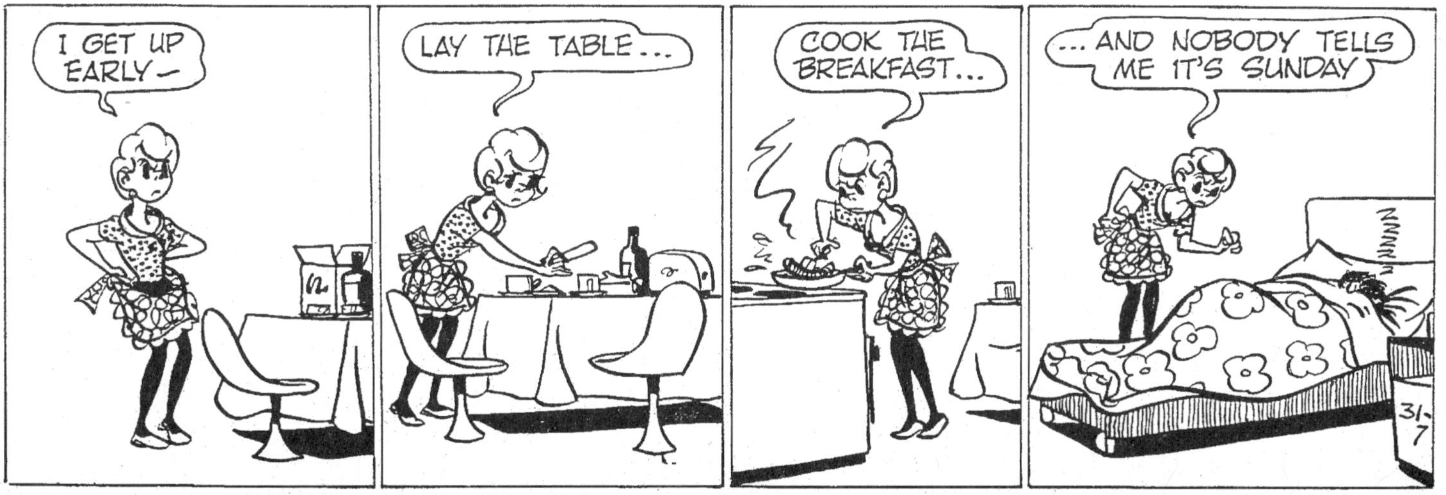
I GET UP EARLY –
LAY THE TABLE...
COOK THE BREAKFAST...
... AND NOBODY TELLS ME IT'S SUNDAY
31-7

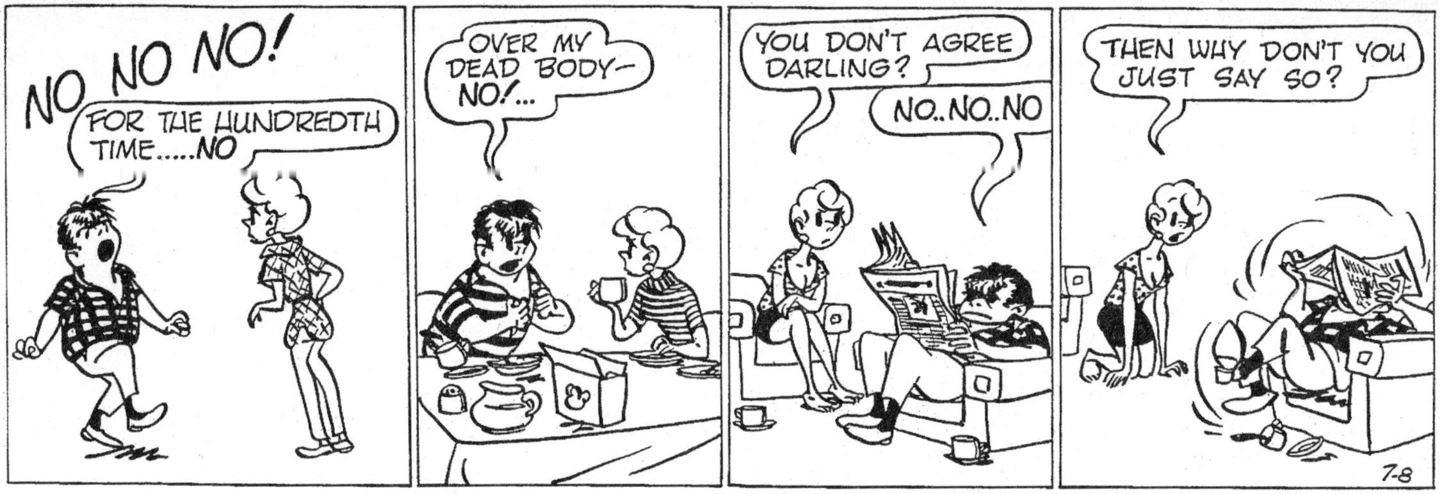
NO NO NO!
FOR THE HUNDREDTH TIME.....NO
OVER MY DEAD BODY— NO!...
YOU DON'T AGREE DARLING?
NO..NO..NO
THEN WHY DON'T YOU JUST SAY SO?
7-8

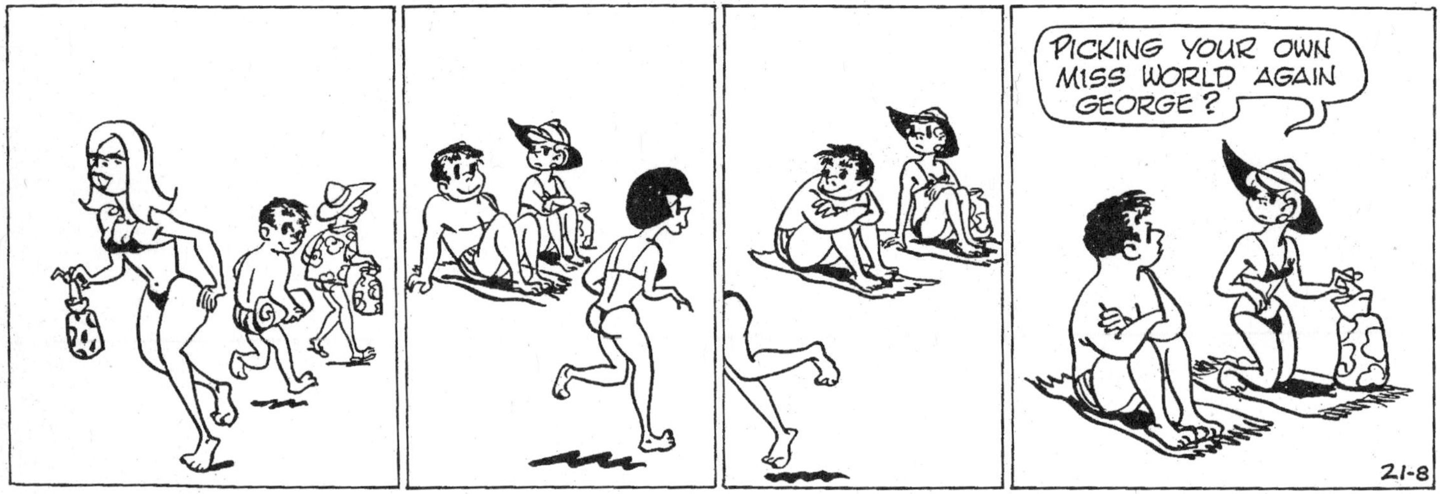
PICKING YOUR OWN MISS WORLD AGAIN GEORGE?
21-8

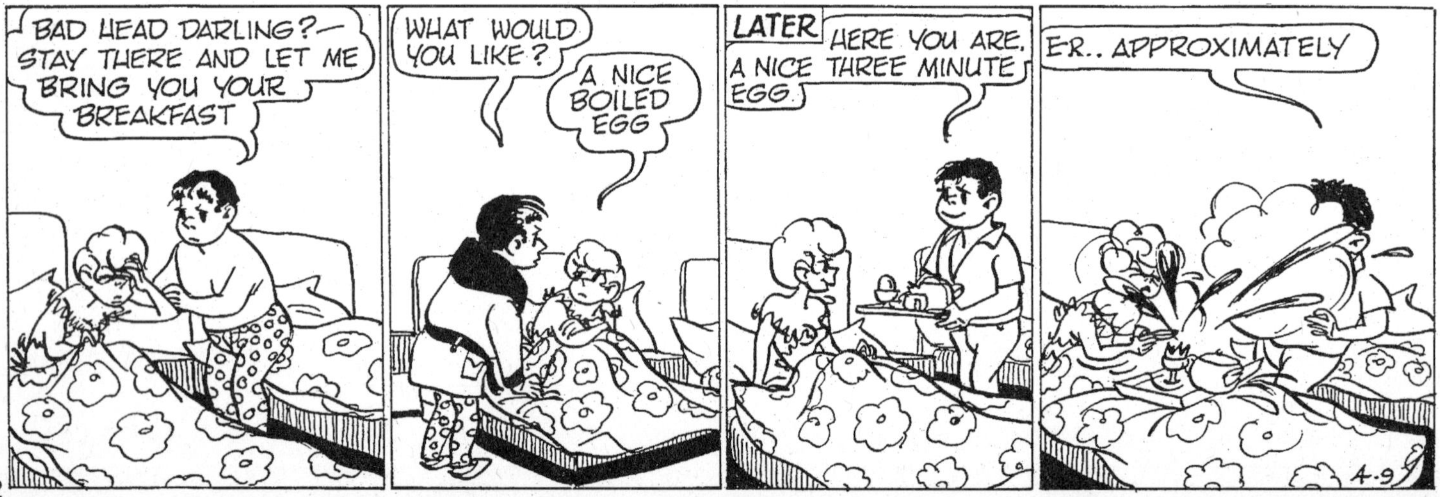
BAD HEAD DARLING?— STAY THERE AND LET ME BRING YOU YOUR BREAKFAST
WHAT WOULD YOU LIKE?
A NICE BOILED EGG
LATER
HERE YOU ARE. A NICE THREE MINUTE EGG.
E-R.. APPROXIMATELY
4-9

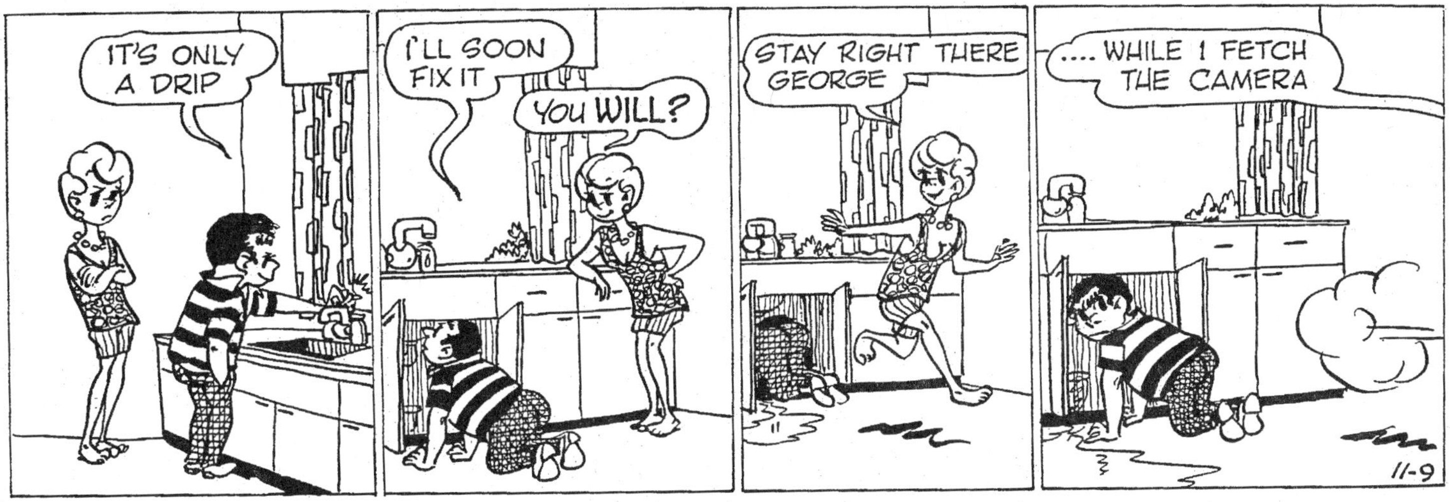
IT'S ONLY A DRIP
I'LL SOON FIX IT
YOU WILL?
STAY RIGHT THERE GEORGE
.... WHILE I FETCH THE CAMERA
11-9

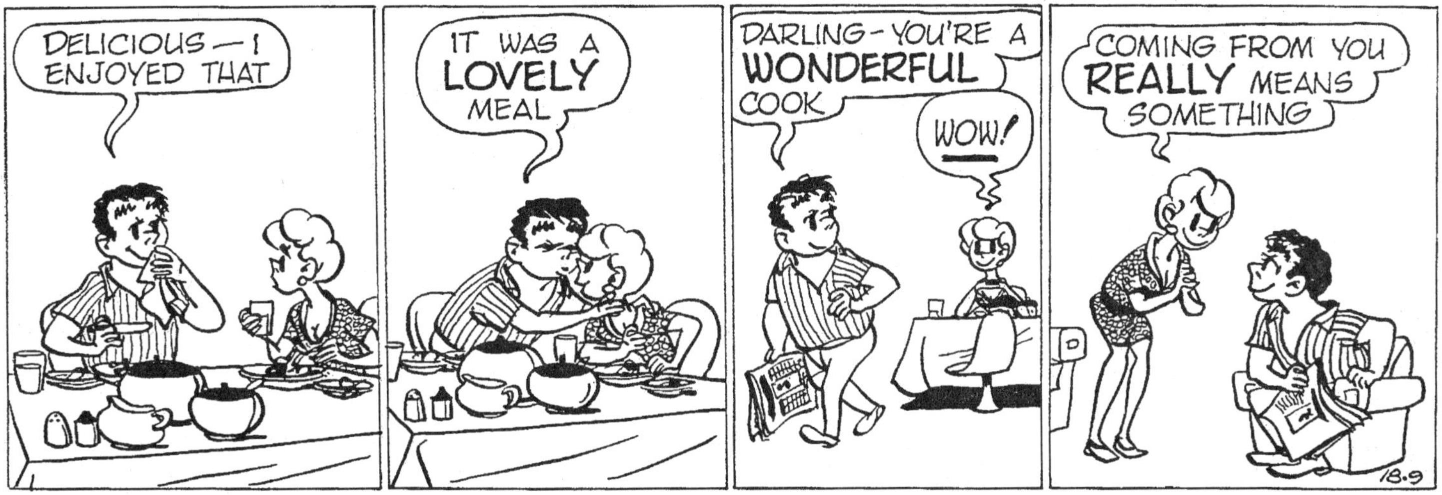
DELICIOUS — I ENJOYED THAT
IT WAS A LOVELY MEAL
DARLING - YOU'RE A WONDERFUL COOK
WOW!
COMING FROM YOU REALLY MEANS SOMETHING
18-9

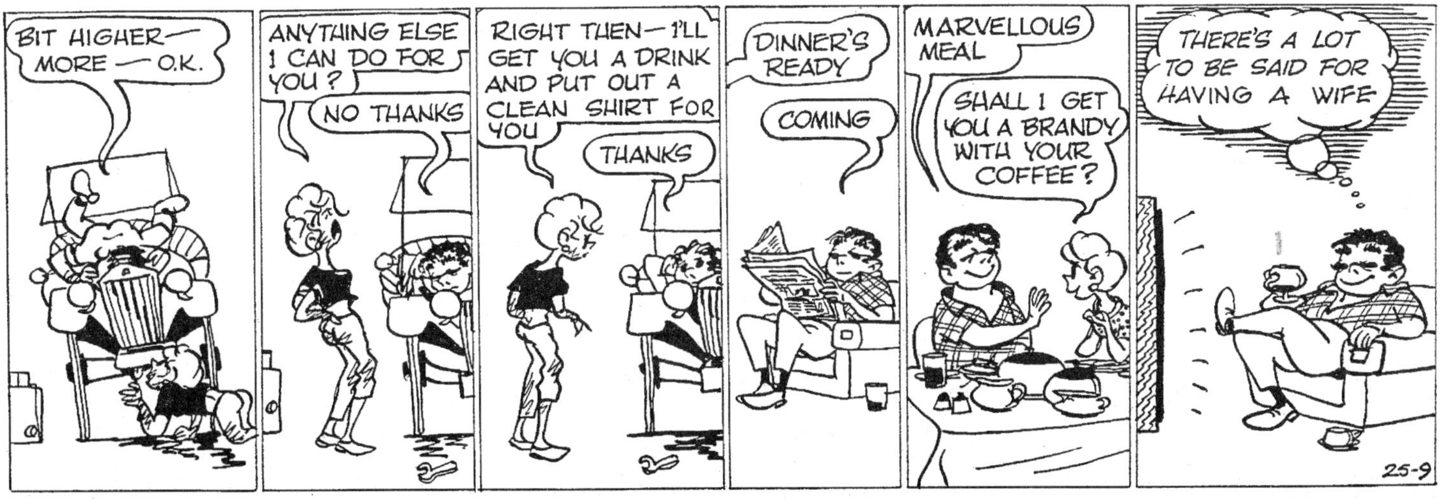
BIT HIGHER— MORE — O.K.
ANYTHING ELSE I CAN DO FOR YOU?
NO THANKS
RIGHT THEN— I'LL GET YOU A DRINK AND PUT OUT A CLEAN SHIRT FOR YOU
THANKS
DINNER'S READY
COMING
MARVELLOUS MEAL
SHALL I GET YOU A BRANDY WITH YOUR COFFEE?
THERE'S A LOT TO BE SAID FOR HAVING A WIFE
25-9

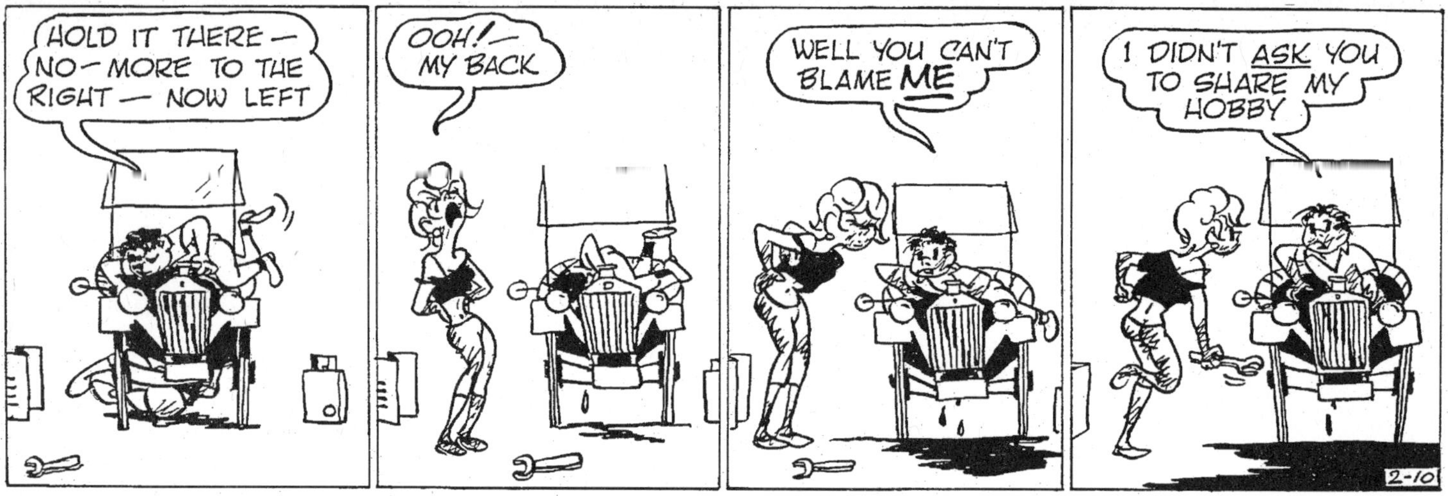
HOLD IT THERE— NO—MORE TO THE RIGHT — NOW LEFT
OOH!— MY BACK
WELL YOU CAN'T BLAME ME
I DIDN'T ASK YOU TO SHARE MY HOBBY
2-10

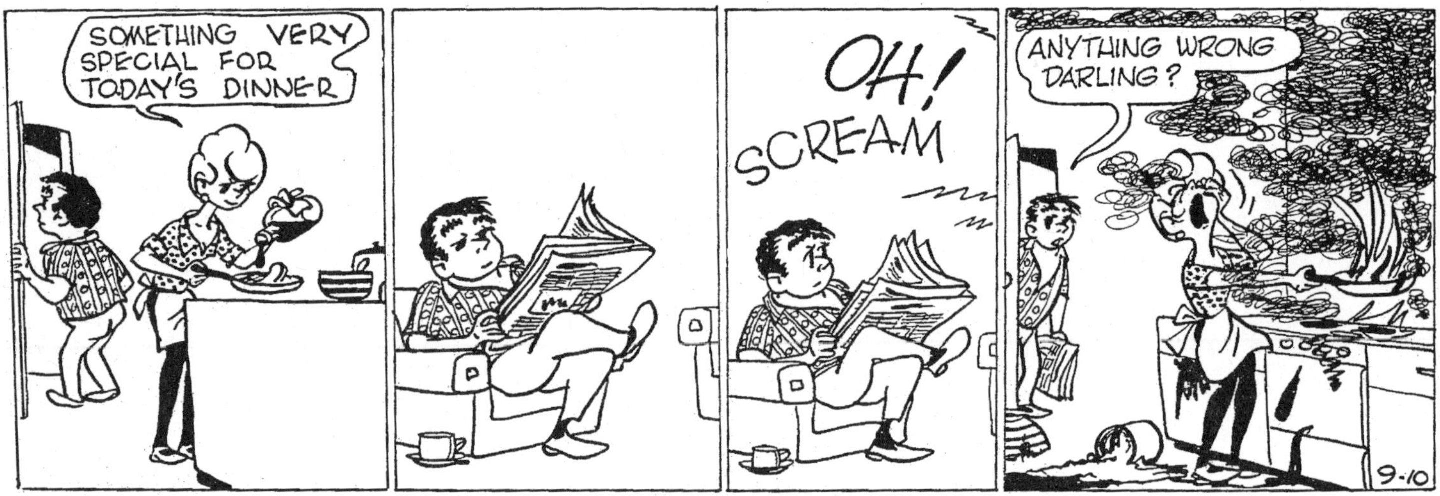
SOMETHING VERY SPECIAL FOR TODAY'S DINNER
OH!
SCREAM
ANYTHING WRONG DARLING?
9-10

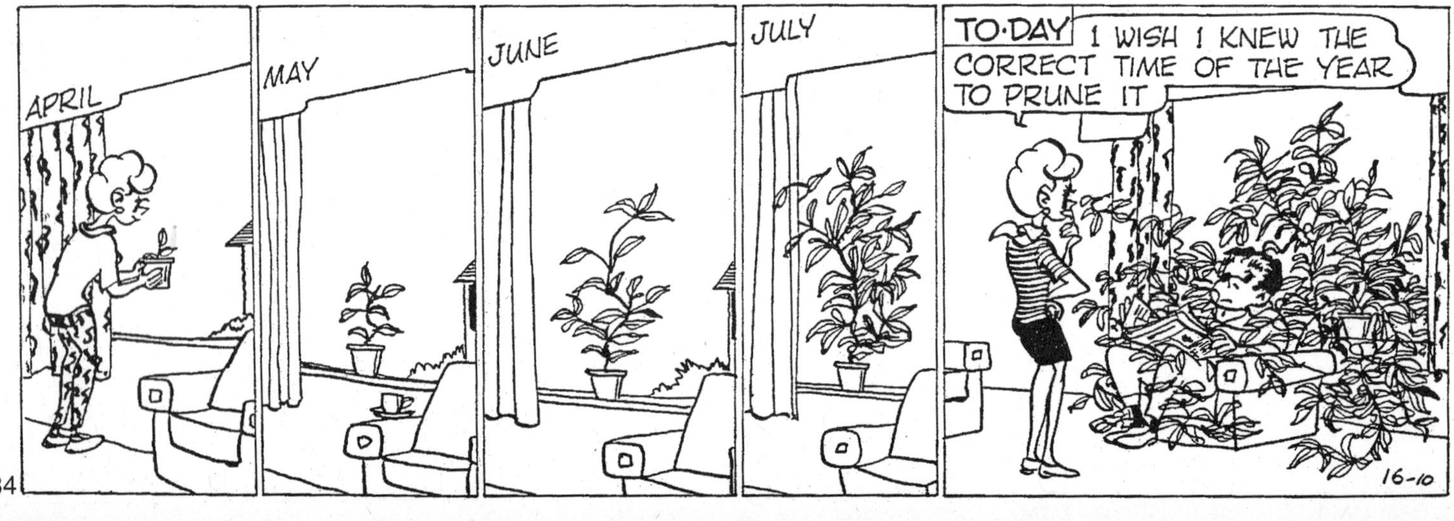
APRIL
MAY
JUNE
JULY
TO·DAY
I WISH I KNEW THE CORRECT TIME OF THE YEAR TO PRUNE IT
16-10

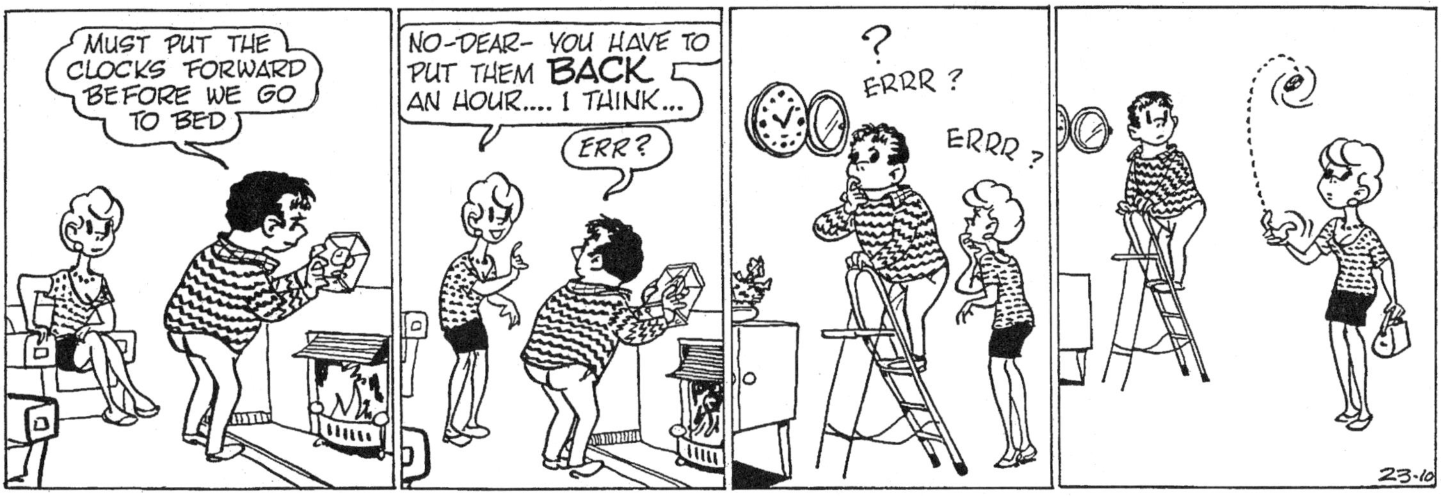
MUST PUT THE CLOCKS FORWARD BEFORE WE GO TO BED
NO-DEAR- YOU HAVE TO PUT THEM BACK AN HOUR.... I THINK...
ERR?
?
ERRR ?
ERRR ?
23-10

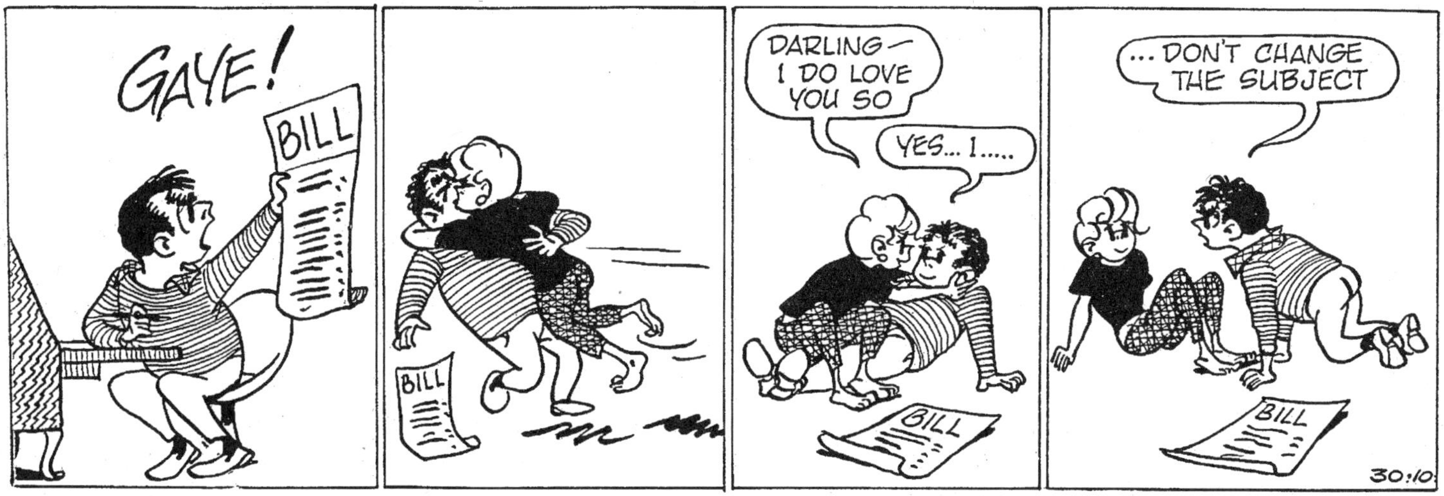
GAYE!
BILL
BILL
DARLING— I DO LOVE YOU SO
YES... I.....
BILL
... DON'T CHANGE THE SUBJECT
BILL
30-10

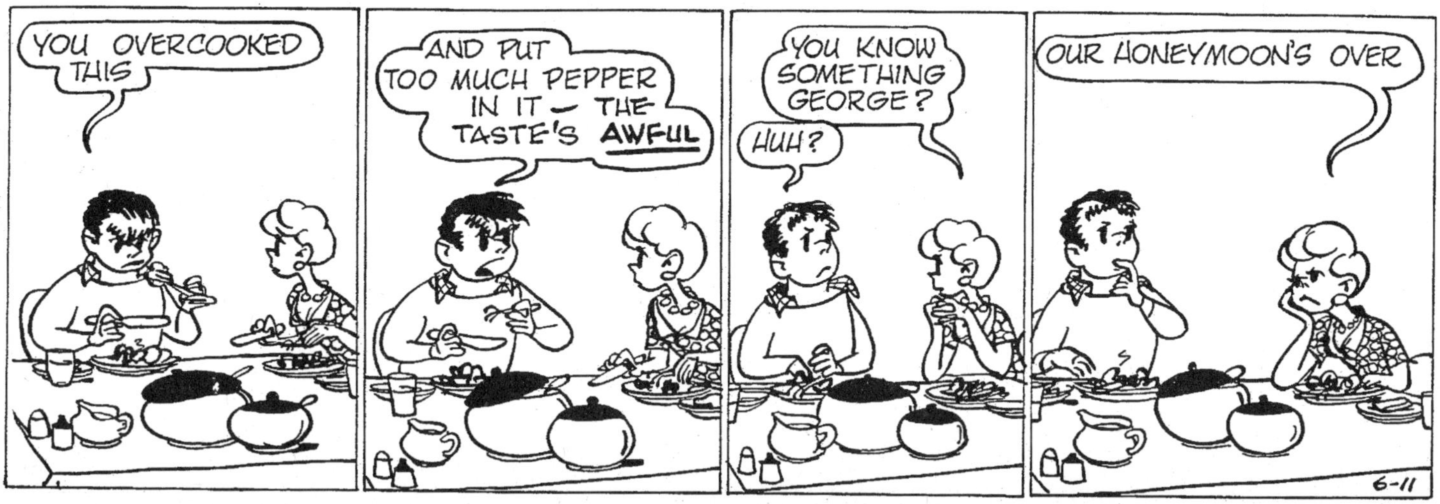
YOU OVERCOOKED THIS
AND PUT TOO MUCH PEPPER IN IT — THE TASTE'S AWFUL
YOU KNOW SOMETHING GEORGE?
HUH?
OUR HONEYMOON'S OVER
6-11

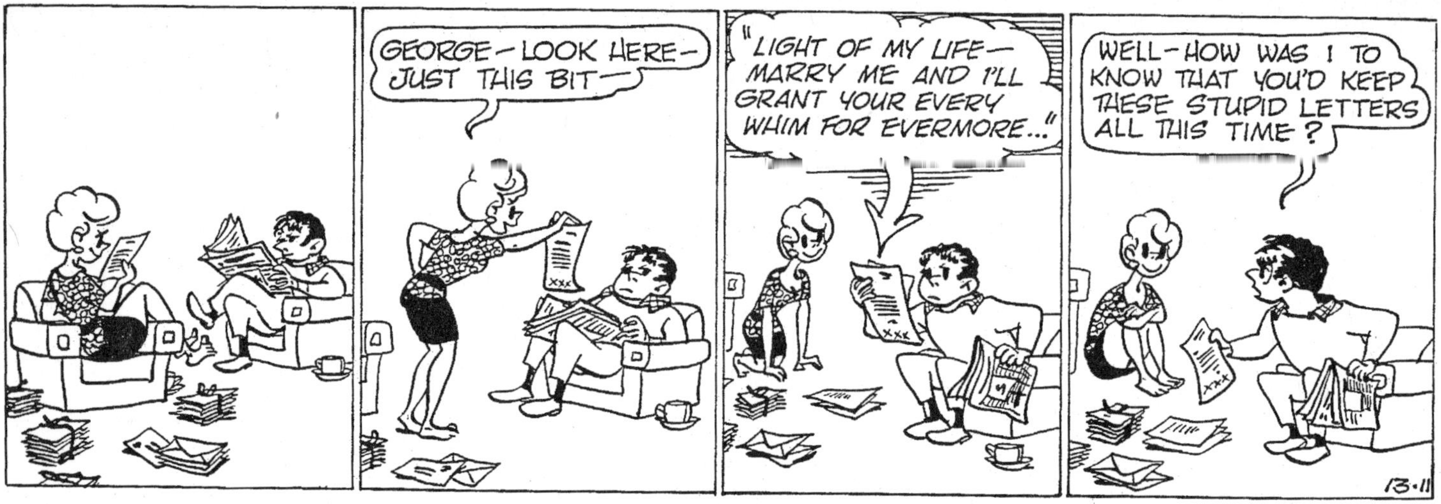
GEORGE – LOOK HERE – JUST THIS BIT –
"LIGHT OF MY LIFE – MARRY ME AND I'LL GRANT YOUR EVERY WHIM FOR EVERMORE..."
WELL – HOW WAS I TO KNOW THAT YOU'D KEEP THESE STUPID LETTERS ALL THIS TIME?
13·11

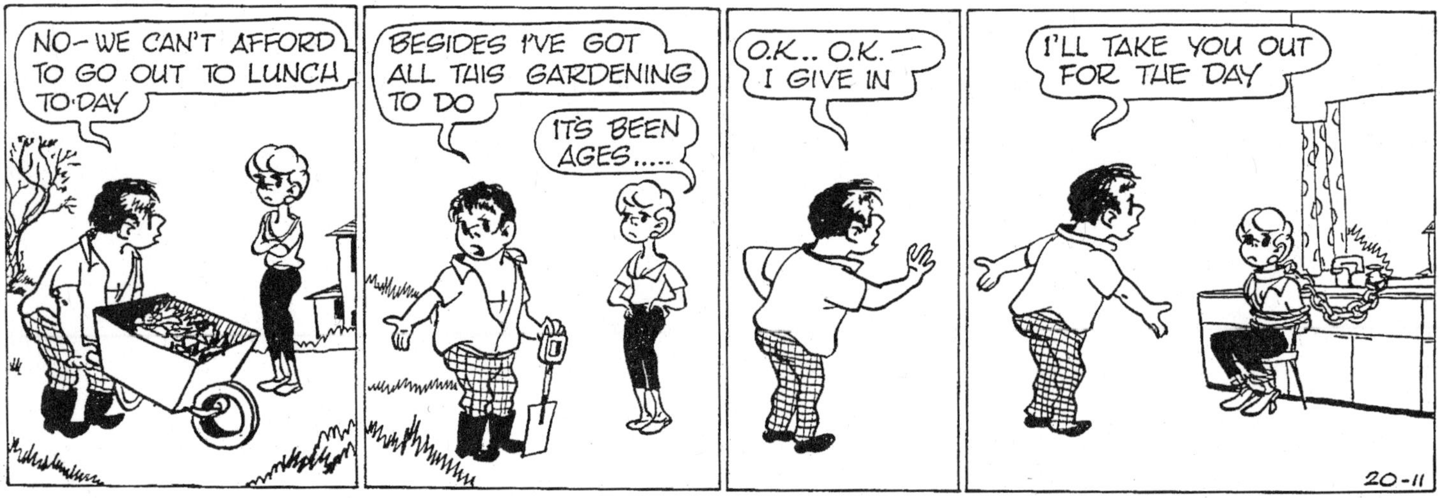
NO – WE CAN'T AFFORD TO GO OUT TO LUNCH TO·DAY
BESIDES I'VE GOT ALL THIS GARDENING TO DO
IT'S BEEN AGES.....
O.K.. O.K. – I GIVE IN
I'LL TAKE YOU OUT FOR THE DAY
20-11

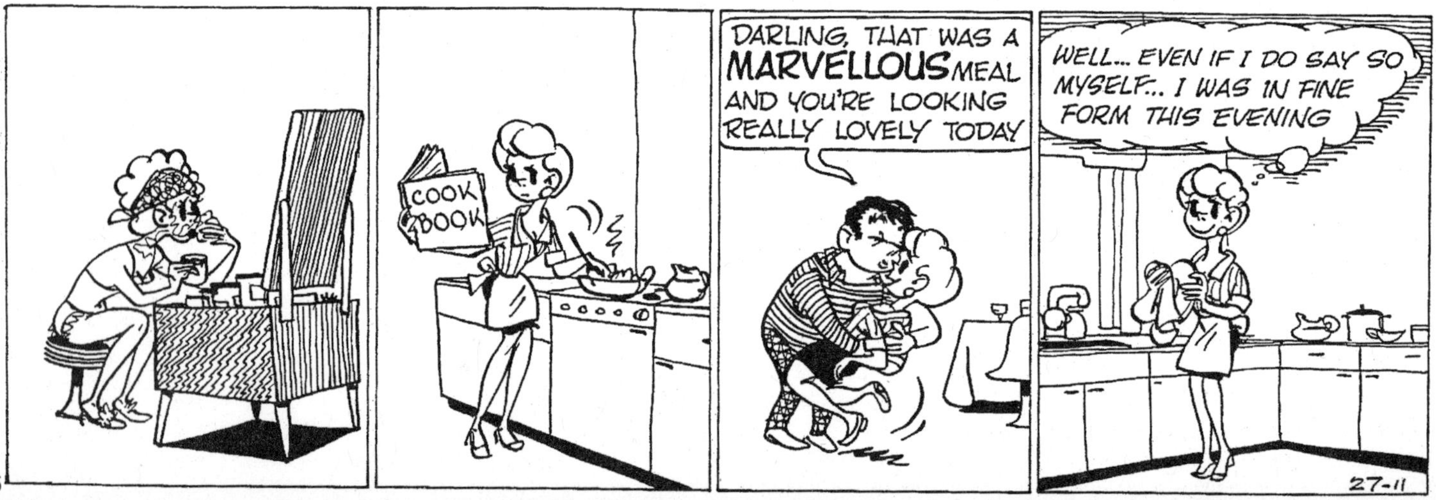
COOK BOOK
DARLING, THAT WAS A MARVELLOUS MEAL AND YOU'RE LOOKING REALLY LOVELY TODAY
WELL... EVEN IF I DO SAY SO MYSELF... I WAS IN FINE FORM THIS EVENING
27-11

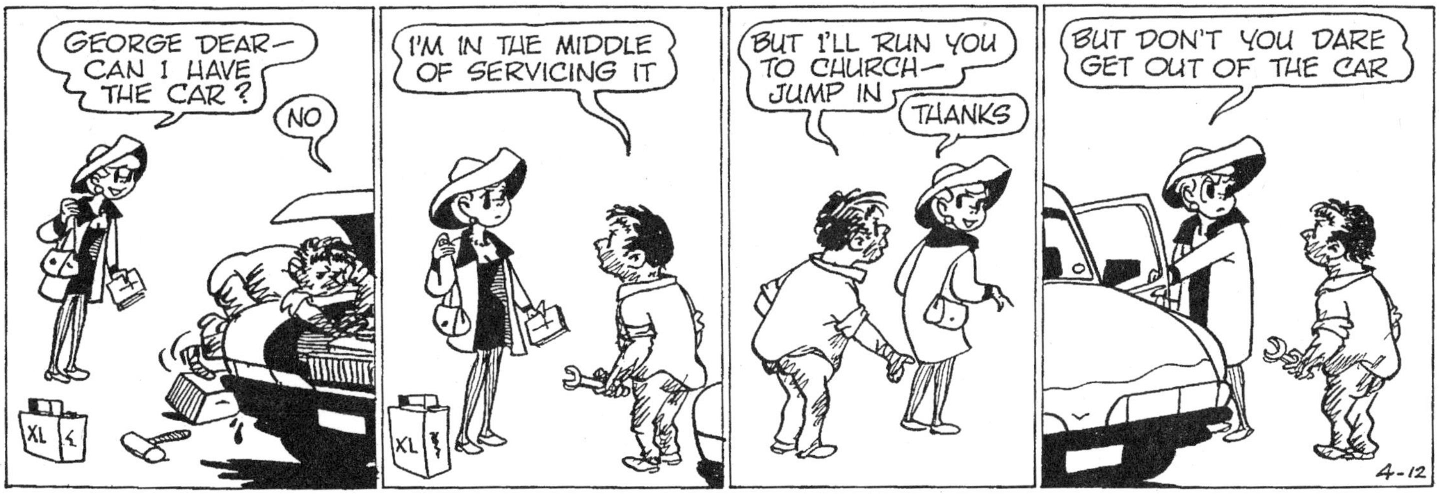
GEORGE DEAR— CAN I HAVE THE CAR?
NO
I'M IN THE MIDDLE OF SERVICING IT
BUT I'LL RUN YOU TO CHURCH— JUMP IN
THANKS
BUT DON'T YOU DARE GET OUT OF THE CAR
4-12

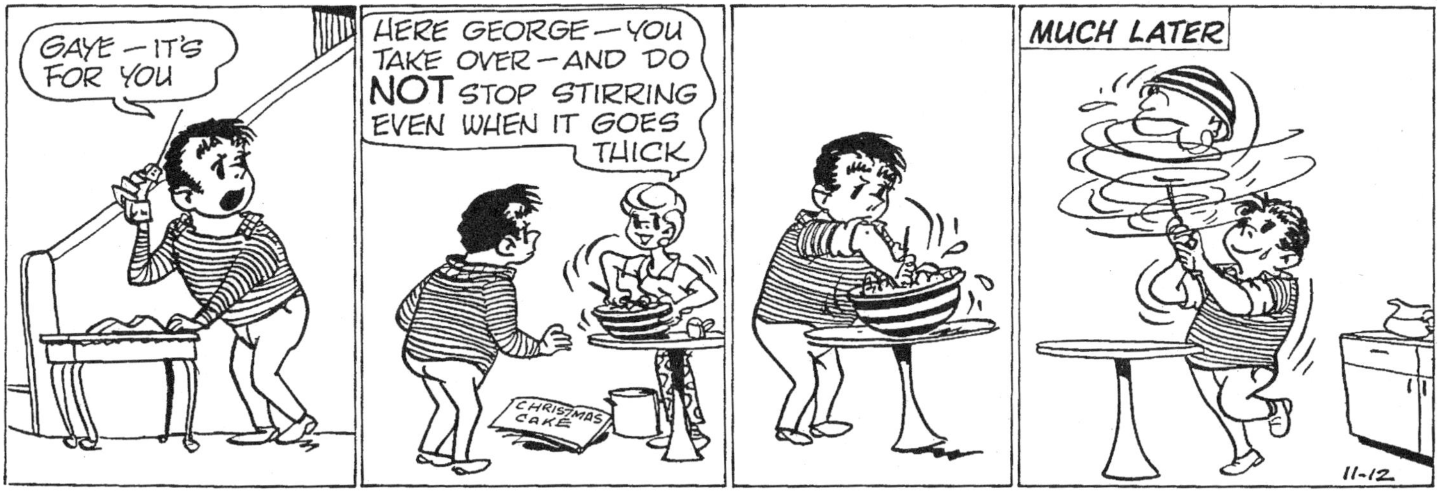
GAYE — IT'S FOR YOU
HERE GEORGE — YOU TAKE OVER — AND DO **NOT** STOP STIRRING EVEN WHEN IT GOES THICK
CHRISTMAS CAKE
MUCH LATER
11-12

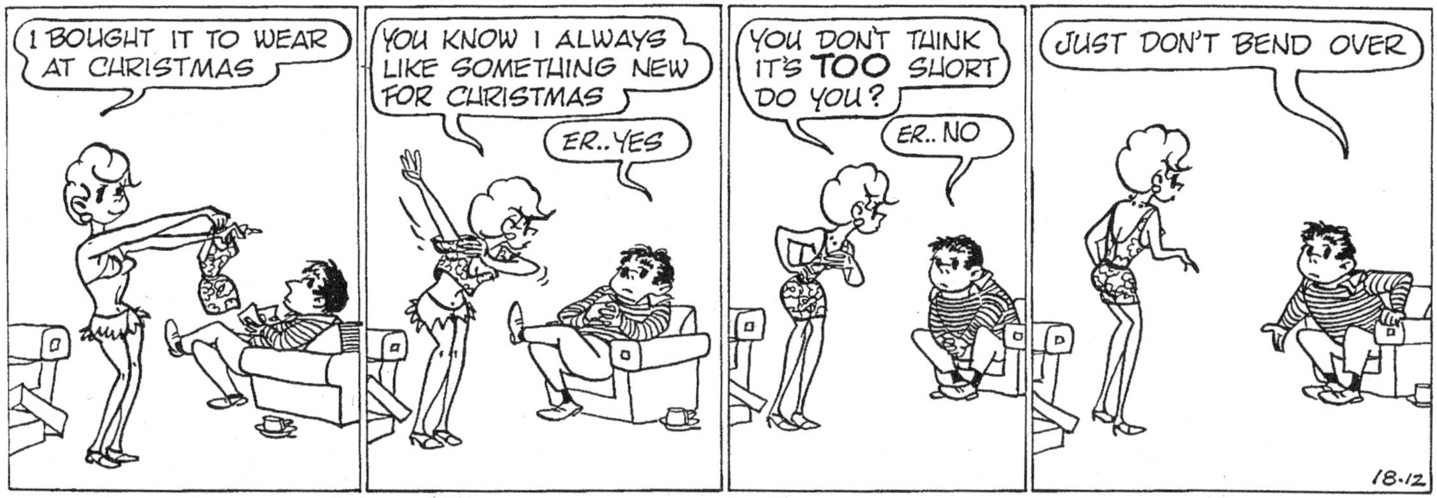
I BOUGHT IT TO WEAR AT CHRISTMAS
YOU KNOW I ALWAYS LIKE SOMETHING NEW FOR CHRISTMAS
ER..YES
YOU DON'T THINK IT'S **TOO** SHORT DO YOU?
ER.. NO
JUST DON'T BEND OVER
18-12

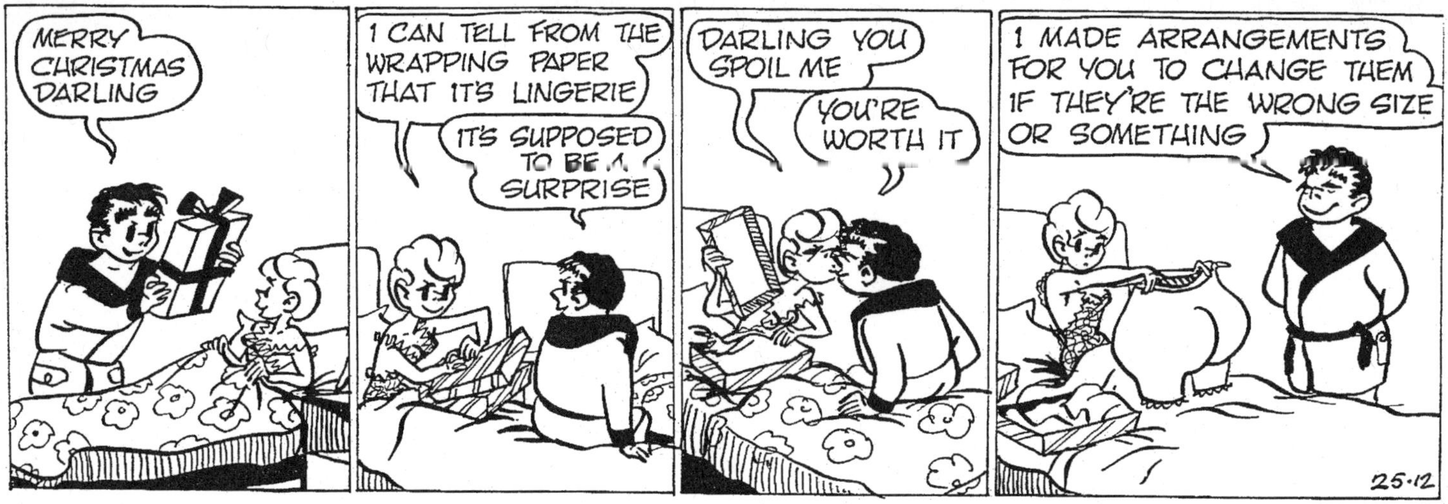
MERRY CHRISTMAS DARLING
I CAN TELL FROM THE WRAPPING PAPER THAT IT'S LINGERIE
IT'S SUPPOSED TO BE A SURPRISE
DARLING YOU SPOIL ME
YOU'RE WORTH IT
I MADE ARRANGEMENTS FOR YOU TO CHANGE THEM IF THEY'RE THE WRONG SIZE OR SOMETHING
25-12

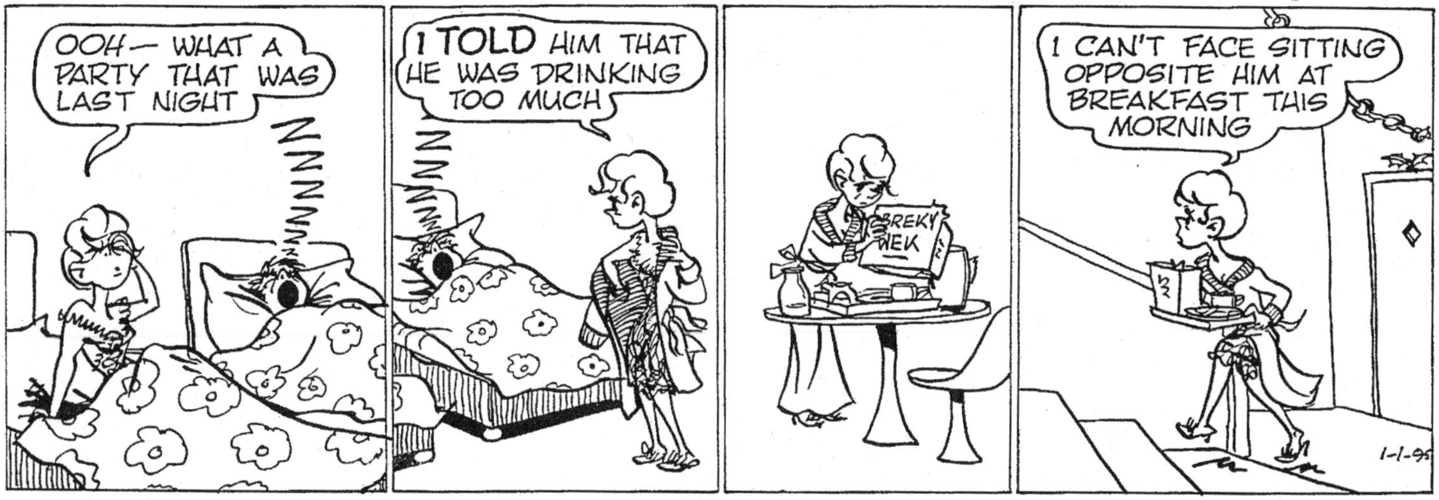
OOH— WHAT A PARTY THAT WAS LAST NIGHT
I TOLD HIM THAT HE WAS DRINKING TOO MUCH
BREKY WEK
I CAN'T FACE SITTING OPPOSITE HIM AT BREAKFAST THIS MORNING
1-1-95

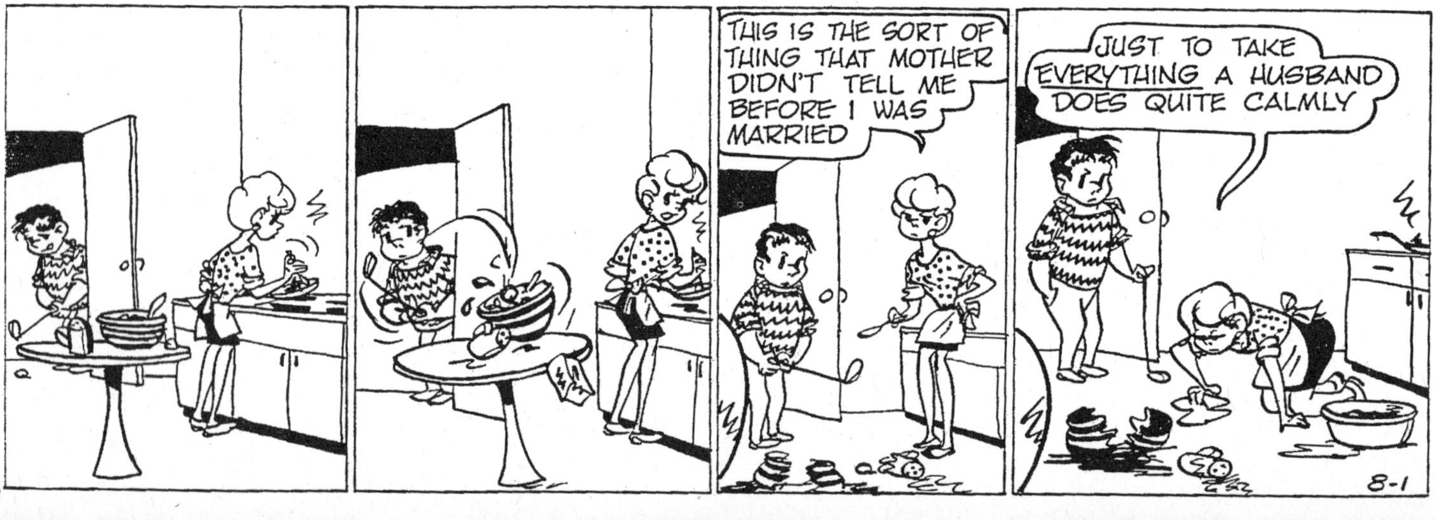
THIS IS THE SORT OF THING THAT MOTHER DIDN'T TELL ME BEFORE I WAS MARRIED
JUST TO TAKE EVERYTHING A HUSBAND DOES QUITE CALMLY
8-1

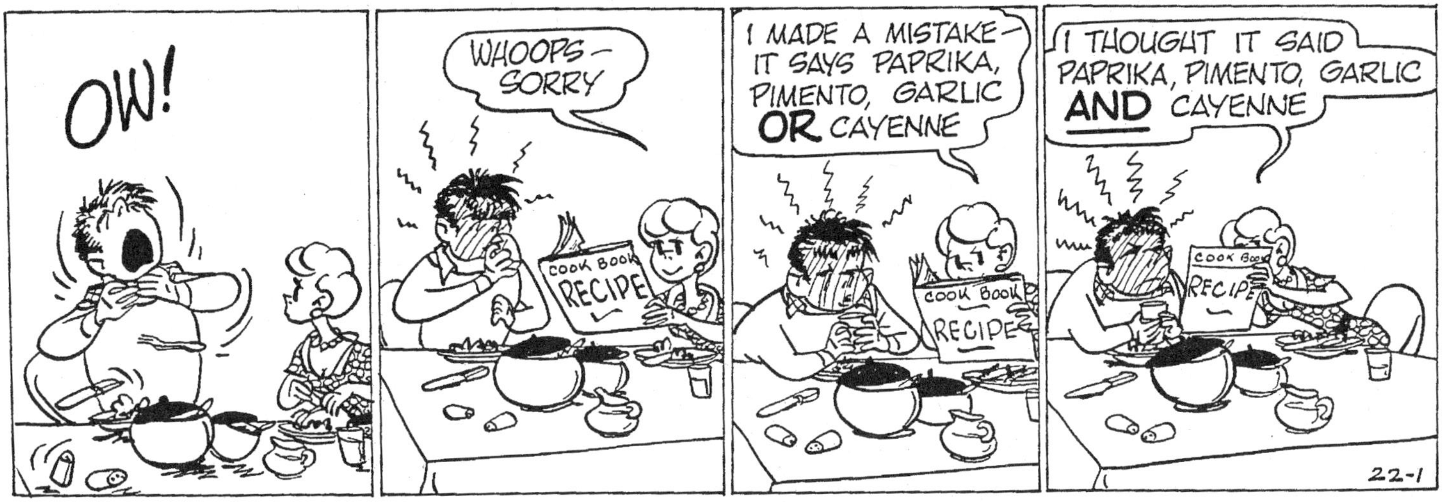
OW!
WHOOPS-
SORRY
COOK BOOK
RECIPE
I MADE A MISTAKE-
IT SAYS PAPRIKA, PIMENTO, GARLIC **OR** CAYENNE
COOK BOOK
RECIPE
I THOUGHT IT SAID PAPRIKA, PIMENTO, GARLIC **AND** CAYENNE
COOK BOOK
RECIPE
22-1

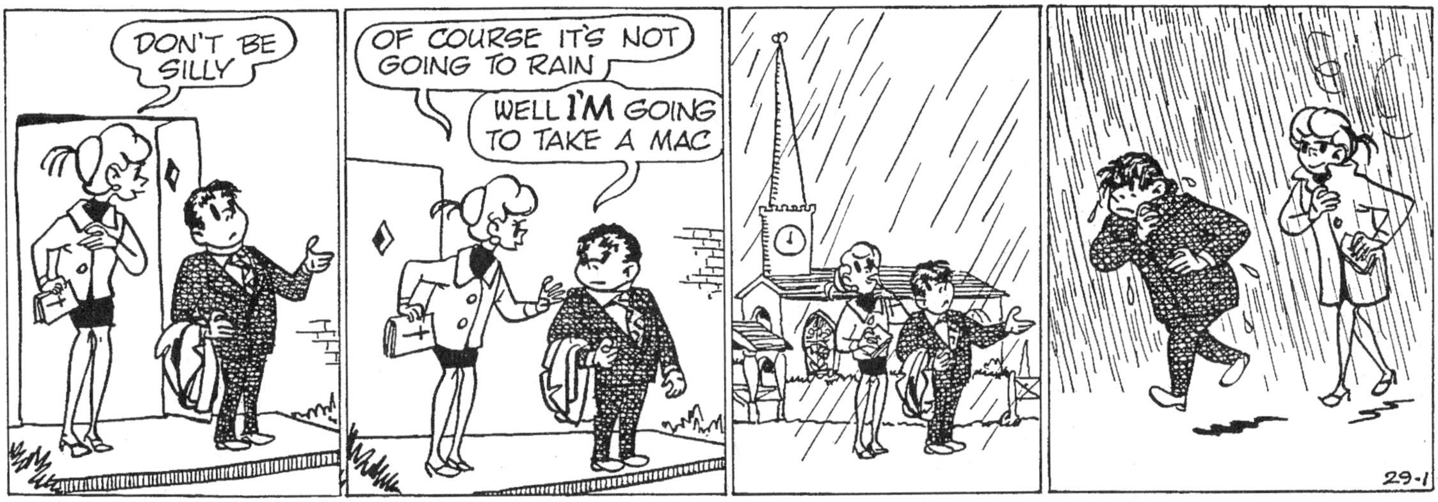
DON'T BE SILLY
OF COURSE IT'S NOT GOING TO RAIN
WELL **I'M** GOING TO TAKE A MAC
29-1

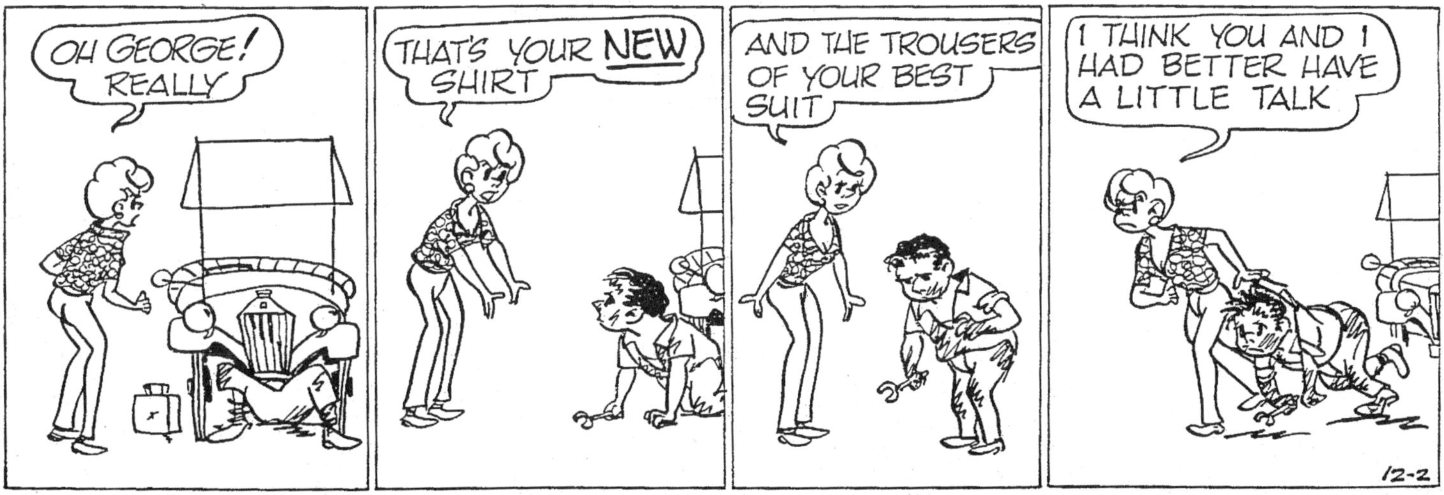
OH GEORGE! REALLY
THAT'S YOUR NEW SHIRT
AND THE TROUSERS OF YOUR BEST SUIT
I THINK YOU AND I HAD BETTER HAVE A LITTLE TALK
12-2

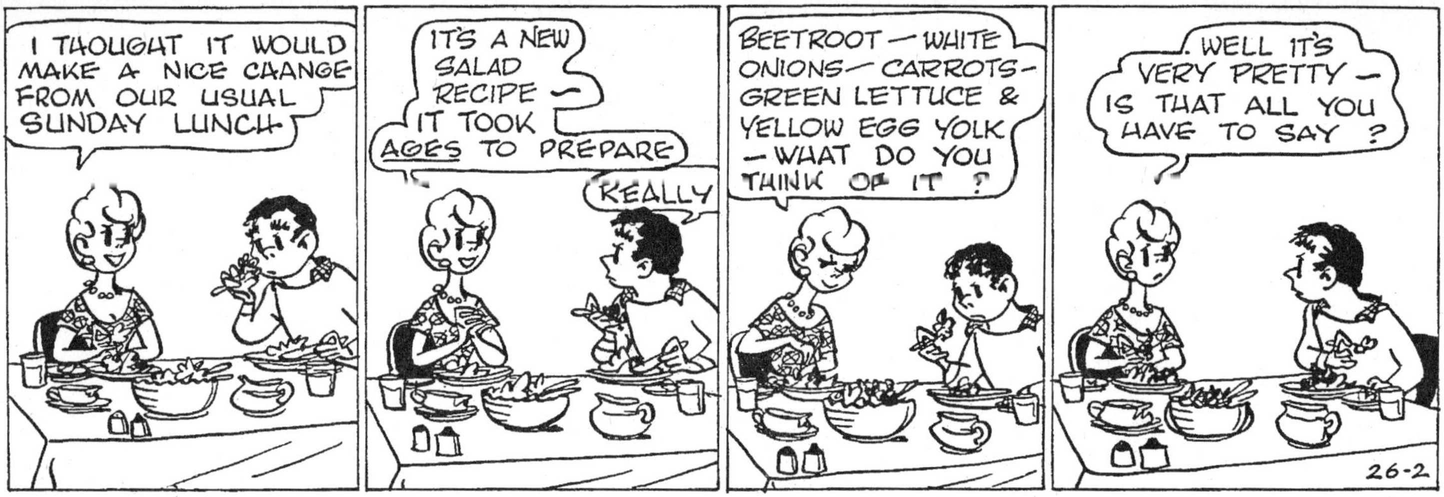
I THOUGHT IT WOULD MAKE A NICE CAANGE FROM OUR USUAL SUNDAY LUNCH
IT'S A NEW SALAD RECIPE — IT TOOK AGES TO PREPARE
KEALLY
BEETROOT — WHITE ONIONS — CARROTS — GREEN LETTUCE & YELLOW EGG YOLK — WHAT DO YOU THINK OF IT ?
. WELL IT'S VERY PRETTY — IS THAT ALL YOU HAVE TO SAY ?
26-2

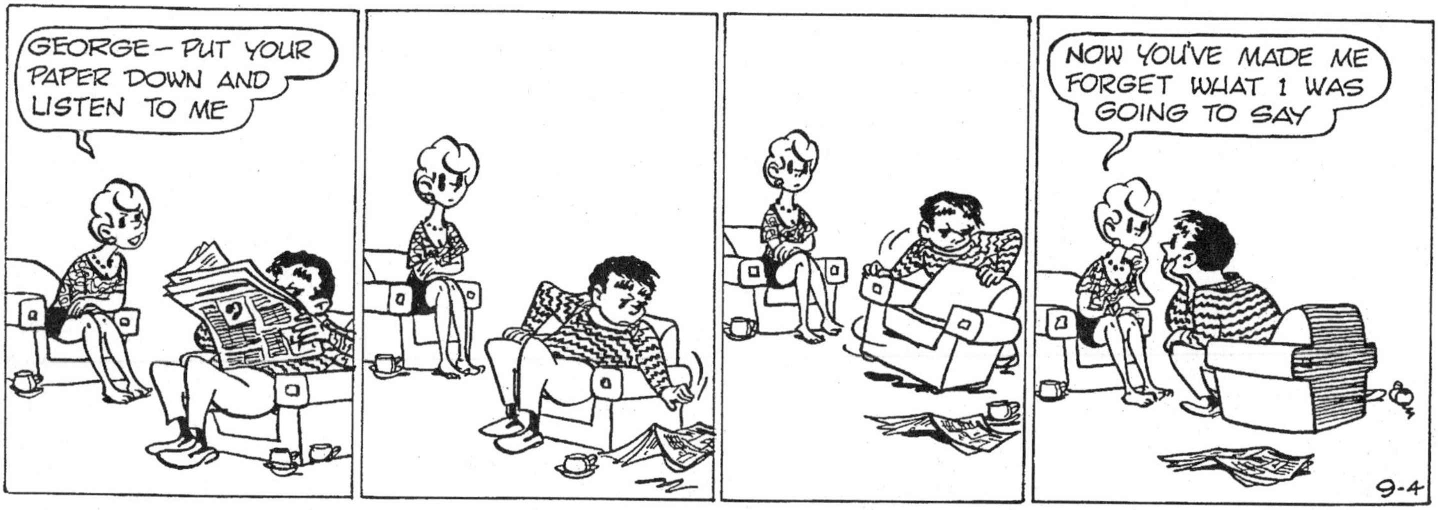
GEORGE — PUT YOUR PAPER DOWN AND LISTEN TO ME
NOW YOU'VE MADE ME FORGET WHAT I WAS GOING TO SAY
9-4

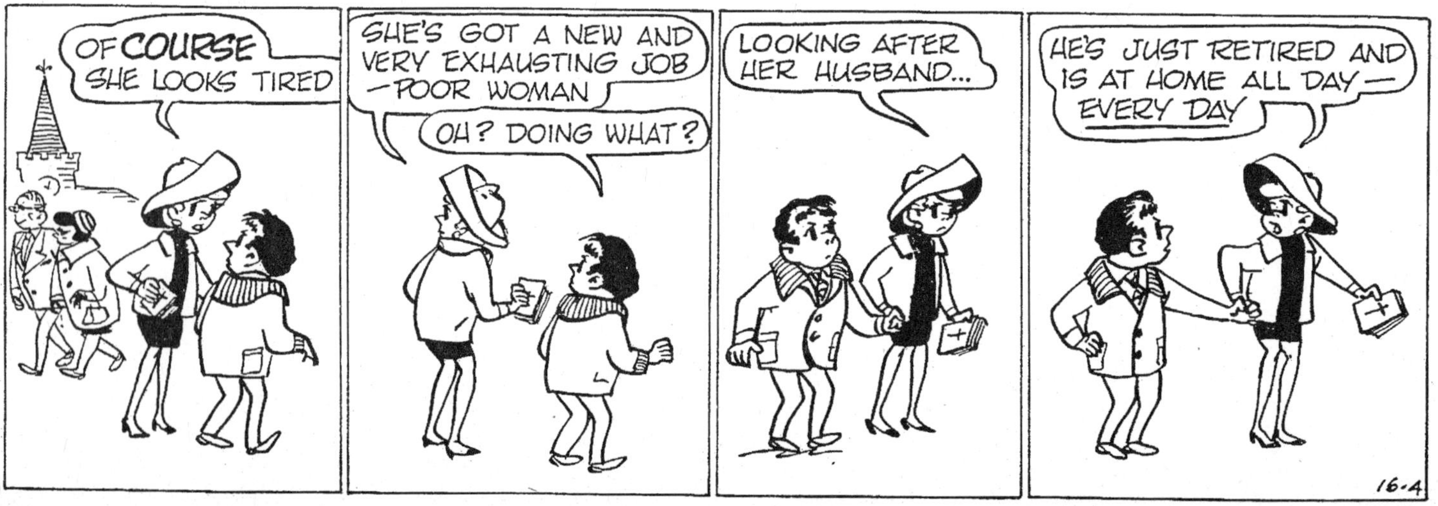
OF COURSE SHE LOOKS TIRED
SHE'S GOT A NEW AND VERY EXHAUSTING JOB — POOR WOMAN
OH? DOING WHAT?
LOOKING AFTER HER HUSBAND...
HE'S JUST RETIRED AND IS AT HOME ALL DAY — EVERY DAY
16-4

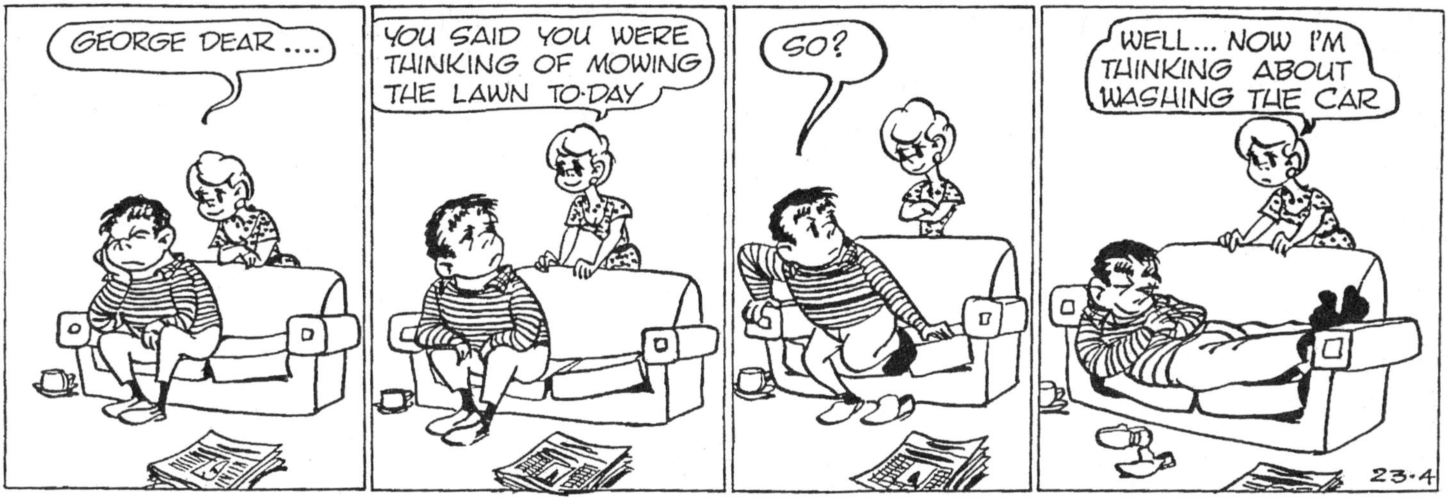
GEORGE DEAR ....
YOU SAID YOU WERE THINKING OF MOWING THE LAWN TO-DAY
SO?
WELL... NOW I'M THINKING ABOUT WASHING THE CAR
23-4

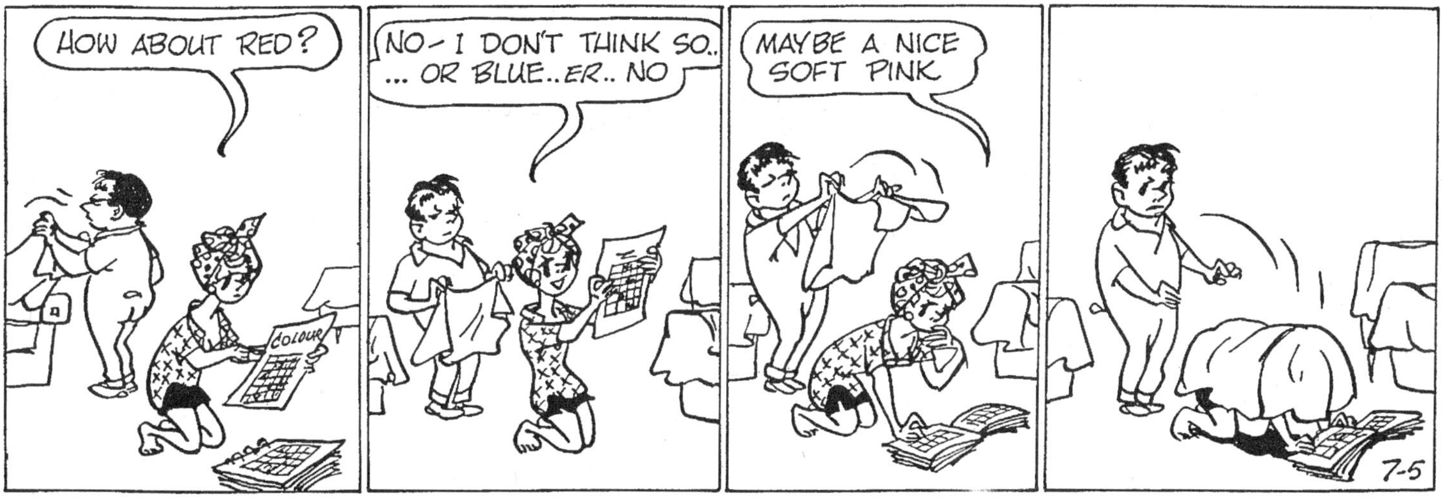
HOW ABOUT RED?
COLOUR
NO- I DON'T THINK SO.. ... OR BLUE..ER.. NO
MAYBE A NICE SOFT PINK
7-5

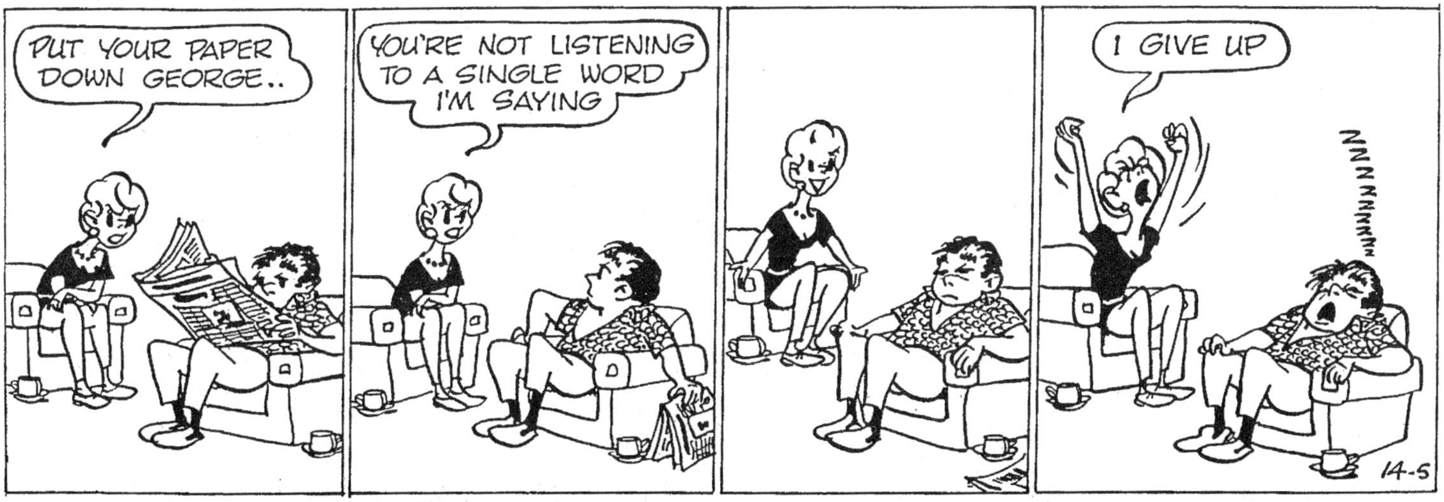
PUT YOUR PAPER DOWN GEORGE..
YOU'RE NOT LISTENING TO A SINGLE WORD I'M SAYING
I GIVE UP
14-5

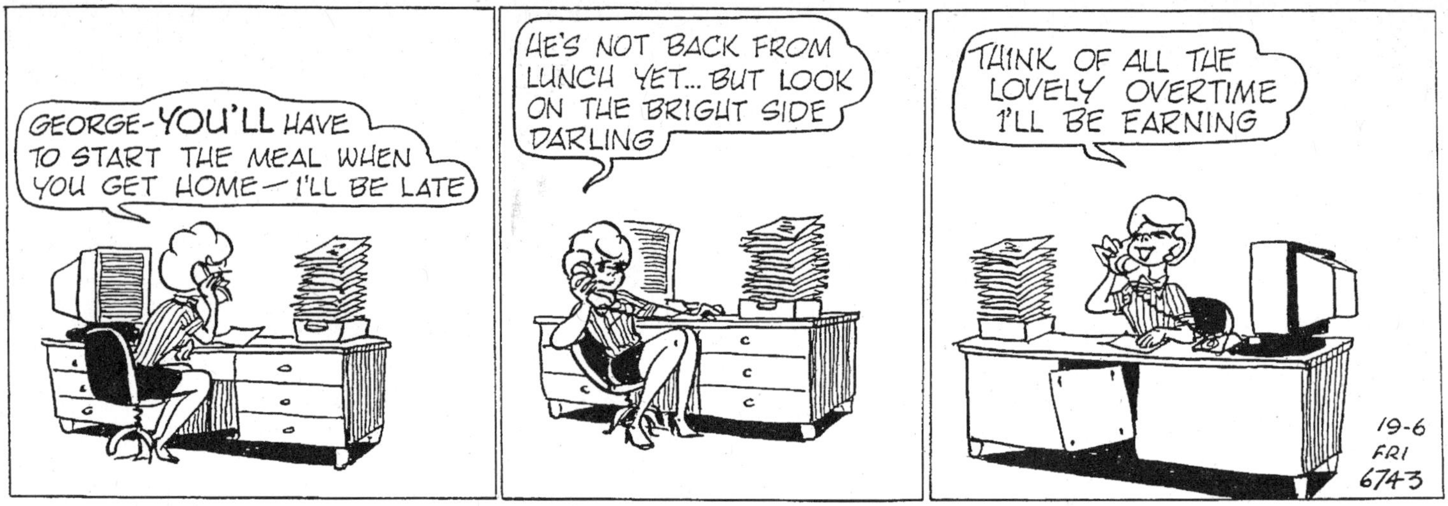
GEORGE-YOU'LL HAVE TO START THE MEAL WHEN YOU GET HOME—I'LL BE LATE
HE'S NOT BACK FROM LUNCH YET... BUT LOOK ON THE BRIGHT SIDE DARLING
THINK OF ALL THE LOVELY OVERTIME I'LL BE EARNING
19-6 FRI 6743

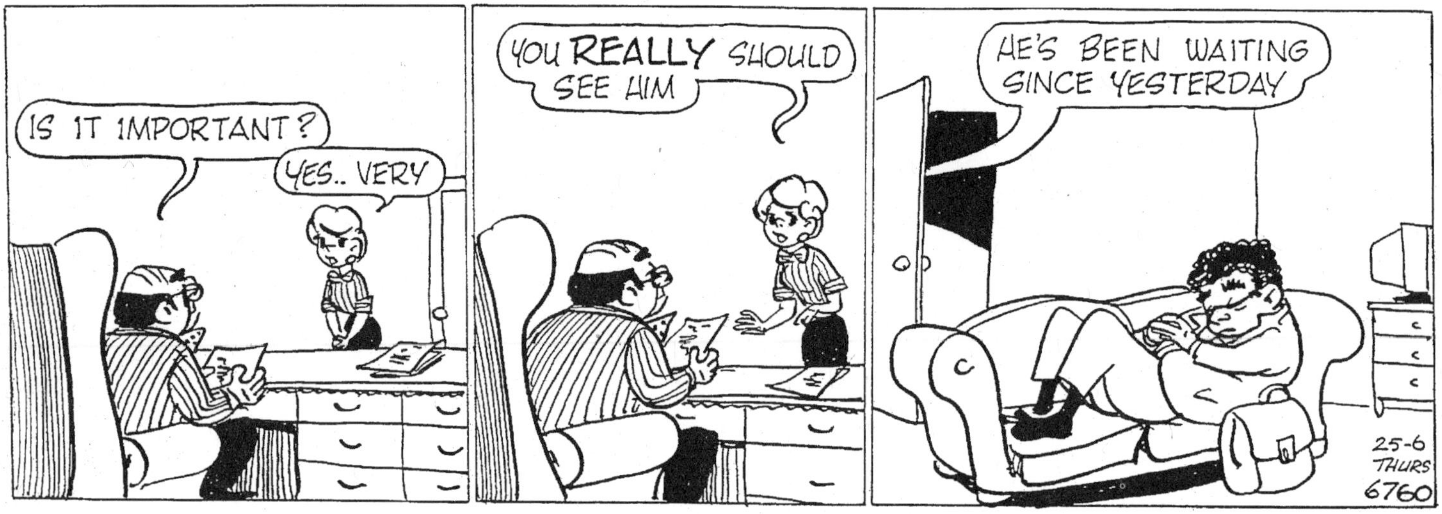
IS IT IMPORTANT?
YES.. VERY
YOU REALLY SHOULD SEE HIM
HE'S BEEN WAITING SINCE YESTERDAY
25-6 THURS 6760

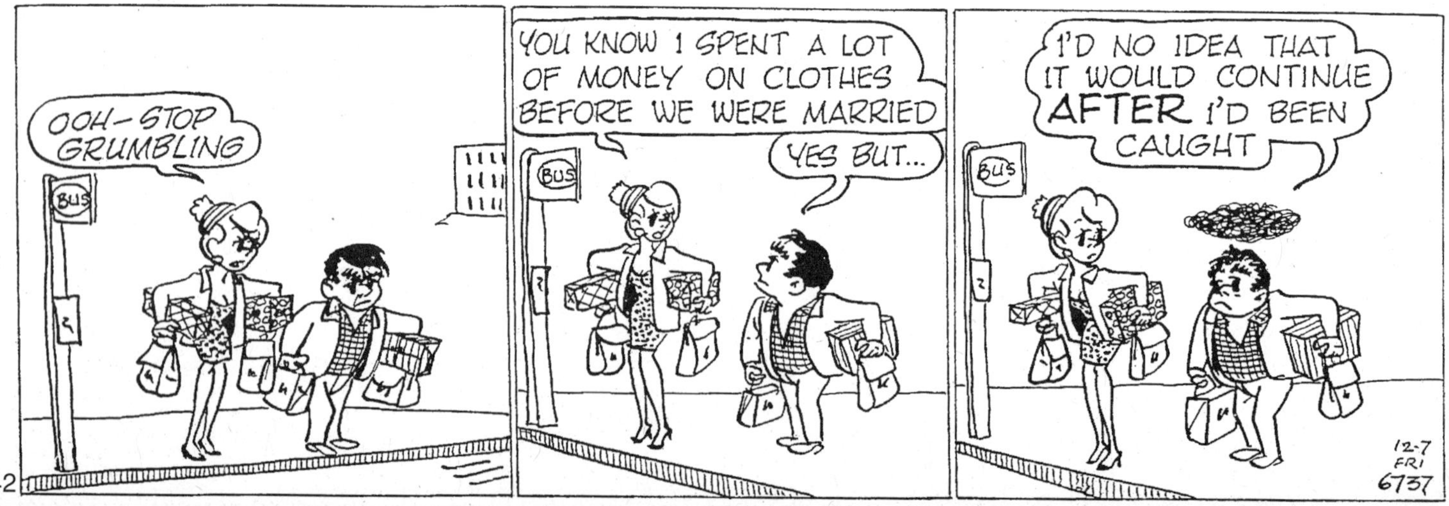
OOH—STOP GRUMBLING
BUS
YOU KNOW I SPENT A LOT OF MONEY ON CLOTHES BEFORE WE WERE MARRIED
YES BUT...
I'D NO IDEA THAT IT WOULD CONTINUE AFTER I'D BEEN CAUGHT
12-7 FRI 6737

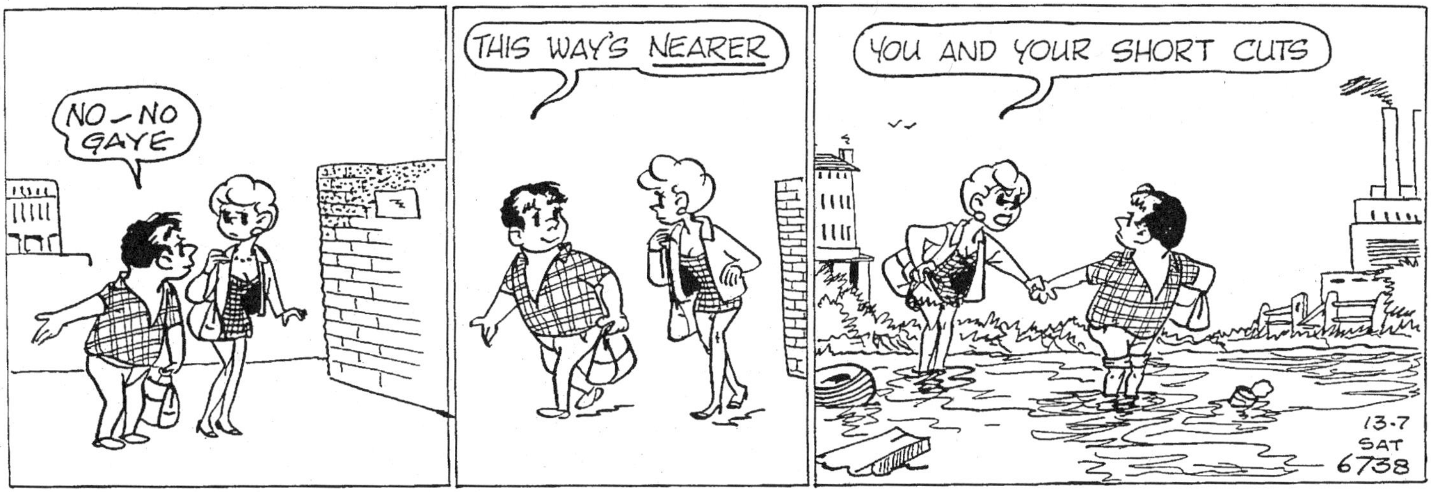
NO-NO GAYE
THIS WAY'S NEARER
YOU AND YOUR SHORT CUTS
13-7 SAT 6738

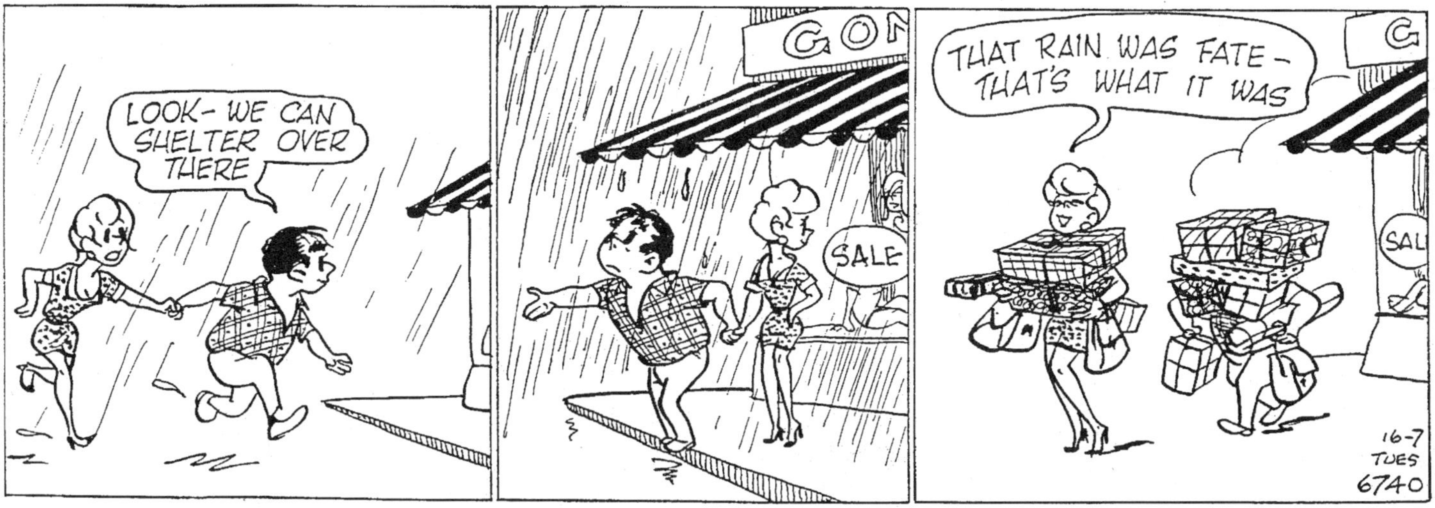
LOOK- WE CAN SHELTER OVER THERE
SALE
THAT RAIN WAS FATE- THAT'S WHAT IT WAS
16-7 TUES 6740

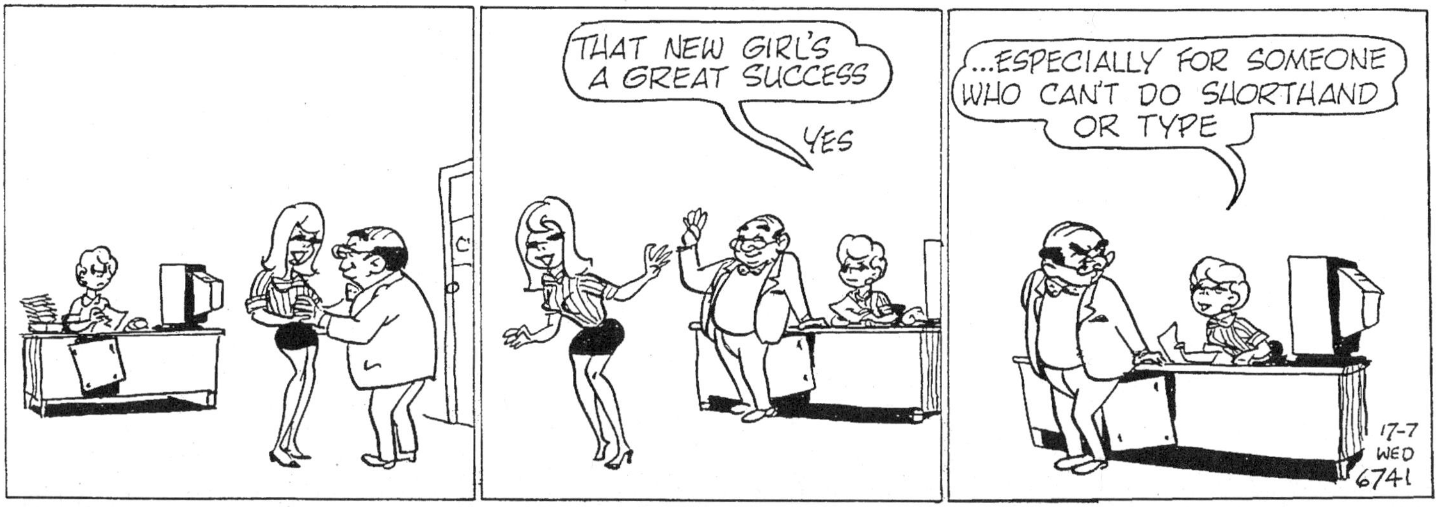
THAT NEW GIRL'S A GREAT SUCCESS
YES
...ESPECIALLY FOR SOMEONE WHO CAN'T DO SHORTHAND OR TYPE
17-7 WED 6741

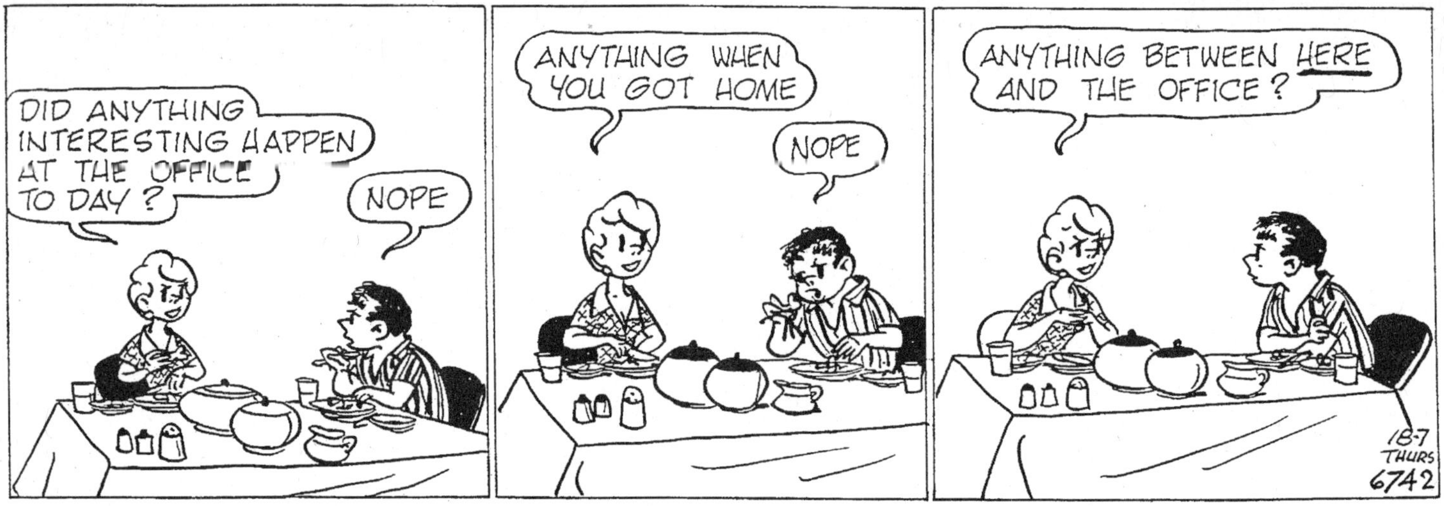
DID ANYTHING INTERESTING HAPPEN AT THE OFFICE TO DAY ?
NOPE
ANYTHING WHEN YOU GOT HOME
NOPE
ANYTHING BETWEEN HERE AND THE OFFICE ?
18-7 THURS
6742

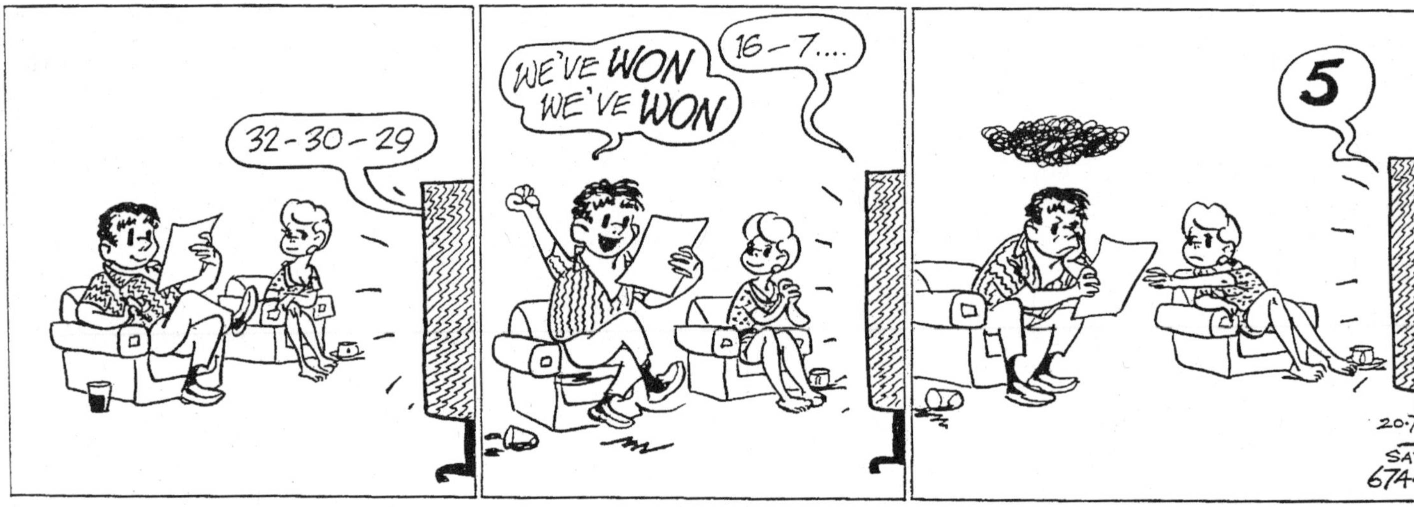
32-30-29
WE'VE WON WE'VE WON
16-7....
5
20-7 SAT
6744

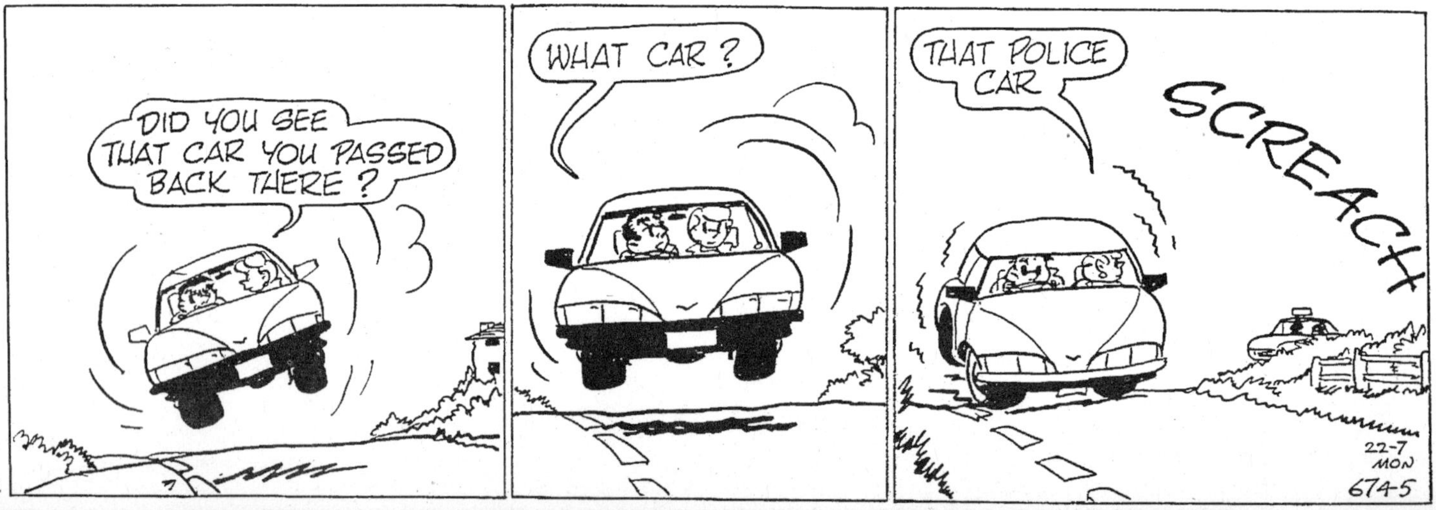
DID YOU SEE THAT CAR YOU PASSED BACK THERE ?
WHAT CAR ?
THAT POLICE CAR
SCREACH
22-7 MON
674-5

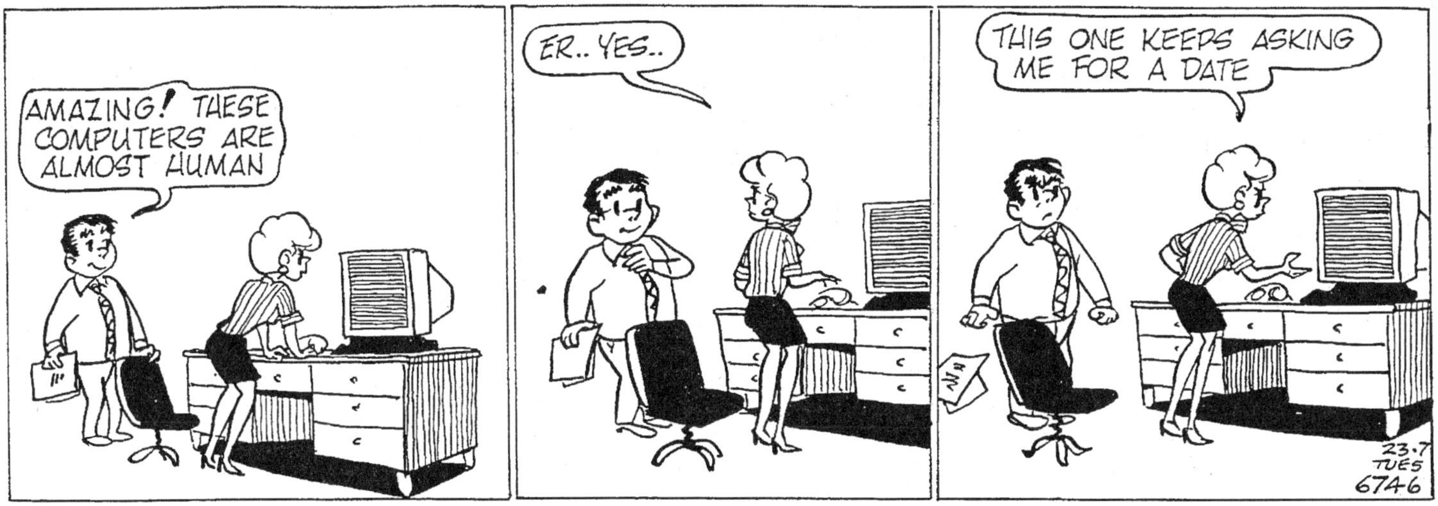
AMAZING! THESE COMPUTERS ARE ALMOST HUMAN
ER.. YES..
THIS ONE KEEPS ASKING ME FOR A DATE
23.7 TUES 6746

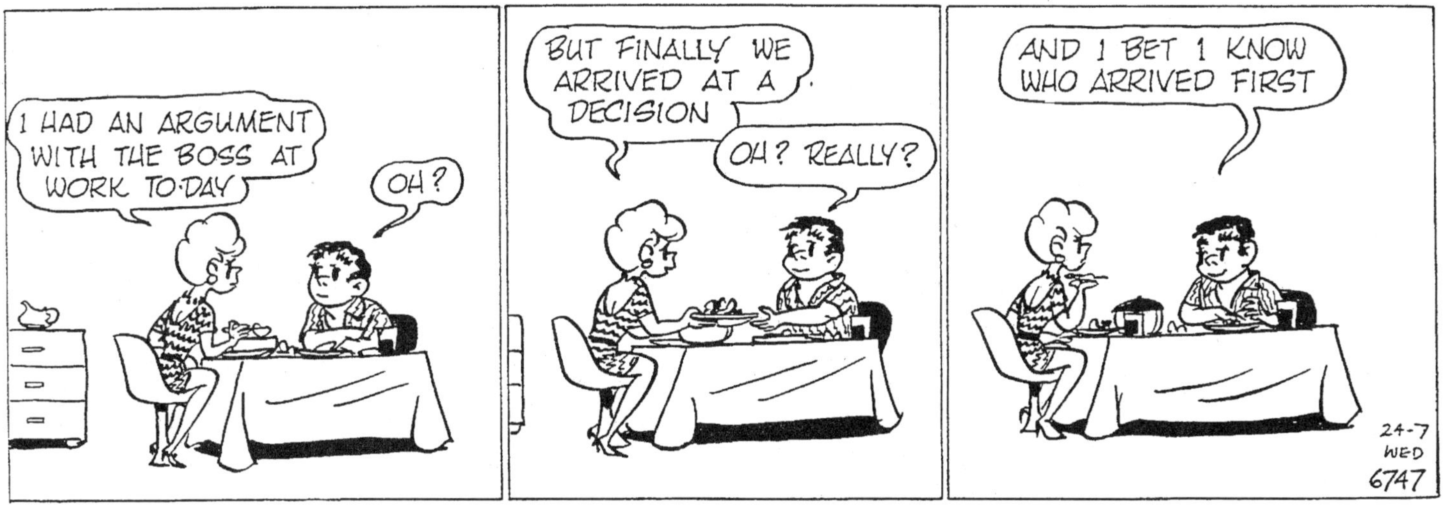
I HAD AN ARGUMENT WITH THE BOSS AT WORK TO-DAY
OH?
BUT FINALLY WE ARRIVED AT A DECISION
OH? REALLY?
AND I BET I KNOW WHO ARRIVED FIRST
24-7 WED 6747

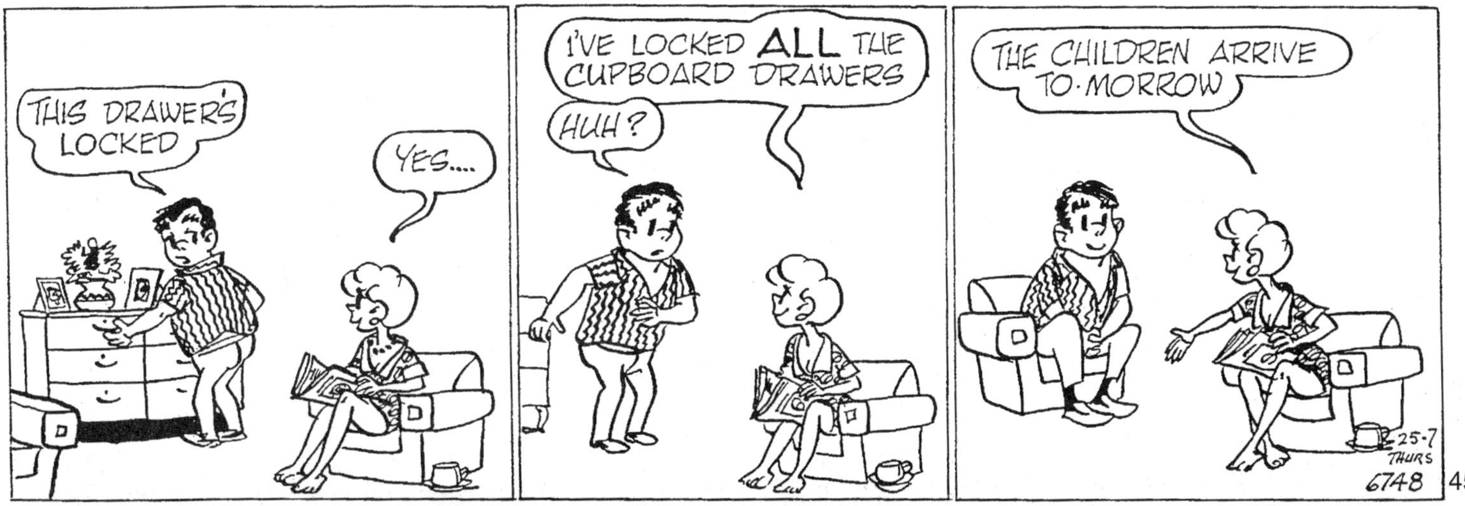
THIS DRAWER'S LOCKED
YES....
I'VE LOCKED ALL THE CUPBOARD DRAWERS
HUH?
THE CHILDREN ARRIVE TO-MORROW
25-7 THURS 6748

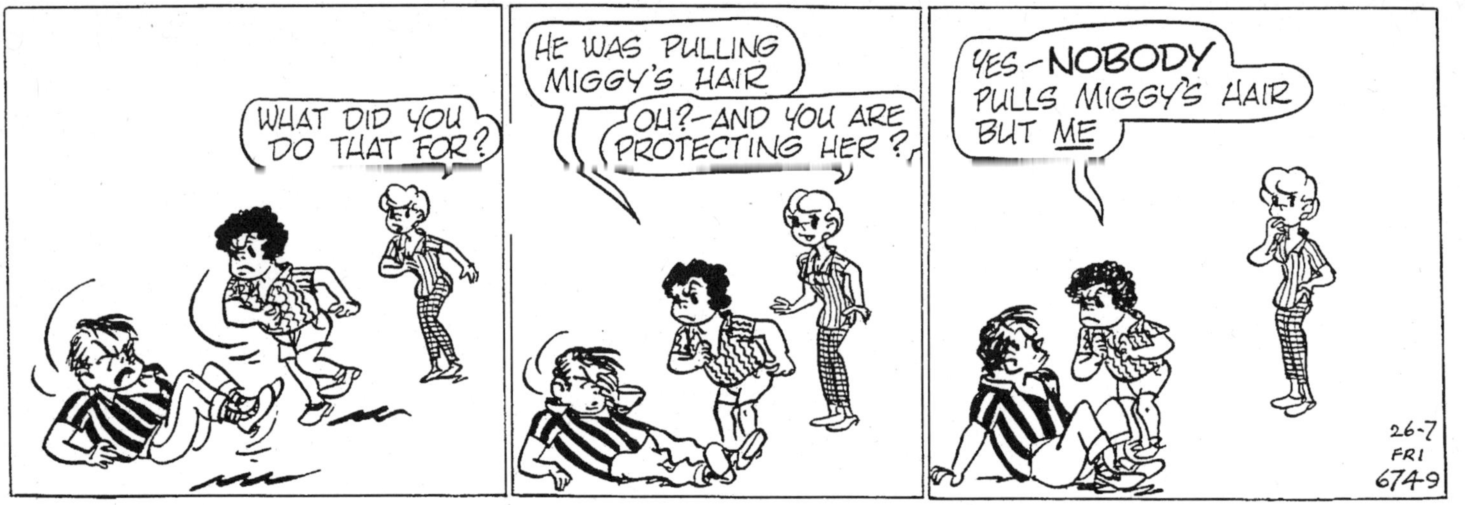
WHAT DID YOU DO THAT FOR?
HE WAS PULLING MIGGY'S HAIR
OH?—AND YOU ARE PROTECTING HER?
YES—NOBODY PULLS MIGGY'S HAIR BUT ME
26-7
FRI
6749

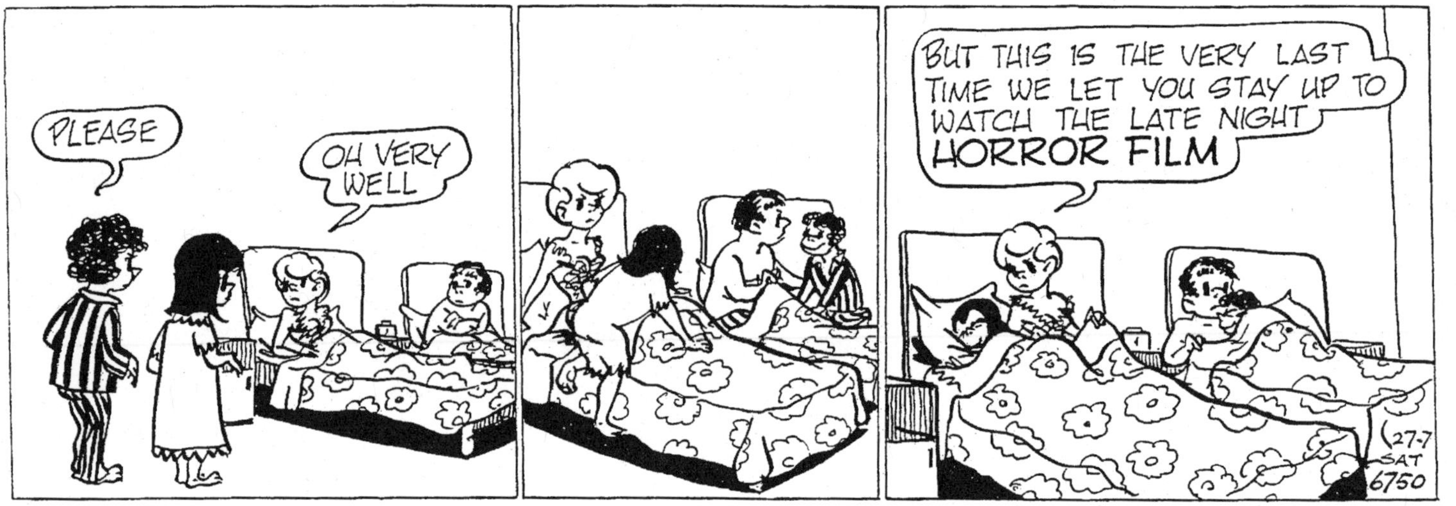
PLEASE
OH VERY WELL
BUT THIS IS THE VERY LAST TIME WE LET YOU STAY UP TO WATCH THE LATE NIGHT HORROR FILM
27-7
SAT
6750

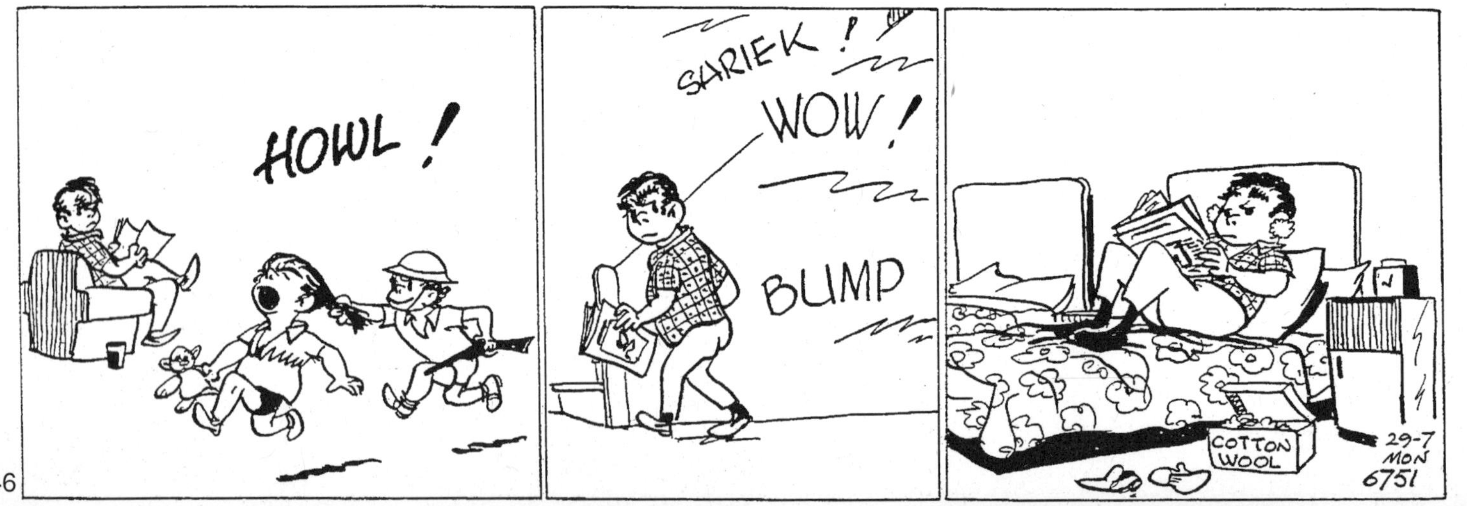
HOWL!
SHRIEK!
WOW!
BUMP
COTTON WOOL
29-7
MON
6751

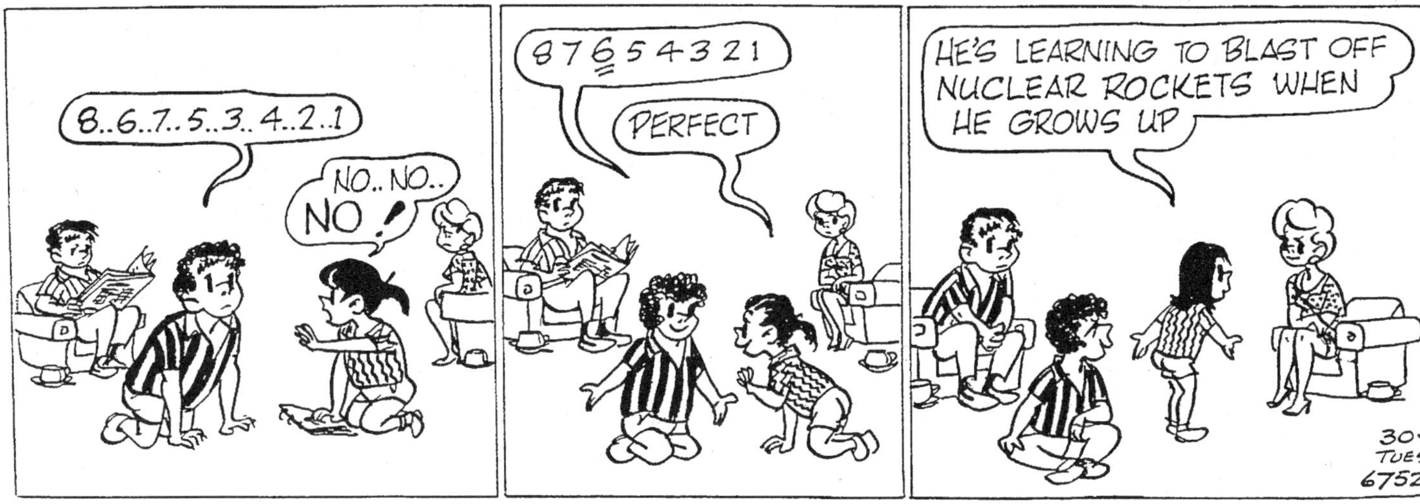
8..6..7..5..3..4..2..1
NO..NO.. NO!
87654321
PERFECT
HE'S LEARNING TO BLAST OFF NUCLEAR ROCKETS WHEN HE GROWS UP
30·7 TUES
6752

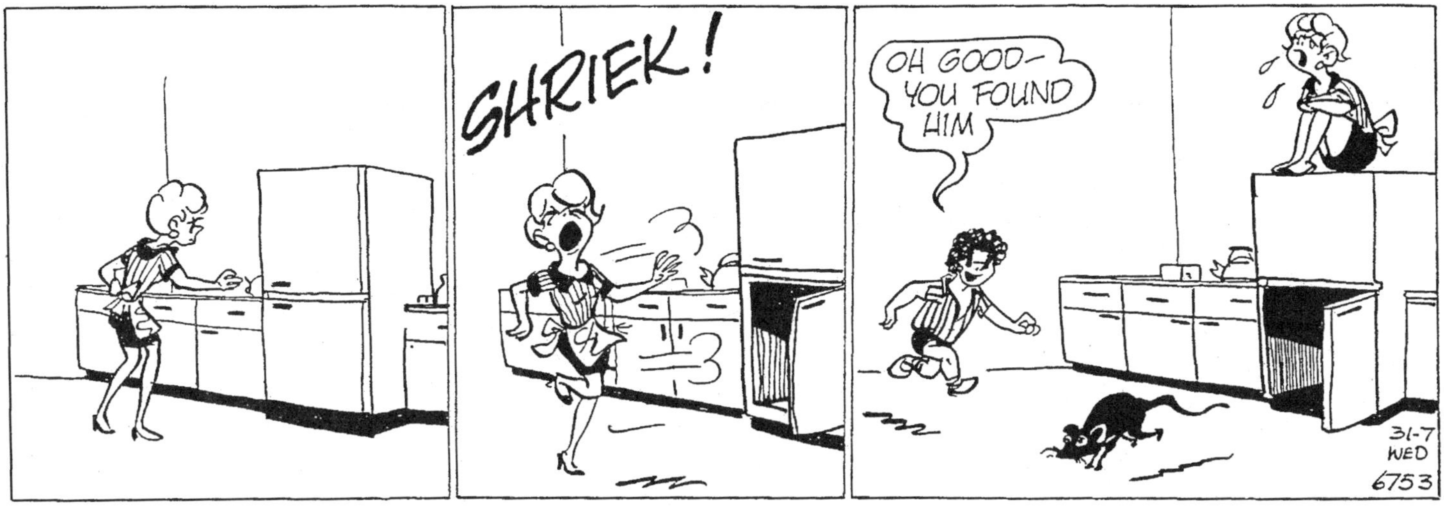
SHRIEK!
OH GOOD- YOU FOUND HIM
31-7 WED
6753

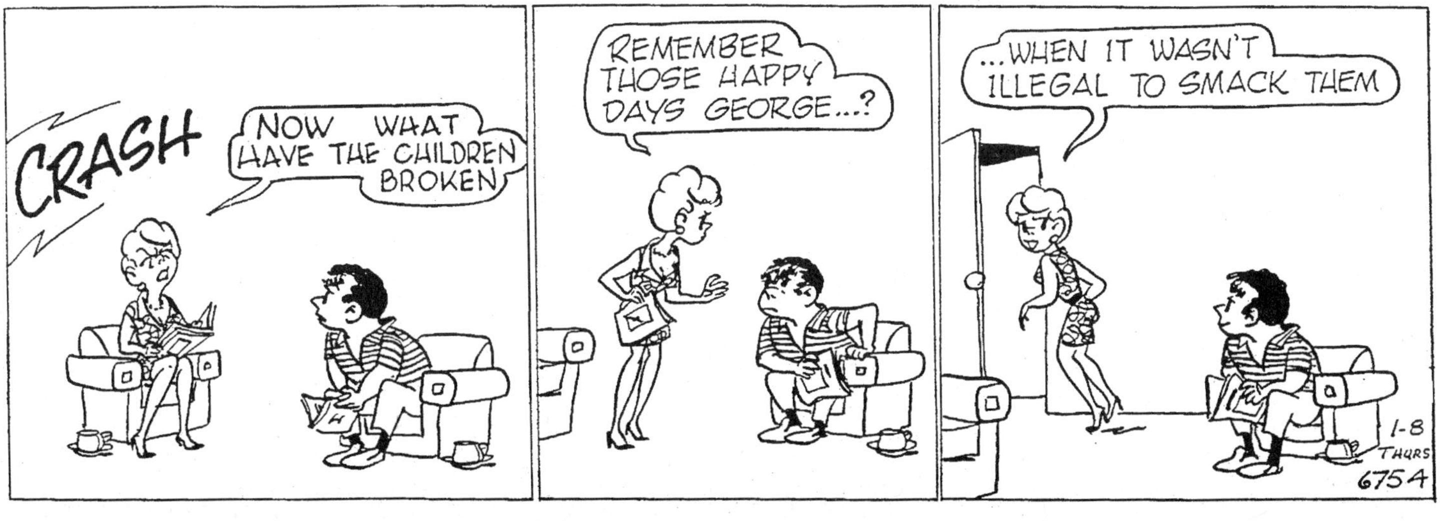
CRASH
NOW WHAT HAVE THE CHILDREN BROKEN
REMEMBER THOSE HAPPY DAYS GEORGE...?
...WHEN IT WASN'T ILLEGAL TO SMACK THEM
1-8 THURS
6754

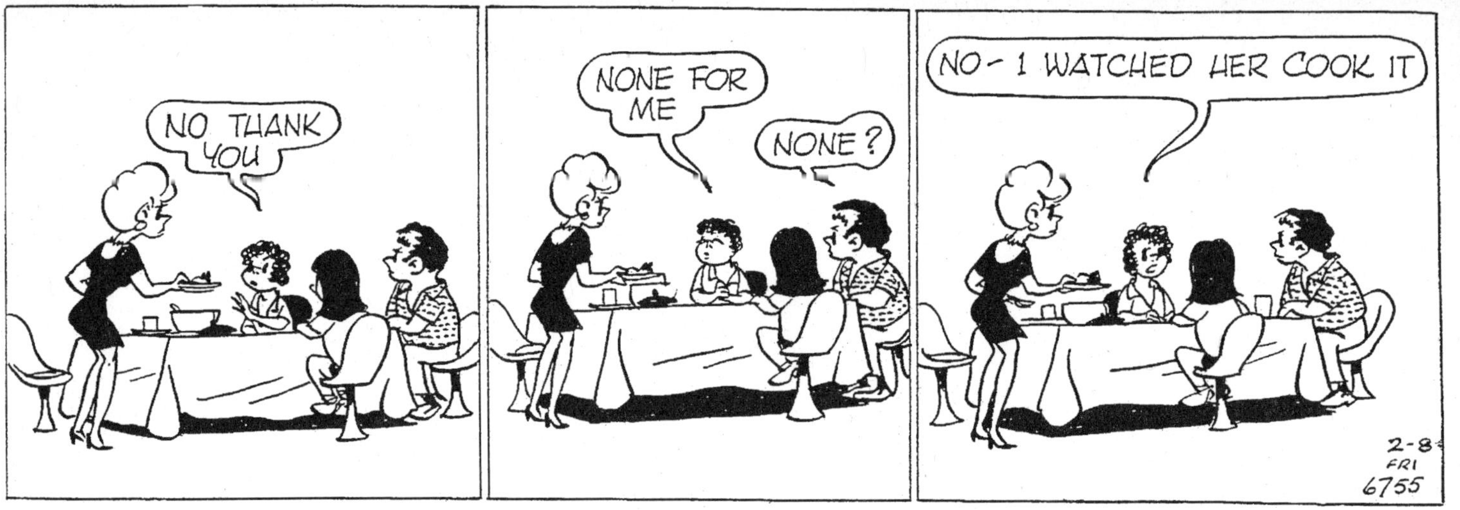
NO THANK YOU
NONE FOR ME
NONE?
NO - 1 WATCHED HER COOK IT
2-8 FRI
6755

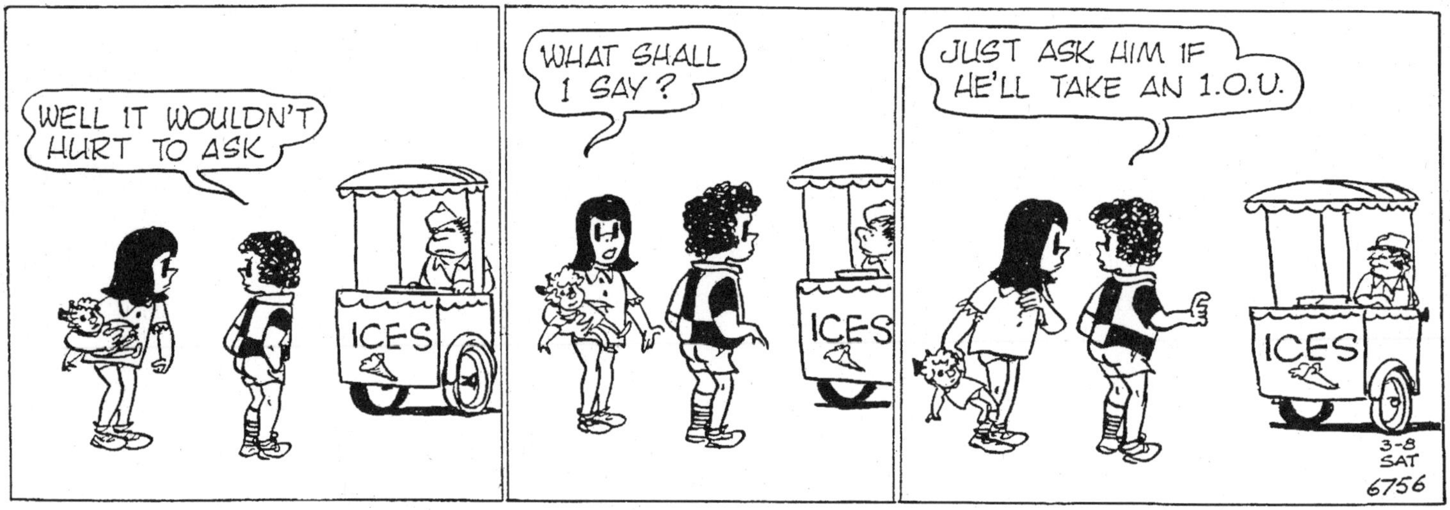
WELL IT WOULDN'T HURT TO ASK
ICES
WHAT SHALL I SAY?
ICES
JUST ASK HIM IF HE'LL TAKE AN I.O.U.
ICES
3-8 SAT
6756

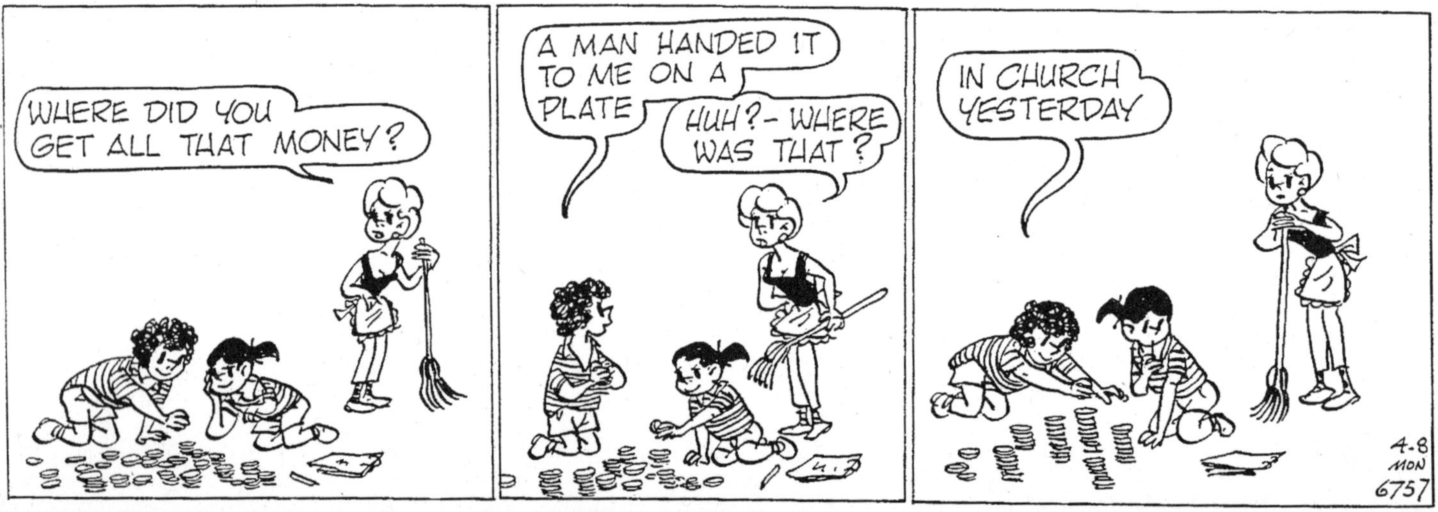
WHERE DID YOU GET ALL THAT MONEY?
A MAN HANDED IT TO ME ON A PLATE
HUH? - WHERE WAS THAT?
IN CHURCH YESTERDAY
4-8 MON
6757

One of the most exciting and enjoyable things about creating a successful cartoon strip is watching your characters build a life of their own just like real people. Then, time goes by and they become household names, not only in this country but in other countries around the world.

And so it has happened for George and Gaye Gambol. Over a period of forty-six. years they have shown us the funny side of everyday life, every day in The Express.

When I first saw George and Gaye arrive on my drawing board and realised their predicament, a great sadness overwhelmed me. After all the warmth and love they have shown us over the years it seemed a cruel blow that they should have had to endure the demise of their brilliant creator Barry Appleby.

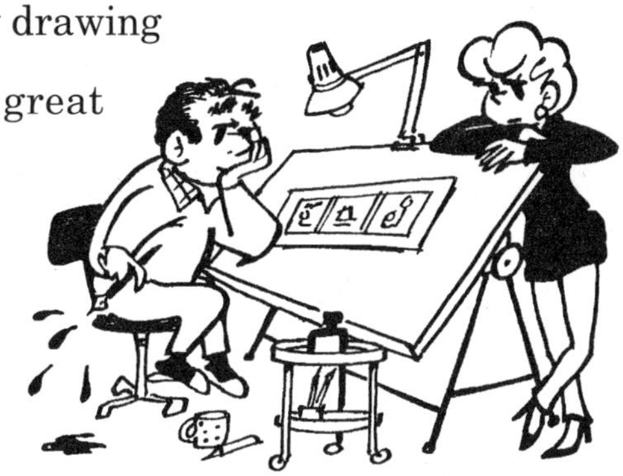

But like all great cartoon characters The Gambols have the strength to carry on in a new era. And in the same way that Barry gave them the spark of life, so he gave me, several years later a young budding cartoonist, the spark of ambition and a burning desire to follow in his footsteps, as a strip cartoonist.

I hope that George and Gaye and all our readers find me worthy of continuing the search for fun in every day life.

Roger Mahoney.

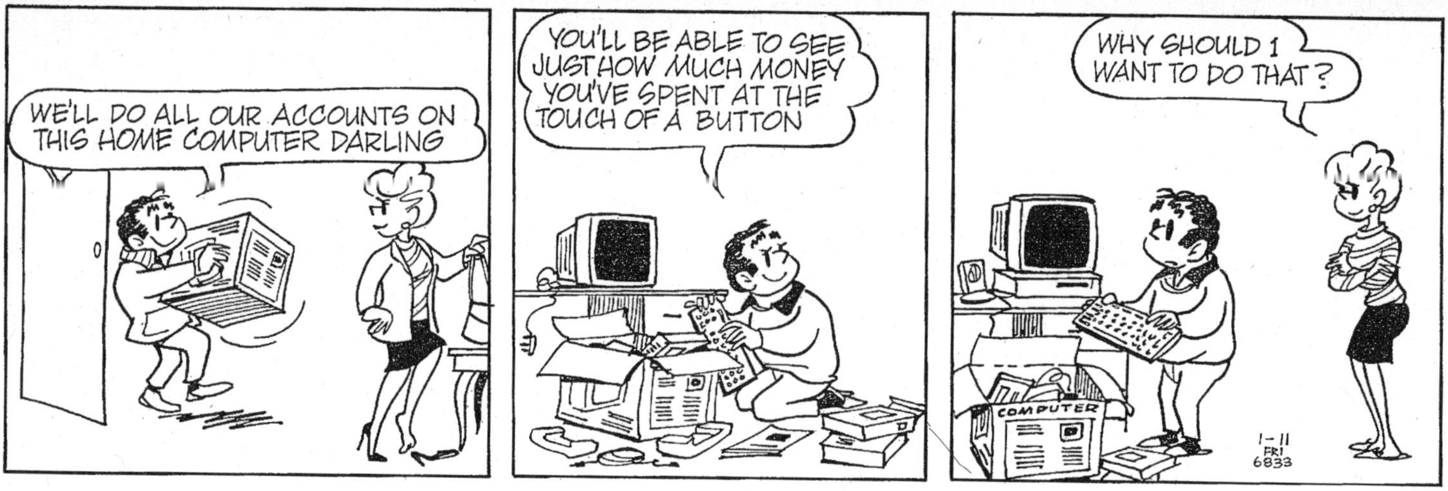
WE'LL DO ALL OUR ACCOUNTS ON THIS HOME COMPUTER DARLING
YOU'LL BE ABLE TO SEE JUST HOW MUCH MONEY YOU'VE SPENT AT THE TOUCH OF A BUTTON
WHY SHOULD I WANT TO DO THAT?
COMPUTER
1-11 FRI 6833

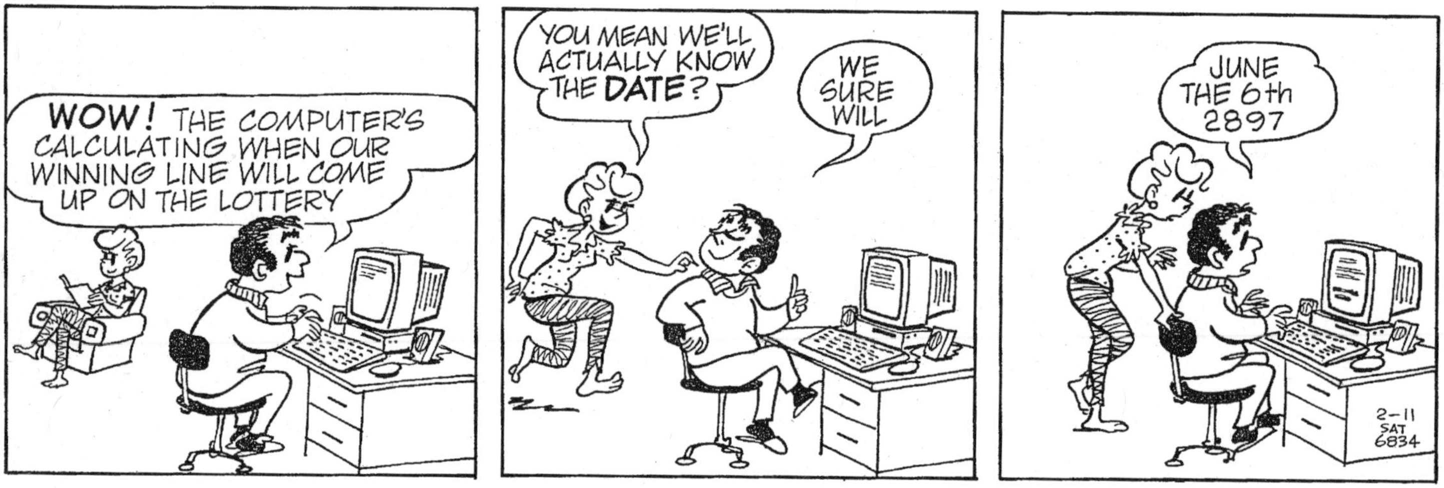
WOW! THE COMPUTER'S CALCULATING WHEN OUR WINNING LINE WILL COME UP ON THE LOTTERY
YOU MEAN WE'LL ACTUALLY KNOW THE DATE?
WE SURE WILL
JUNE THE 6th 2897
2-11 SAT 6834

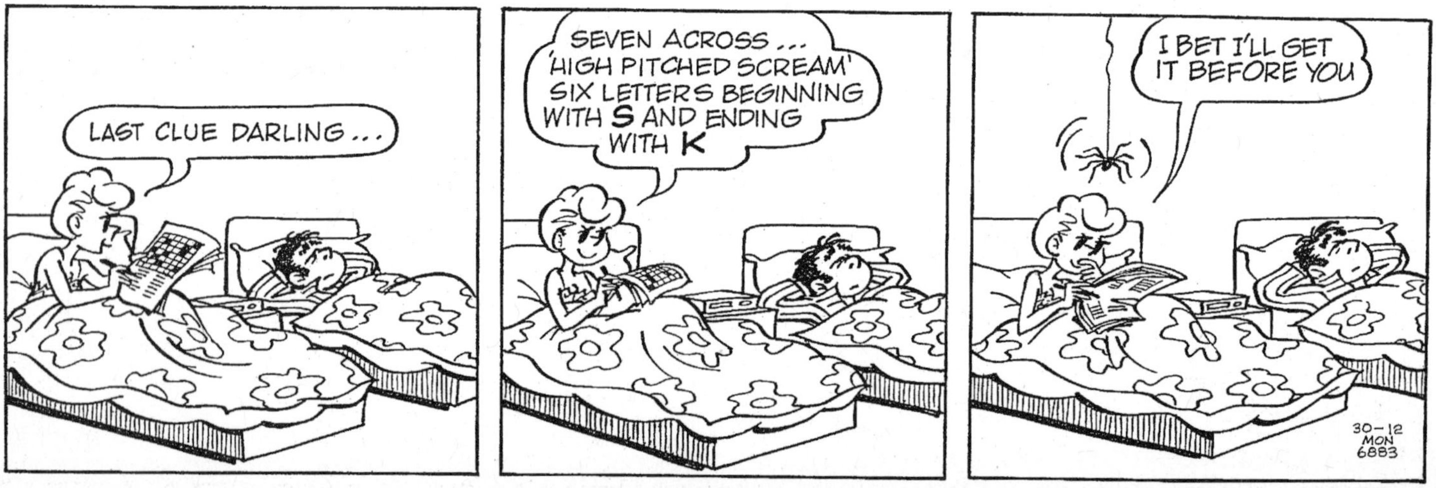
LAST CLUE DARLING...
SEVEN ACROSS... 'HIGH PITCHED SCREAM' SIX LETTERS BEGINNING WITH S AND ENDING WITH K
I BET I'LL GET IT BEFORE YOU
30-12 MON 6883

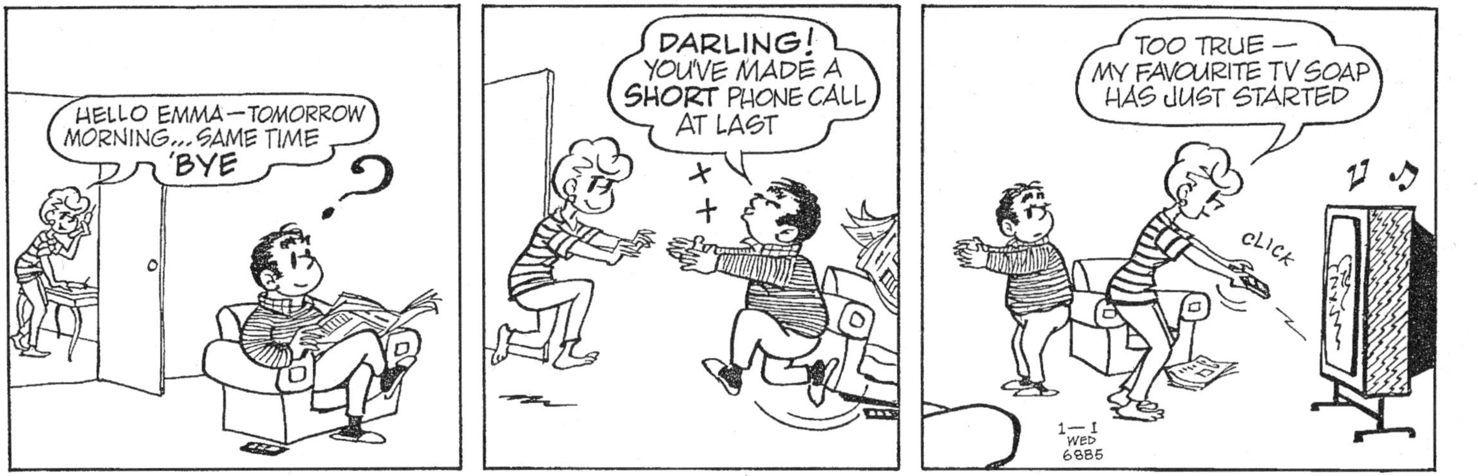
HELLO EMMA—TOMORROW MORNING... SAME TIME 'BYE
DARLING! YOU'VE MADE A **SHORT** PHONE CALL AT LAST
TOO TRUE — MY FAVOURITE TV SOAP HAS JUST STARTED
CLICK
1—I WED 6885

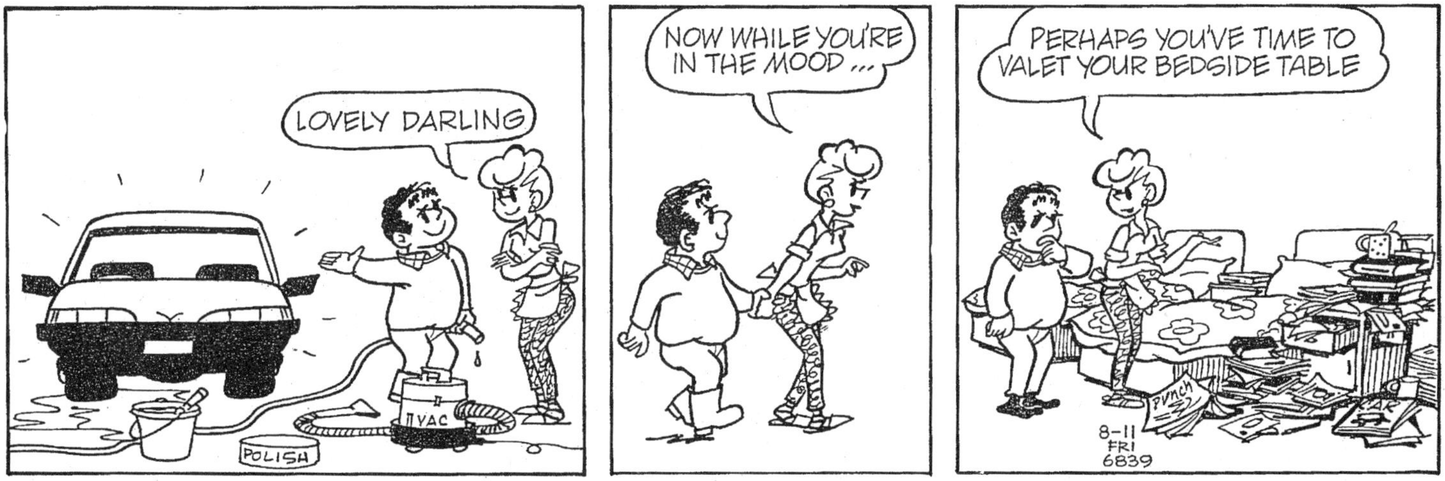
LOVELY DARLING
VAC
POLISH
NOW WHILE YOU'RE IN THE MOOD...
PERHAPS YOU'VE TIME TO VALET YOUR BEDSIDE TABLE
PUNCH
8-11 FRI 6839

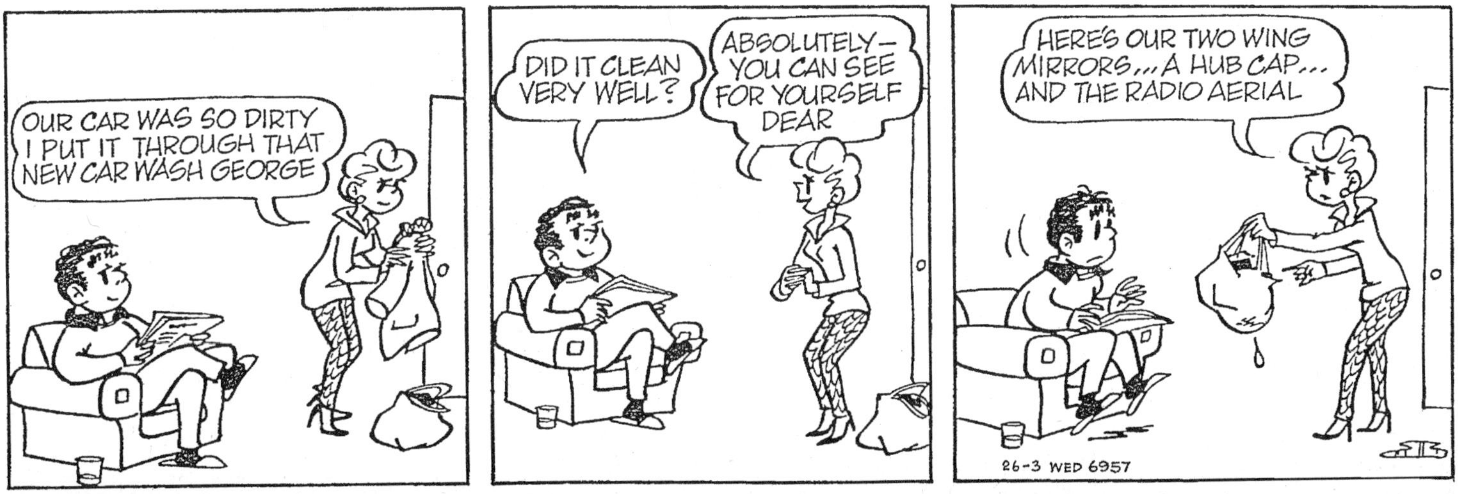
OUR CAR WAS SO DIRTY I PUT IT THROUGH THAT NEW CAR WASH GEORGE
DID IT CLEAN VERY WELL?
ABSOLUTELY— YOU CAN SEE FOR YOURSELF DEAR
HERE'S OUR TWO WING MIRRORS... A HUB CAP... AND THE RADIO AERIAL
26-3 WED 6957

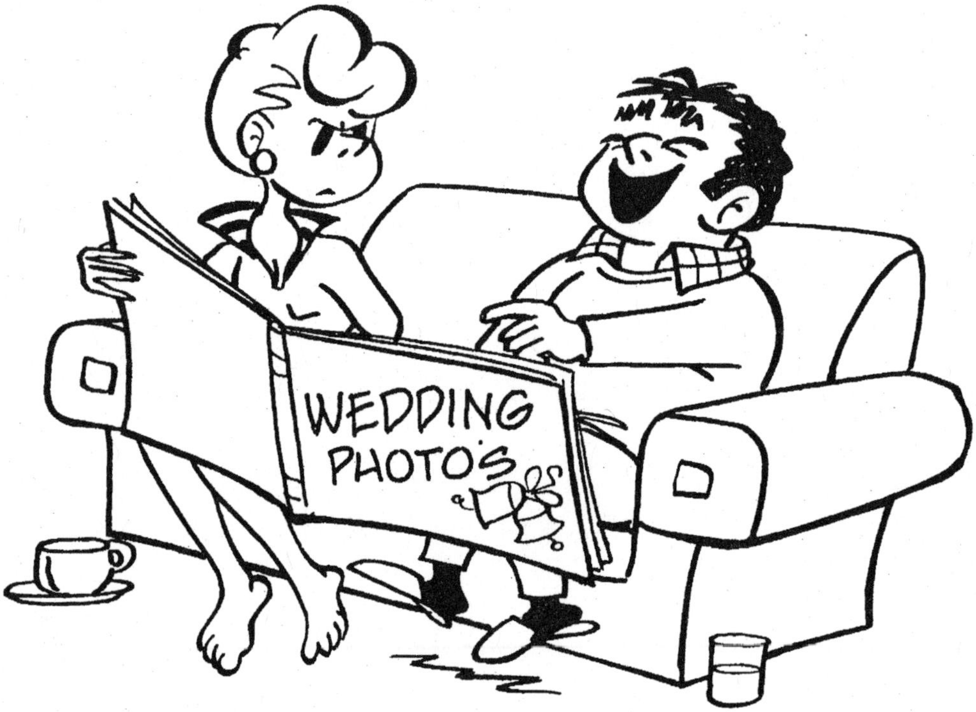
WEDDING
PHOTO'S

SOME PEOPLE SAY YOU CAN NEVER RECAPTURE THE ROMANCE OF YOUR HONEYMOON — NEVERTHELESS — GEORGE AND GAYE DECIDED TO FIND OUT FOR THEMSELVES

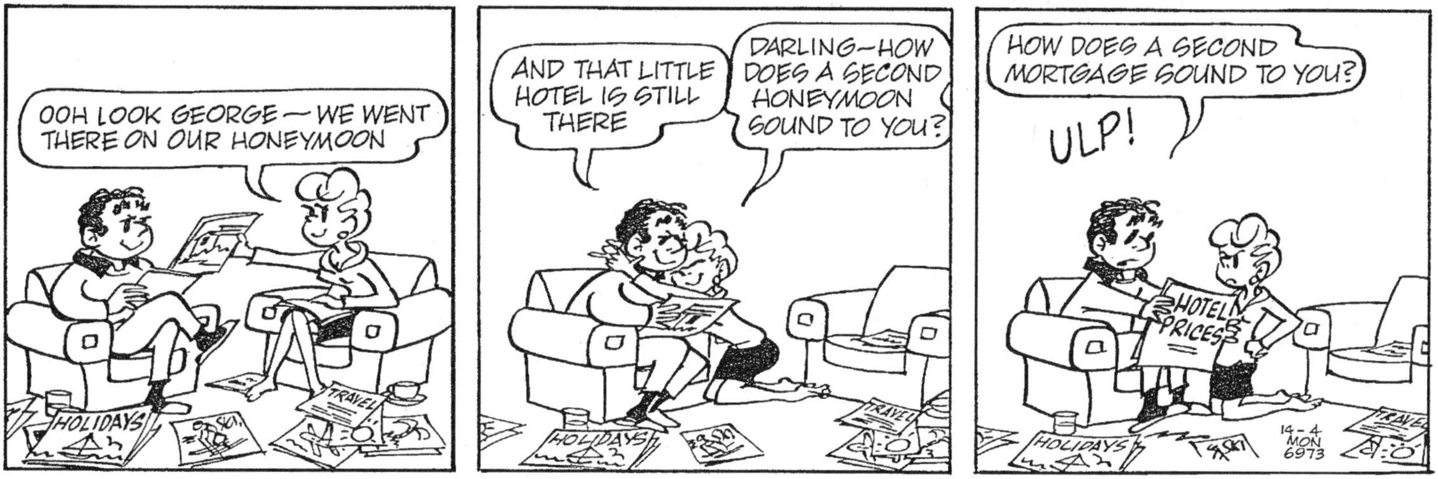
OOH LOOK GEORGE — WE WENT THERE ON OUR HONEYMOON
HOLIDAYS
TRAVEL
AND THAT LITTLE HOTEL IS STILL THERE
DARLING—HOW DOES A SECOND HONEYMOON SOUND TO YOU?
HOW DOES A SECOND MORTGAGE SOUND TO YOU?
ULP!
HOTEL PRICES
14-4 MON 6973

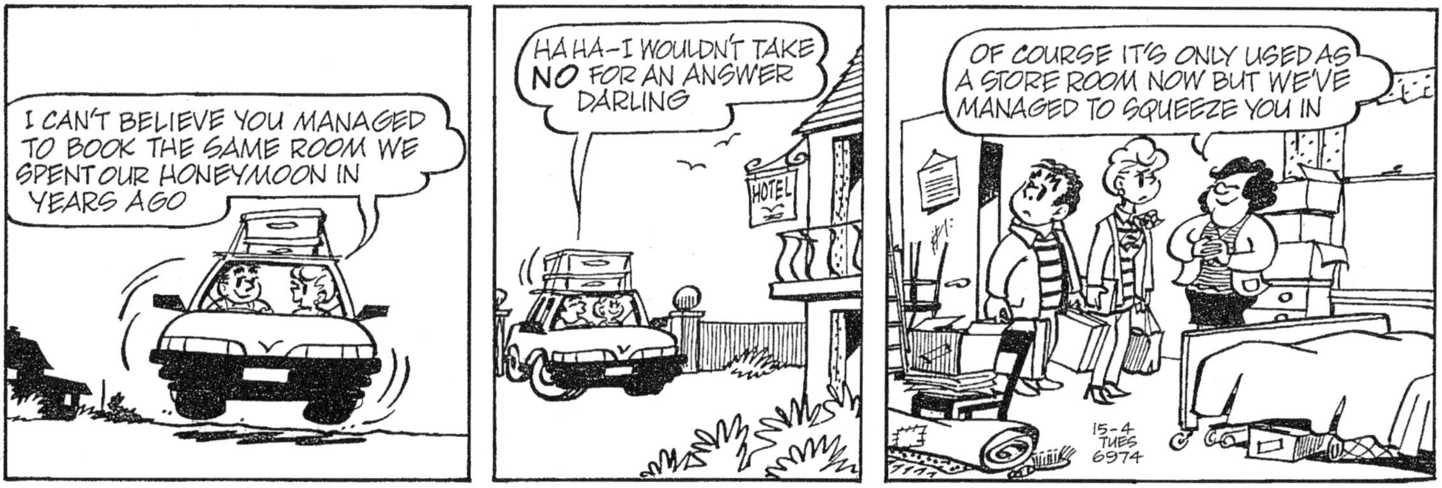
I CAN'T BELIEVE YOU MANAGED TO BOOK THE SAME ROOM WE SPENT OUR HONEYMOON IN YEARS AGO
HA HA-I WOULDN'T TAKE NO FOR AN ANSWER DARLING
HOTEL
OF COURSE IT'S ONLY USED AS A STORE ROOM NOW BUT WE'VE MANAGED TO SQUEEZE YOU IN
15-4 TUES 6974

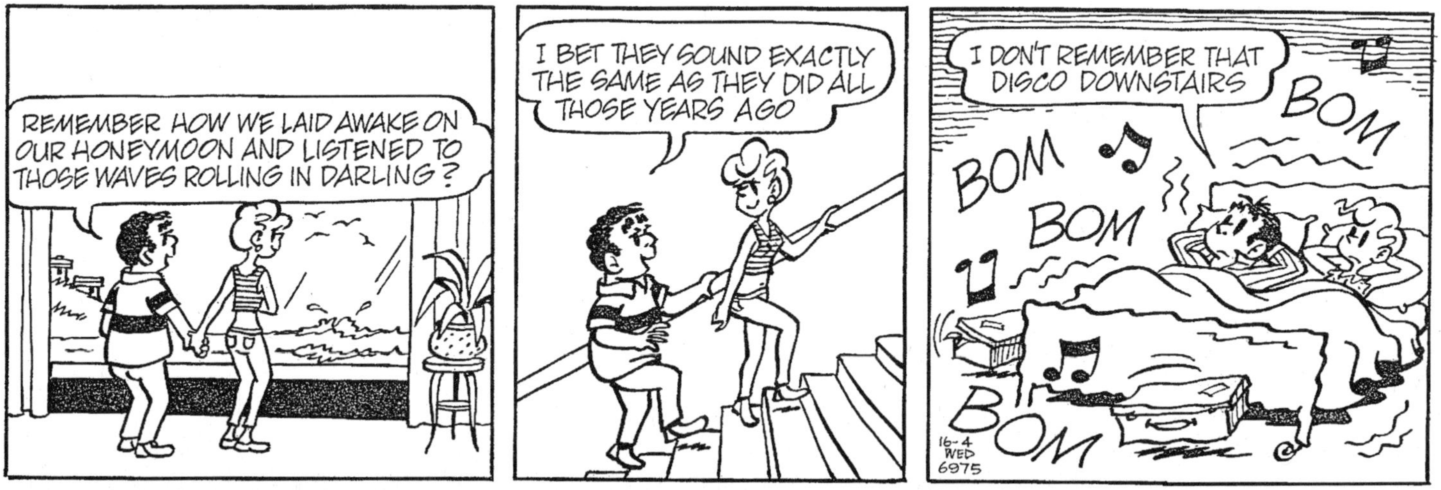
REMEMBER HOW WE LAID AWAKE ON OUR HONEYMOON AND LISTENED TO THOSE WAVES ROLLING IN DARLING?
I BET THEY SOUND EXACTLY THE SAME AS THEY DID ALL THOSE YEARS AGO
I DON'T REMEMBER THAT DISCO DOWNSTAIRS
BOM
BOM
BOM
BOM
16-4 WED 6975

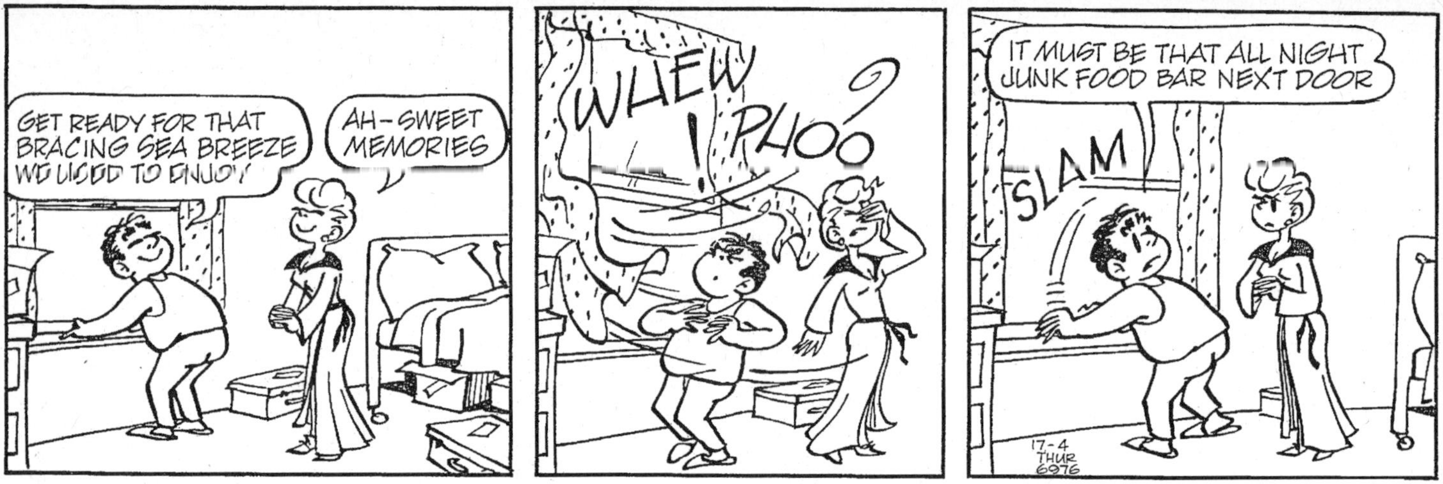
GET READY FOR THAT BRACING SEA BREEZE WE USED TO ENJOY
AH – SWEET MEMORIES
WHEW
!
PHOO
IT MUST BE THAT ALL NIGHT JUNK FOOD BAR NEXT DOOR
SLAM
17-4 THUR 6976

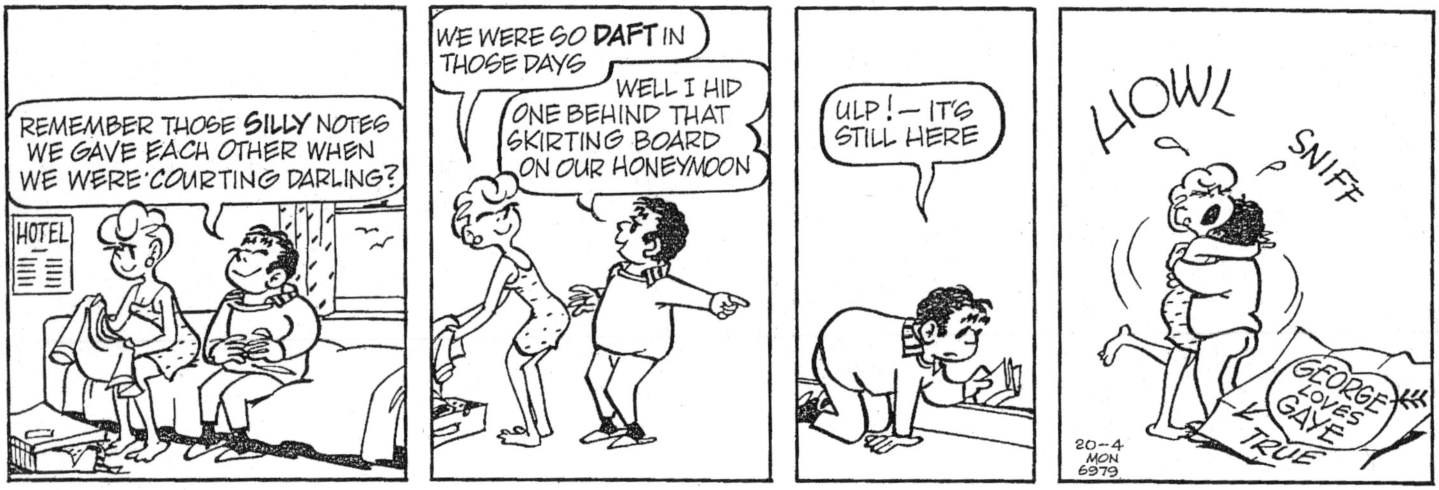
REMEMBER THOSE **SILLY** NOTES WE GAVE EACH OTHER WHEN WE WERE COURTING DARLING?
HOTEL
WE WERE SO **DAFT** IN THOSE DAYS
WELL I HID ONE BEHIND THAT SKIRTING BOARD ON OUR HONEYMOON
ULP! – IT'S STILL HERE
HOWL
SNIFF
GEORGE LOVES GAYE
TRUE
20-4 MON 6979

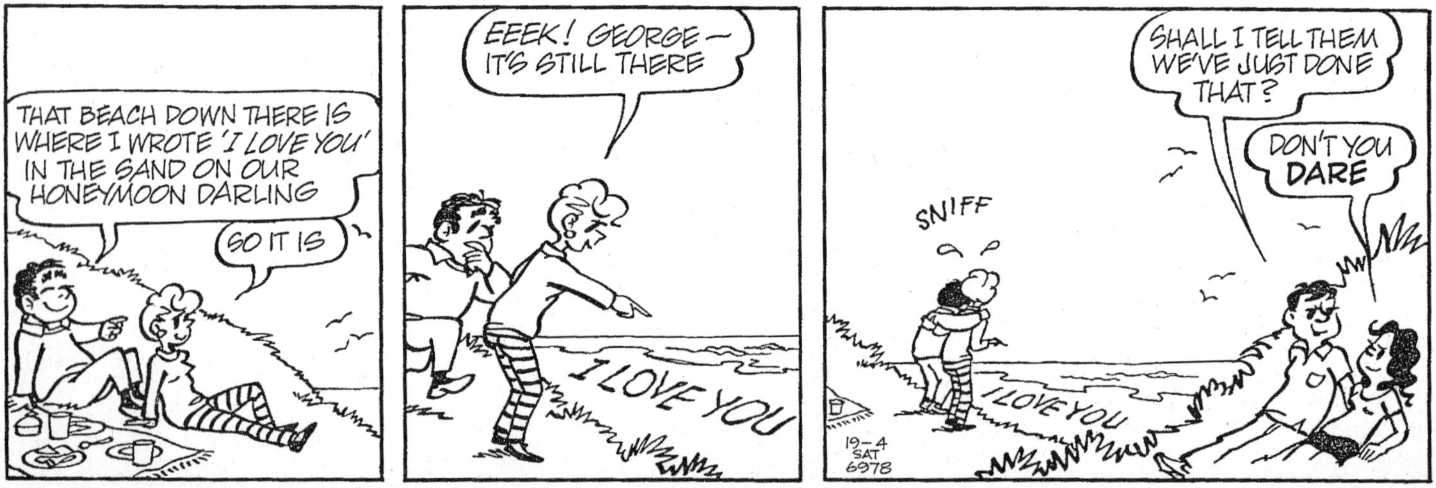
THAT BEACH DOWN THERE IS WHERE I WROTE '*I LOVE YOU*' IN THE SAND ON OUR HONEYMOON DARLING
SO IT IS
EEEK! GEORGE – IT'S STILL THERE
I LOVE YOU
SHALL I TELL THEM WE'VE JUST DONE THAT?
DON'T YOU **DARE**
SNIFF
I LOVE YOU
19-4 SAT 6978

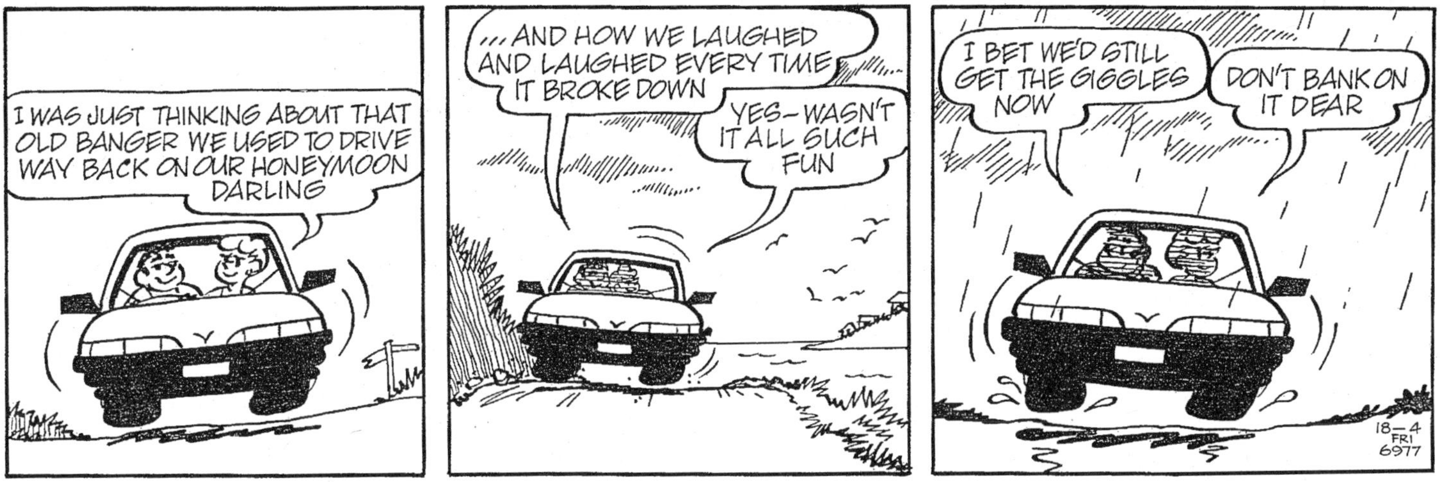
I WAS JUST THINKING ABOUT THAT OLD BANGER WE USED TO DRIVE WAY BACK ON OUR HONEYMOON DARLING
...AND HOW WE LAUGHED AND LAUGHED EVERY TIME IT BROKE DOWN
YES–WASN'T IT ALL SUCH FUN
I BET WE'D STILL GET THE GIGGLES NOW
DON'T BANK ON IT DEAR
18–4 FRI 6977

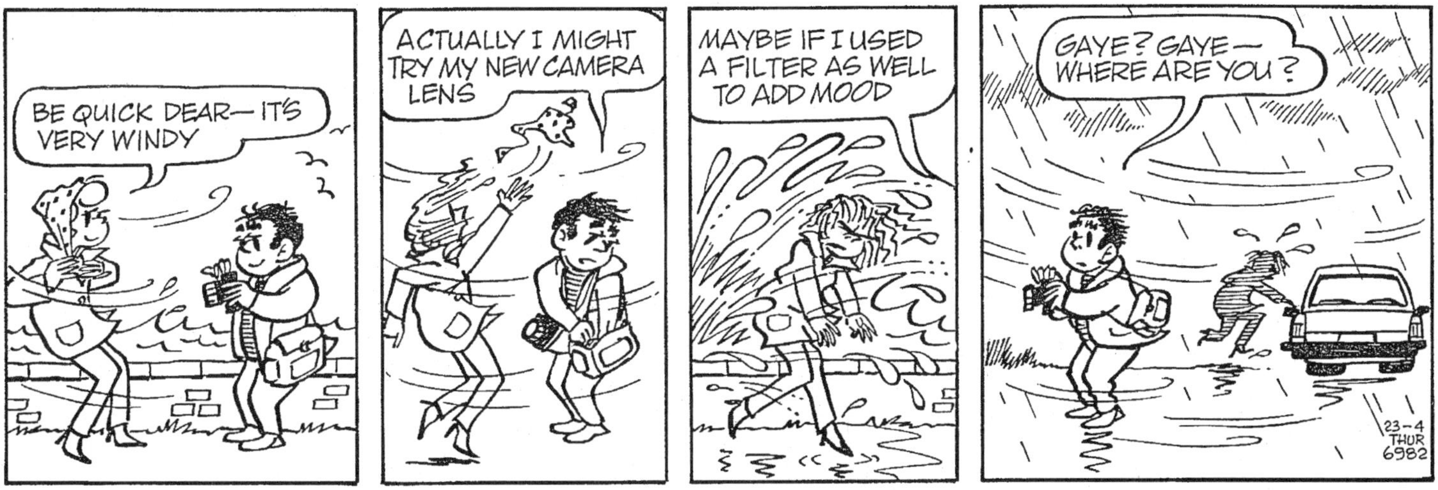
BE QUICK DEAR–IT'S VERY WINDY
ACTUALLY I MIGHT TRY MY NEW CAMERA LENS
MAYBE IF I USED A FILTER AS WELL TO ADD MOOD
GAYE? GAYE– WHERE ARE YOU?
23–4 THUR 6982

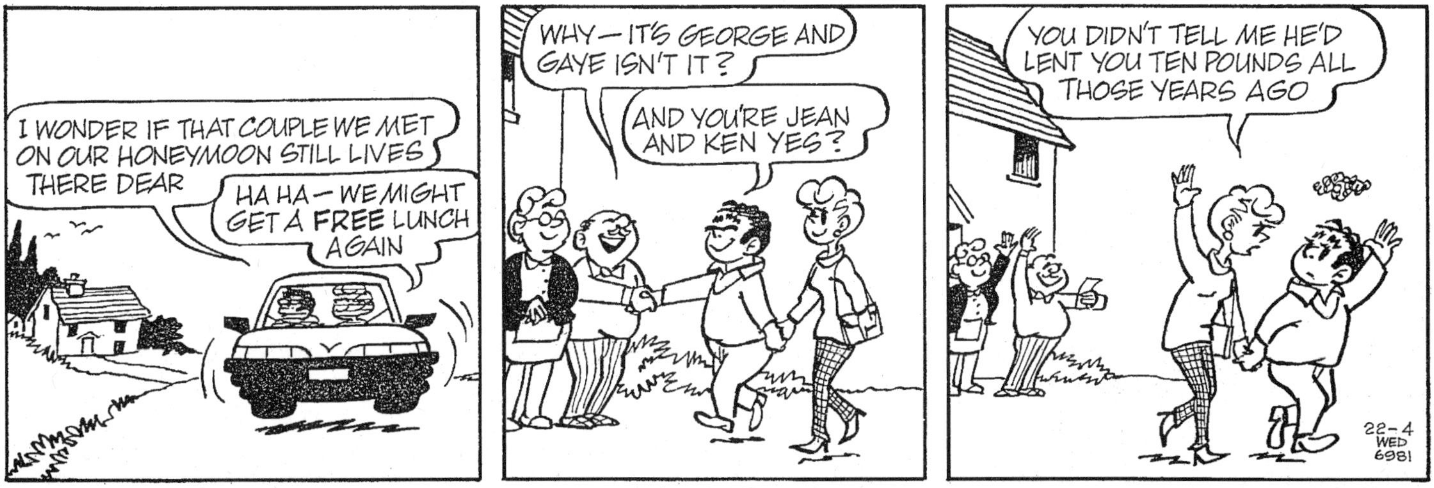
I WONDER IF THAT COUPLE WE MET ON OUR HONEYMOON STILL LIVES THERE DEAR
HA HA–WE MIGHT GET A **FREE** LUNCH AGAIN
WHY–IT'S GEORGE AND GAYE ISN'T IT?
AND YOU'RE JEAN AND KEN YES?
YOU DIDN'T TELL ME HE'D LENT YOU TEN POUNDS ALL THOSE YEARS AGO
22–4 WED 6981

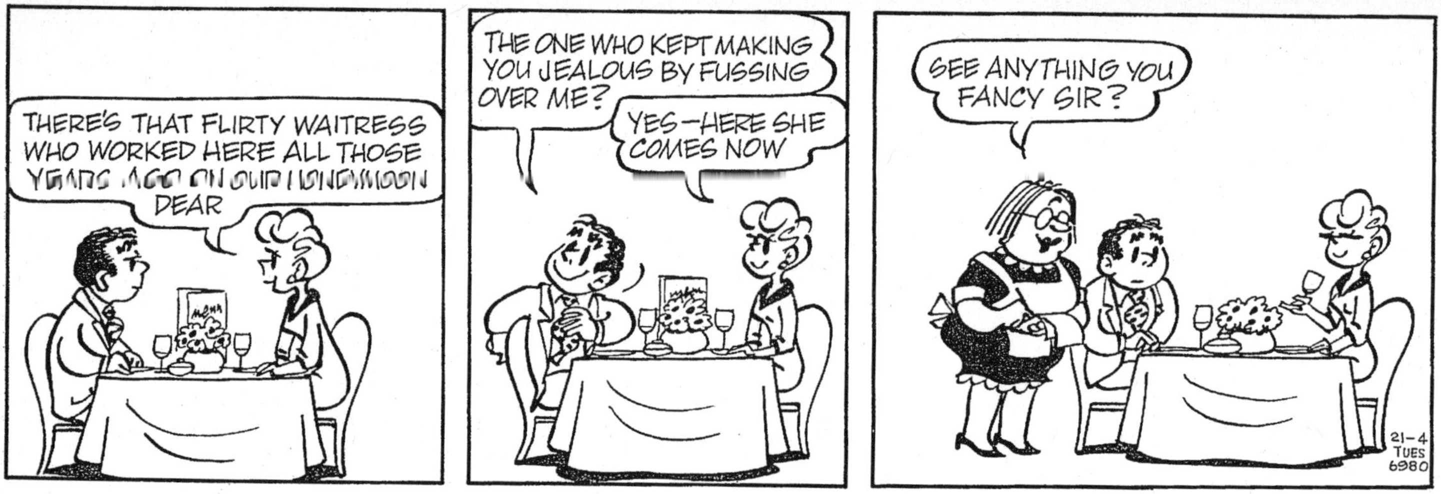
THERE'S THAT FLIRTY WAITRESS WHO WORKED HERE ALL THOSE YEARS AGO ON OUR HONEYMOON DEAR
THE ONE WHO KEPT MAKING YOU JEALOUS BY FUSSING OVER ME?
YES—HERE SHE COMES NOW
SEE ANYTHING YOU FANCY SIR?
21–4 TUES 6980

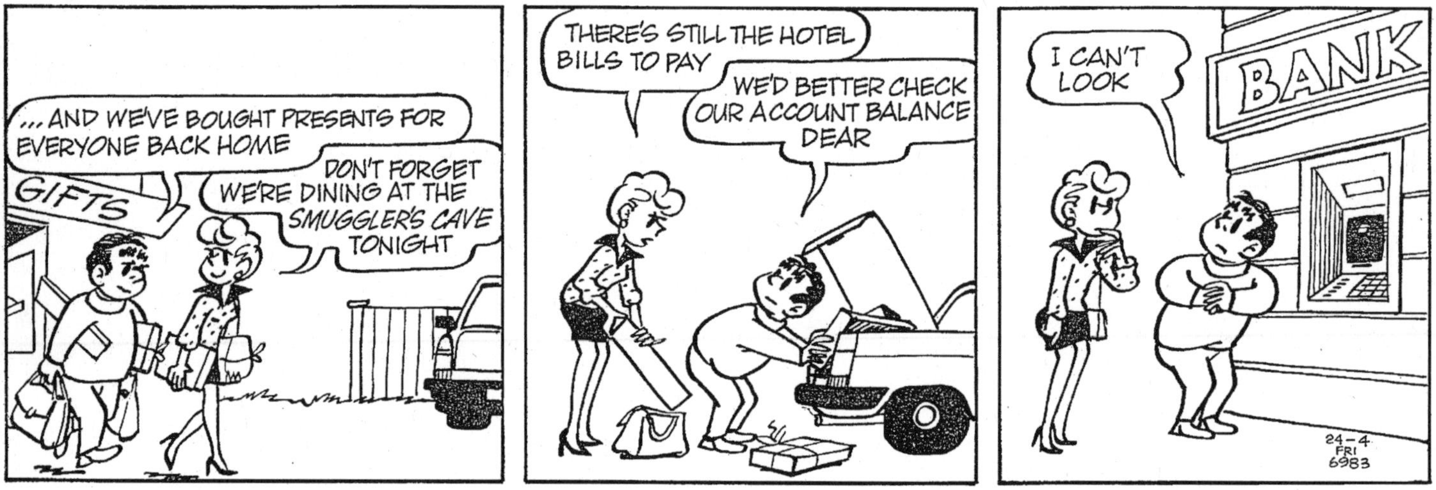
...AND WE'VE BOUGHT PRESENTS FOR EVERYONE BACK HOME
GIFTS
DON'T FORGET WE'RE DINING AT THE SMUGGLER'S CAVE TONIGHT
THERE'S STILL THE HOTEL BILLS TO PAY
WE'D BETTER CHECK OUR ACCOUNT BALANCE DEAR
I CAN'T LOOK
BANK
24–4 FRI 6983

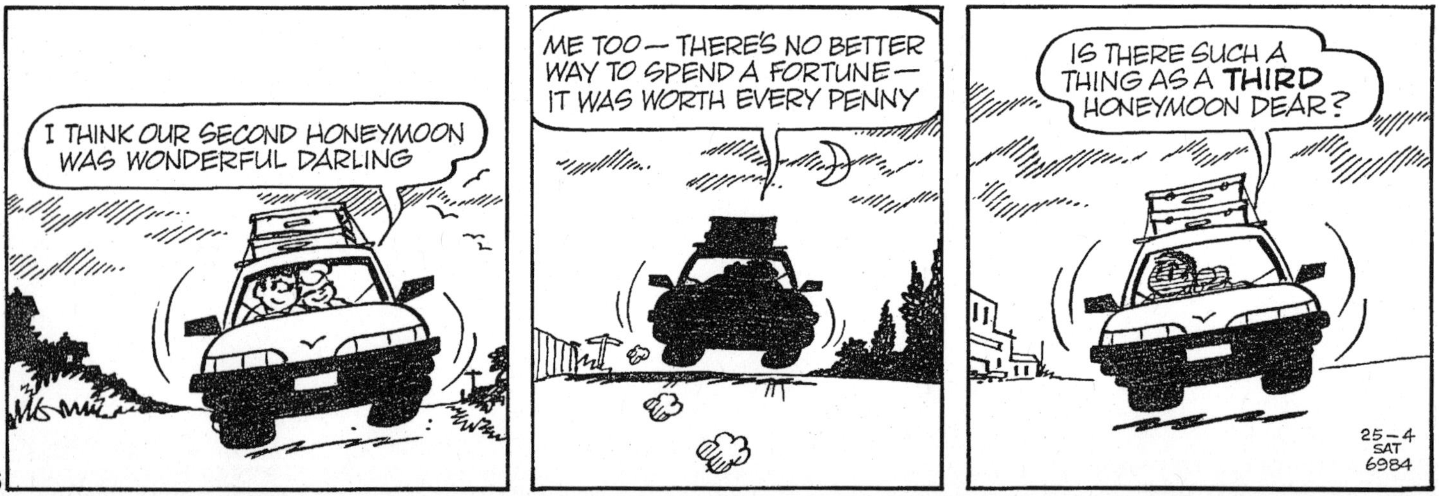
I THINK OUR SECOND HONEYMOON WAS WONDERFUL DARLING
ME TOO— THERE'S NO BETTER WAY TO SPEND A FORTUNE— IT WAS WORTH EVERY PENNY
IS THERE SUCH A THING AS A THIRD HONEYMOON DEAR?
25–4 SAT 6984

LUCKY FOR MIGGY AND FLIVVER THAT
UNCLE GEORGE AND AUNTIE GAYE
ARE SO YOUNG — OR AT LEAST THAT'S
HOW MIGGY AND FLIVVER SEE THEM

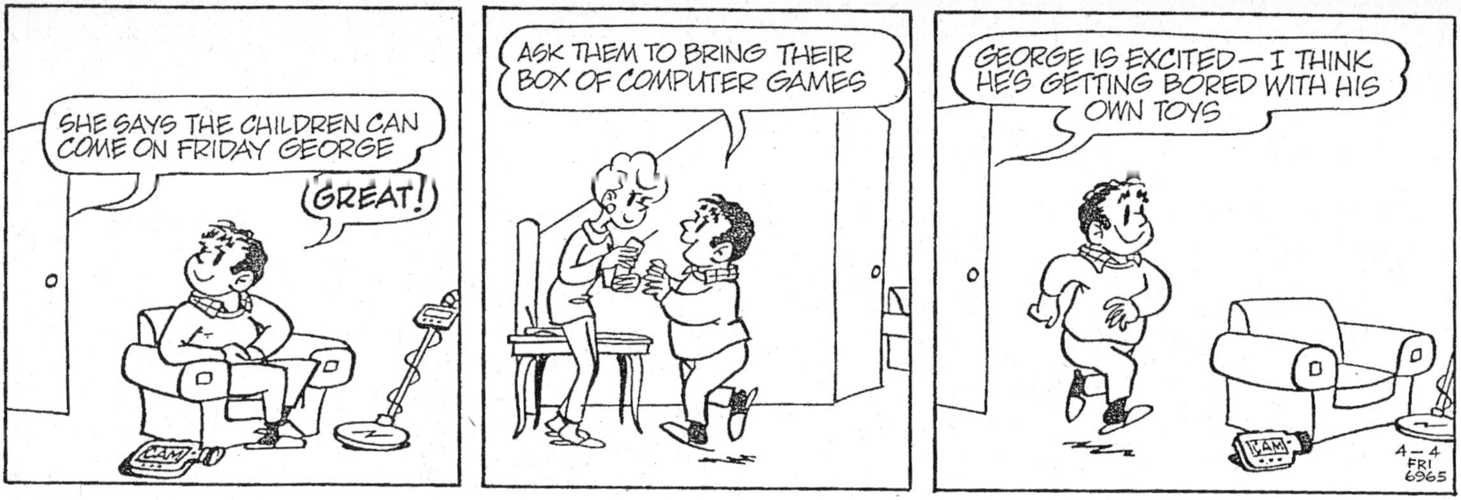
SHE SAYS THE CHILDREN CAN COME ON FRIDAY GEORGE
GREAT!
ASK THEM TO BRING THEIR BOX OF COMPUTER GAMES
GEORGE IS EXCITED— I THINK HE'S GETTING BORED WITH HIS OWN TOYS
GAM
4—4 FRI 6965

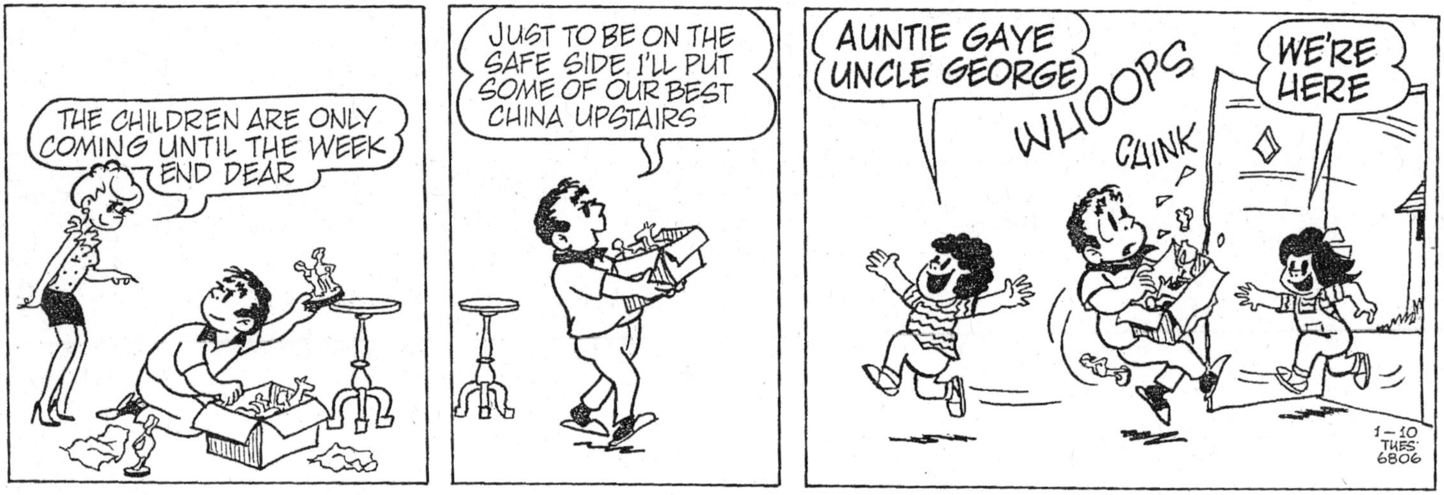
THE CHILDREN ARE ONLY COMING UNTIL THE WEEK END DEAR
JUST TO BE ON THE SAFE SIDE I'LL PUT SOME OF OUR BEST CHINA UPSTAIRS
AUNTIE GAYE UNCLE GEORGE
WHOOPS
CLINK
WE'RE HERE
1—10 THES. 6806

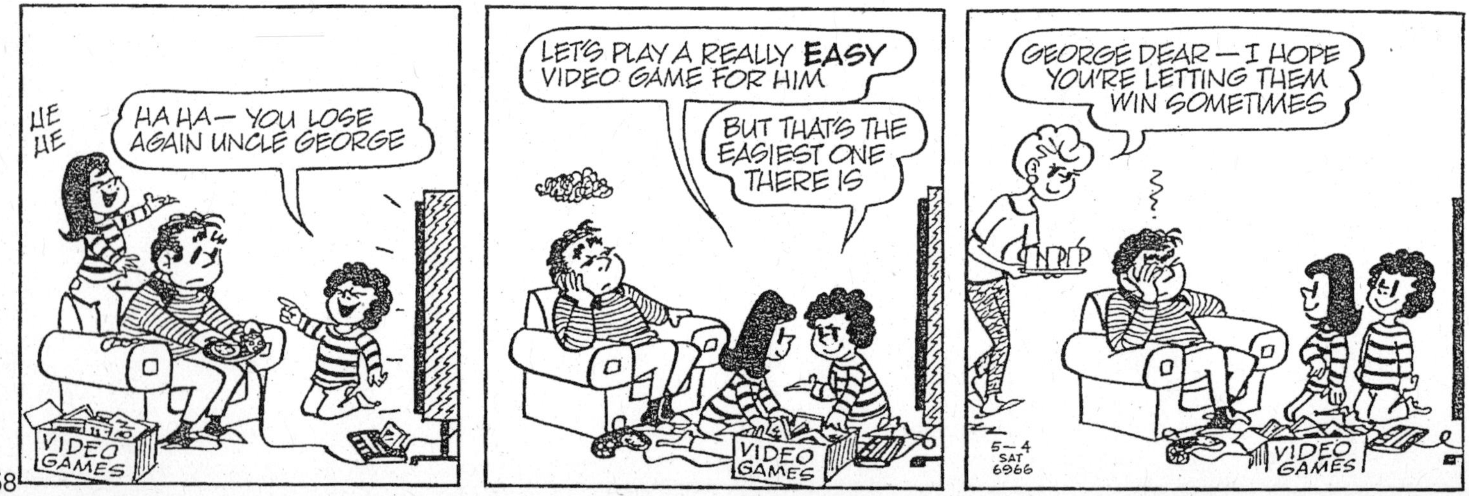
HE HE
HA HA— YOU LOSE AGAIN UNCLE GEORGE
VIDEO GAMES
LET'S PLAY A REALLY EASY VIDEO GAME FOR HIM
BUT THAT'S THE EASIEST ONE THERE IS
VIDEO GAMES
GEORGE DEAR— I HOPE YOU'RE LETTING THEM WIN SOMETIMES
VIDEO GAMES
5—4 SAT 6966

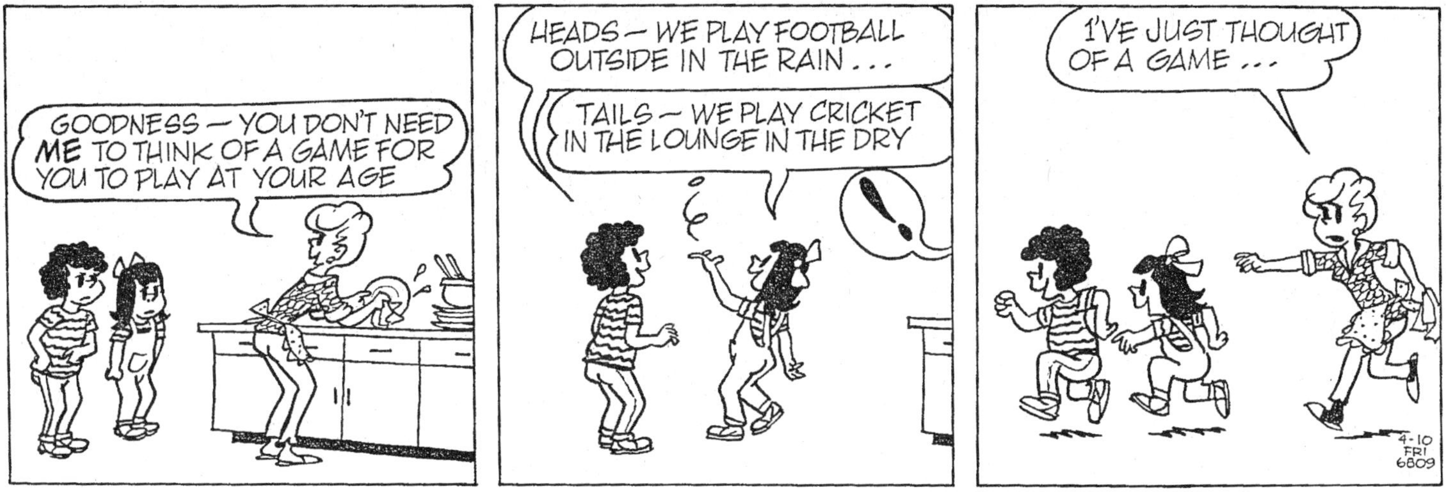
GOODNESS — YOU DON'T NEED ME TO THINK OF A GAME FOR YOU TO PLAY AT YOUR AGE
HEADS — WE PLAY FOOTBALL OUTSIDE IN THE RAIN . . .
TAILS — WE PLAY CRICKET IN THE LOUNGE IN THE DRY
!
I'VE JUST THOUGHT OF A GAME . . .
4-10 FRI 6809

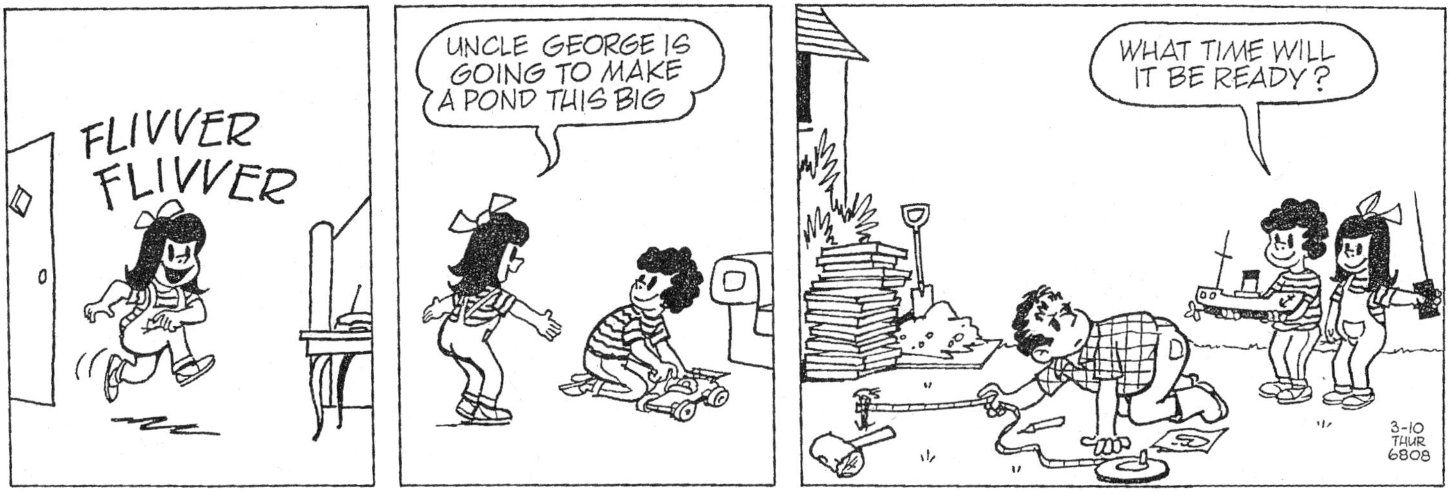
FLIVVER FLIVVER
UNCLE GEORGE IS GOING TO MAKE A POND THIS BIG
WHAT TIME WILL IT BE READY ?
3-10 THUR 6808

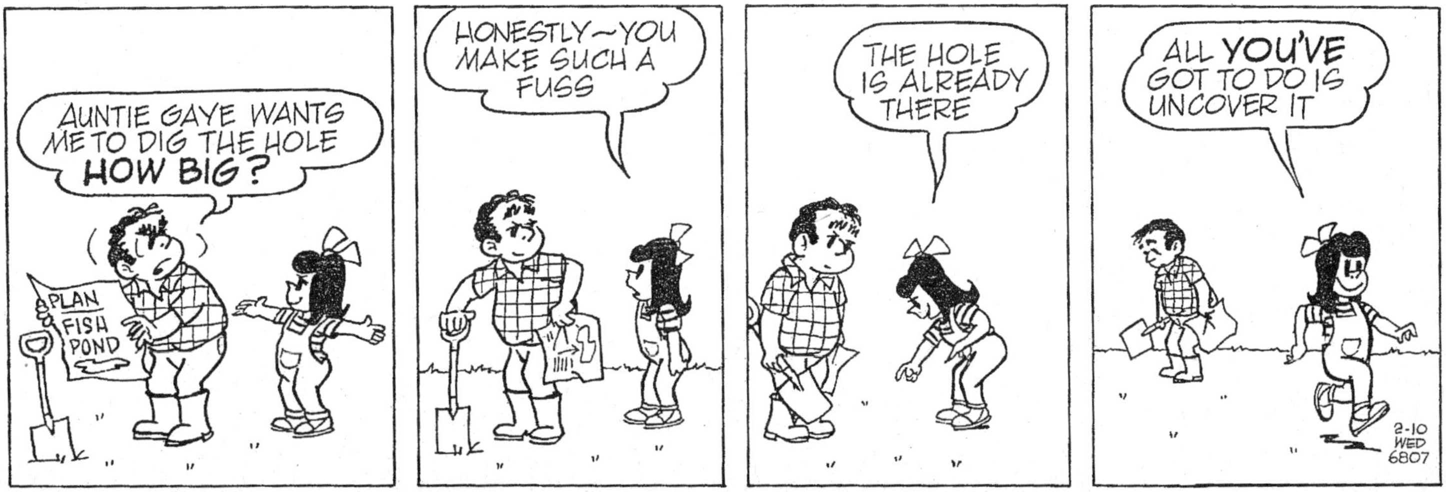
AUNTIE GAYE WANTS ME TO DIG THE HOLE HOW BIG ?
PLAN FISH POND
HONESTLY — YOU MAKE SUCH A FUSS
THE HOLE IS ALREADY THERE
ALL YOU'VE GOT TO DO IS UNCOVER IT
2-10 WED 6807

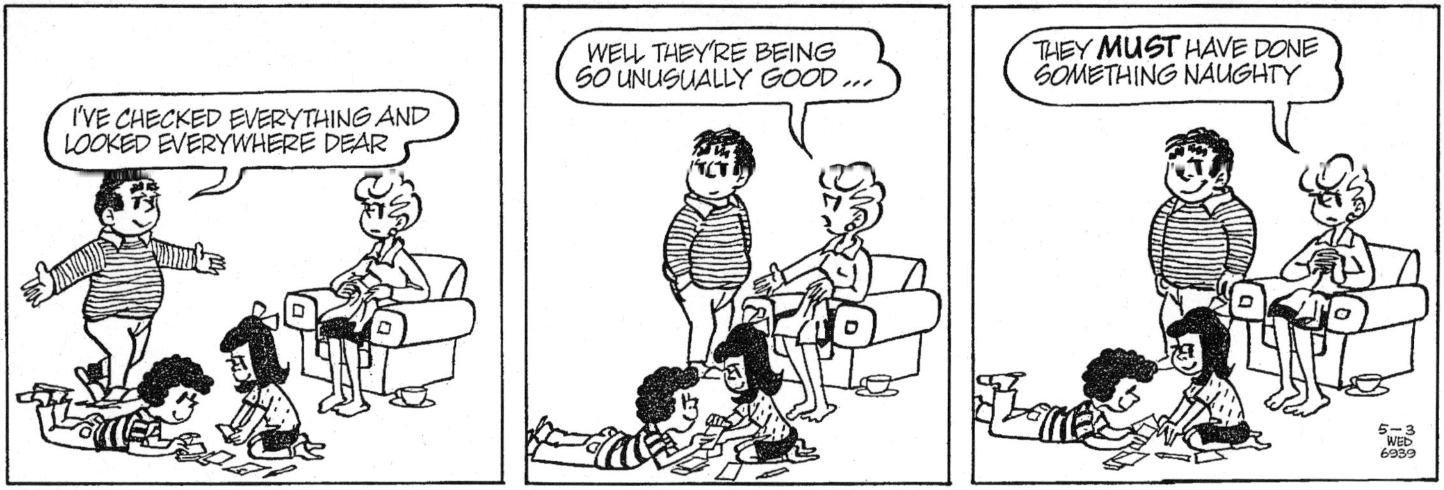
I'VE CHECKED EVERYTHING AND LOOKED EVERYWHERE DEAR
WELL THEY'RE BEING SO UNUSUALLY GOOD ...
THEY MUST HAVE DONE SOMETHING NAUGHTY
5-3 WED 6939

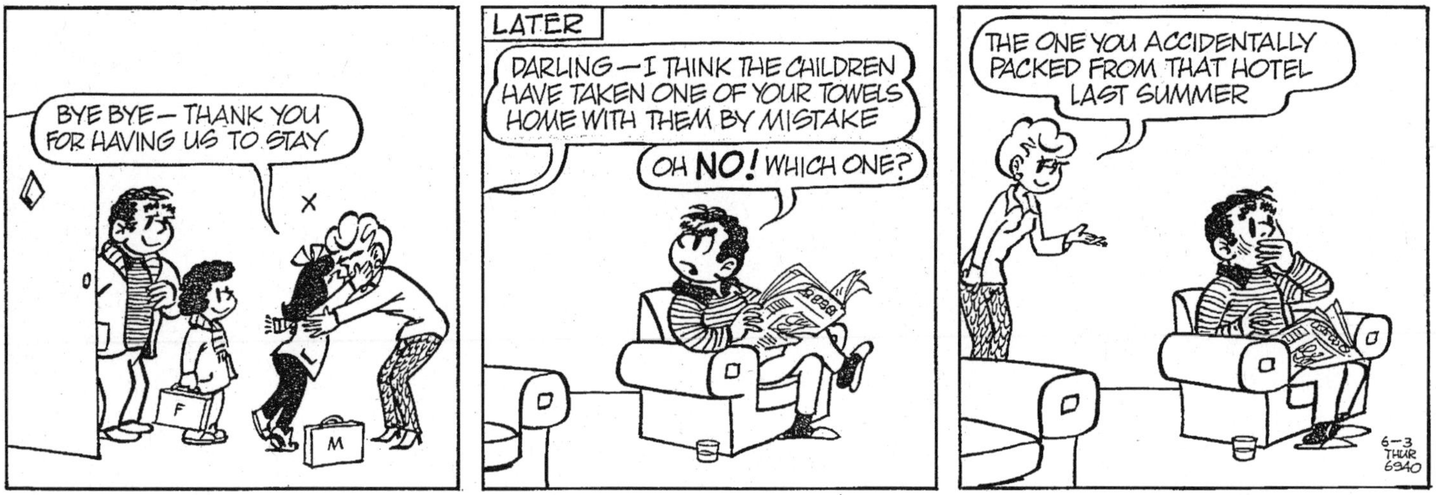
BYE BYE— THANK YOU FOR HAVING US TO STAY
F
M
LATER
DARLING—I THINK THE CHILDREN HAVE TAKEN ONE OF YOUR TOWELS HOME WITH THEM BY MISTAKE
OH NO! WHICH ONE?
THE ONE YOU ACCIDENTALLY PACKED FROM THAT HOTEL LAST SUMMER
6-3 THUR 6940

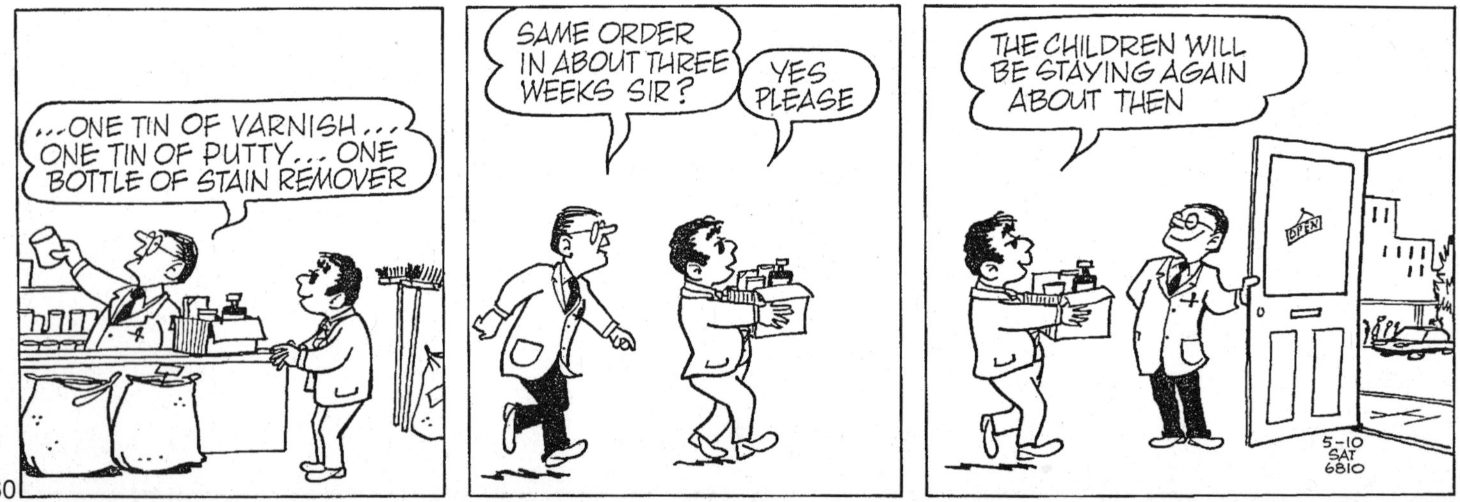
...ONE TIN OF VARNISH... ONE TIN OF PUTTY... ONE BOTTLE OF STAIN REMOVER
SAME ORDER IN ABOUT THREE WEEKS SIR?
YES PLEASE
THE CHILDREN WILL BE STAYING AGAIN ABOUT THEN
OPEN
5-10 SAT 6810

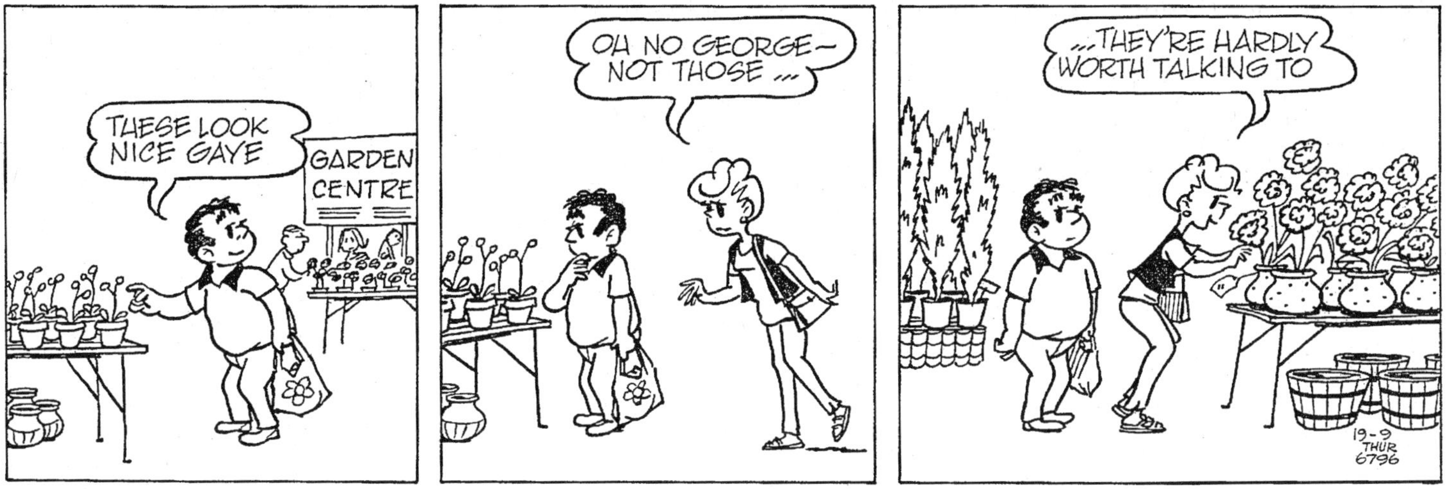
THESE LOOK NICE GAYE
GARDEN CENTRE
OH NO GEORGE— NOT THOSE ...
...THEY'RE HARDLY WORTH TALKING TO
19-9 THUR 6796

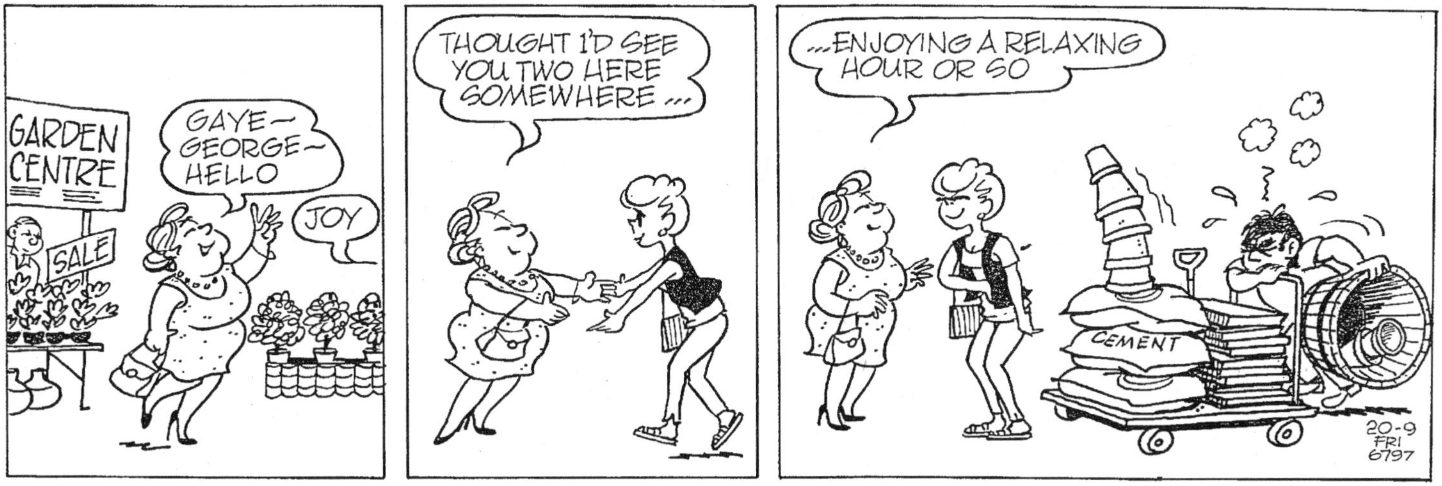
GARDEN CENTRE
SALE
GAYE— GEORGE— HELLO
JOY
THOUGHT I'D SEE YOU TWO HERE SOMEWHERE ...
...ENJOYING A RELAXING HOUR OR SO
CEMENT
20-9 FRI 6797

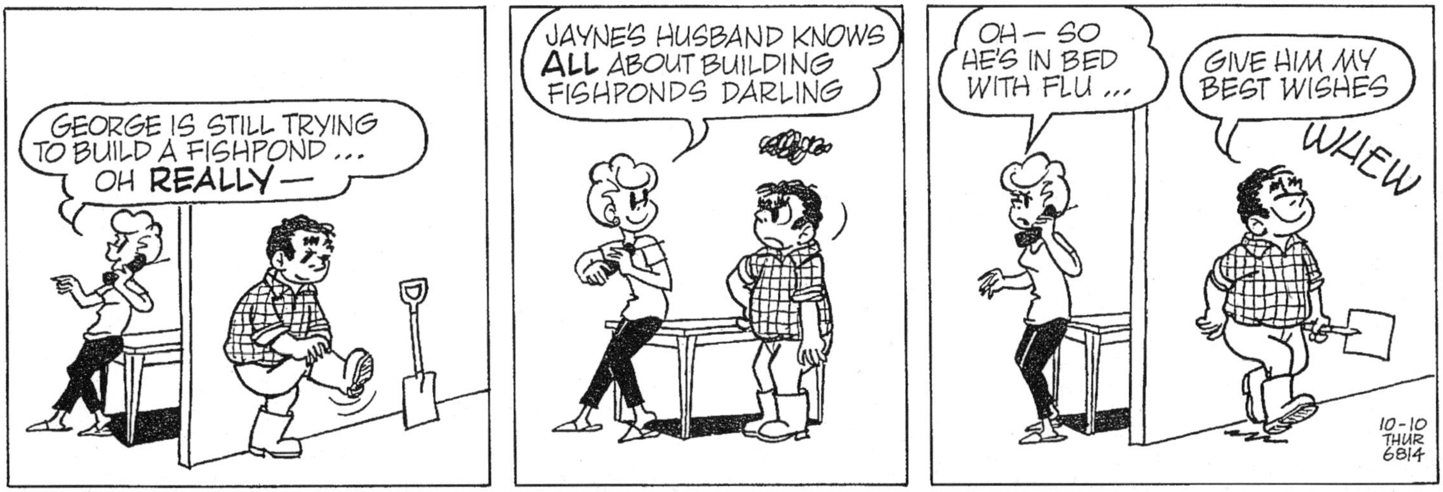
GEORGE IS STILL TRYING TO BUILD A FISHPOND ... OH **REALLY**—
JAYNE'S HUSBAND KNOWS **ALL** ABOUT BUILDING FISHPONDS DARLING
OH— SO HE'S IN BED WITH FLU ...
GIVE HIM MY BEST WISHES
WHEW
10-10 THUR 6814

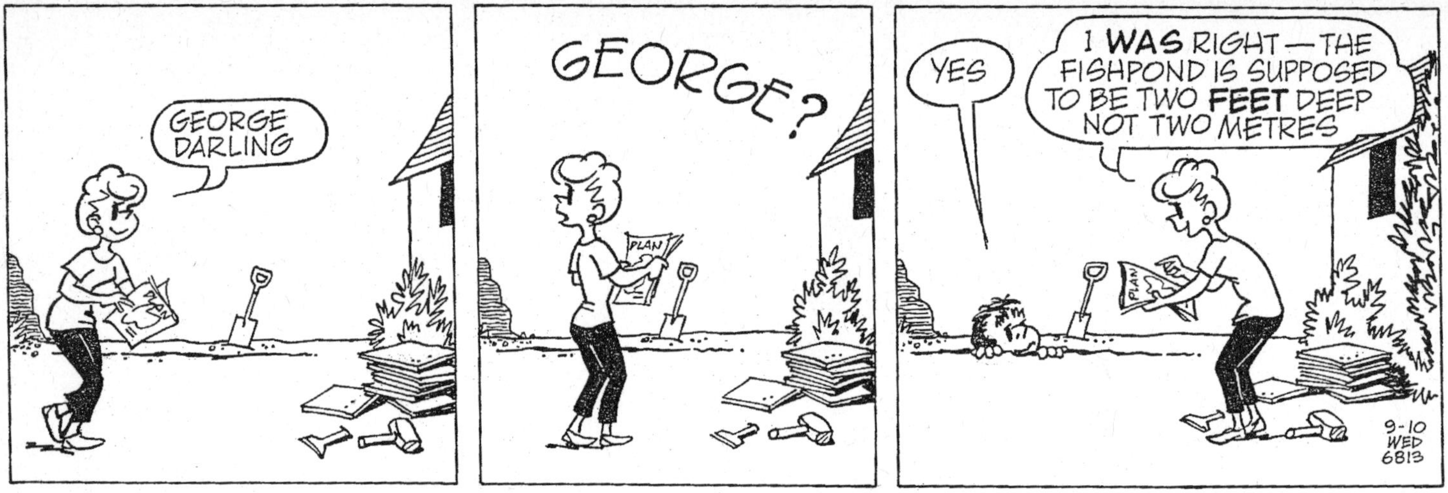
GEORGE DARLING
GEORGE?
YES
I WAS RIGHT—THE FISHPOND IS SUPPOSED TO BE TWO FEET DEEP NOT TWO METRES
PLAN
9-10 WED 6813

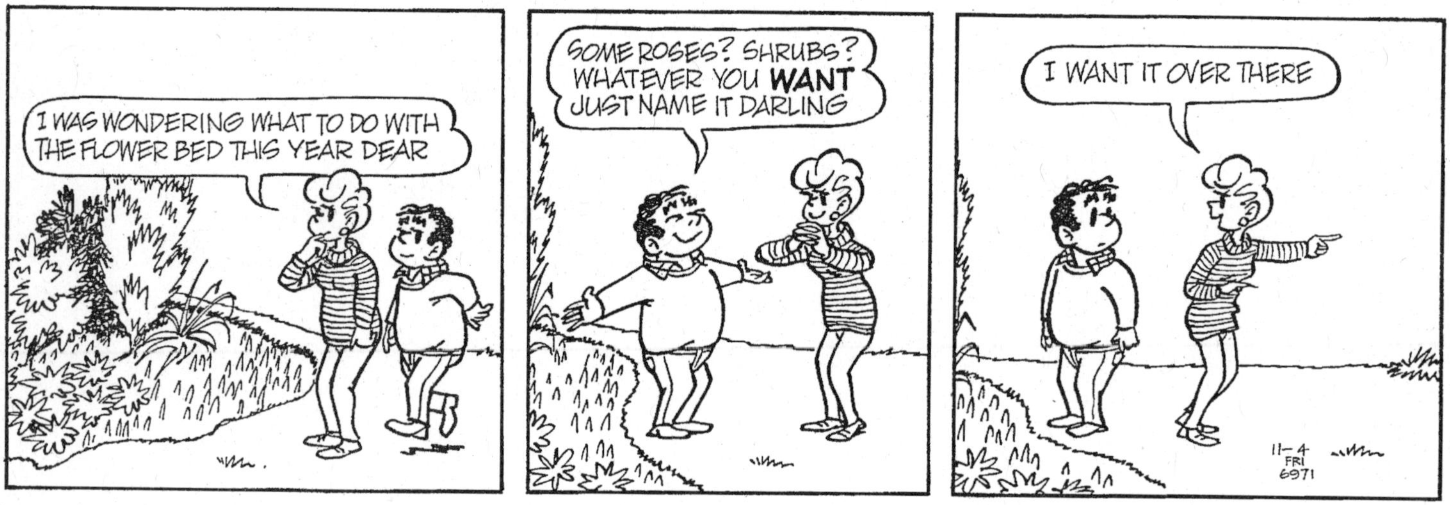
I WAS WONDERING WHAT TO DO WITH THE FLOWER BED THIS YEAR DEAR
SOME ROSES? SHRUBS? WHATEVER YOU WANT JUST NAME IT DARLING
I WANT IT OVER THERE
11-4 FRI 6971

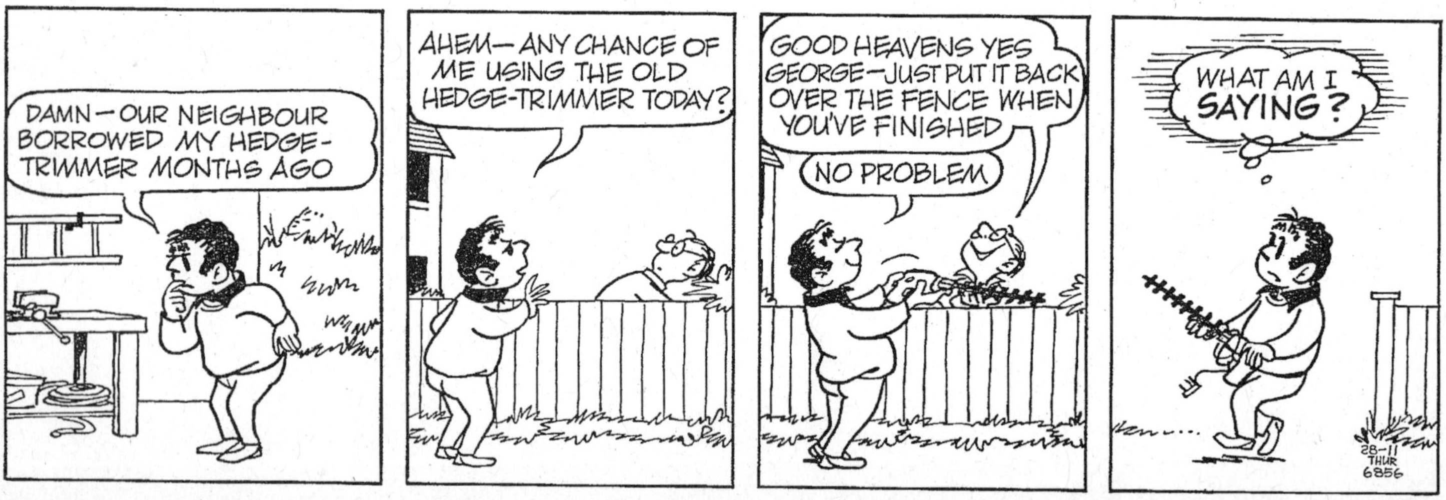
DAMN—OUR NEIGHBOUR BORROWED MY HEDGE-TRIMMER MONTHS AGO
AHEM—ANY CHANCE OF ME USING THE OLD HEDGE-TRIMMER TODAY?
GOOD HEAVENS YES GEORGE—JUST PUT IT BACK OVER THE FENCE WHEN YOU'VE FINISHED
NO PROBLEM
WHAT AM I SAYING?
28-11 THUR 6856

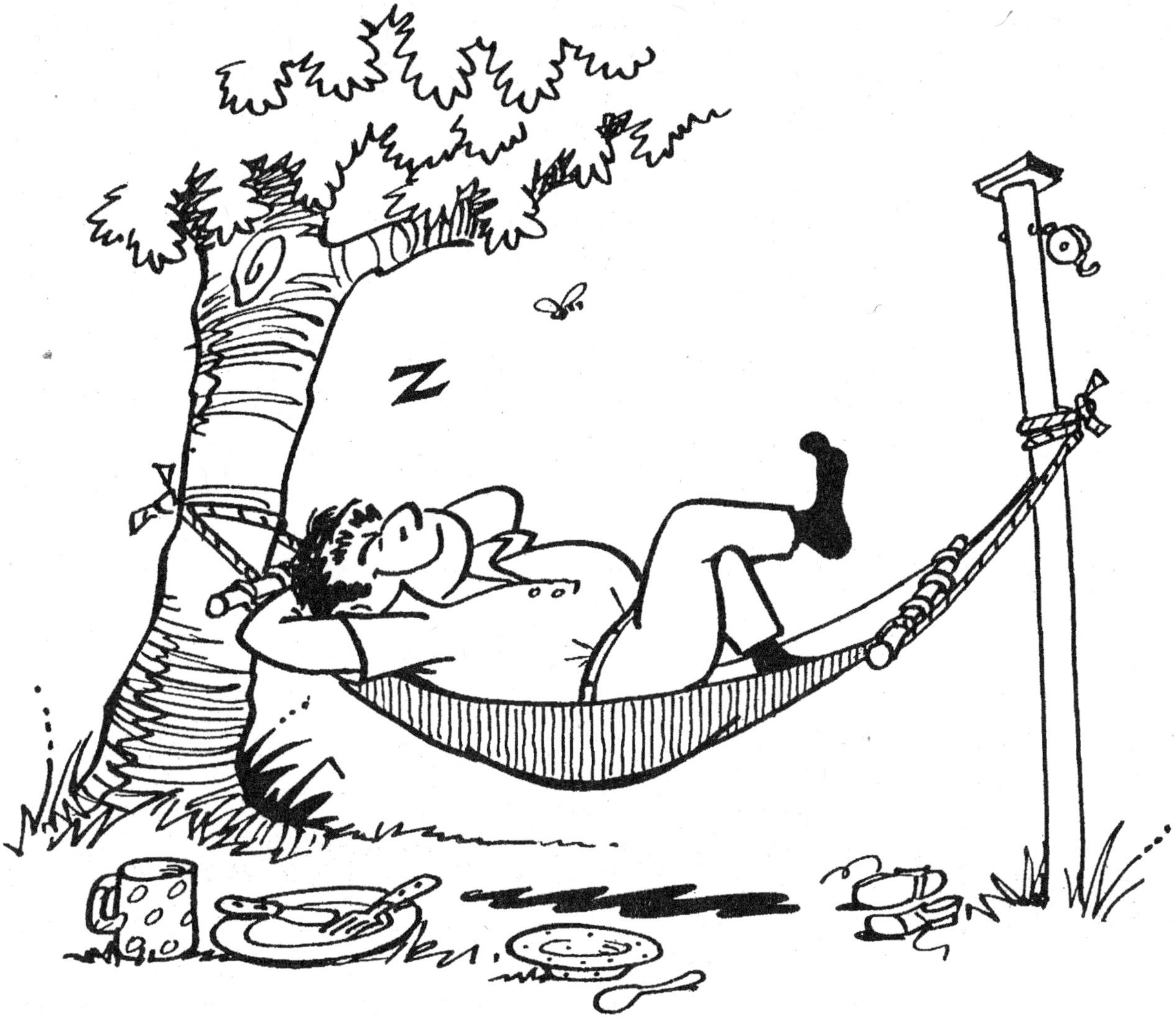
Z

KEEP FIT—EXERCISE—DIETS—
GEORGE REALLY PREFERS THE
WELL FED LOOK

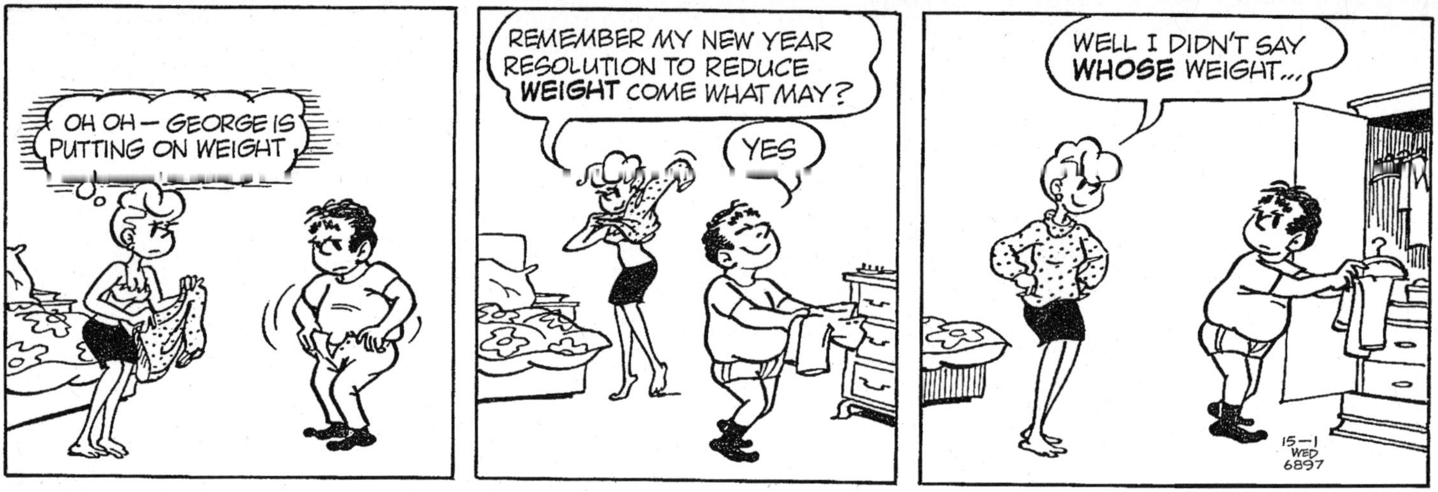
OH OH — GEORGE IS PUTTING ON WEIGHT
REMEMBER MY NEW YEAR RESOLUTION TO REDUCE **WEIGHT** COME WHAT MAY?
YES
WELL I DIDN'T SAY **WHOSE** WEIGHT...
15—1 WED 6897

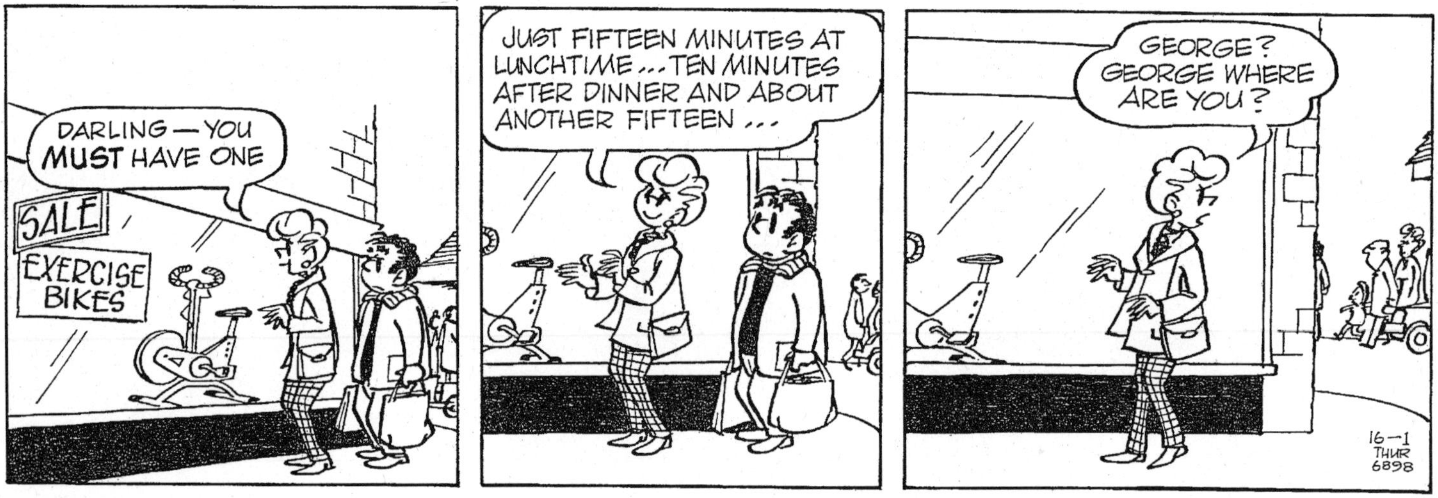
SALE
EXERCISE BIKES
DARLING — YOU **MUST** HAVE ONE
JUST FIFTEEN MINUTES AT LUNCHTIME... TEN MINUTES AFTER DINNER AND ABOUT ANOTHER FIFTEEN ...
GEORGE? GEORGE WHERE ARE YOU?
16—1 THUR 6898

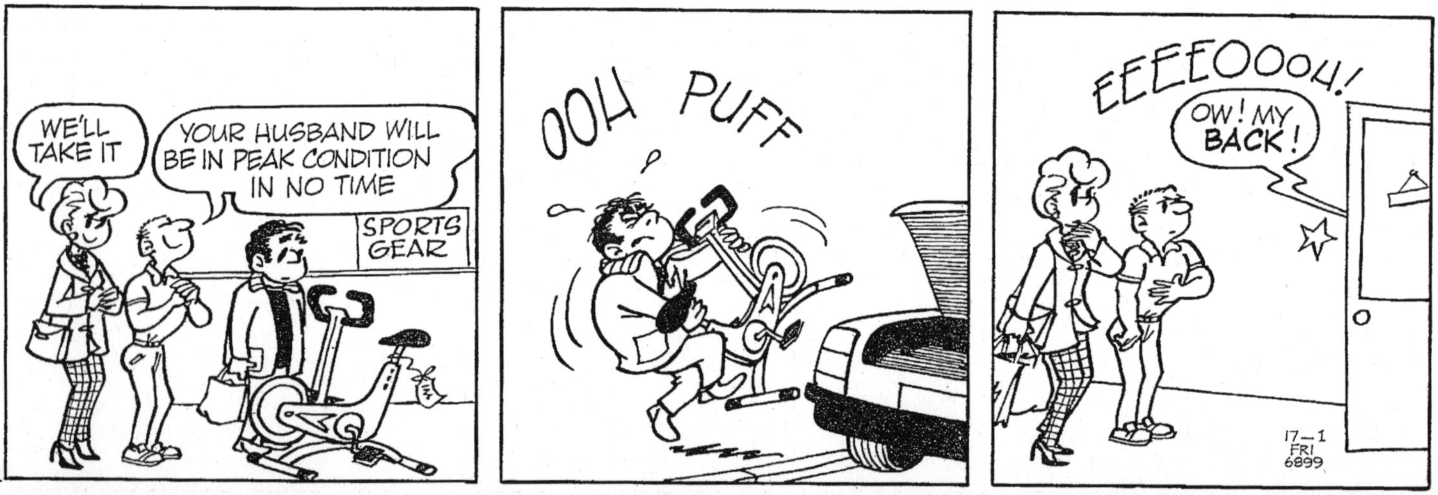
WE'LL TAKE IT
YOUR HUSBAND WILL BE IN PEAK CONDITION IN NO TIME
SPORTS GEAR
OOH PUFF
EEEEOOOOH!
OW! MY **BACK**!
17—1 FRI 6899

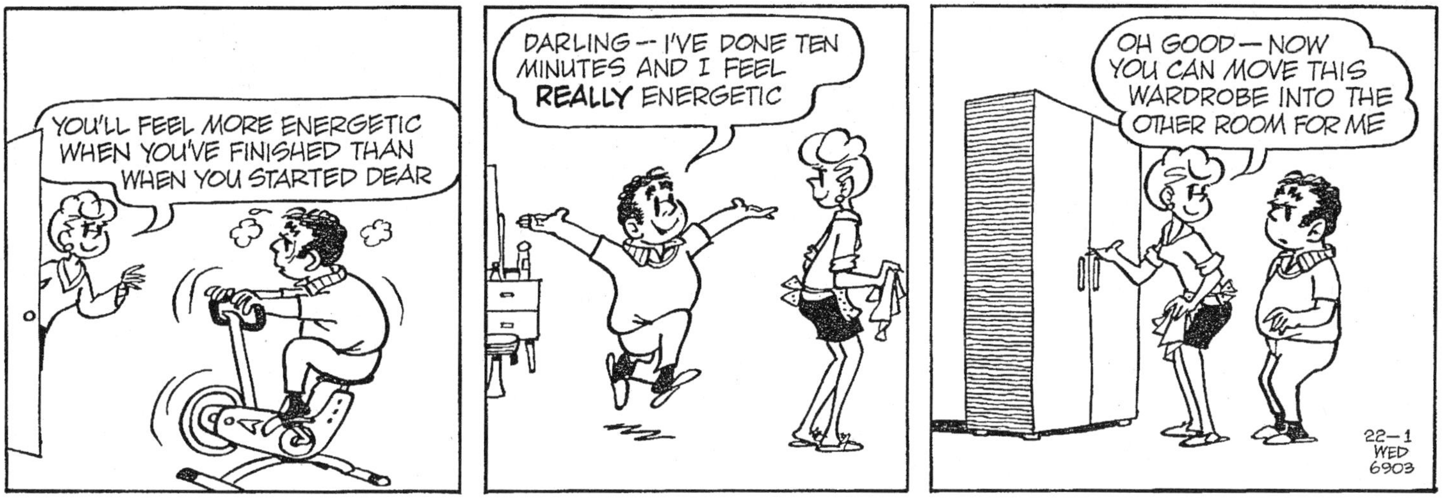
YOU'LL FEEL MORE ENERGETIC WHEN YOU'VE FINISHED THAN WHEN YOU STARTED DEAR
DARLING -- I'VE DONE TEN MINUTES AND I FEEL **REALLY** ENERGETIC
OH GOOD — NOW YOU CAN MOVE THIS WARDROBE INTO THE OTHER ROOM FOR ME
22—1 WED 6903

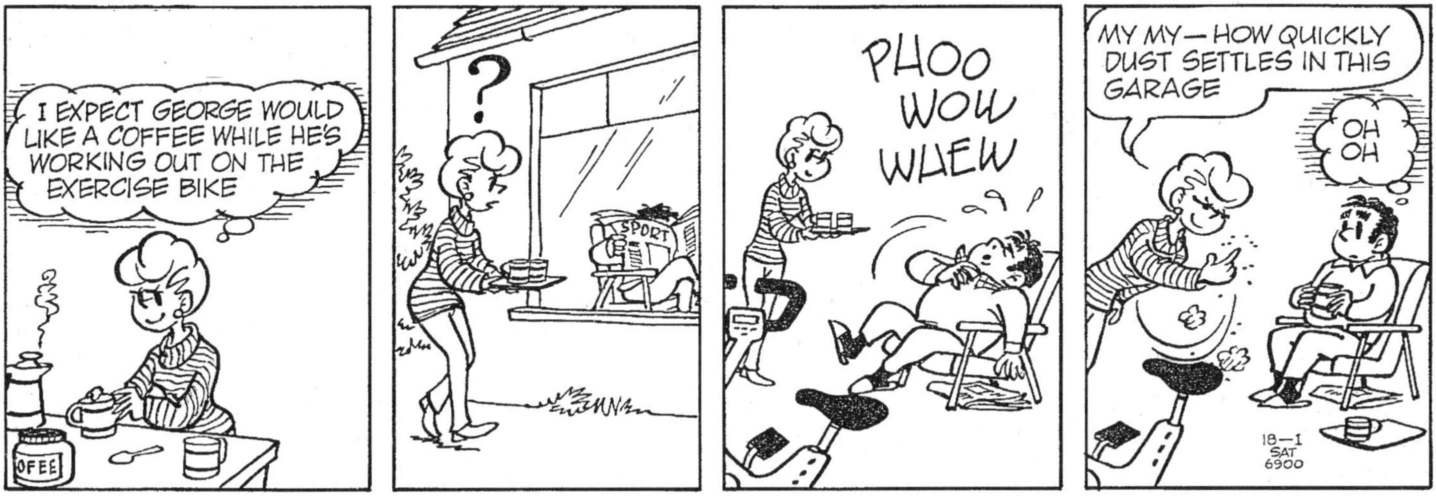
I EXPECT GEORGE WOULD LIKE A COFFEE WHILE HE'S WORKING OUT ON THE EXERCISE BIKE
OFEE
?
SPORT
PHOO WOW WHEW
MY MY — HOW QUICKLY DUST SETTLES IN THIS GARAGE
OH OH
18—1 SAT 6900

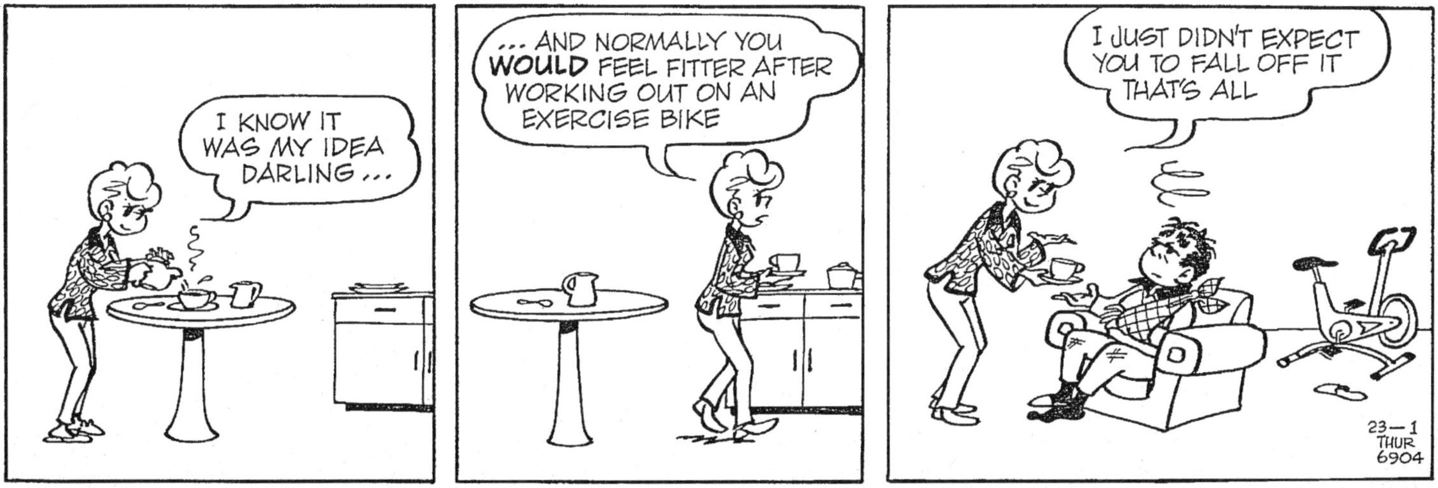
I KNOW IT WAS MY IDEA DARLING ...
... AND NORMALLY YOU **WOULD** FEEL FITTER AFTER WORKING OUT ON AN EXERCISE BIKE
I JUST DIDN'T EXPECT YOU TO FALL OFF IT THAT'S ALL
23—1 THUR 6904

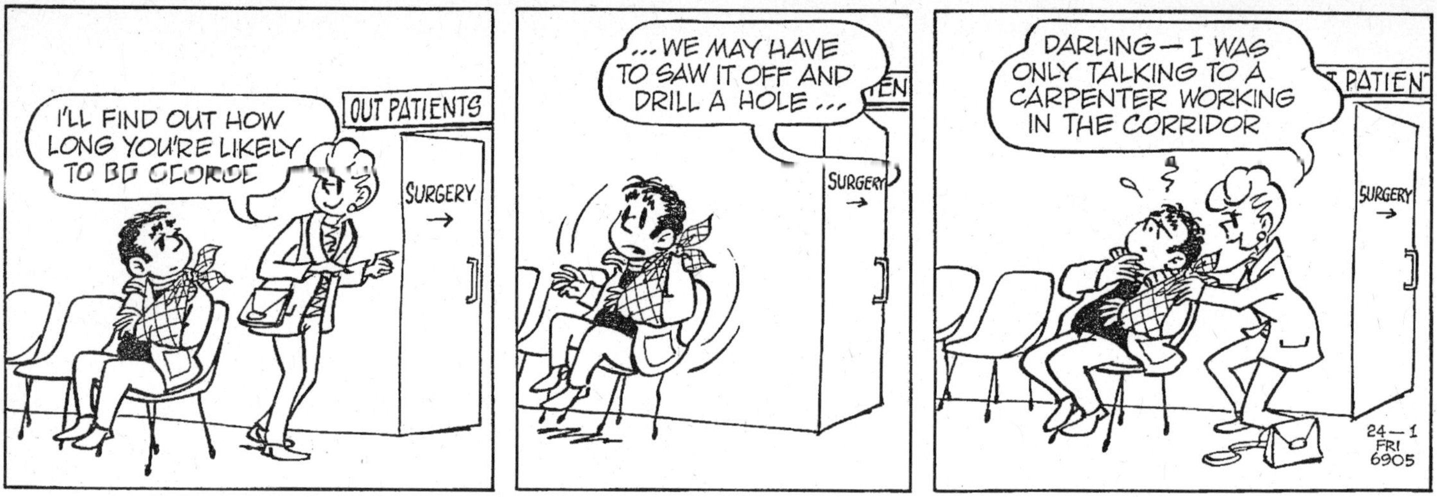
I'LL FIND OUT HOW LONG YOU'RE LIKELY TO BE GEORGE
OUT PATIENTS
SURGERY →
...WE MAY HAVE TO SAW IT OFF AND DRILL A HOLE...
SURGERY →
DARLING — I WAS ONLY TALKING TO A CARPENTER WORKING IN THE CORRIDOR
SURGERY →
24—1 FRI 6905

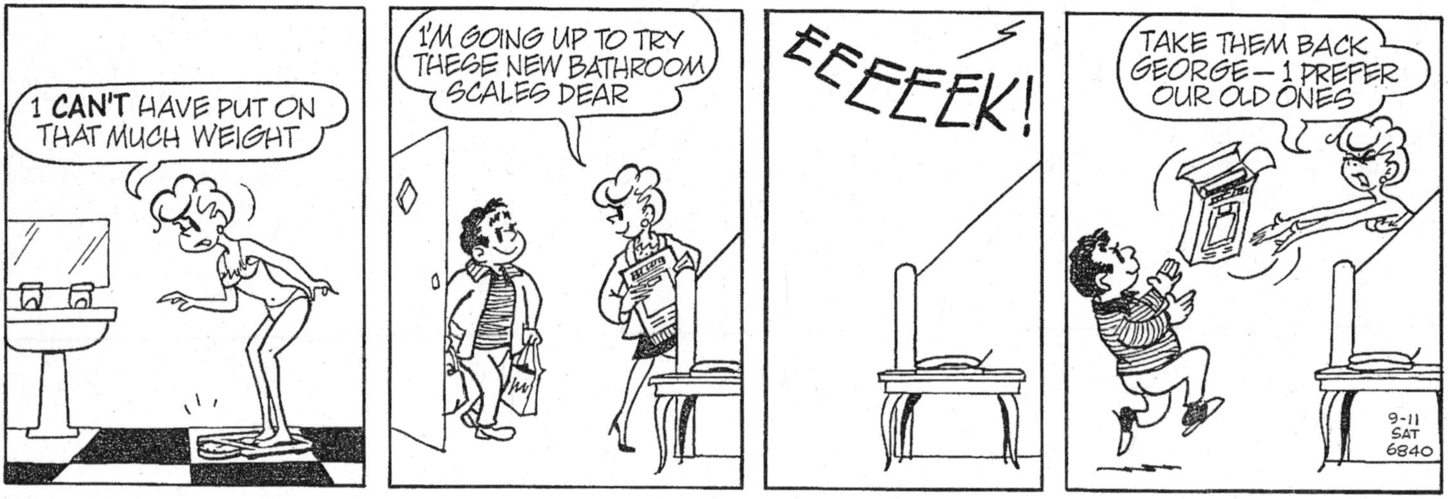
I CAN'T HAVE PUT ON THAT MUCH WEIGHT
I'M GOING UP TO TRY THESE NEW BATHROOM SCALES DEAR
EEEEEK!
TAKE THEM BACK GEORGE — I PREFER OUR OLD ONES
9-11 SAT 6840

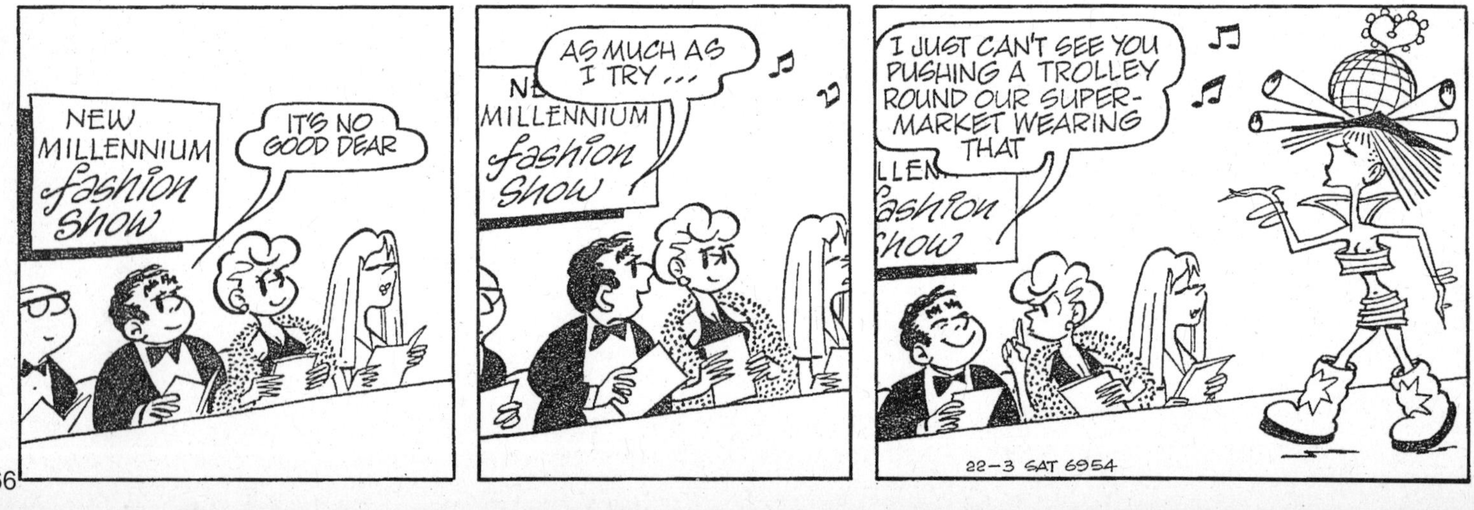
NEW MILLENNIUM fashion show
IT'S NO GOOD DEAR
AS MUCH AS I TRY...
I JUST CAN'T SEE YOU PUSHING A TROLLEY ROUND OUR SUPER-MARKET WEARING THAT
22-3 SAT 6954

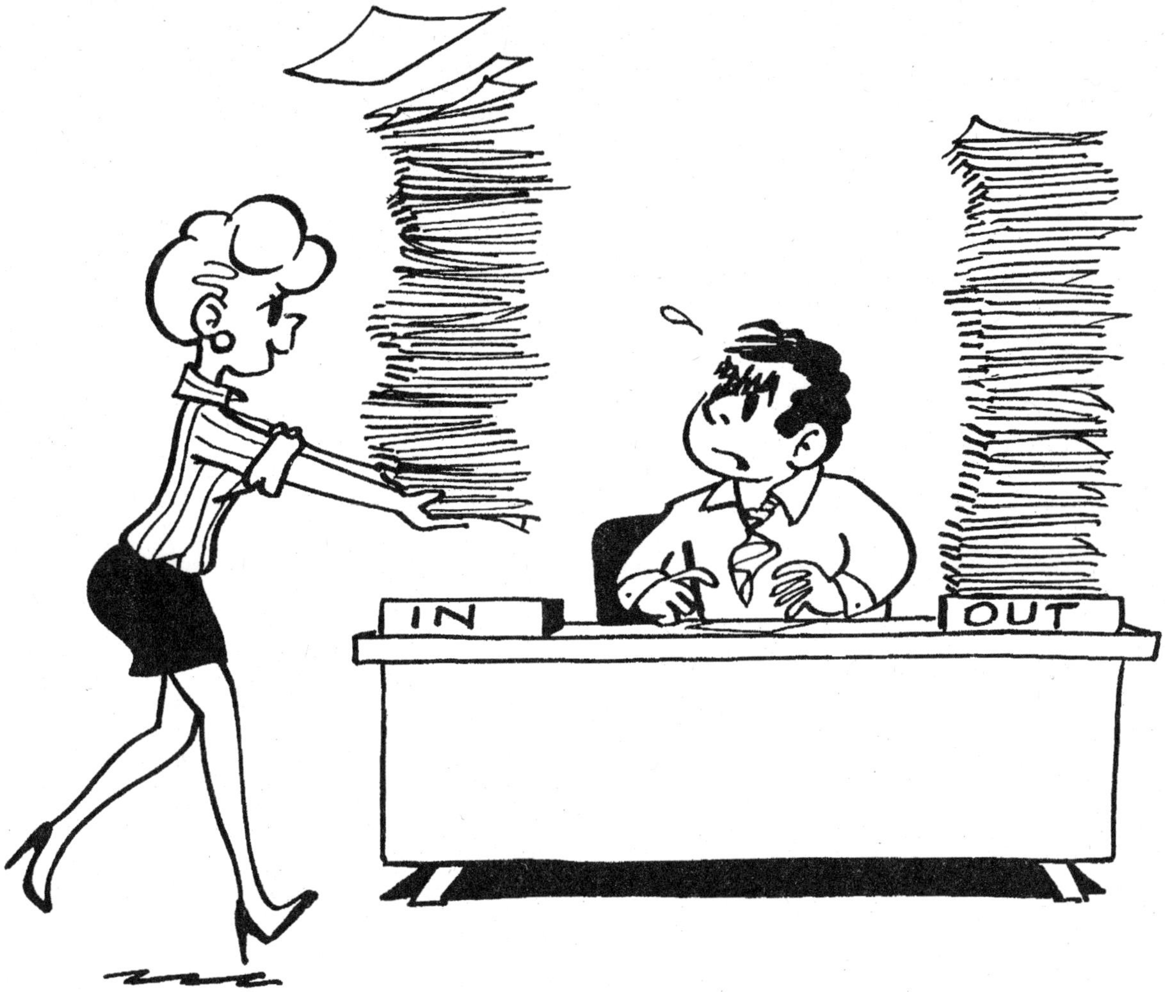
IN
OUT

GAYE ENJOYS WORKING AS
PERSONAL ASSISTANT TO GEORGES' BOSS

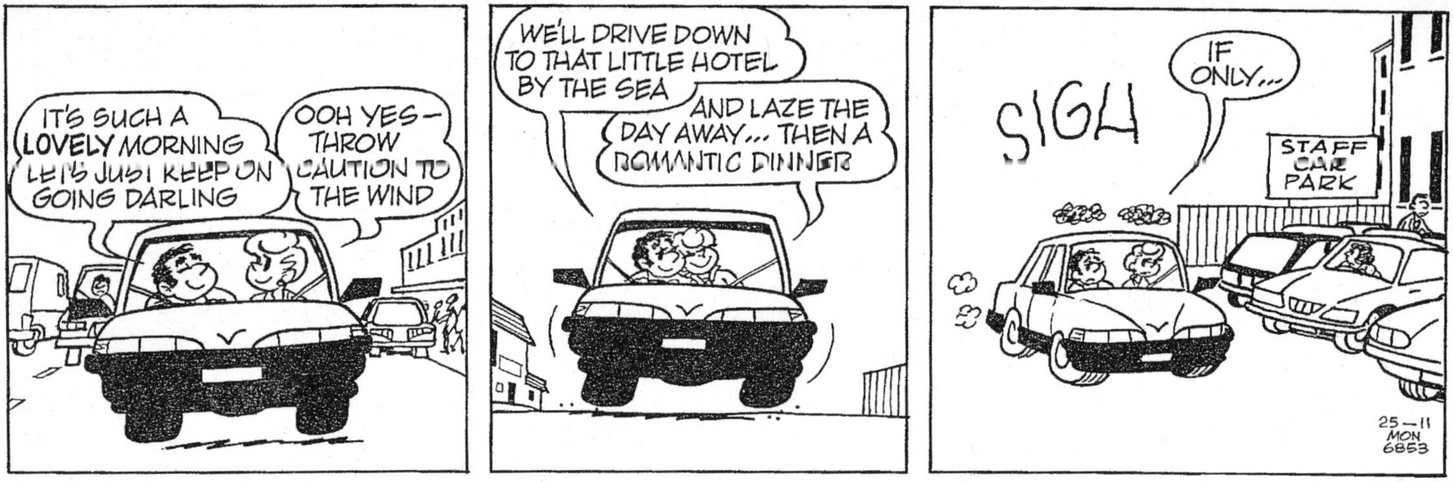
IT'S SUCH A LOVELY MORNING LET'S JUST KEEP ON GOING DARLING
OOH YES— THROW CAUTION TO THE WIND
WE'LL DRIVE DOWN TO THAT LITTLE HOTEL BY THE SEA
AND LAZE THE DAY AWAY... THEN A ROMANTIC DINNER
SIGH
IF ONLY...
STAFF CAR PARK
25—11 MON 6853

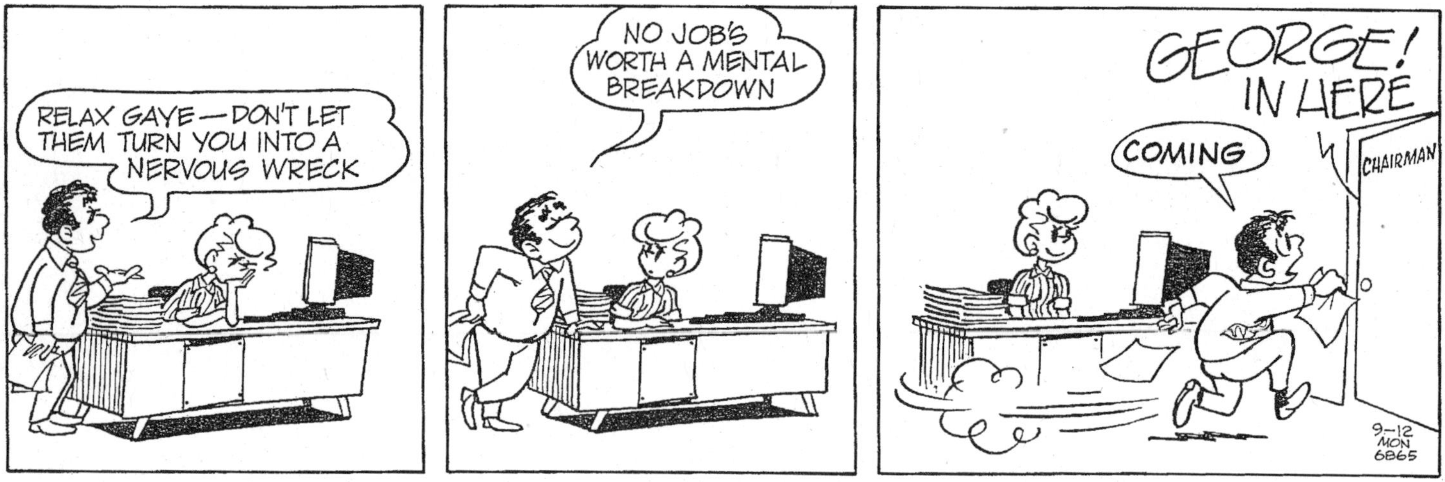
RELAX GAYE—DON'T LET THEM TURN YOU INTO A NERVOUS WRECK
NO JOB'S WORTH A MENTAL BREAKDOWN
GEORGE! IN HERE
COMING
CHAIRMAN
9—12 MON 6865

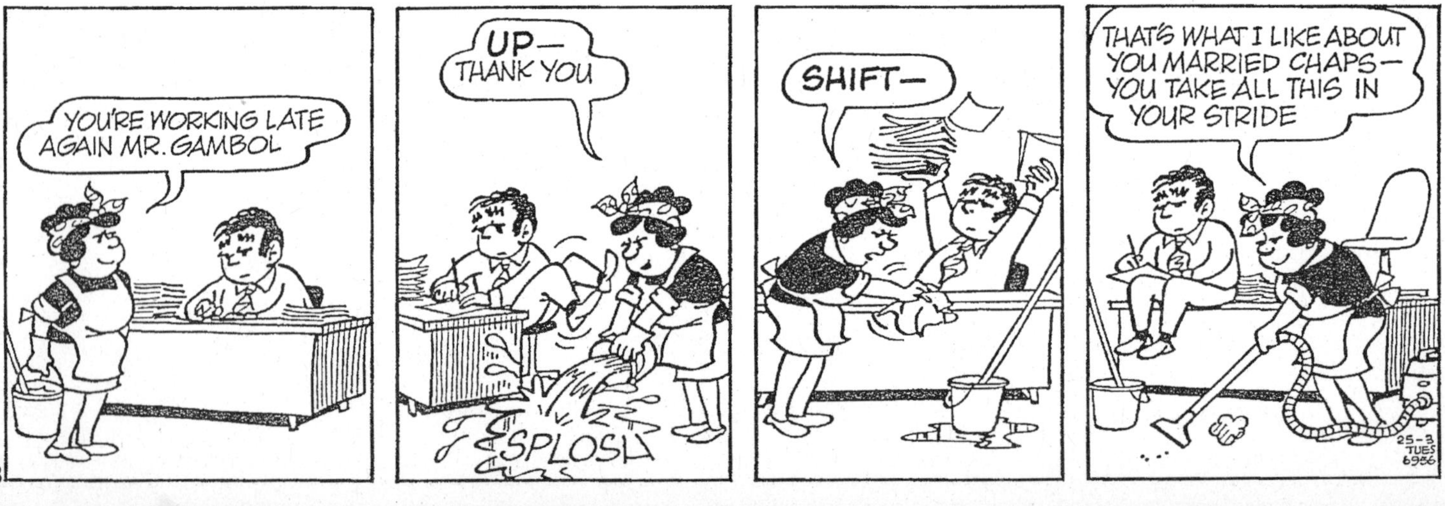
YOU'RE WORKING LATE AGAIN MR. GAMBOL
UP— THANK YOU
SPLOSH
SHIFT—
THAT'S WHAT I LIKE ABOUT YOU MARRIED CHAPS— YOU TAKE ALL THIS IN YOUR STRIDE
25—3 TUES 6956

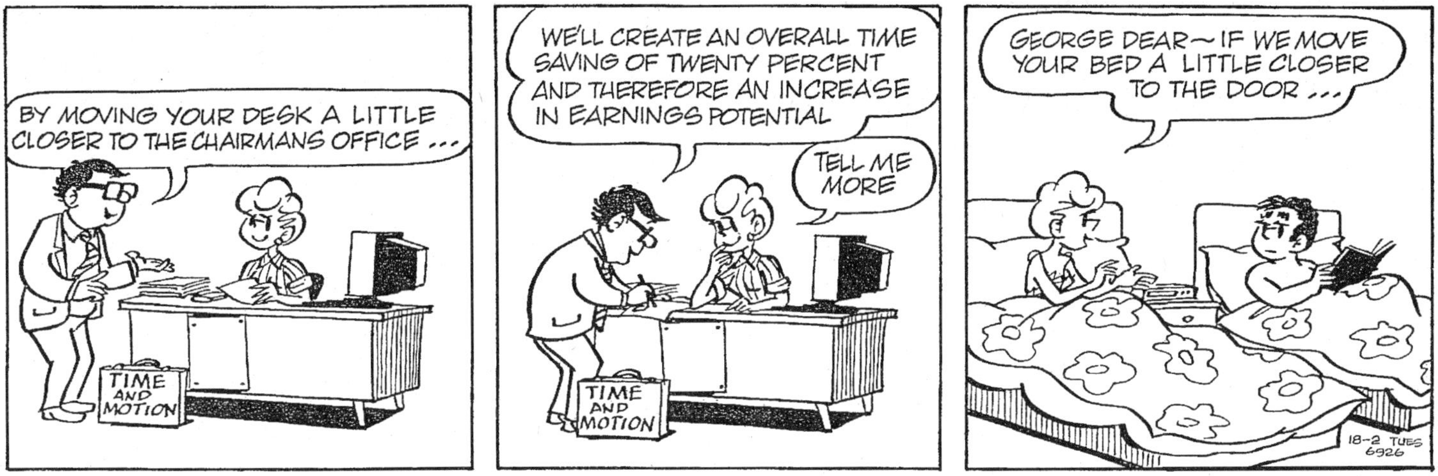
BY MOVING YOUR DESK A LITTLE CLOSER TO THE CHAIRMANS OFFICE ...
TIME AND MOTION
WE'LL CREATE AN OVERALL TIME SAVING OF TWENTY PERCENT AND THEREFORE AN INCREASE IN EARNINGS POTENTIAL
TELL ME MORE
TIME AND MOTION
GEORGE DEAR ~ IF WE MOVE YOUR BED A LITTLE CLOSER TO THE DOOR ...
18-2 TUES 6926

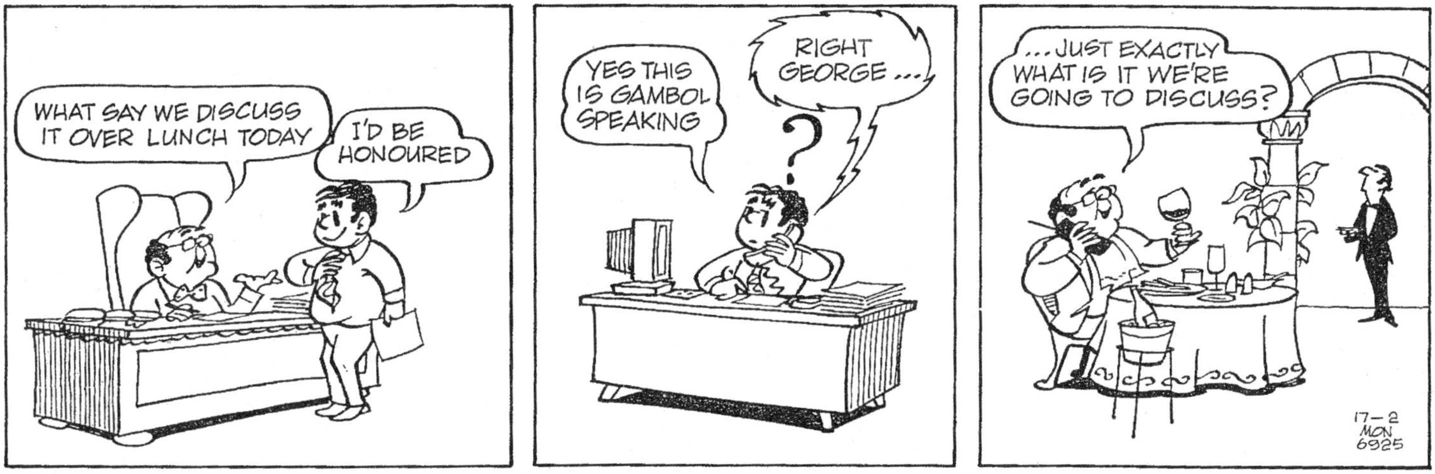
WHAT SAY WE DISCUSS IT OVER LUNCH TODAY
I'D BE HONOURED
YES THIS IS GAMBOL SPEAKING
RIGHT GEORGE ...
?
... JUST EXACTLY WHAT IS IT WE'RE GOING TO DISCUSS?
17-2 MON 6925

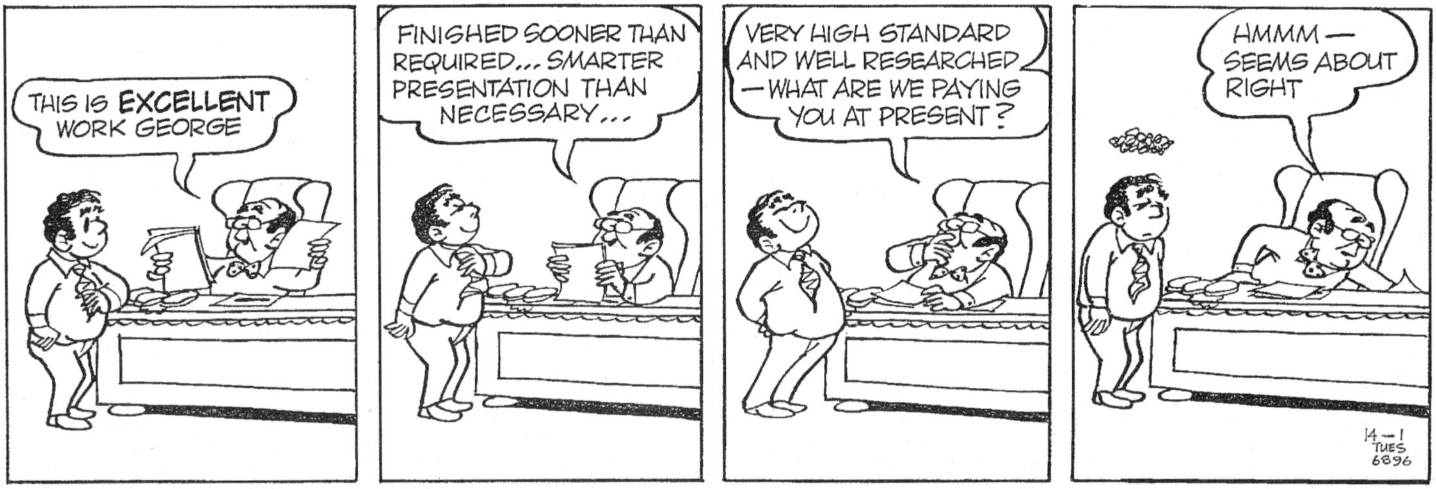
THIS IS **EXCELLENT** WORK GEORGE
FINISHED SOONER THAN REQUIRED... SMARTER PRESENTATION THAN NECESSARY...
VERY HIGH STANDARD AND WELL RESEARCHED — WHAT ARE WE PAYING YOU AT PRESENT ?
HMMM — SEEMS ABOUT RIGHT
14-1 TUES 6896

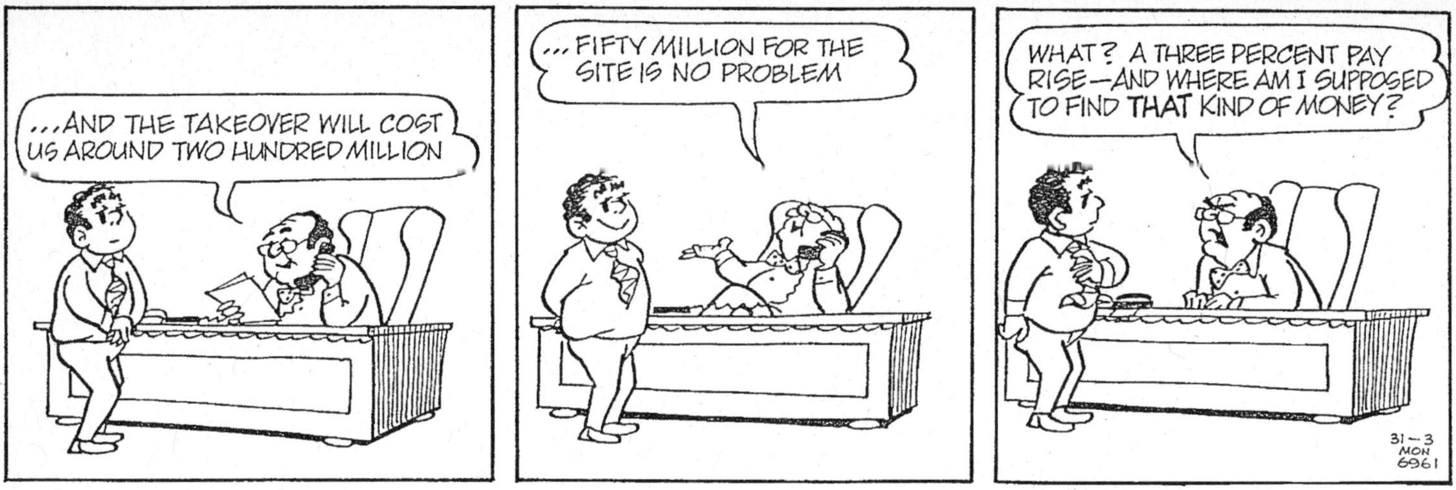

...AND THE TAKEOVER WILL COST US AROUND TWO HUNDRED MILLION
...FIFTY MILLION FOR THE SITE IS NO PROBLEM
WHAT? A THREE PERCENT PAY RISE—AND WHERE AM I SUPPOSED TO FIND **THAT** KIND OF MONEY?
31—3 MON 6961

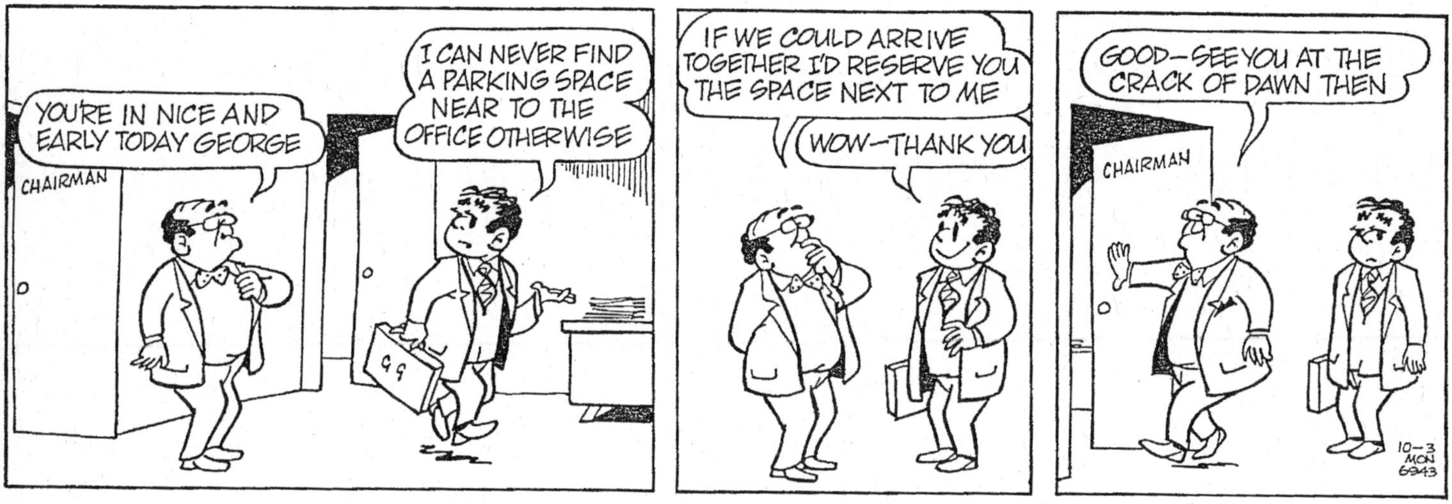

CHAIRMAN
YOU'RE IN NICE AND EARLY TODAY GEORGE
I CAN NEVER FIND A PARKING SPACE NEAR TO THE OFFICE OTHERWISE
IF WE COULD ARRIVE TOGETHER I'D RESERVE YOU THE SPACE NEXT TO ME
WOW—THANK YOU
CHAIRMAN
GOOD—SEE YOU AT THE CRACK OF DAWN THEN
10—3 MON 6943

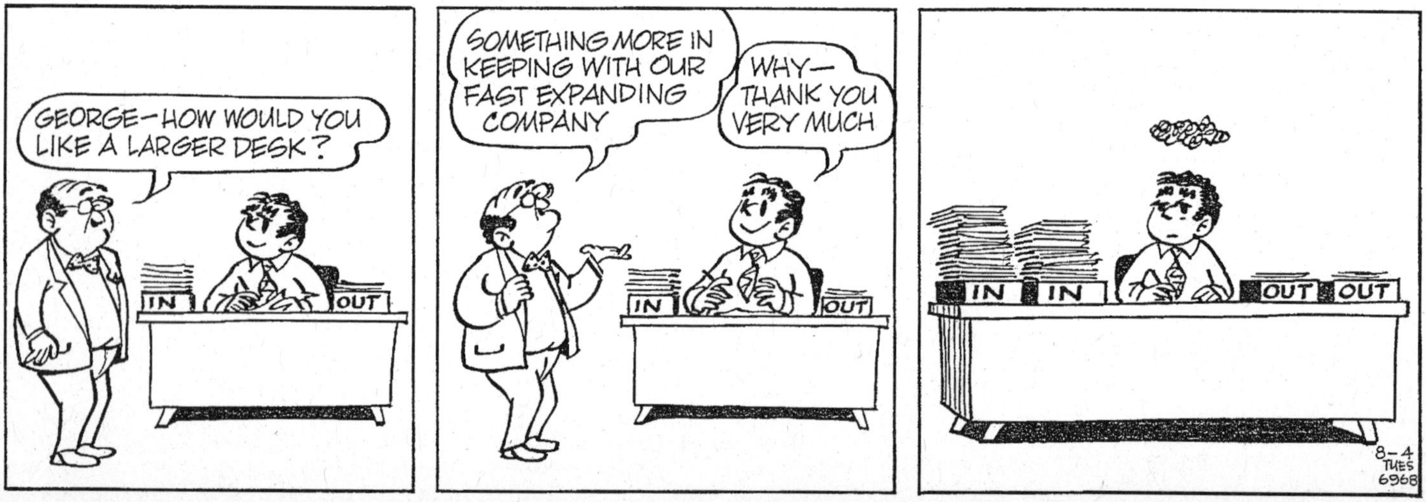

GEORGE—HOW WOULD YOU LIKE A LARGER DESK?
IN
OUT
SOMETHING MORE IN KEEPING WITH OUR FAST EXPANDING COMPANY
WHY—THANK YOU VERY MUCH
IN
OUT
IN
IN
OUT
OUT
8—4 TUES 6968

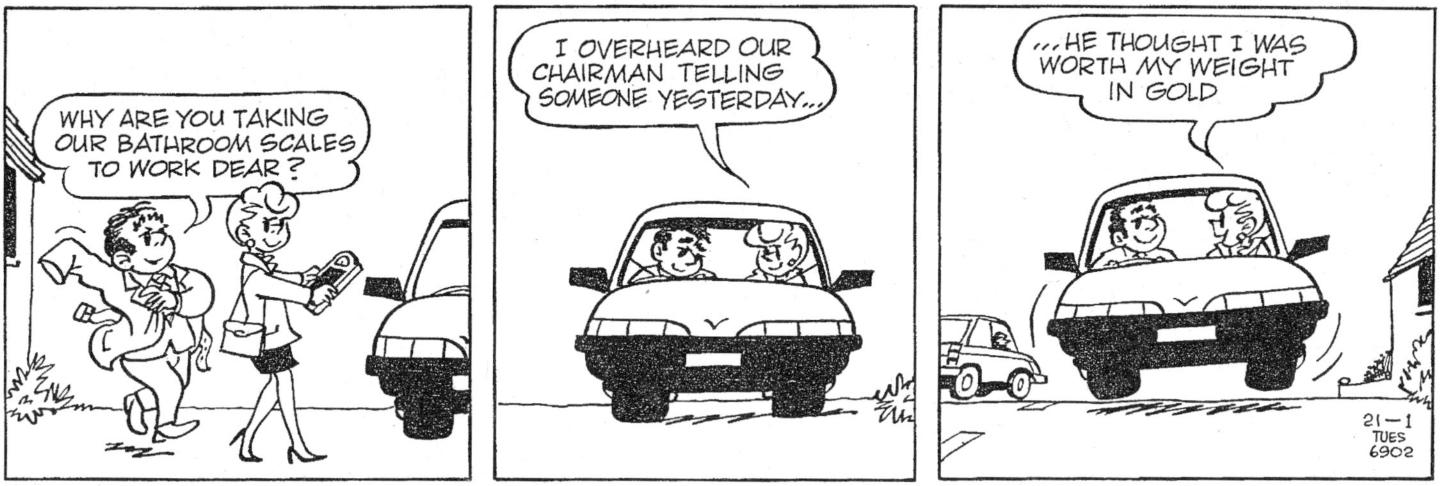
WHY ARE YOU TAKING OUR BATHROOM SCALES TO WORK DEAR?
I OVERHEARD OUR CHAIRMAN TELLING SOMEONE YESTERDAY...
...HE THOUGHT I WAS WORTH MY WEIGHT IN GOLD
21—1 TUES 6902

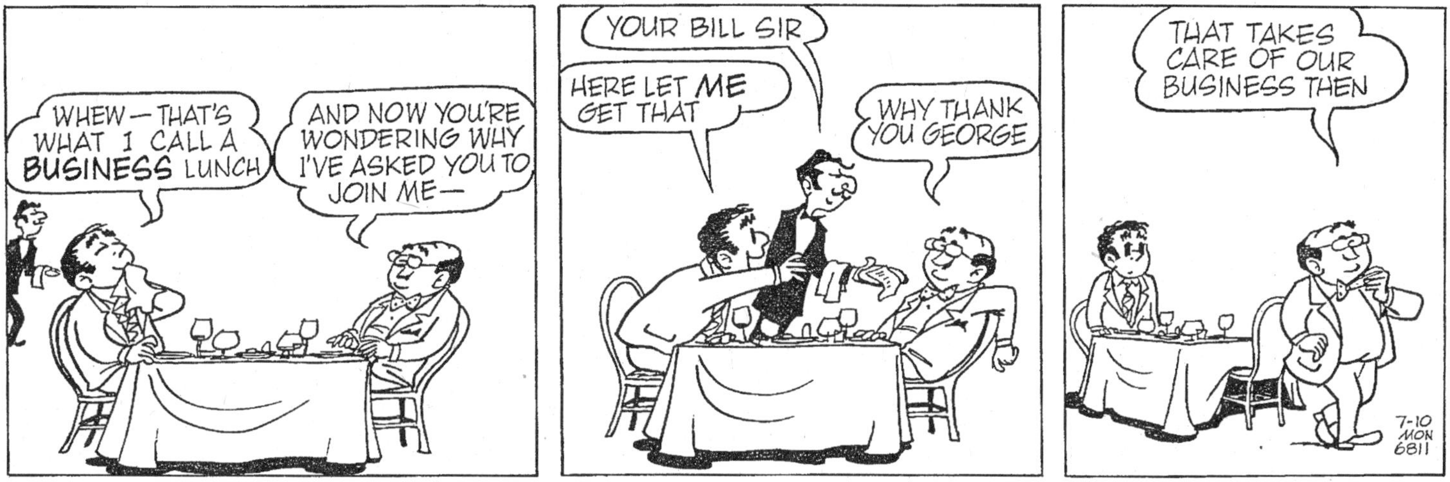
WHEW—THAT'S WHAT I CALL A BUSINESS LUNCH
AND NOW YOU'RE WONDERING WHY I'VE ASKED YOU TO JOIN ME—
YOUR BILL SIR
HERE LET ME GET THAT
WHY THANK YOU GEORGE
THAT TAKES CARE OF OUR BUSINESS THEN
7-10 MON 6811

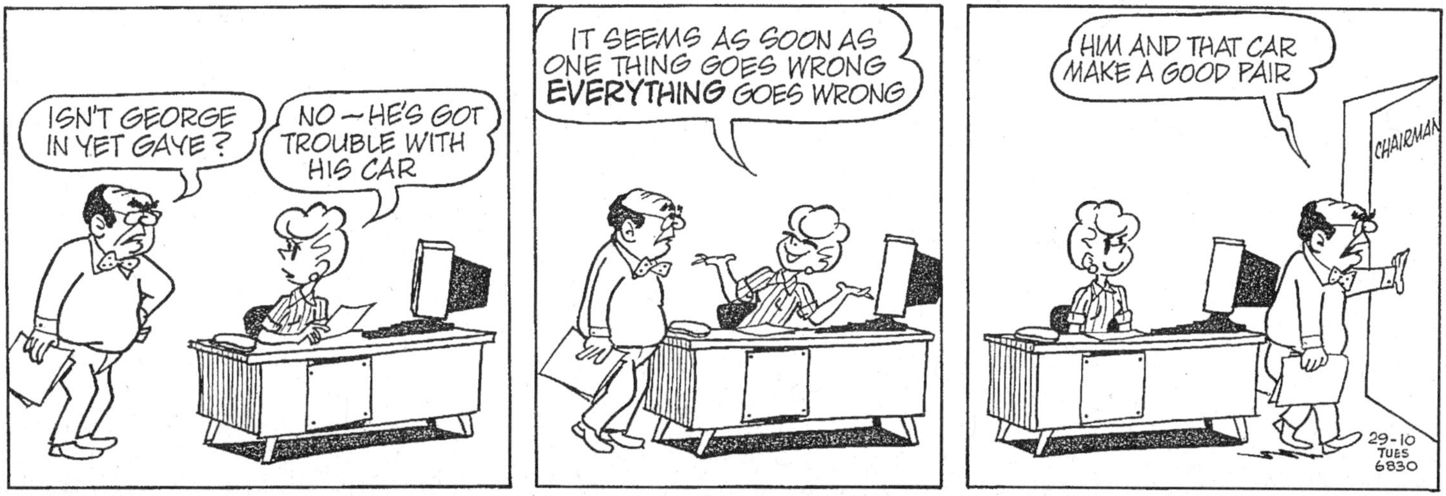
ISN'T GEORGE IN YET GAYE?
NO—HE'S GOT TROUBLE WITH HIS CAR
IT SEEMS AS SOON AS ONE THING GOES WRONG EVERYTHING GOES WRONG
HIM AND THAT CAR MAKE A GOOD PAIR
CHAIRMAN
29-10 TUES 6830

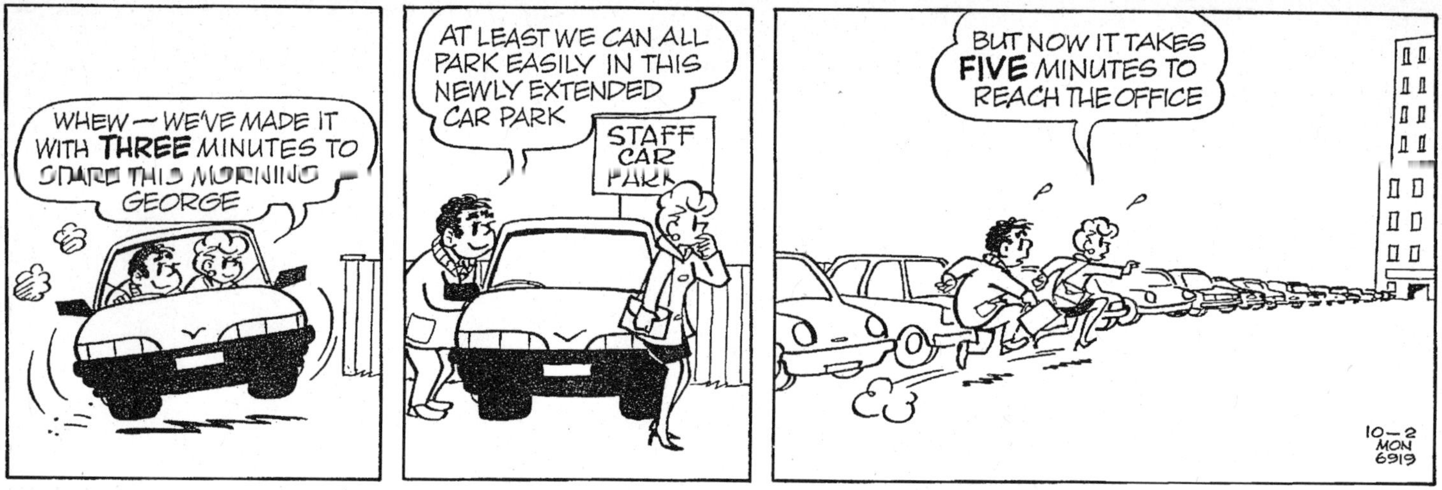
WHEW — WE'VE MADE IT WITH THREE MINUTES TO SPARE THIS MORNING GEORGE
AT LEAST WE CAN ALL PARK EASILY IN THIS NEWLY EXTENDED CAR PARK
STAFF CAR PARK
BUT NOW IT TAKES FIVE MINUTES TO REACH THE OFFICE
10—2 MON 6919

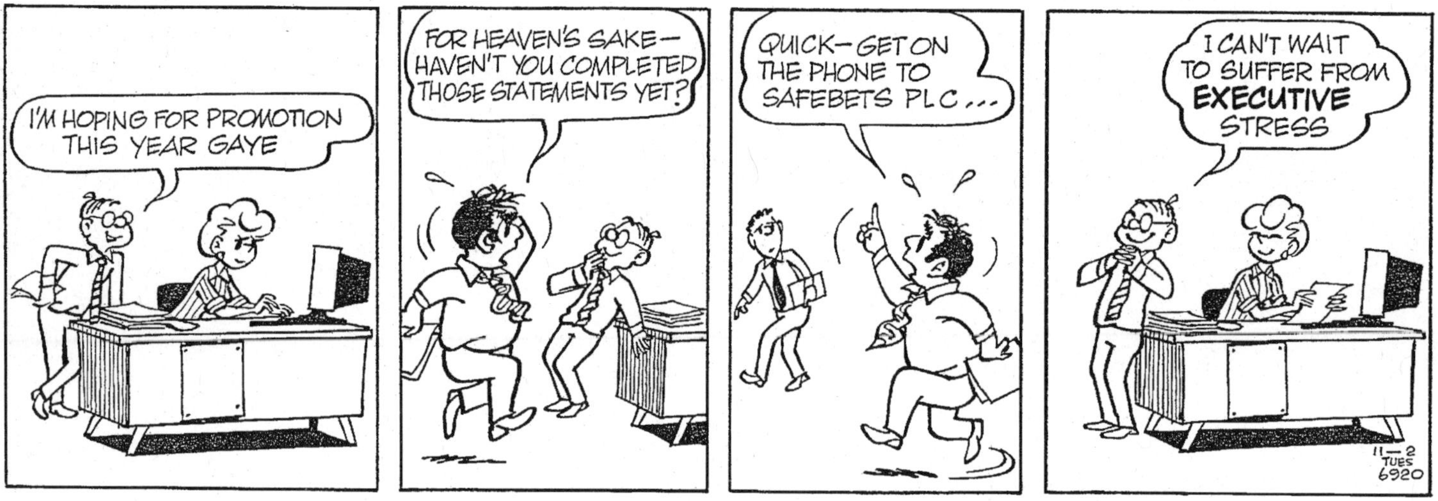
I'M HOPING FOR PROMOTION THIS YEAR GAYE
FOR HEAVEN'S SAKE— HAVEN'T YOU COMPLETED THOSE STATEMENTS YET?
QUICK— GET ON THE PHONE TO SAFEBETS PLC...
I CAN'T WAIT TO SUFFER FROM EXECUTIVE STRESS
11—2 TUES 6920

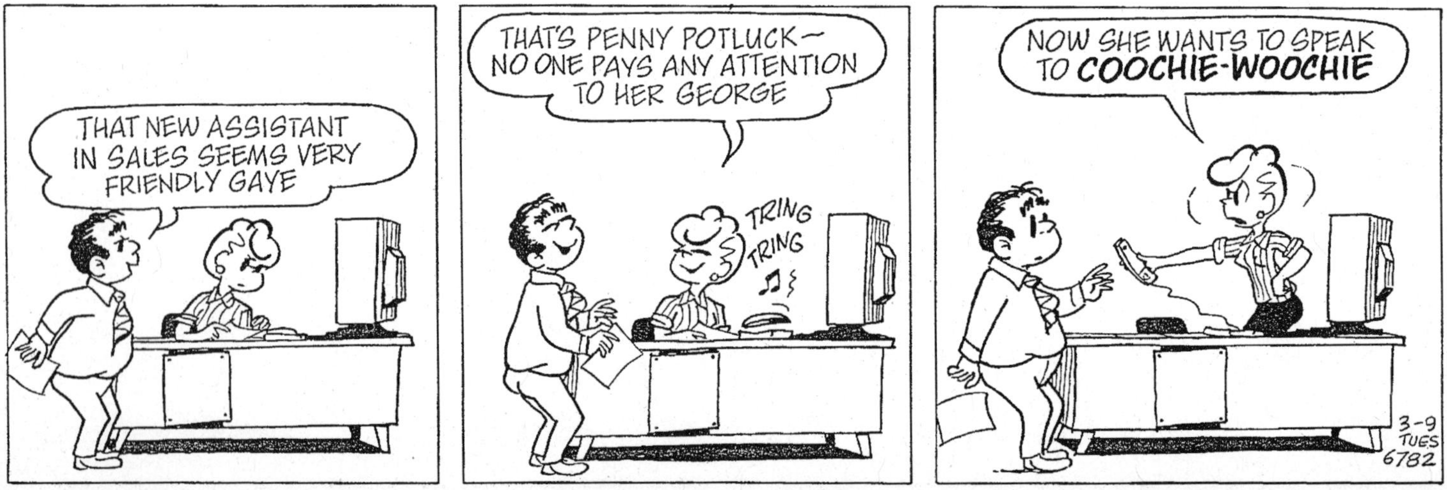
THAT NEW ASSISTANT IN SALES SEEMS VERY FRIENDLY GAYE
THAT'S PENNY POTLUCK— NO ONE PAYS ANY ATTENTION TO HER GEORGE
TRING TRING
NOW SHE WANTS TO SPEAK TO COOCHIE-WOOCHIE
3-9 TUES 6782

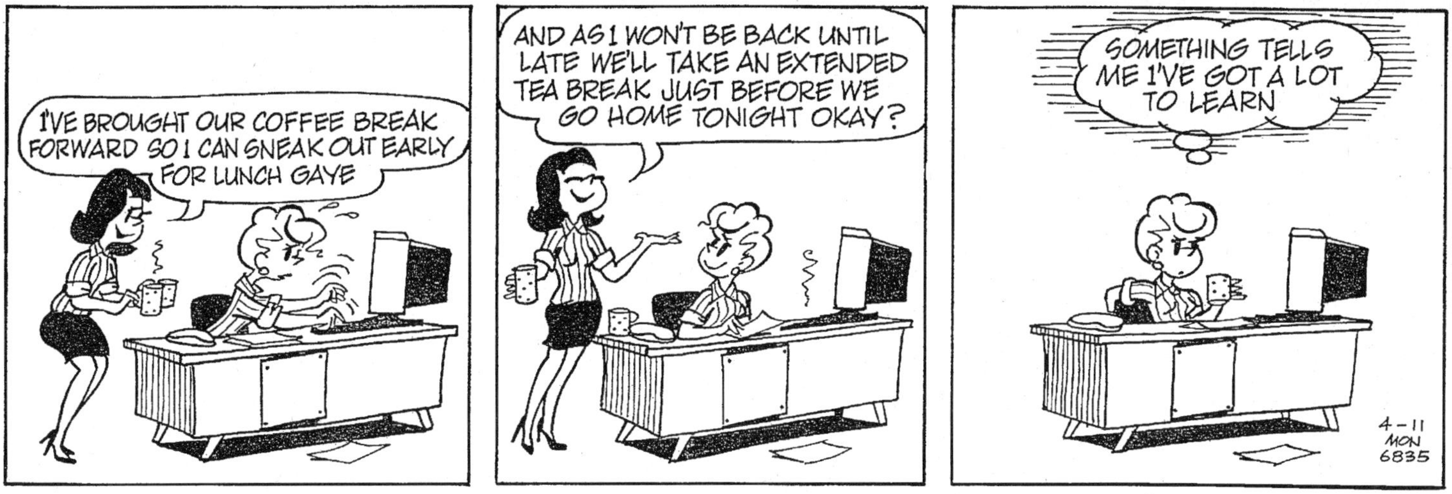
I'VE BROUGHT OUR COFFEE BREAK FORWARD SO I CAN SNEAK OUT EARLY FOR LUNCH GAYE
AND AS I WON'T BE BACK UNTIL LATE WE'LL TAKE AN EXTENDED TEA BREAK JUST BEFORE WE GO HOME TONIGHT OKAY?
SOMETHING TELLS ME I'VE GOT A LOT TO LEARN
4-11 MON 6835

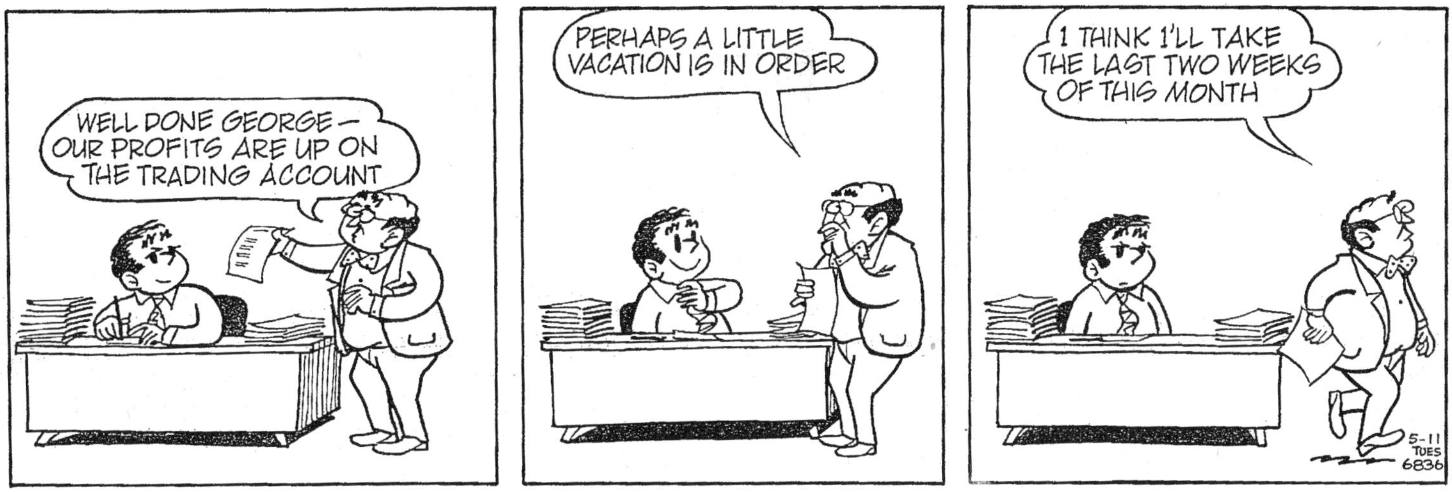
WELL DONE GEORGE— OUR PROFITS ARE UP ON THE TRADING ACCOUNT
PERHAPS A LITTLE VACATION IS IN ORDER
I THINK I'LL TAKE THE LAST TWO WEEKS OF THIS MONTH
5-11 TUES 6836

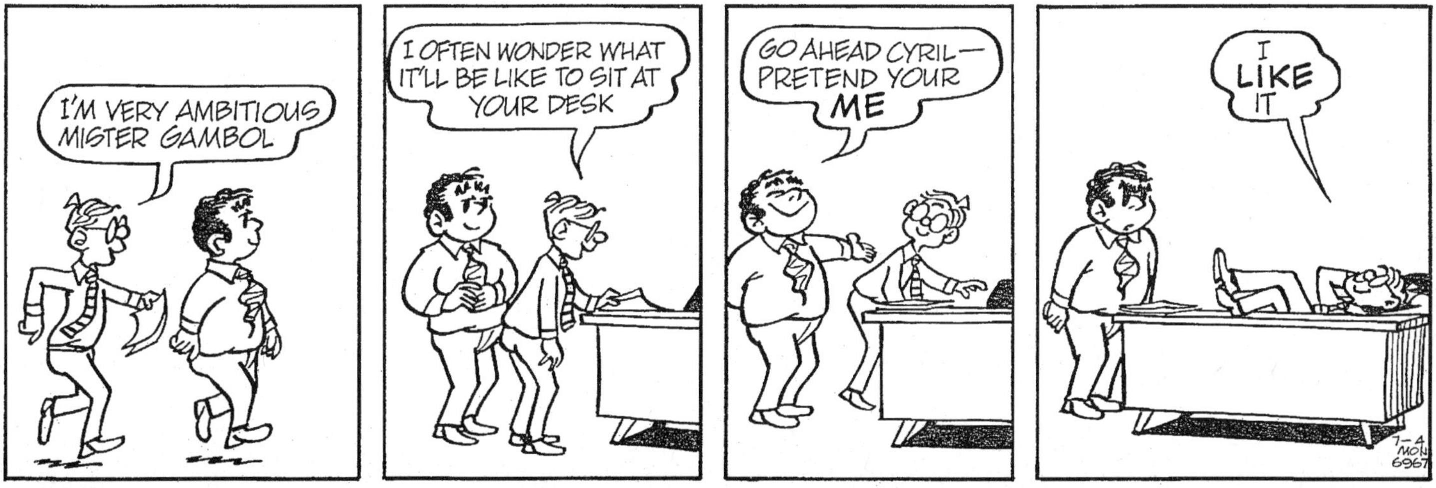
I'M VERY AMBITIOUS MISTER GAMBOL
I OFTEN WONDER WHAT IT'LL BE LIKE TO SIT AT YOUR DESK
GO AHEAD CYRIL— PRETEND YOUR ME
I LIKE IT
7-4 MON 6967

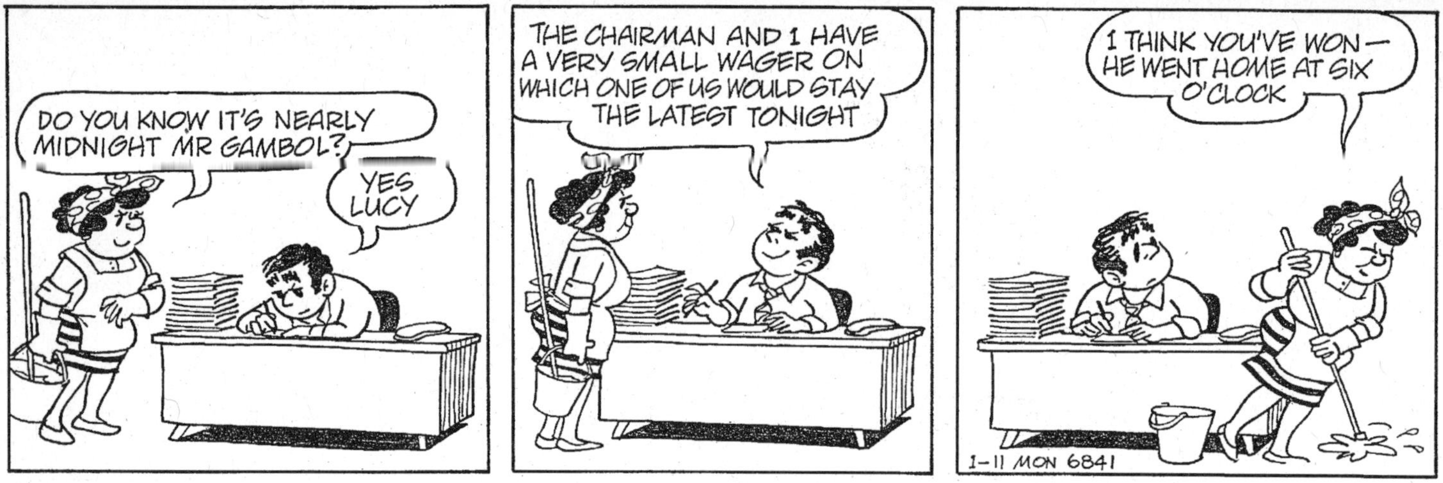
DO YOU KNOW IT'S NEARLY MIDNIGHT MR GAMBOL?
YES LUCY
THE CHAIRMAN AND I HAVE A VERY SMALL WAGER ON WHICH ONE OF US WOULD STAY THE LATEST TONIGHT
I THINK YOU'VE WON — HE WENT HOME AT SIX O'CLOCK
1-11 MON 6841

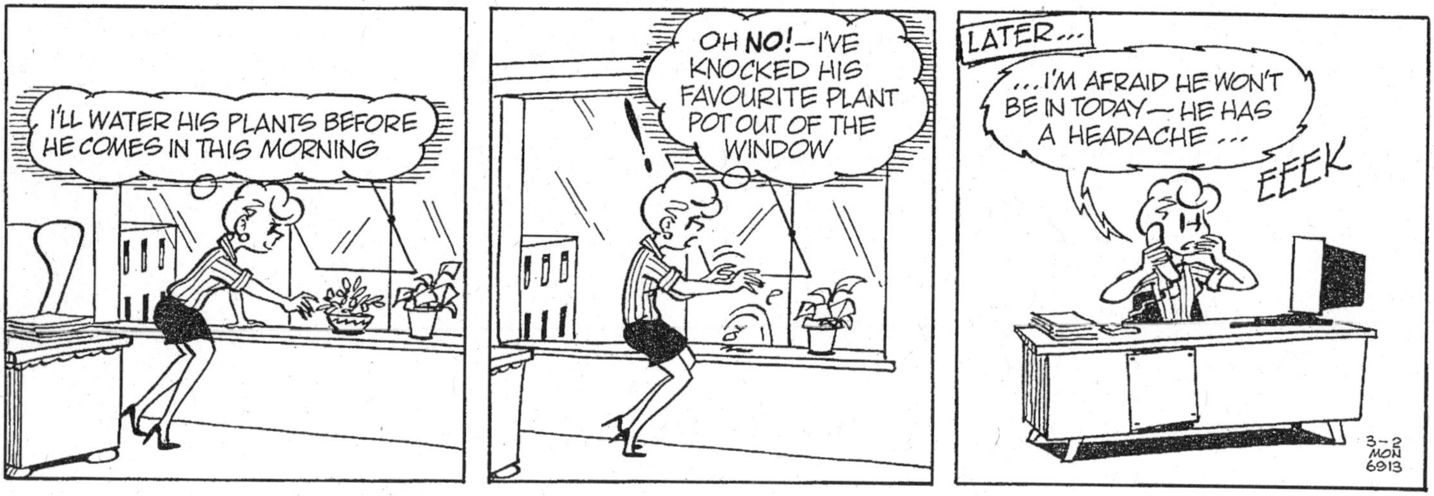
I'LL WATER HIS PLANTS BEFORE HE COMES IN THIS MORNING
OH NO! — I'VE KNOCKED HIS FAVOURITE PLANT POT OUT OF THE WINDOW
!
LATER...
...I'M AFRAID HE WON'T BE IN TODAY — HE HAS A HEADACHE ...
EEEK
3-2 MON 6913

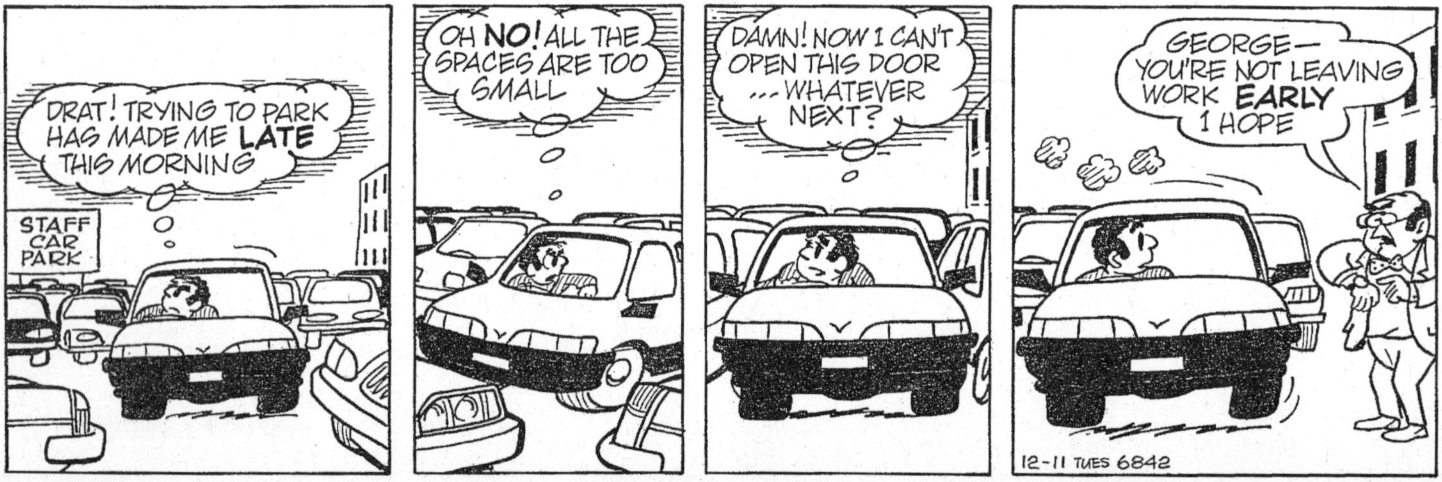
DRAT! TRYING TO PARK HAS MADE ME LATE THIS MORNING
STAFF CAR PARK
OH NO! ALL THE SPACES ARE TOO SMALL
DAMN! NOW I CAN'T OPEN THIS DOOR ... WHATEVER NEXT?
GEORGE — YOU'RE NOT LEAVING WORK EARLY I HOPE
12-11 TUES 6842

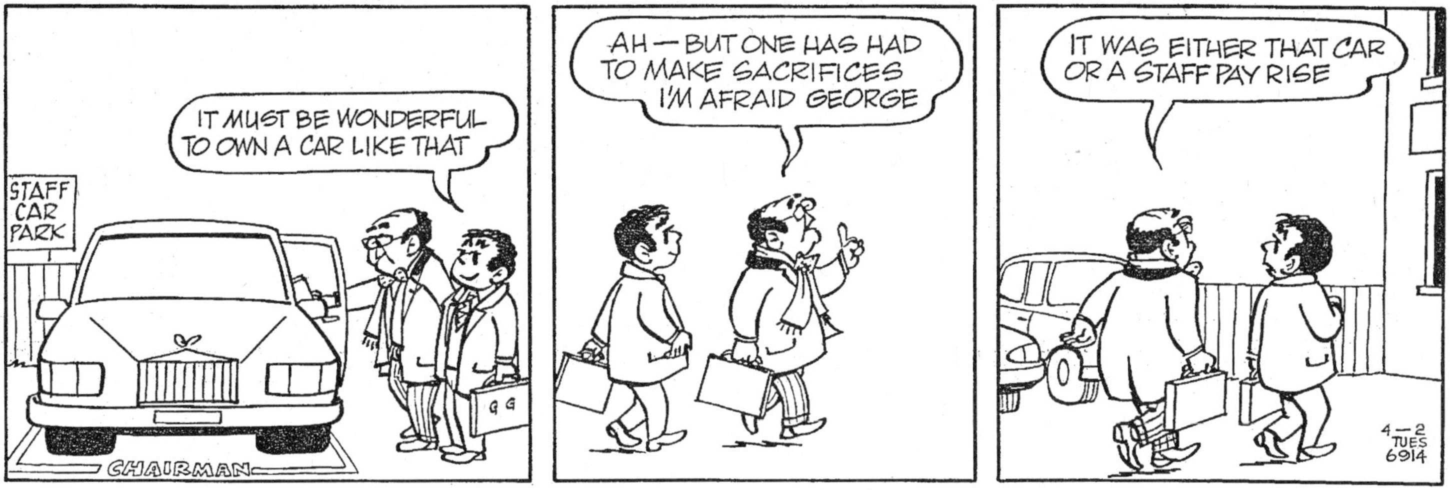
STAFF CAR PARK
CHAIRMAN
IT MUST BE WONDERFUL TO OWN A CAR LIKE THAT
G G
AH — BUT ONE HAS HAD TO MAKE SACRIFICES I'M AFRAID GEORGE
IT WAS EITHER THAT CAR OR A STAFF PAY RISE
4—2 TUES 6914

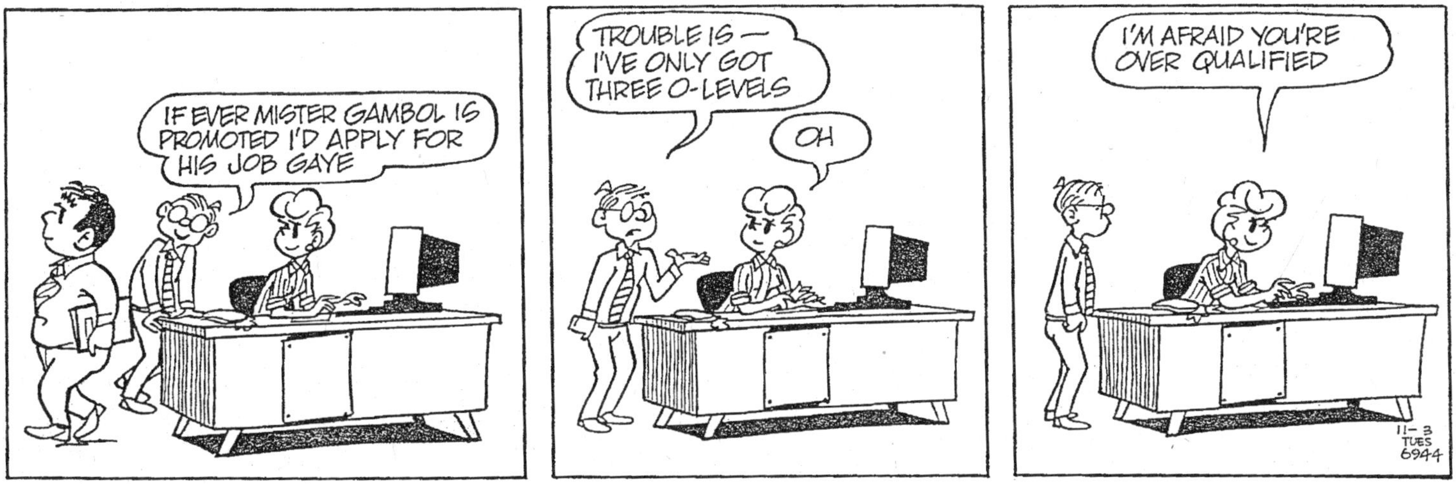
IF EVER MISTER GAMBOL IS PROMOTED I'D APPLY FOR HIS JOB GAYE
TROUBLE IS — I'VE ONLY GOT THREE O-LEVELS
OH
I'M AFRAID YOU'RE OVER QUALIFIED
11—3 TUES 6944

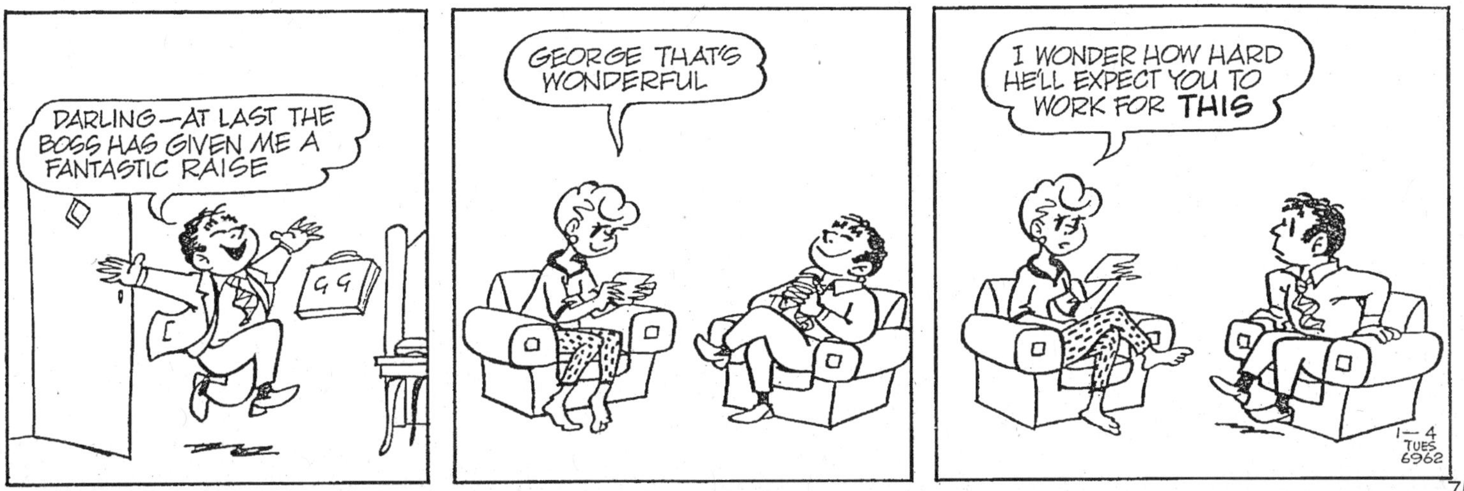
DARLING — AT LAST THE BOSS HAS GIVEN ME A FANTASTIC RAISE
G G
GEORGE THAT'S WONDERFUL
I WONDER HOW HARD HE'LL EXPECT YOU TO WORK FOR THIS
1—4 TUES 6962

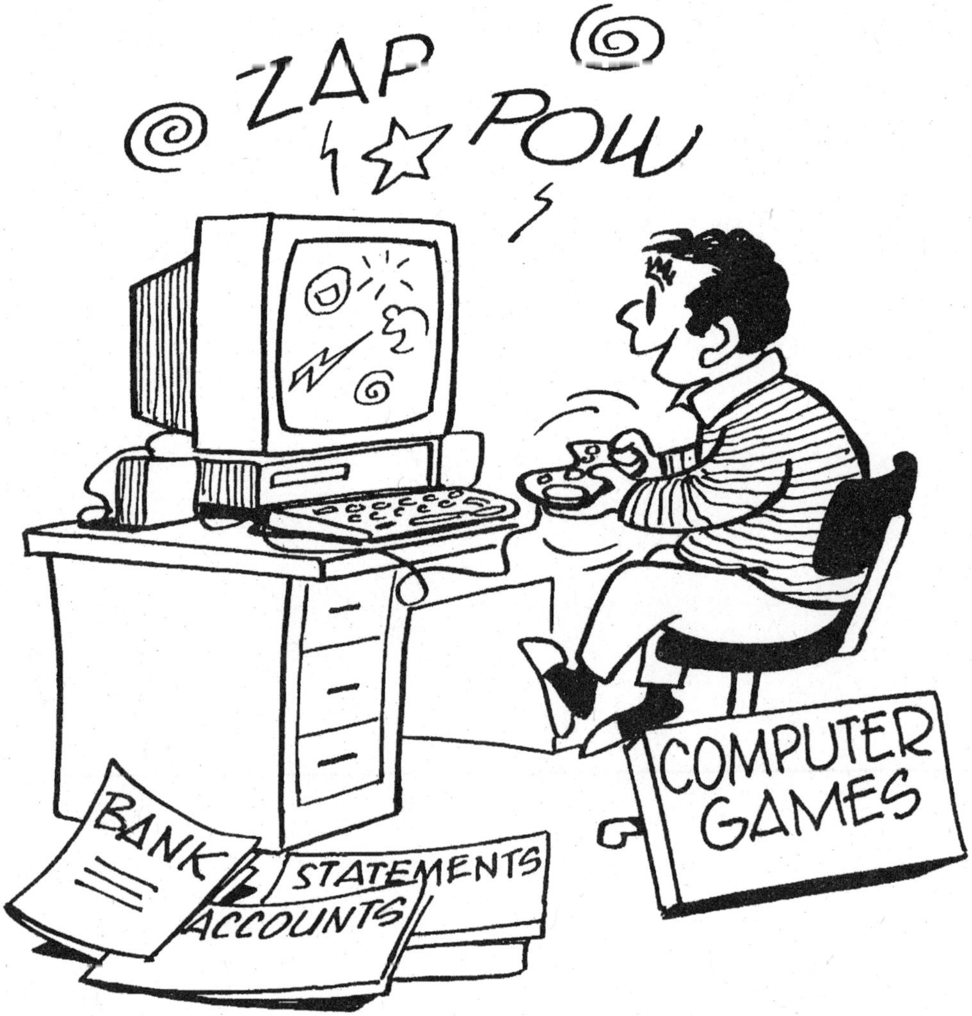
ZAP
POW
COMPUTER GAMES
BANK
STATEMENTS
ACCOUNTS

AT LAST GEORGE HAS BOUGHT HIMSELF A COMPUTER TO DO THEIR ACCOUNTS ON— AT LEAST THAT'S WHAT HE SAYS IT'S FOR

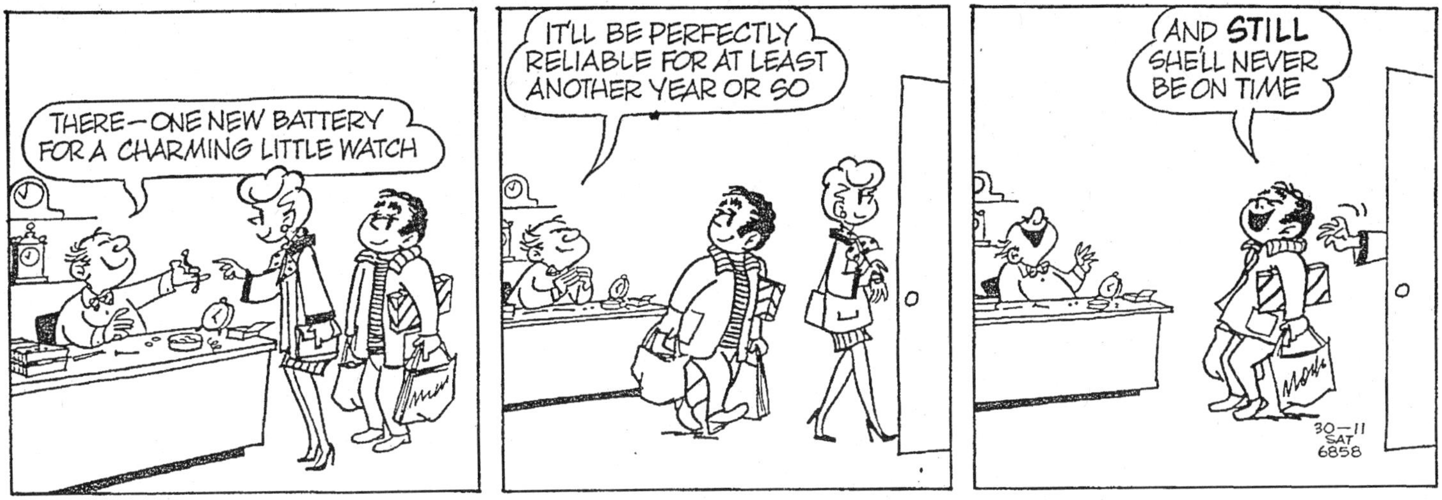
THERE—ONE NEW BATTERY FOR A CHARMING LITTLE WATCH
IT'LL BE PERFECTLY RELIABLE FOR AT LEAST ANOTHER YEAR OR SO
AND **STILL** SHE'LL NEVER BE ON TIME
30—11 SAT 6858

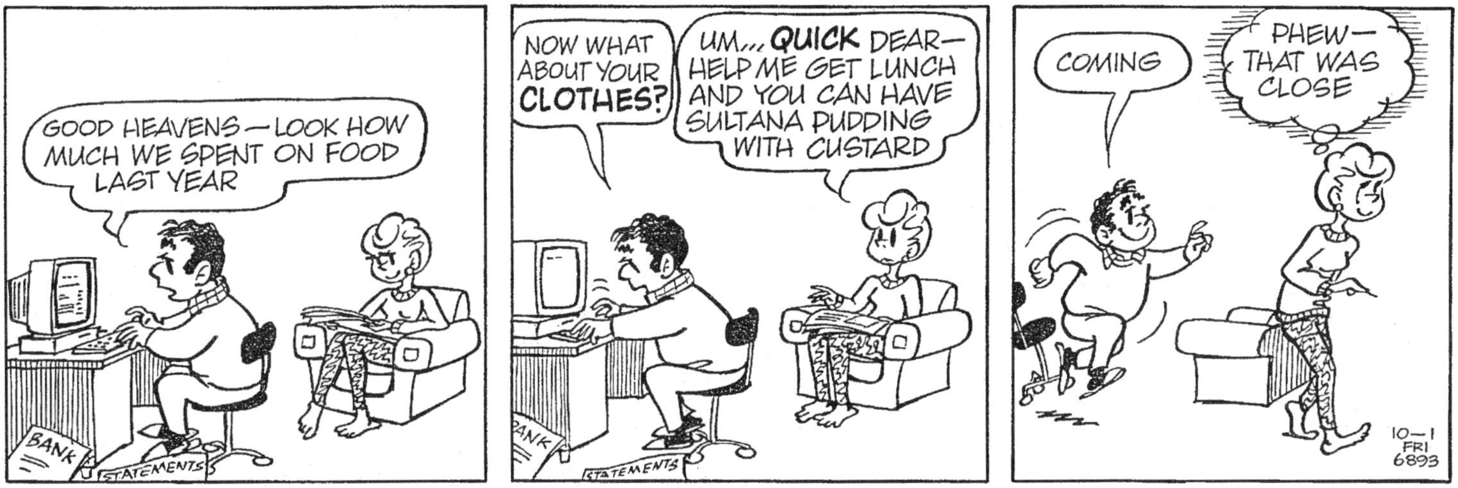
GOOD HEAVENS—LOOK HOW MUCH WE SPENT ON FOOD LAST YEAR
BANK STATEMENTS
NOW WHAT ABOUT YOUR **CLOTHES?**
UM,,, **QUICK** DEAR—HELP ME GET LUNCH AND YOU CAN HAVE SULTANA PUDDING WITH CUSTARD
COMING
PHEW—THAT WAS CLOSE
10—1 FRI 6893

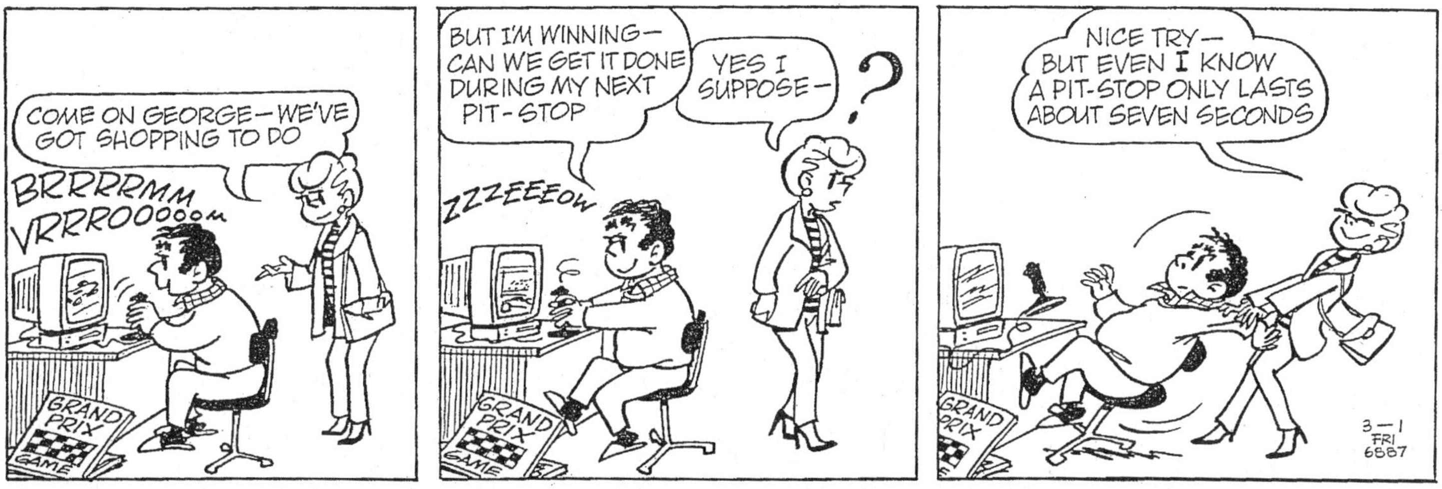
COME ON GEORGE—WE'VE GOT SHOPPING TO DO
BRRRRMM VRRROOOOOOM
GRAND PRIX GAME
BUT I'M WINNING—CAN WE GET IT DONE DURING MY NEXT PIT-STOP
YES I SUPPOSE—
?
ZZZEEEEOW
NICE TRY—BUT EVEN **I** KNOW A PIT-STOP ONLY LASTS ABOUT SEVEN SECONDS
3—1 FRI 6887

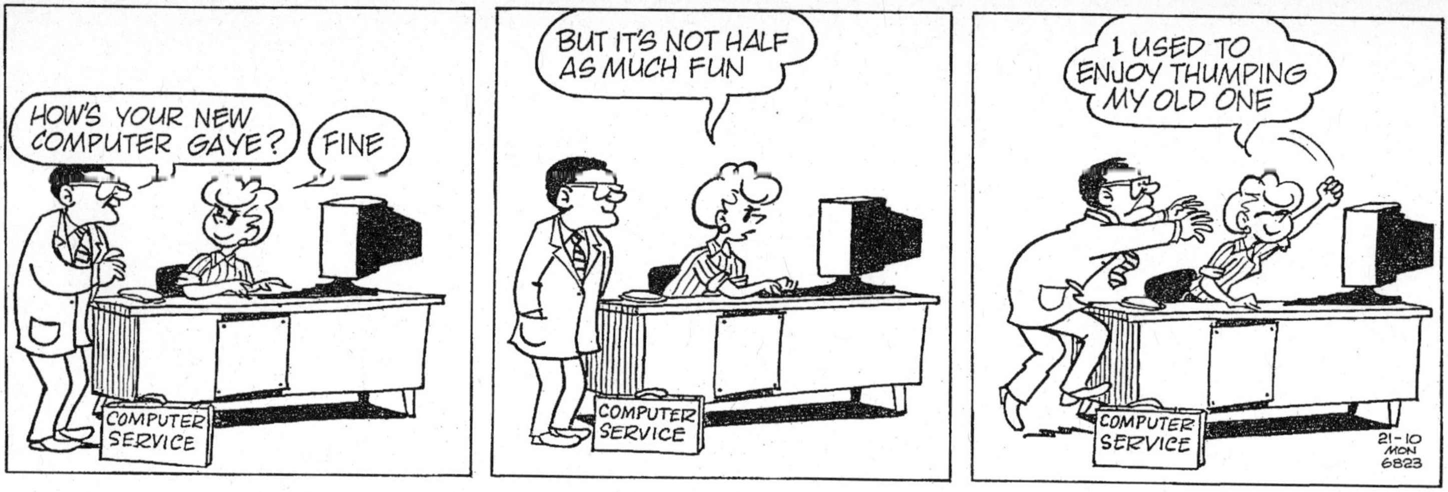
HOW'S YOUR NEW COMPUTER GAYE?
FINE
COMPUTER SERVICE
BUT IT'S NOT HALF AS MUCH FUN
COMPUTER SERVICE
I USED TO ENJOY THUMPING MY OLD ONE
COMPUTER SERVICE
21-10 MON 6823

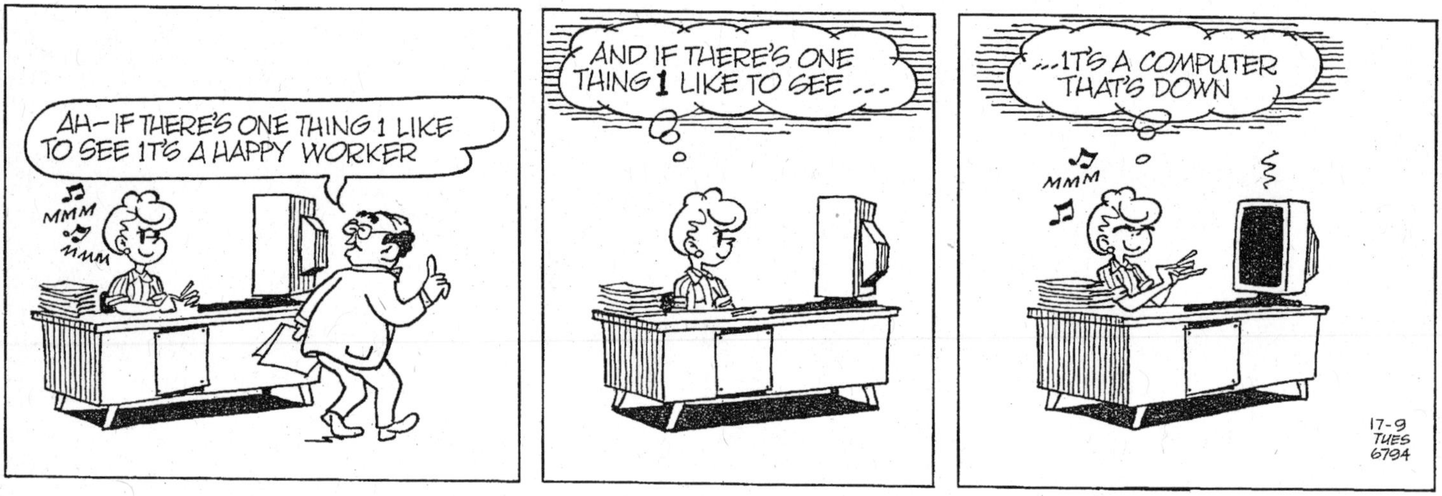
AH– IF THERE'S ONE THING I LIKE TO SEE IT'S A HAPPY WORKER
MMM
MMM
AND IF THERE'S ONE THING I LIKE TO SEE ...
...IT'S A COMPUTER THAT'S DOWN
MMM
17-9 TUES 6794

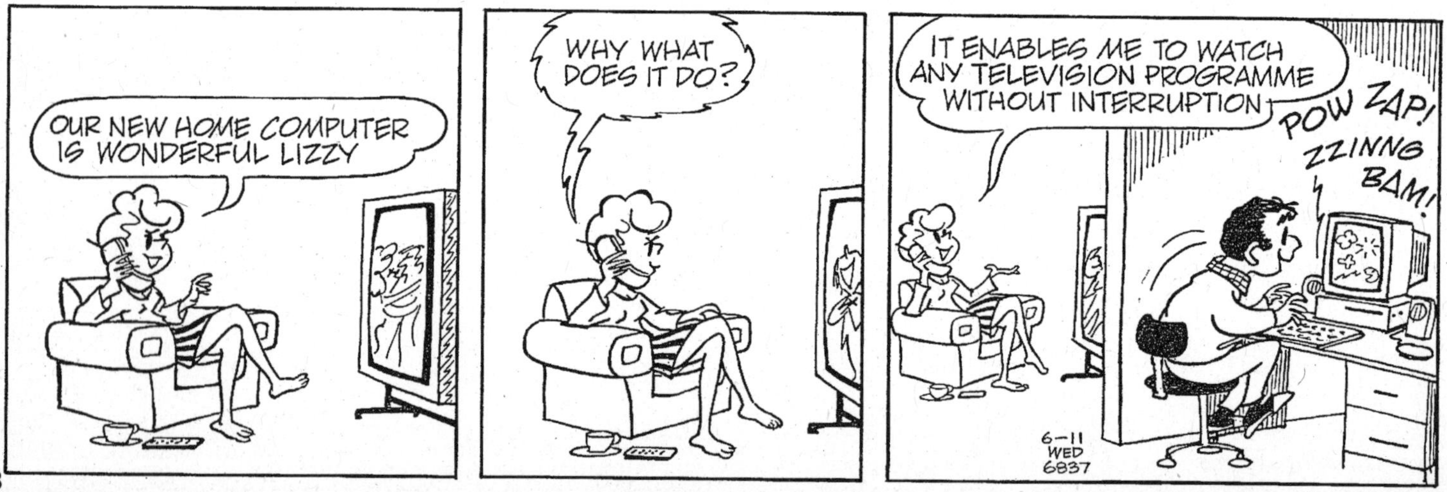
OUR NEW HOME COMPUTER IS WONDERFUL LIZZY
WHY WHAT DOES IT DO?
IT ENABLES ME TO WATCH ANY TELEVISION PROGRAMME WITHOUT INTERRUPTION
POW ZAP!
ZZINNG
BAM!
6-11 WED 6837

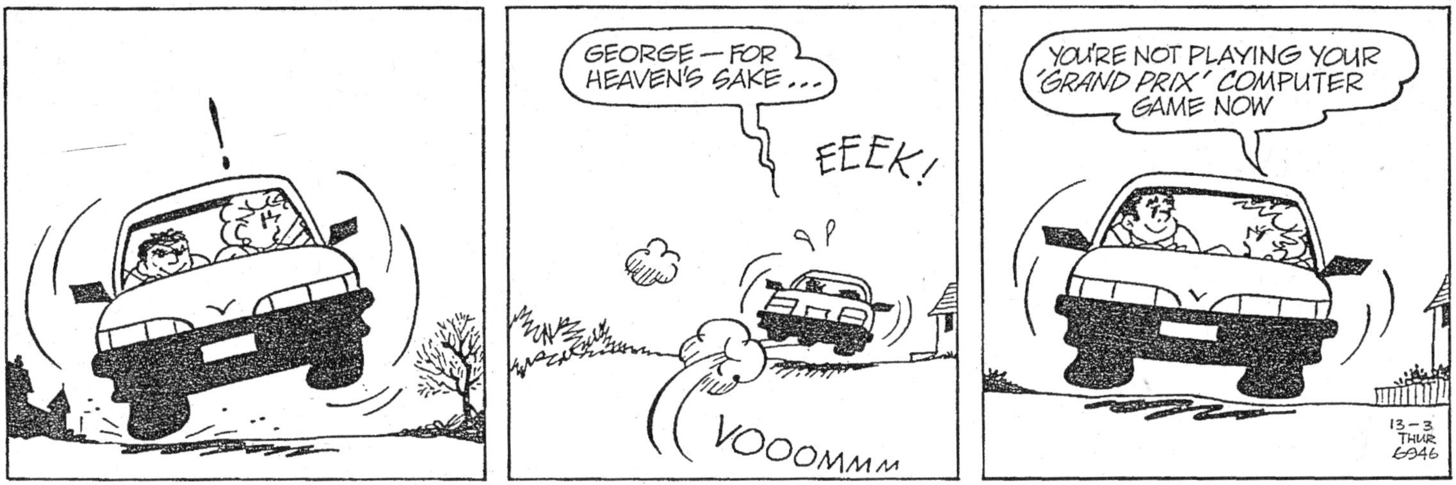
!
GEORGE — FOR HEAVEN'S SAKE ...
EEEK!
VOOOMMMM
YOU'RE NOT PLAYING YOUR 'GRAND PRIX' COMPUTER GAME NOW
13-3 THUR 6946

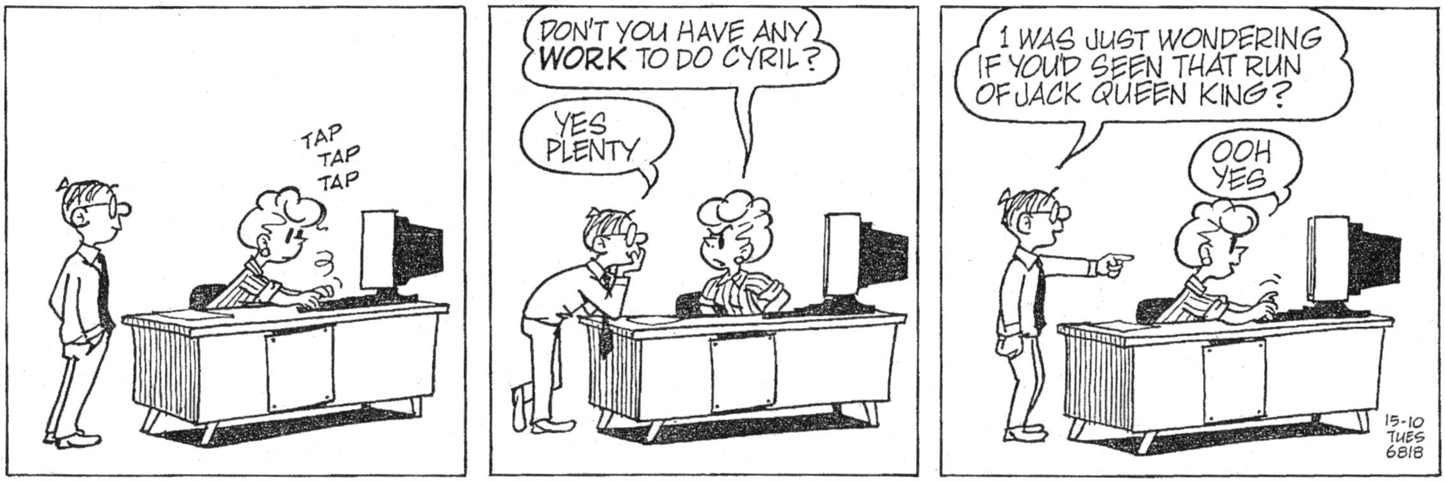
TAP TAP TAP
DON'T YOU HAVE ANY **WORK** TO DO CYRIL?
YES PLENTY
I WAS JUST WONDERING IF YOU'D SEEN THAT RUN OF JACK QUEEN KING?
OOH YES
15-10 TUES 6818

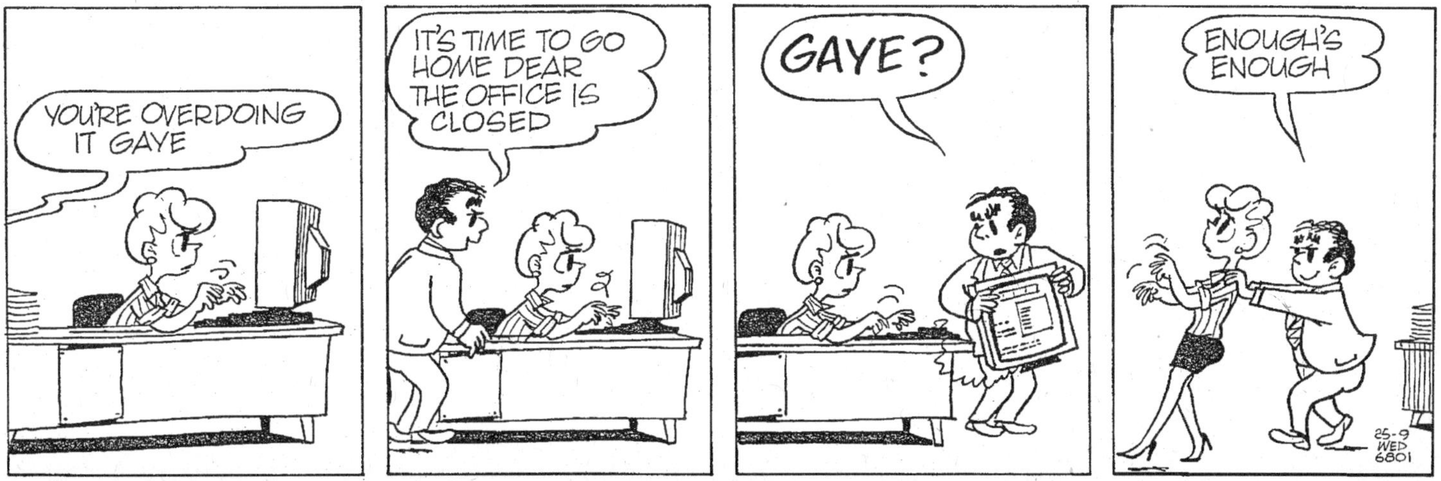
YOU'RE OVERDOING IT GAYE
IT'S TIME TO GO HOME DEAR THE OFFICE IS CLOSED
GAYE?
ENOUGH'S ENOUGH
25-9 WED 6801

THE ONLY THING THAT KEEPS GEORGE
AWAKE DURING THE WEEKEND SHOPPING
IS A TROLLEY WITH A MIND OF ITS OWN

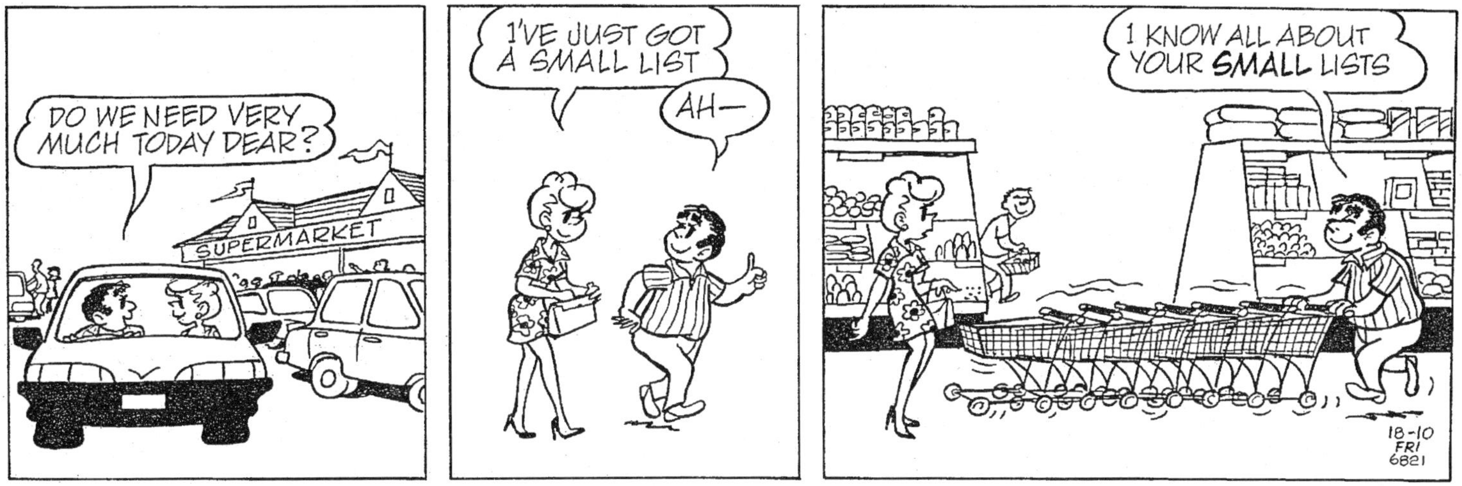
DO WE NEED VERY MUCH TODAY DEAR?
SUPERMARKET
I'VE JUST GOT A SMALL LIST
AH—
I KNOW ALL ABOUT YOUR **SMALL** LISTS
18-10 FRI 6821

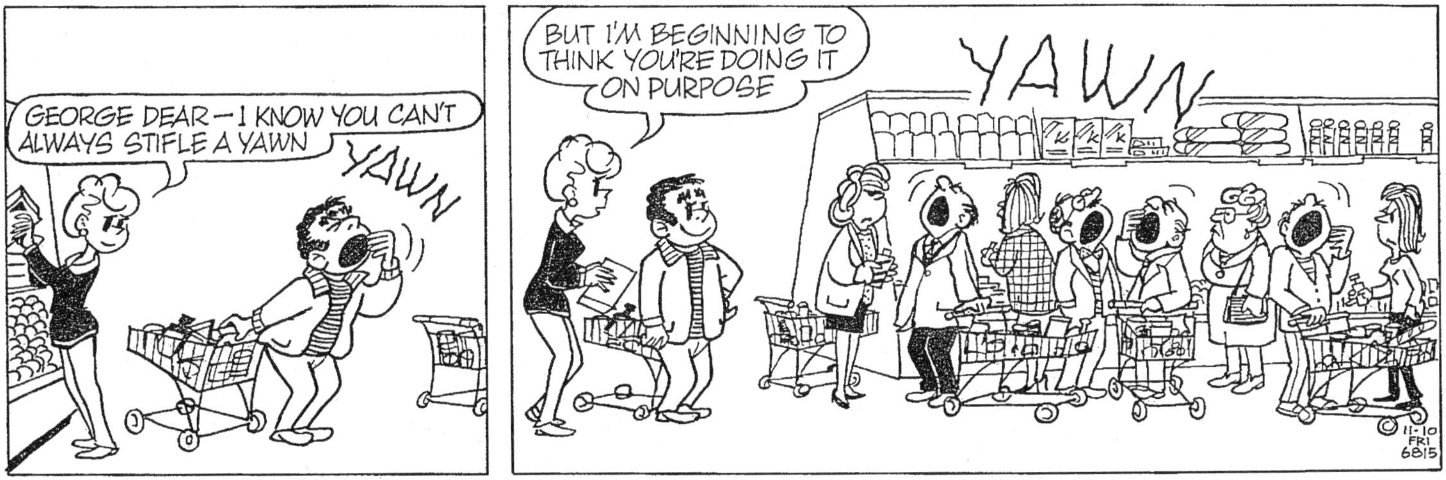
GEORGE DEAR—I KNOW YOU CAN'T ALWAYS STIFLE A YAWN
YAWN
BUT I'M BEGINNING TO THINK YOU'RE DOING IT ON PURPOSE
YAWN
© 11-10 FRI 6815

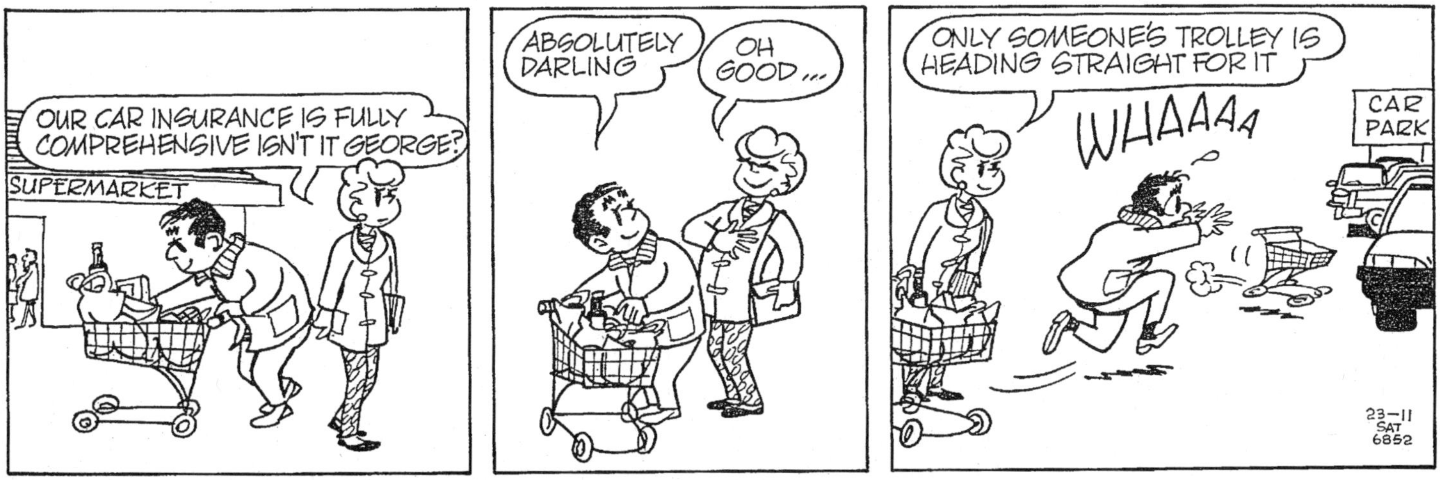
OUR CAR INSURANCE IS FULLY COMPREHENSIVE ISN'T IT GEORGE?
SUPERMARKET
ABSOLUTELY DARLING
OH GOOD...
ONLY SOMEONE'S TROLLEY IS HEADING STRAIGHT FOR IT
WHAAAA
CAR PARK
23-11 SAT 6852

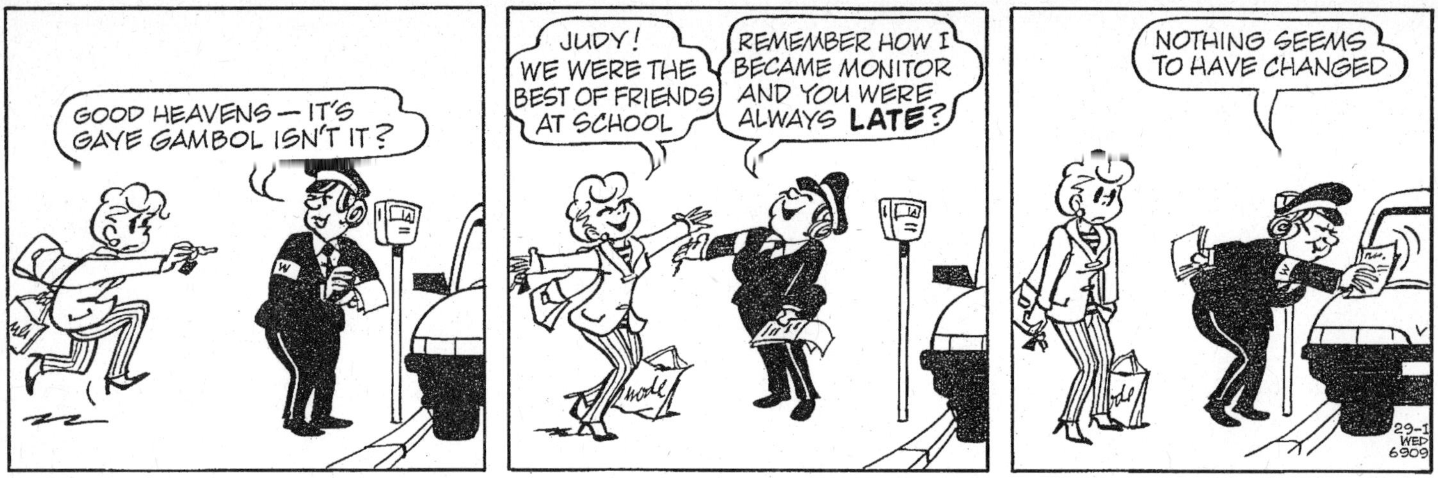
GOOD HEAVENS — IT'S GAYE GAMBOL ISN'T IT?
JUDY! WE WERE THE BEST OF FRIENDS AT SCHOOL
REMEMBER HOW I BECAME MONITOR AND YOU WERE ALWAYS **LATE**?
NOTHING SEEMS TO HAVE CHANGED
29-1 WED 6909

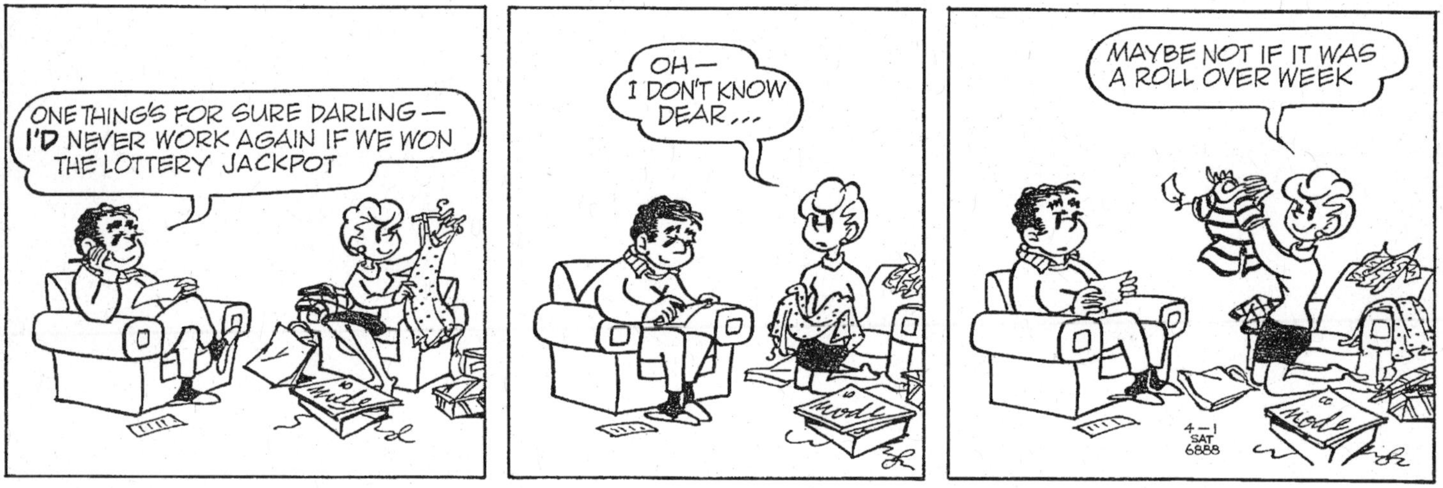
ONE THING'S FOR SURE DARLING — **I'D** NEVER WORK AGAIN IF WE WON THE LOTTERY JACKPOT
OH — I DON'T KNOW DEAR...
MAYBE NOT IF IT WAS A ROLL OVER WEEK
4-1 SAT 6888

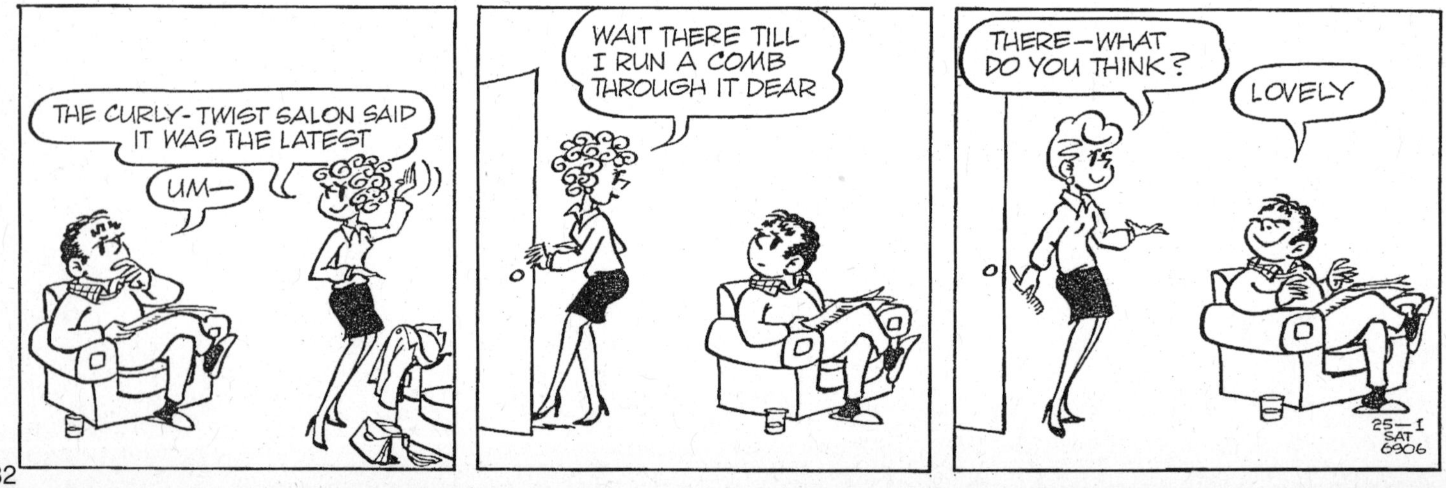
THE CURLY-TWIST SALON SAID IT WAS THE LATEST
UM—
WAIT THERE TILL I RUN A COMB THROUGH IT DEAR
THERE—WHAT DO YOU THINK?
LOVELY
25-1 SAT 6906

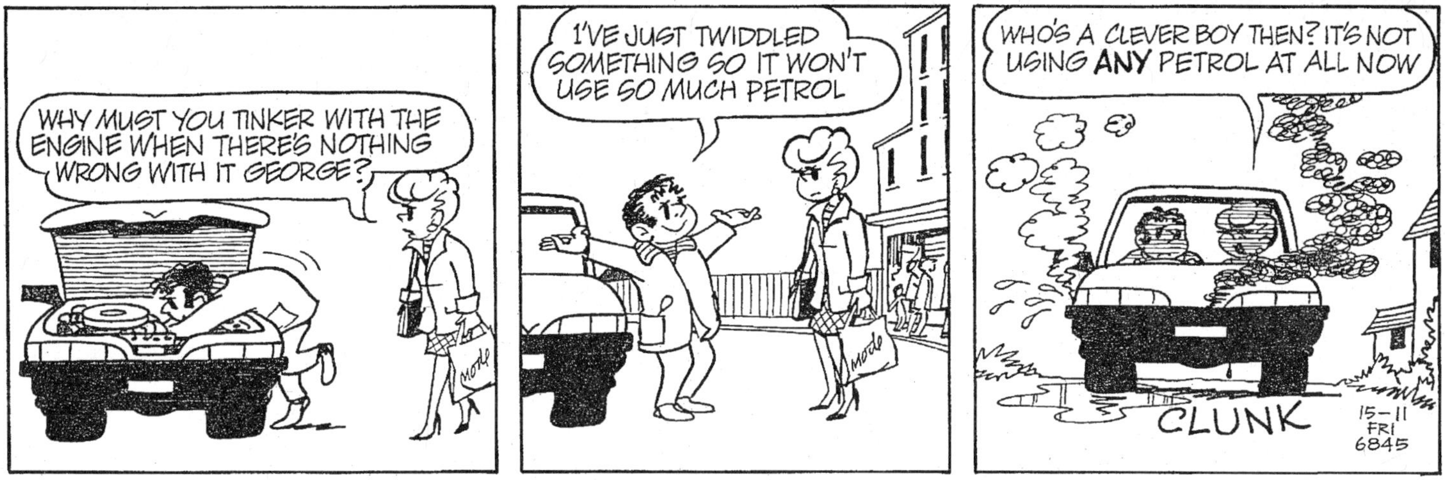
WHY MUST YOU TINKER WITH THE ENGINE WHEN THERE'S NOTHING WRONG WITH IT GEORGE?
MODE
I'VE JUST TWIDDLED SOMETHING SO IT WON'T USE SO MUCH PETROL
MODE
WHO'S A CLEVER BOY THEN? IT'S NOT USING **ANY** PETROL AT ALL NOW
CLUNK
15-11 FRI 6845

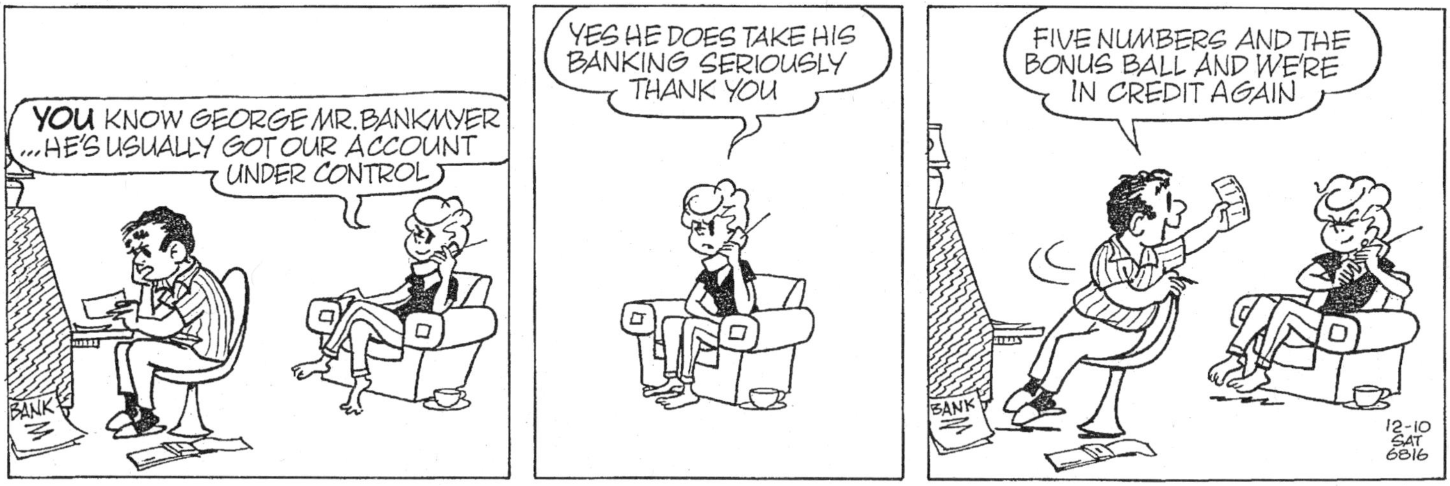
YOU KNOW GEORGE MR. BANKMYER ...HE'S USUALLY GOT OUR ACCOUNT UNDER CONTROL
BANK
YES HE DOES TAKE HIS BANKING SERIOUSLY THANK YOU
FIVE NUMBERS AND THE BONUS BALL AND WE'RE IN CREDIT AGAIN
BANK
12-10 SAT 6816

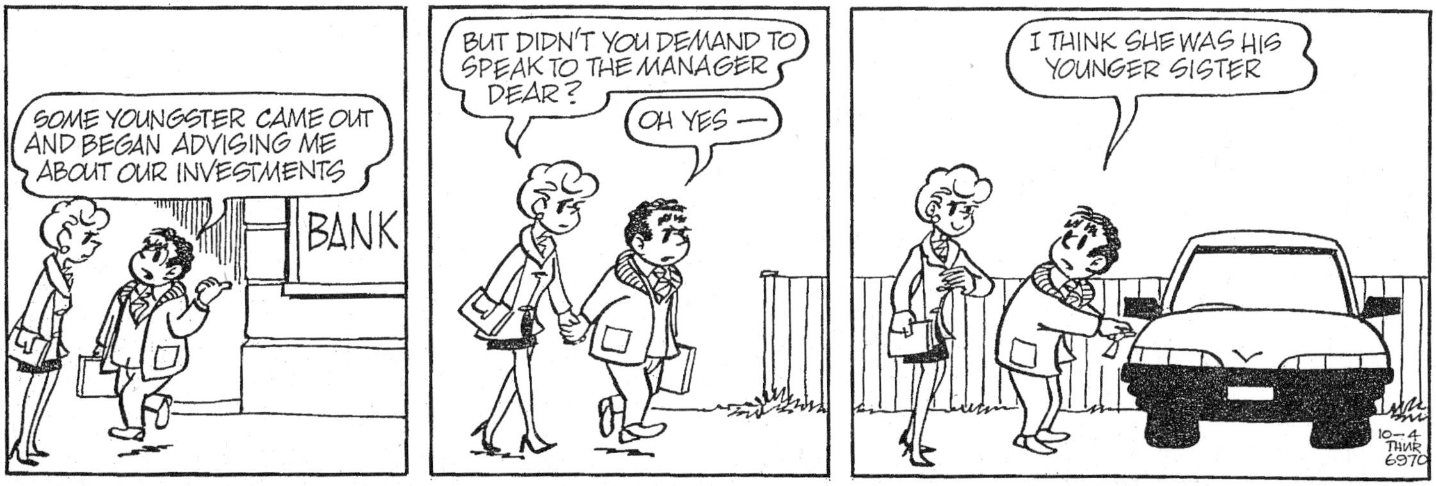
SOME YOUNGSTER CAME OUT AND BEGAN ADVISING ME ABOUT OUR INVESTMENTS
BANK
BUT DIDN'T YOU DEMAND TO SPEAK TO THE MANAGER DEAR?
OH YES —
I THINK SHE WAS HIS YOUNGER SISTER
10-4 THUR 6970

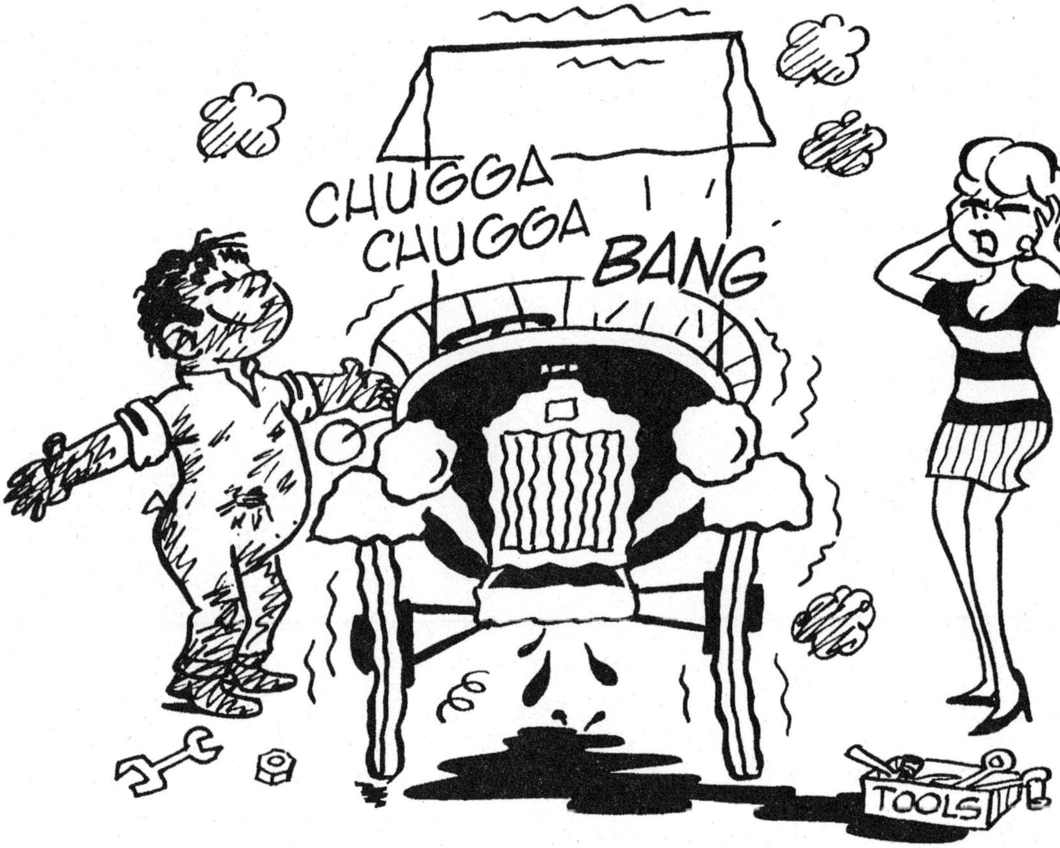
CHUGGA
CHUGGA
BANG
TOOLS

A LOVE-HATE RELATIONSHIP EXISTS BETWEEN THEM AND THAT OLD CAR — GEORGE LOVES IT AND GAYE HATES IT

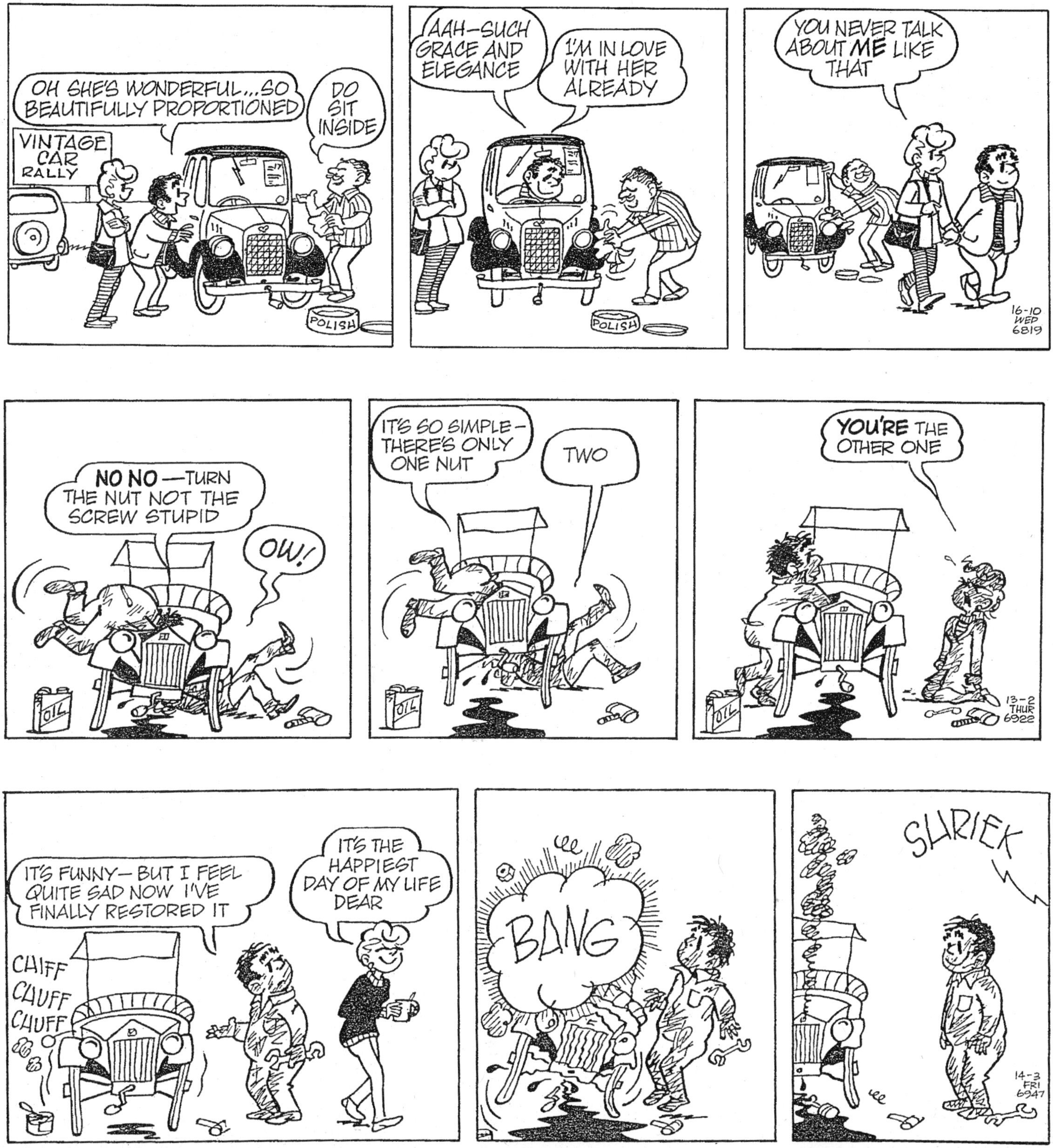
VINTAGE CAR RALLY
OH SHE'S WONDERFUL...SO BEAUTIFULLY PROPORTIONED
DO SIT INSIDE
POLISH
AAH—SUCH GRACE AND ELEGANCE
I'M IN LOVE WITH HER ALREADY
POLISH
YOU NEVER TALK ABOUT **ME** LIKE THAT
16-10 WED 6819
NO NO—TURN THE NUT NOT THE SCREW STUPID
OW!
OIL
IT'S SO SIMPLE—THERE'S ONLY ONE NUT
TWO
OIL
YOU'RE THE OTHER ONE
OIL
13-2 THUR 6922
CHIFF CHUFF CHUFF
IT'S FUNNY—BUT I FEEL QUITE SAD NOW I'VE FINALLY RESTORED IT
IT'S THE HAPPIEST DAY OF MY LIFE DEAR
BANG
SHRIEK
14-3 FRI 6947

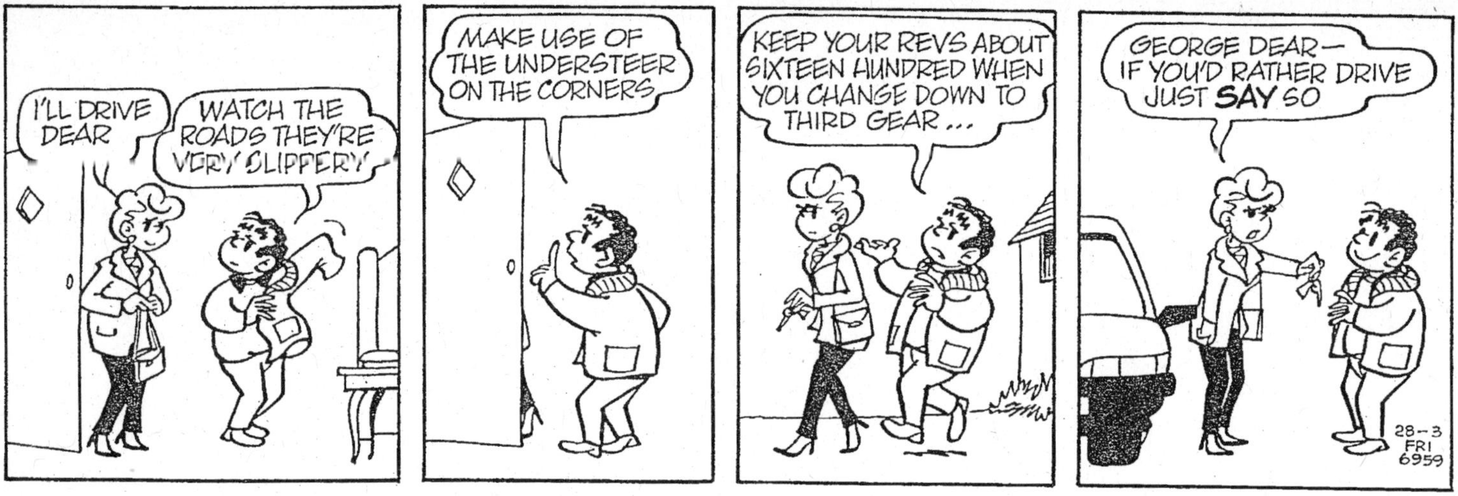
I'LL DRIVE DEAR
WATCH THE ROADS THEY'RE VERY SLIPPERY
MAKE USE OF THE UNDERSTEER ON THE CORNERS
KEEP YOUR REVS ABOUT SIXTEEN HUNDRED WHEN YOU CHANGE DOWN TO THIRD GEAR ...
GEORGE DEAR— IF YOU'D RATHER DRIVE JUST **SAY** SO
28—3 FRI 6959

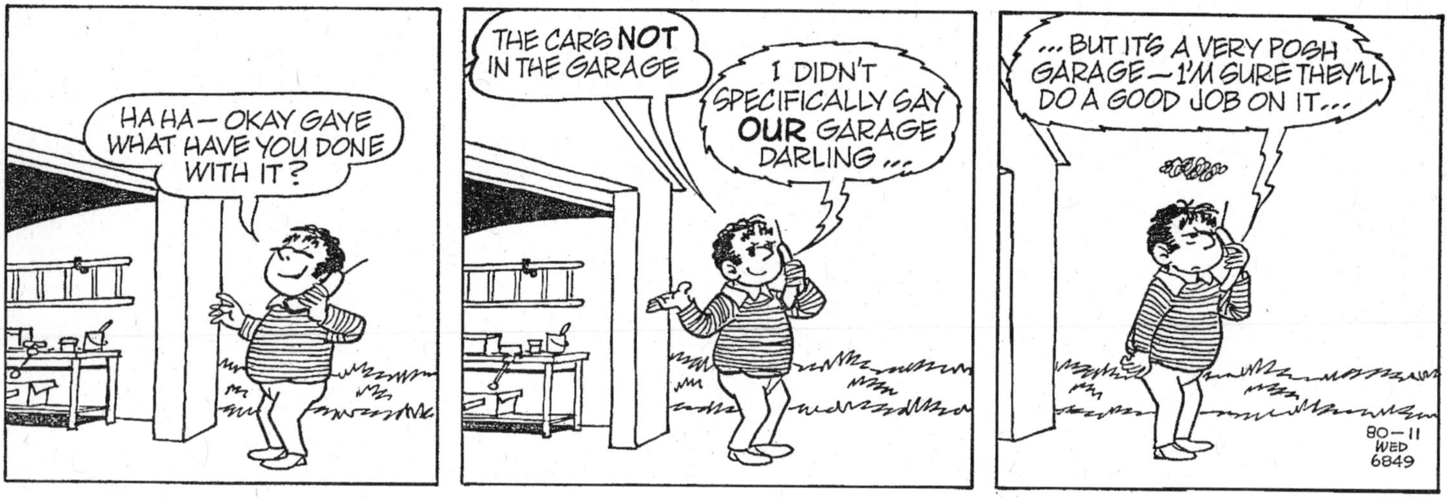
HA HA— OKAY GAYE WHAT HAVE YOU DONE WITH IT?
THE CAR'S **NOT** IN THE GARAGE
I DIDN'T SPECIFICALLY SAY **OUR** GARAGE DARLING ...
... BUT IT'S A VERY POSH GARAGE— I'M SURE THEY'LL DO A GOOD JOB ON IT ...
30—11 WED 6849

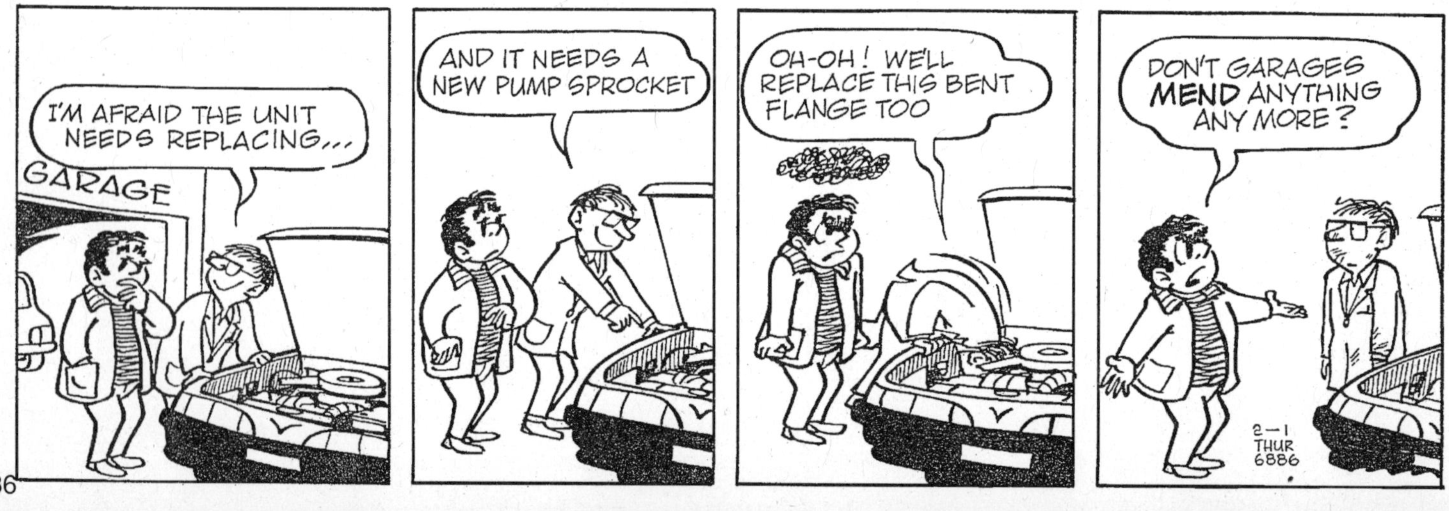
I'M AFRAID THE UNIT NEEDS REPLACING ...
GARAGE
AND IT NEEDS A NEW PUMP SPROCKET
OH-OH! WE'LL REPLACE THIS BENT FLANGE TOO
DON'T GARAGES **MEND** ANYTHING ANY MORE?
2—1 THUR 6886

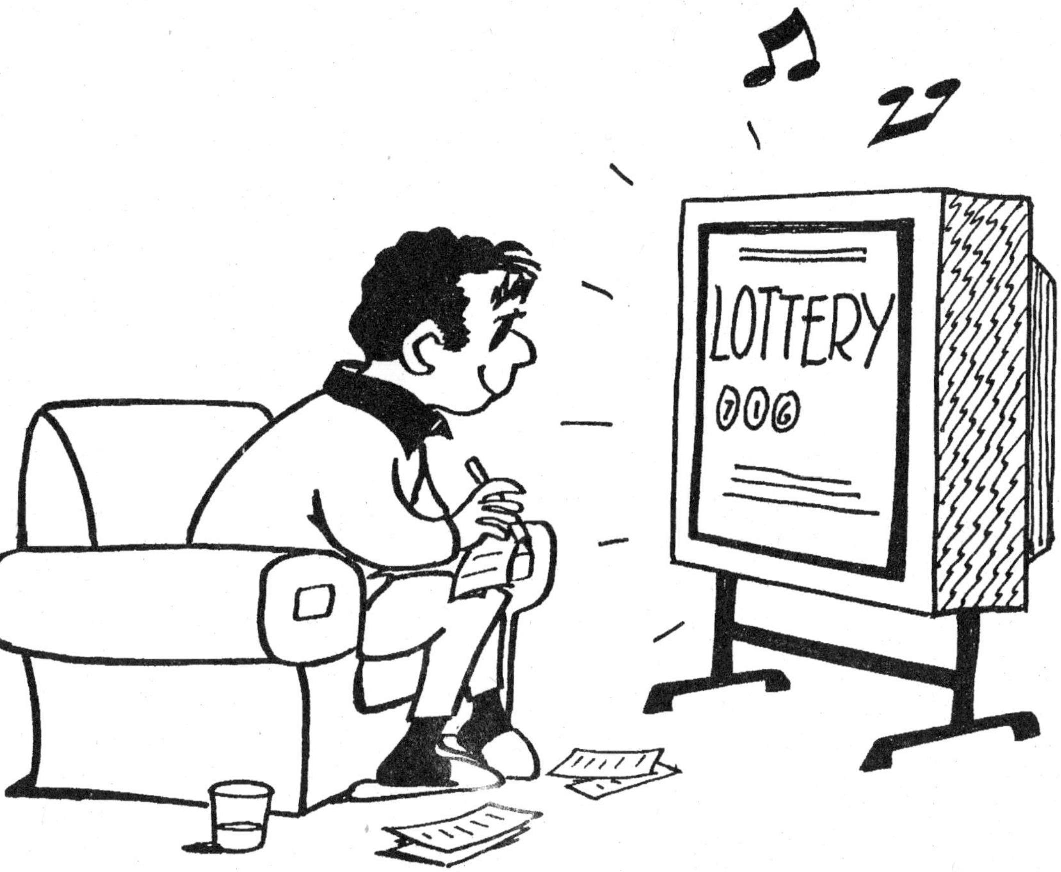
LOTTERY
7
1
6

MOST OF US ENJOY A SERIOUS ATTEMPT AT CLEARING OUR OVERDRAFTS

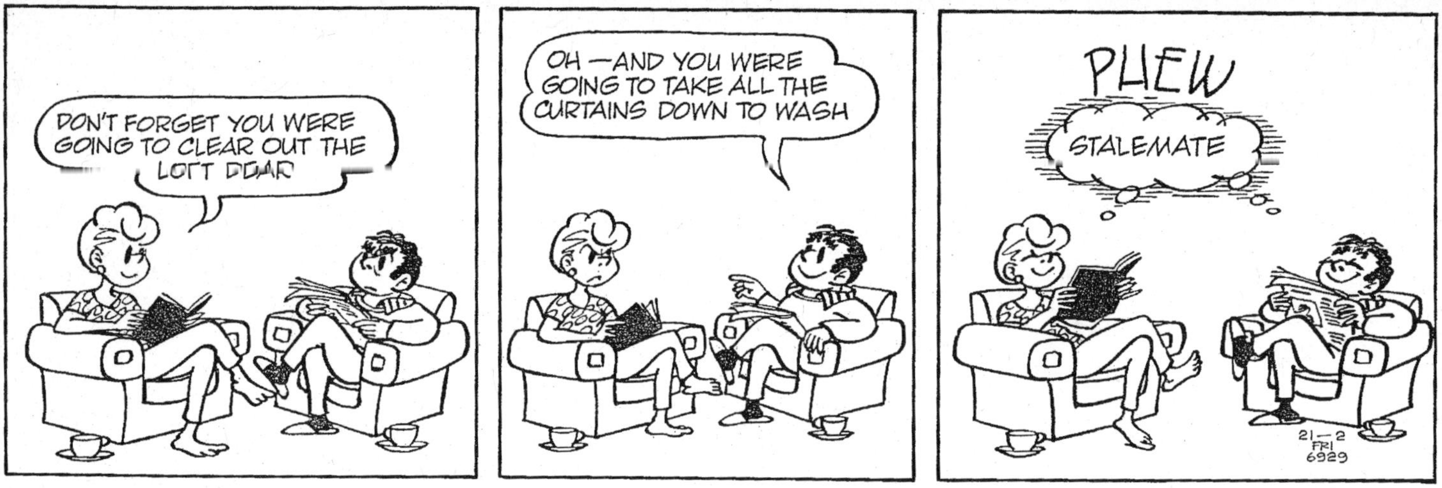
DON'T FORGET YOU WERE GOING TO CLEAR OUT THE LOFT DEAR
OH —AND YOU WERE GOING TO TAKE ALL THE CURTAINS DOWN TO WASH
PHEW
STALEMATE
21—2 FRI 6929

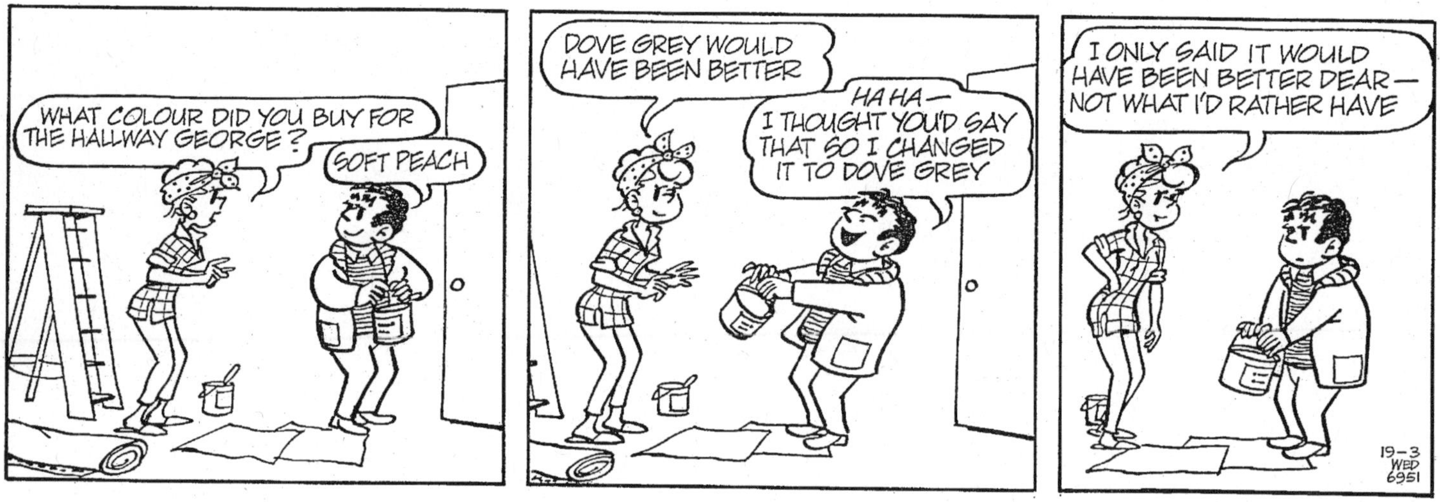
WHAT COLOUR DID YOU BUY FOR THE HALLWAY GEORGE?
SOFT PEACH
DOVE GREY WOULD HAVE BEEN BETTER
HA HA— I THOUGHT YOU'D SAY THAT SO I CHANGED IT TO DOVE GREY
I ONLY SAID IT WOULD HAVE BEEN BETTER DEAR— NOT WHAT I'D RATHER HAVE
19—3 WED 6951

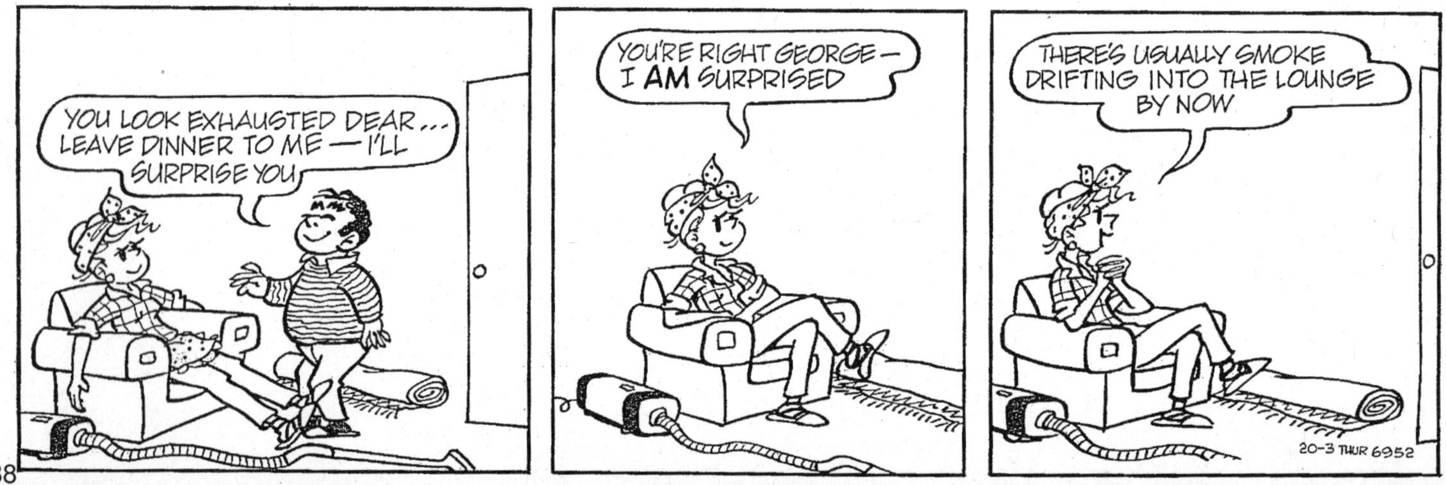
YOU LOOK EXHAUSTED DEAR... LEAVE DINNER TO ME — I'LL SURPRISE YOU
YOU'RE RIGHT GEORGE— I AM SURPRISED
THERE'S USUALLY SMOKE DRIFTING INTO THE LOUNGE BY NOW
20-3 THUR 6952

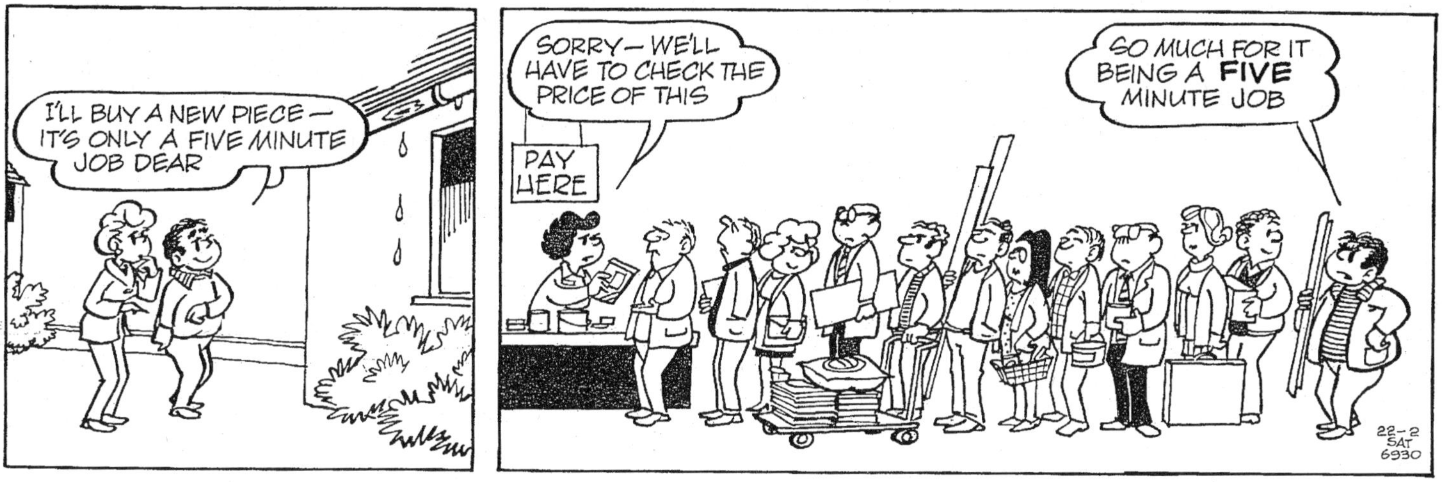
I'LL BUY A NEW PIECE — IT'S ONLY A FIVE MINUTE JOB DEAR
SORRY — WE'LL HAVE TO CHECK THE PRICE OF THIS
PAY HERE
SO MUCH FOR IT BEING A **FIVE** MINUTE JOB
22-2 SAT 6930

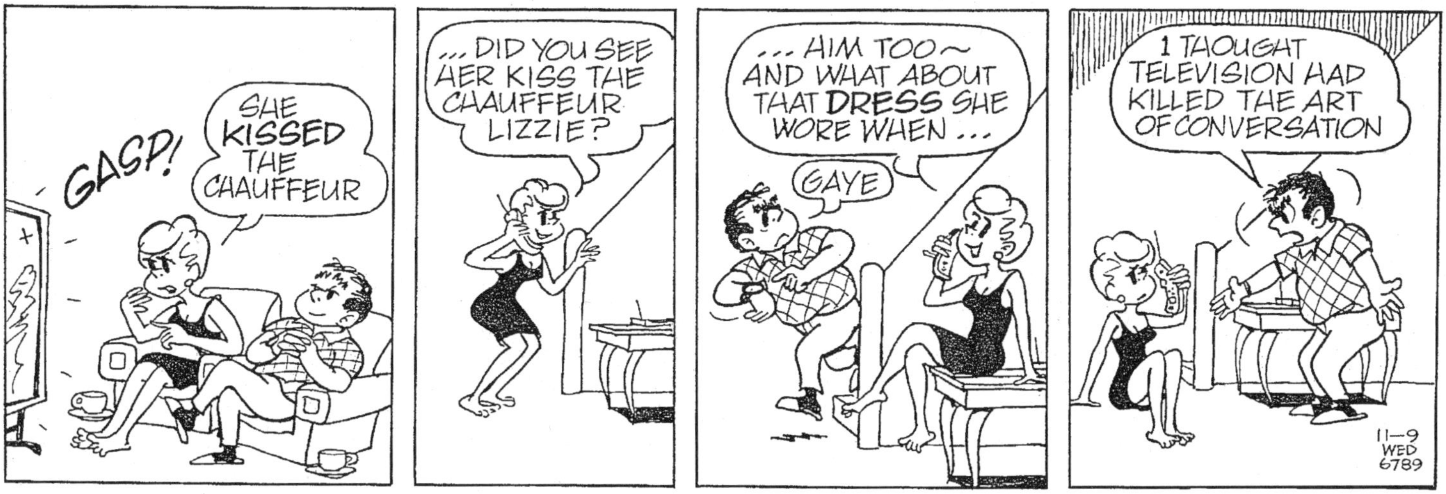
GASP!
SHE **KISSED** THE CHAUFFEUR
... DID YOU SEE HER KISS THE CHAUFFEUR LIZZIE?
... HIM TOO ~ AND WHAT ABOUT THAT **DRESS** SHE WORE WHEN ...
GAYE
I THOUGHT TELEVISION HAD KILLED THE ART OF CONVERSATION
11-9 WED 6789

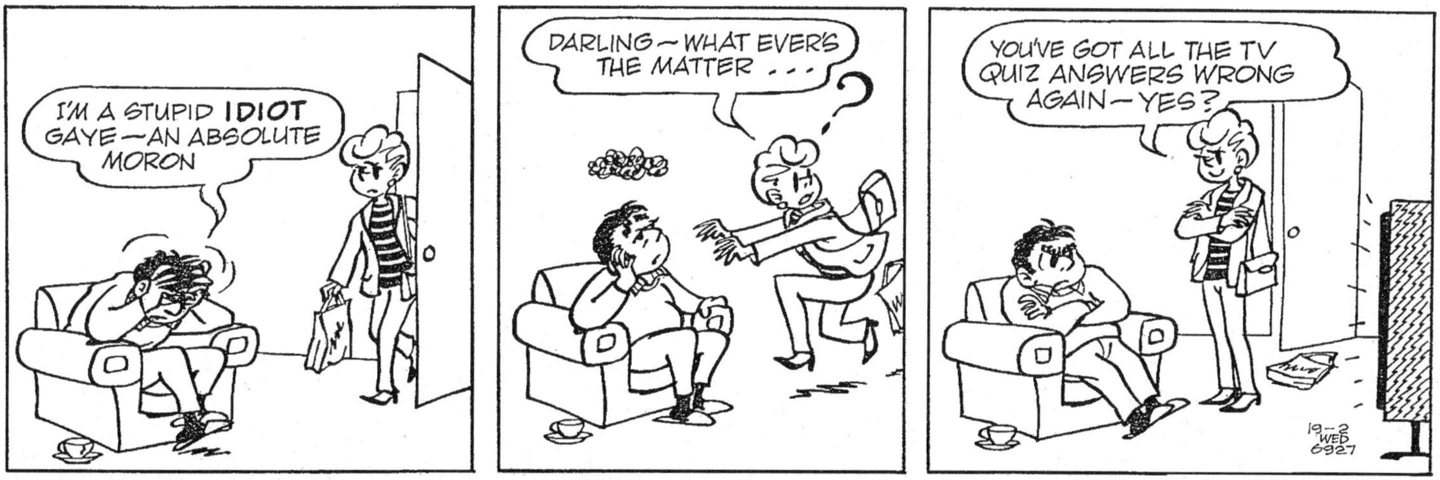
I'M A STUPID **IDIOT** GAYE — AN ABSOLUTE MORON
DARLING ~ WHAT EVER'S THE MATTER ...
?
YOU'VE GOT ALL THE TV QUIZ ANSWERS WRONG AGAIN — YES?
19-2 WED 6927

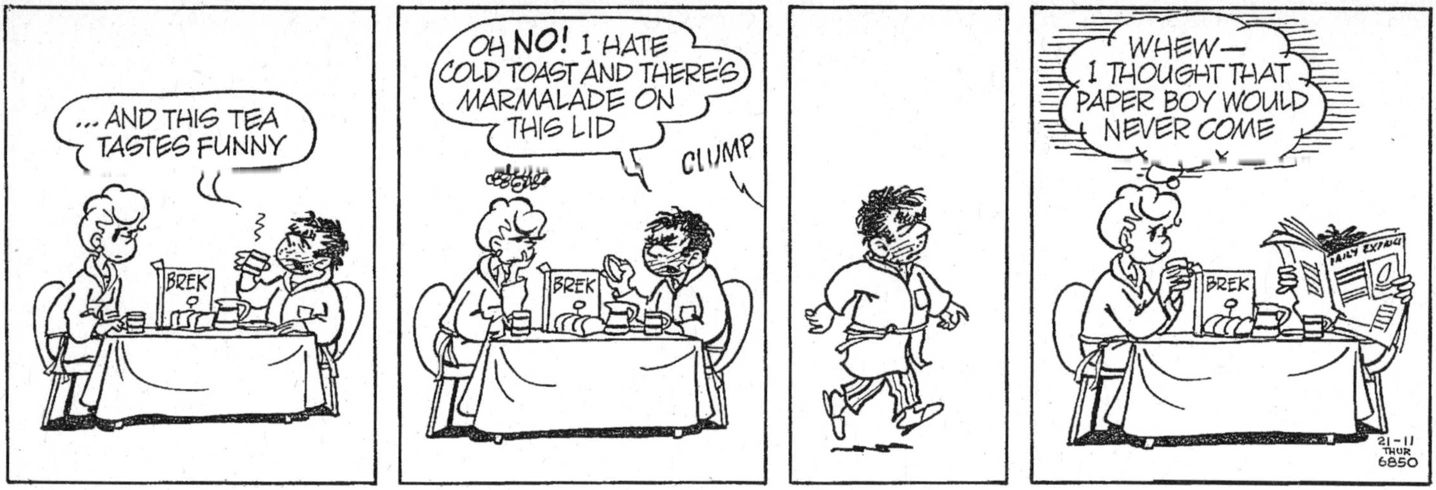
...AND THIS TEA TASTES FUNNY
BREK
OH NO! I HATE COLD TOAST AND THERE'S MARMALADE ON THIS LID
CLUMP
WHEW— I THOUGHT THAT PAPER BOY WOULD NEVER COME
21-11 THUR 6850

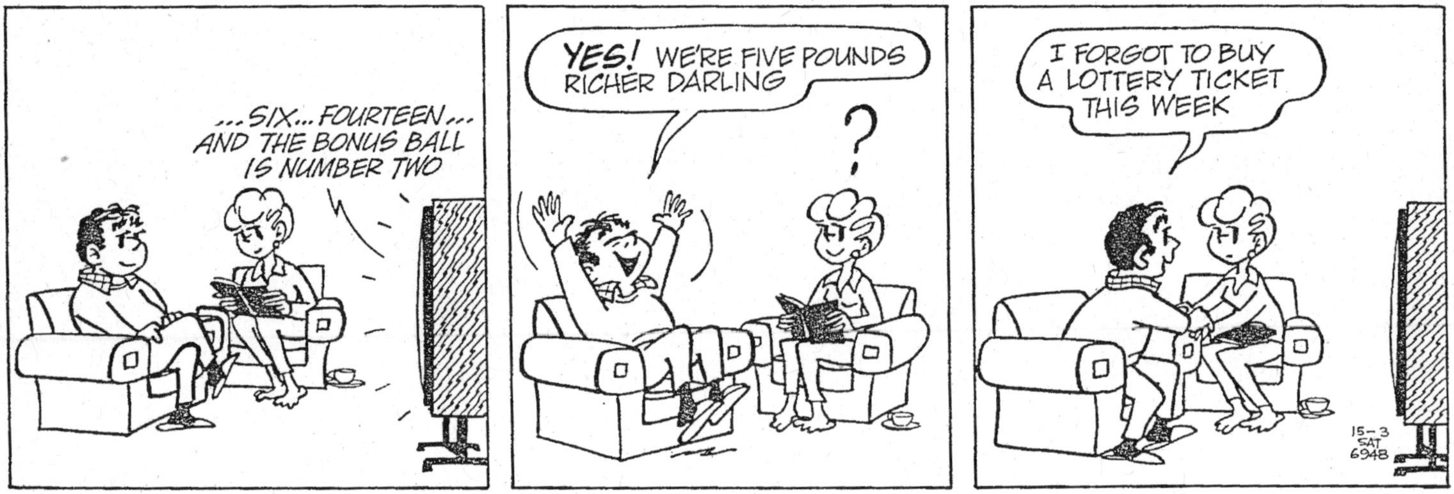
...SIX...FOURTEEN... AND THE BONUS BALL IS NUMBER TWO
YES! WE'RE FIVE POUNDS RICHER DARLING
?
I FORGOT TO BUY A LOTTERY TICKET THIS WEEK
15-3 SAT 6948

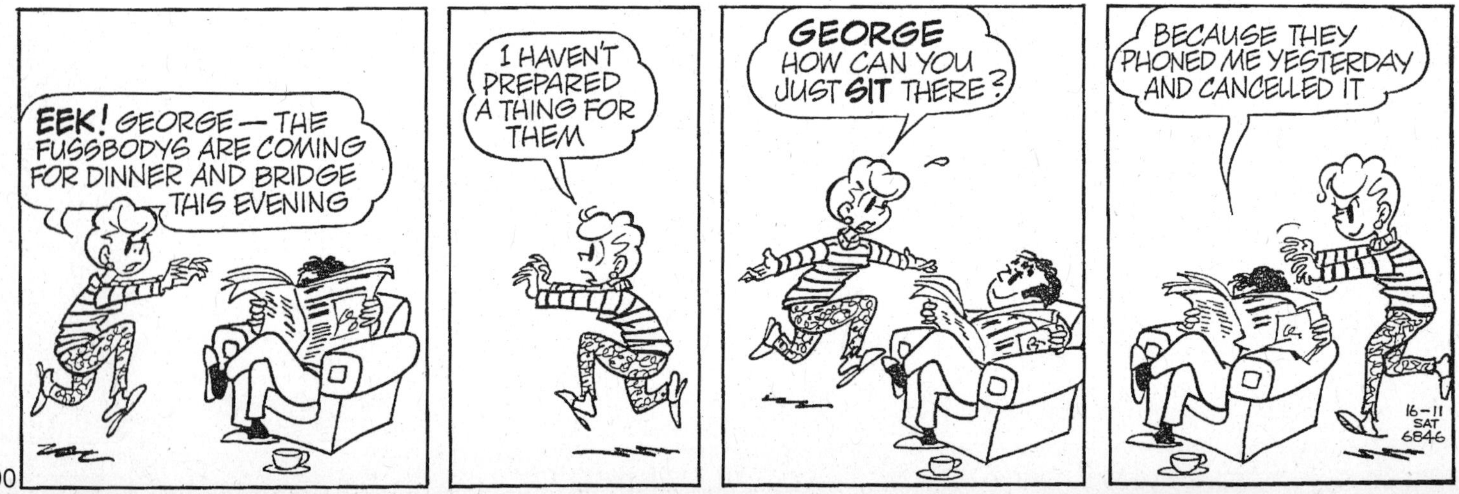
EEK! GEORGE—THE FUSSBODYS ARE COMING FOR DINNER AND BRIDGE THIS EVENING
I HAVEN'T PREPARED A THING FOR THEM
GEORGE HOW CAN YOU JUST SIT THERE?
BECAUSE THEY PHONED ME YESTERDAY AND CANCELLED IT
16-11 SAT 6846

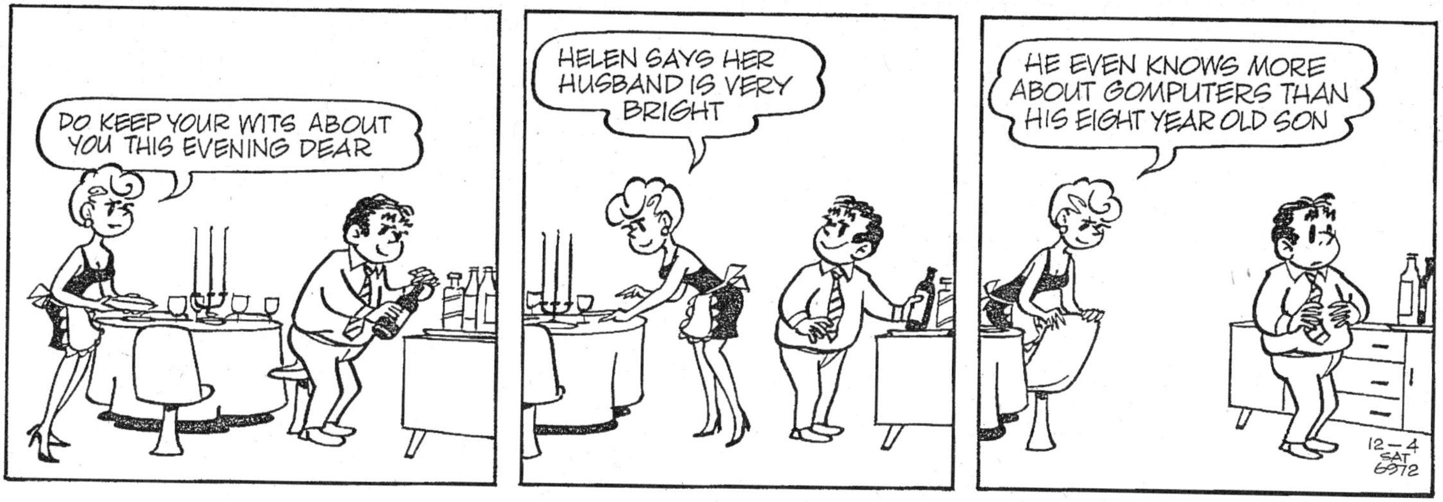
DO KEEP YOUR WITS ABOUT YOU THIS EVENING DEAR
HELEN SAYS HER HUSBAND IS VERY BRIGHT
HE EVEN KNOWS MORE ABOUT COMPUTERS THAN HIS EIGHT YEAR OLD SON
12—4 SAT 6972

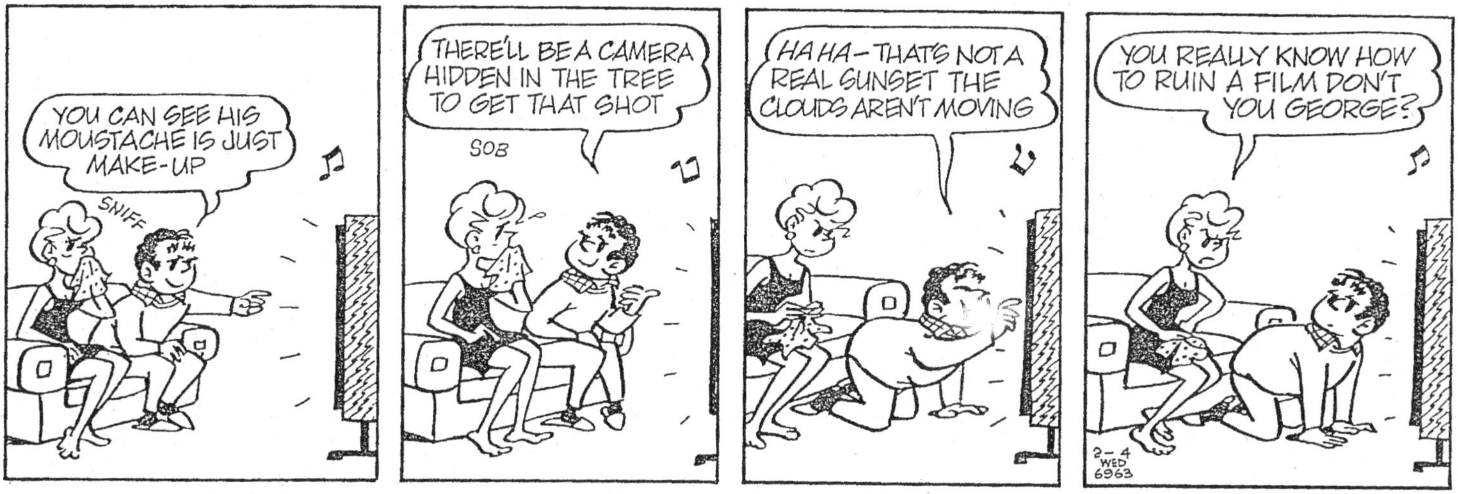
YOU CAN SEE HIS MOUSTACHE IS JUST MAKE-UP
SNIFF
THERE'LL BE A CAMERA HIDDEN IN THE TREE TO GET THAT SHOT
SOB
HA HA – THAT'S NOT A REAL SUNSET THE CLOUDS AREN'T MOVING
YOU REALLY KNOW HOW TO RUIN A FILM DON'T YOU GEORGE?
2–4 WED 6963

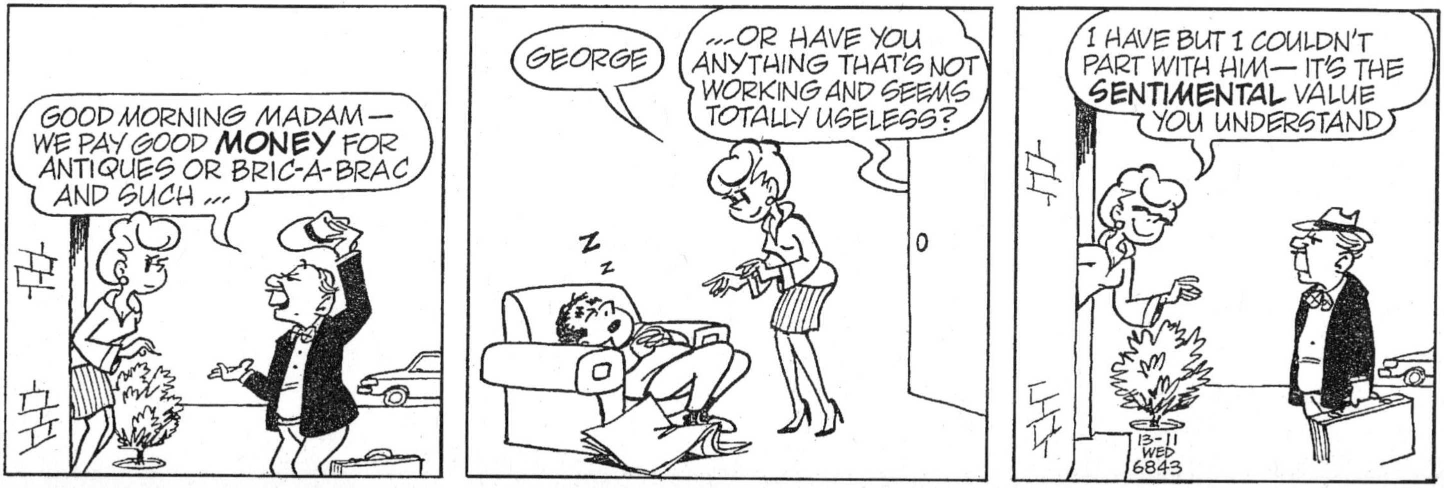
GOOD MORNING MADAM — WE PAY GOOD MONEY FOR ANTIQUES OR BRIC-A-BRAC AND SUCH ...
GEORGE
...OR HAVE YOU ANYTHING THAT'S NOT WORKING AND SEEMS TOTALLY USELESS?
Z Z
I HAVE BUT I COULDN'T PART WITH HIM — IT'S THE SENTIMENTAL VALUE YOU UNDERSTAND
13-11 WED 6843

GAYE OFTEN DRIVES HER BOSS TO
DISTRACTION — BUT WHAT WOULD
HE DO WITHOUT HER ?

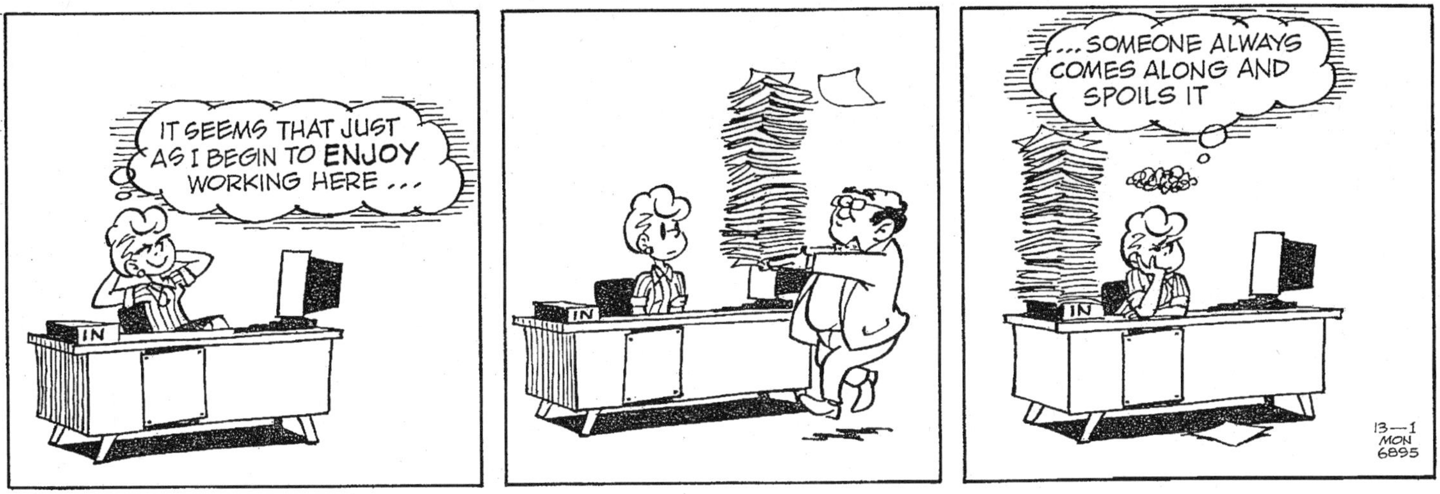
IT SEEMS THAT JUST AS I BEGIN TO ENJOY WORKING HERE . . .
IN
IN
. . . SOMEONE ALWAYS COMES ALONG AND SPOILS IT
IN
13—1 MON 6895

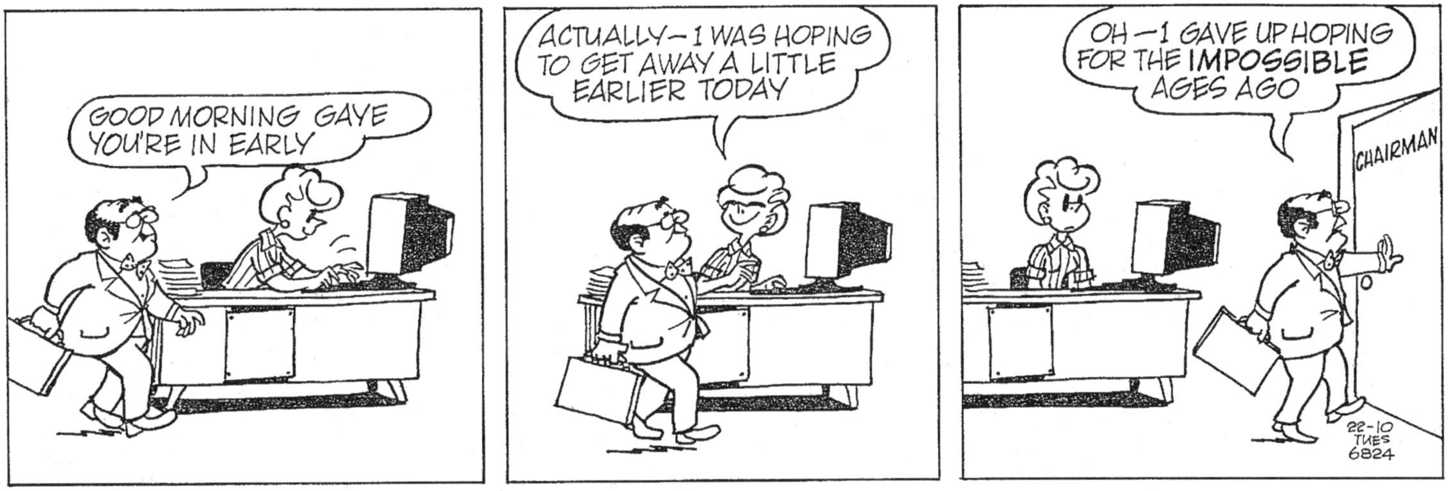
GOOD MORNING GAYE YOU'RE IN EARLY
ACTUALLY—I WAS HOPING TO GET AWAY A LITTLE EARLIER TODAY
OH—I GAVE UP HOPING FOR THE IMPOSSIBLE AGES AGO
CHAIRMAN
22-10 TUES 6824

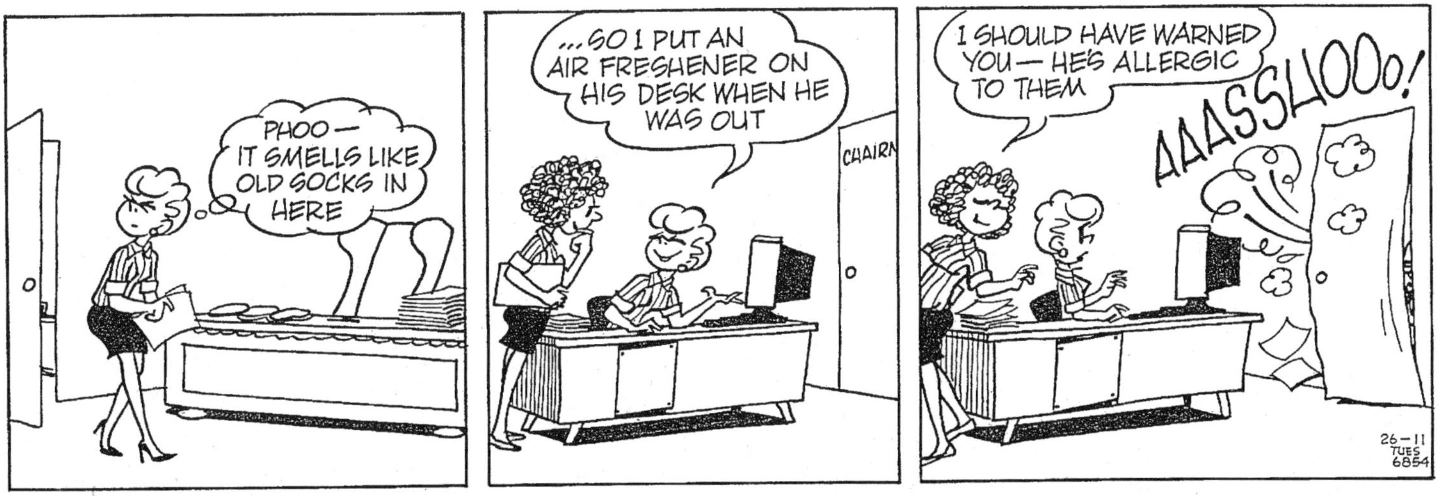
PHOO— IT SMELLS LIKE OLD SOCKS IN HERE
...SO I PUT AN AIR FRESHENER ON HIS DESK WHEN HE WAS OUT
CHAIRN
I SHOULD HAVE WARNED YOU—HE'S ALLERGIC TO THEM
AAASSHOOo!
26—11 TUES 6854

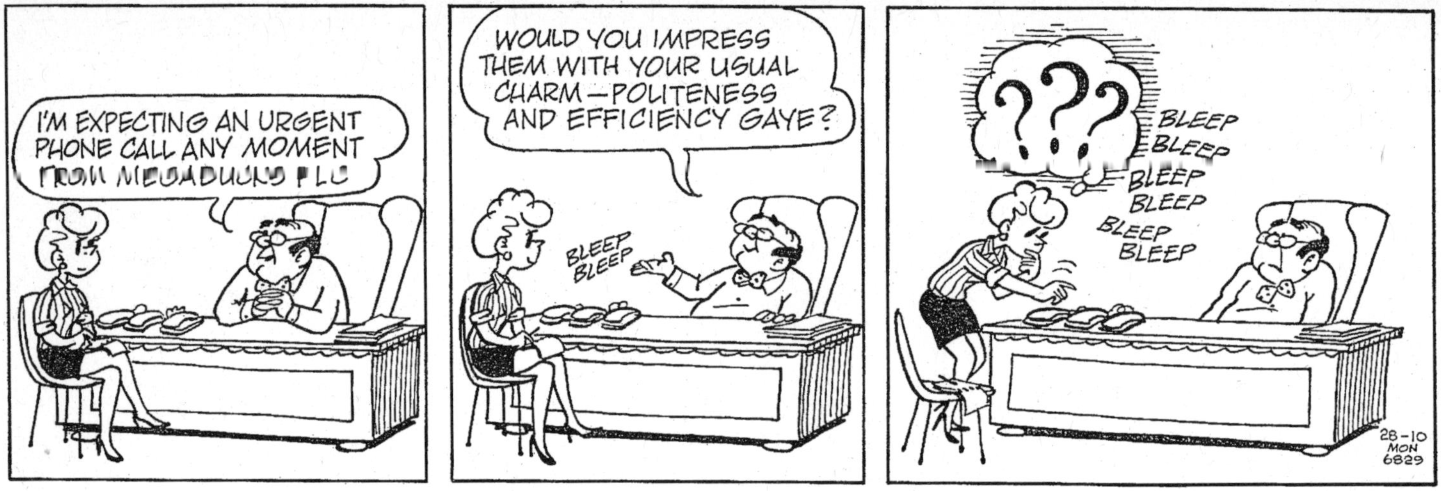
I'M EXPECTING AN URGENT PHONE CALL ANY MOMENT FROM MEGABUCKS PLC
WOULD YOU IMPRESS THEM WITH YOUR USUAL CHARM—POLITENESS AND EFFICIENCY GAYE?
BLEEP BLEEP
???
BLEEP BLEEP BLEEP BLEEP BLEEP BLEEP
28-10 MON 6829

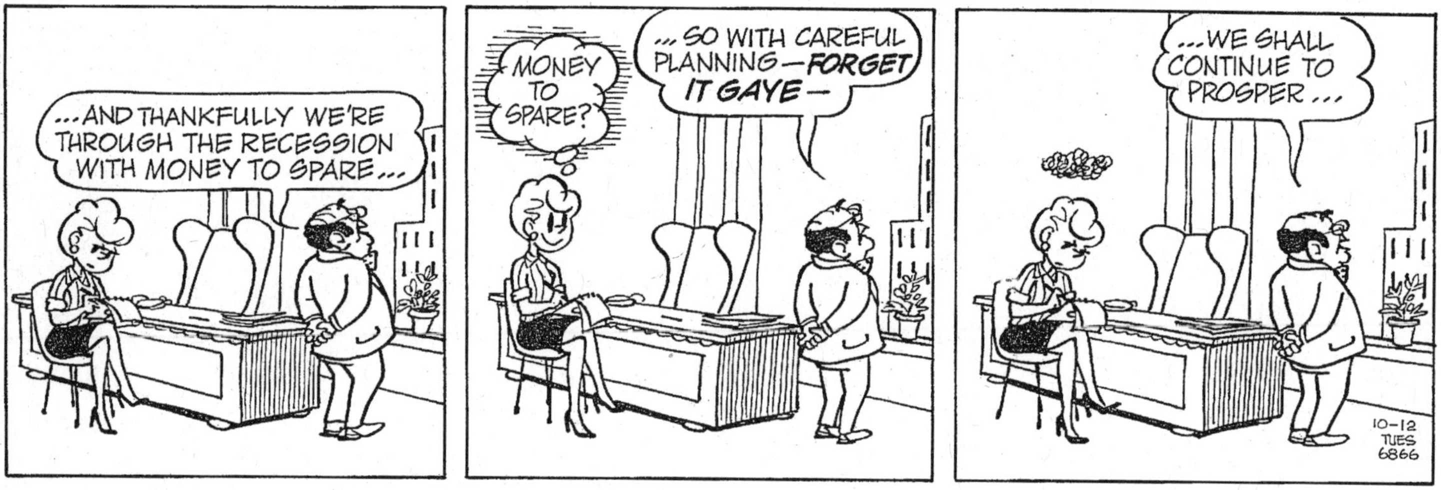
...AND THANKFULLY WE'RE THROUGH THE RECESSION WITH MONEY TO SPARE...
MONEY TO SPARE?
...SO WITH CAREFUL PLANNING—**FORGET IT GAYE**—
...WE SHALL CONTINUE TO PROSPER...
10-12 TUES 6866

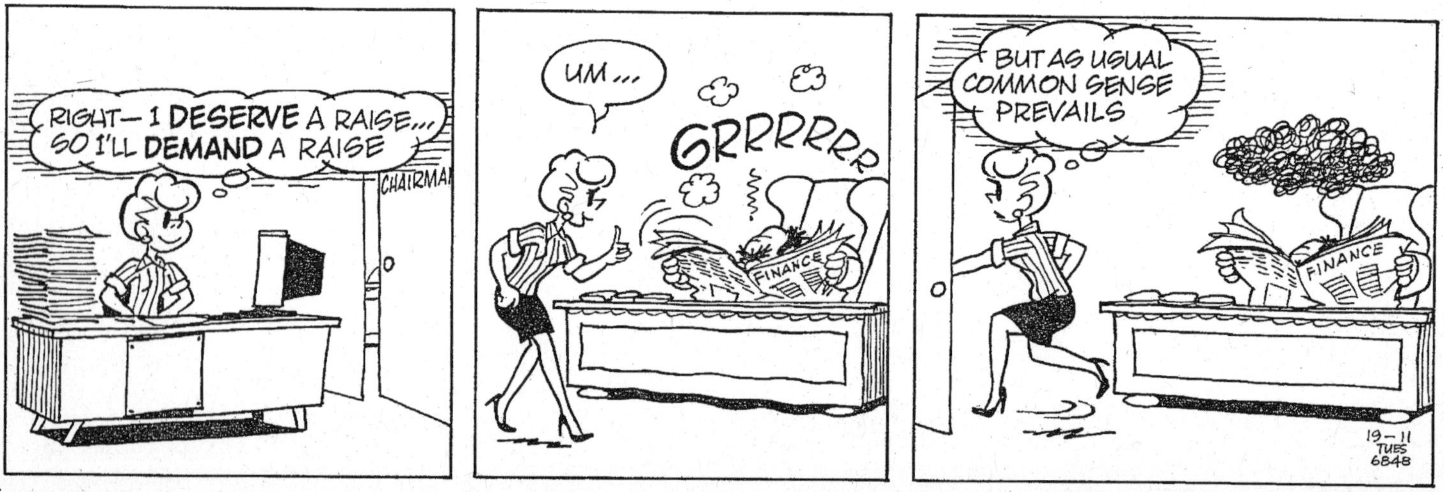
RIGHT—I **DESERVE** A RAISE... SO I'LL **DEMAND** A RAISE
CHAIRMAN
UM...
GRRRRRR
FINANCE
BUT AS USUAL COMMON SENSE PREVAILS
FINANCE
19-11 TUES 6848

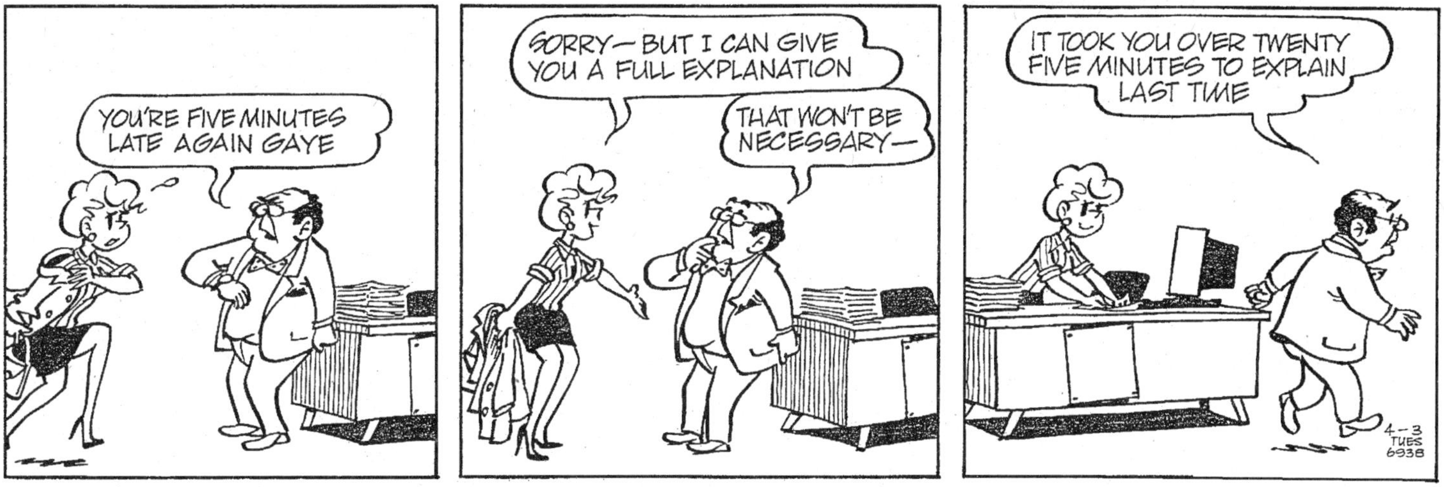
YOU'RE FIVE MINUTES LATE AGAIN GAYE
SORRY— BUT I CAN GIVE YOU A FULL EXPLANATION
THAT WON'T BE NECESSARY—
IT TOOK YOU OVER TWENTY FIVE MINUTES TO EXPLAIN LAST TIME
4-3 TUES 6938

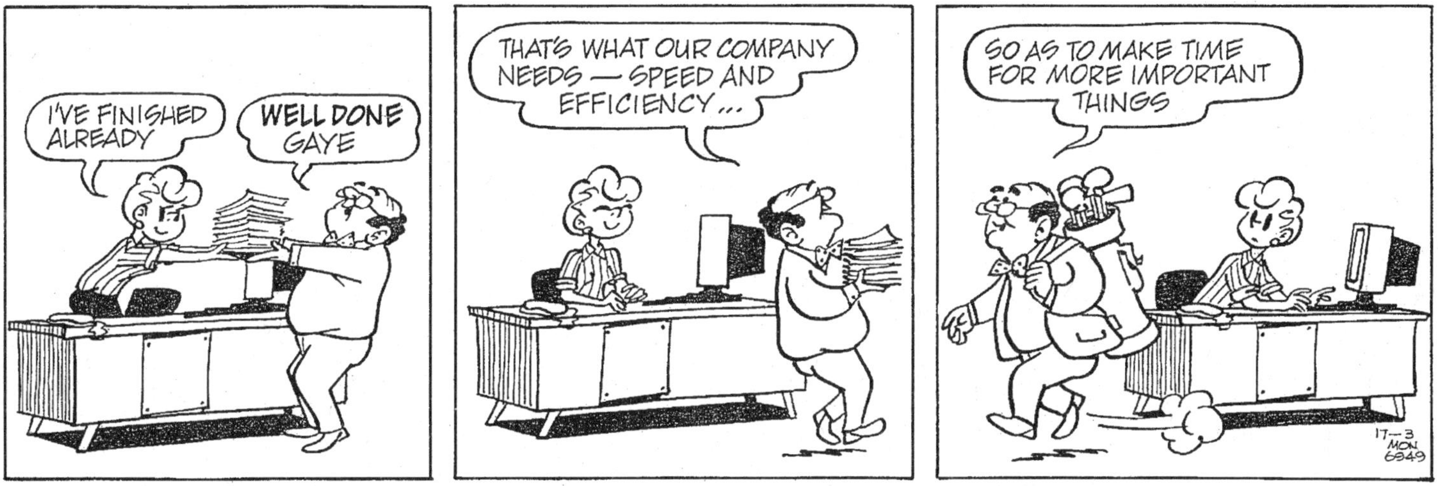
I'VE FINISHED ALREADY
WELL DONE GAYE
THAT'S WHAT OUR COMPANY NEEDS — SPEED AND EFFICIENCY ...
SO AS TO MAKE TIME FOR MORE IMPORTANT THINGS
17-3 MON 6949

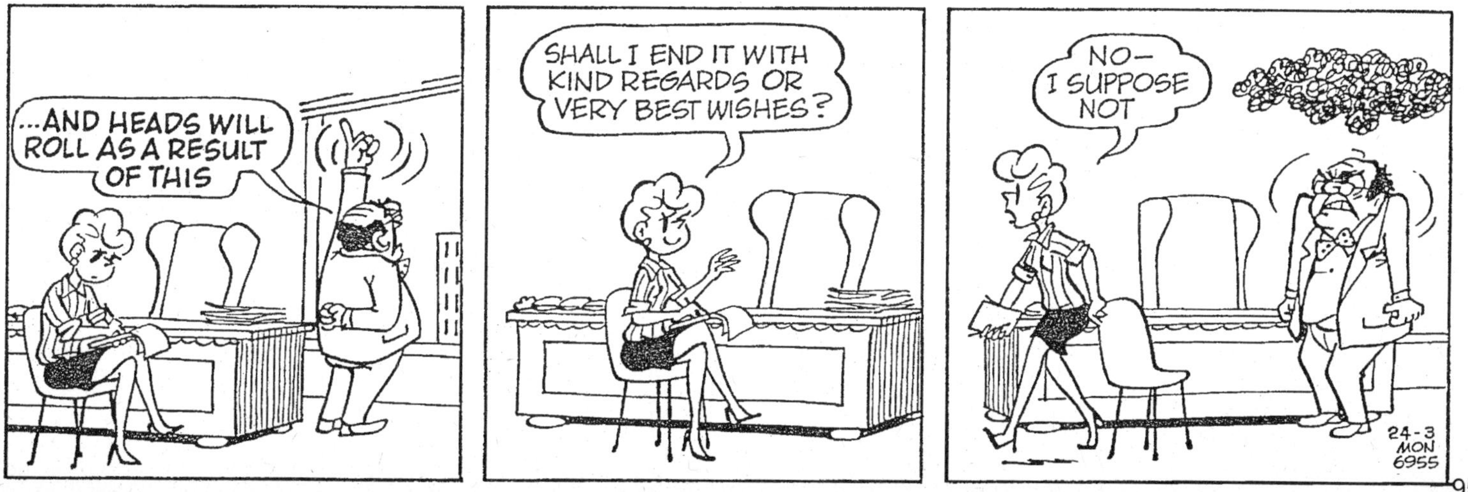
...AND HEADS WILL ROLL AS A RESULT OF THIS
SHALL I END IT WITH KIND REGARDS OR VERY BEST WISHES?
NO— I SUPPOSE NOT
24-3 MON 6955

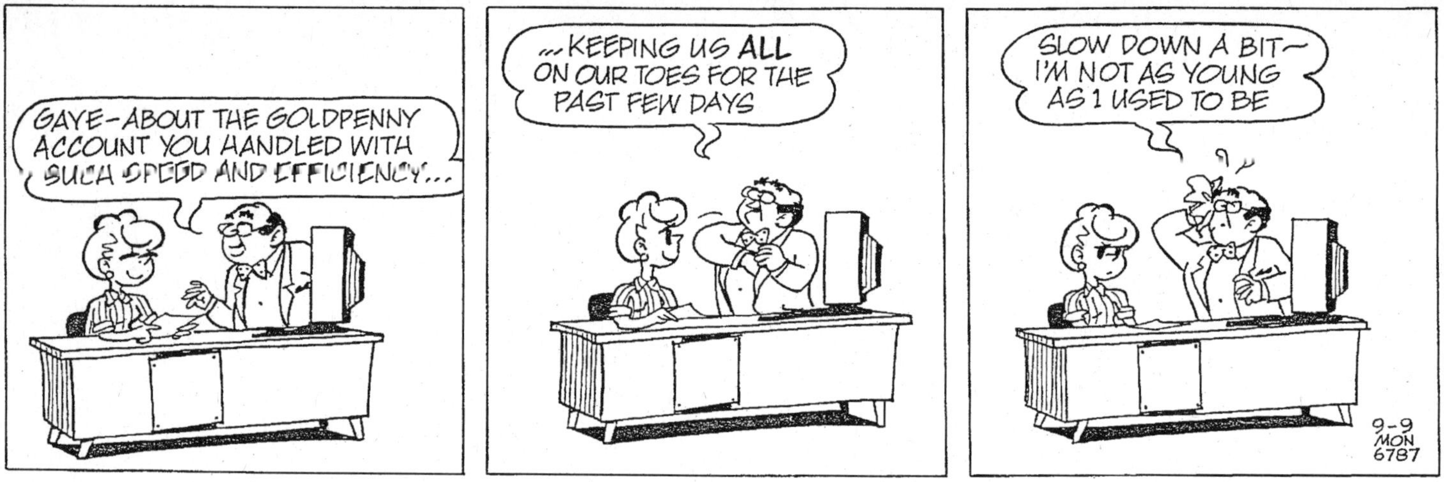
GAYE–ABOUT THE GOLDPENNY ACCOUNT YOU HANDLED WITH SUCH SPEED AND EFFICIENCY...
...KEEPING US ALL ON OUR TOES FOR THE PAST FEW DAYS
SLOW DOWN A BIT— I'M NOT AS YOUNG AS I USED TO BE
9-9 MON 6787

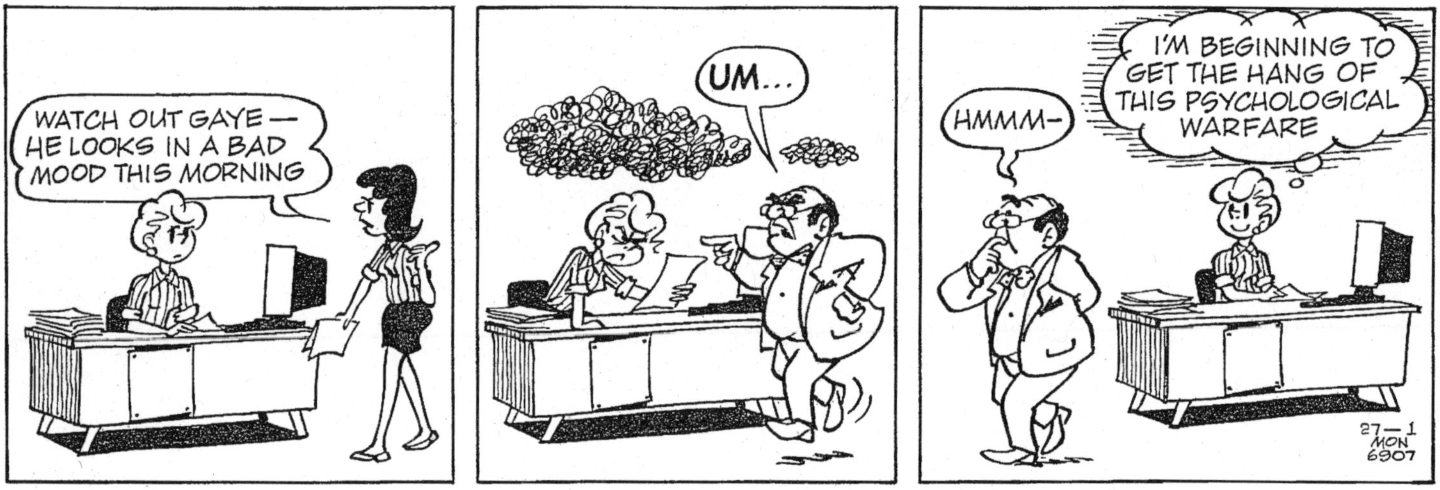
WATCH OUT GAYE— HE LOOKS IN A BAD MOOD THIS MORNING
UM...
HMMM-
I'M BEGINNING TO GET THE HANG OF THIS PSYCHOLOGICAL WARFARE
27—1 MON 6907

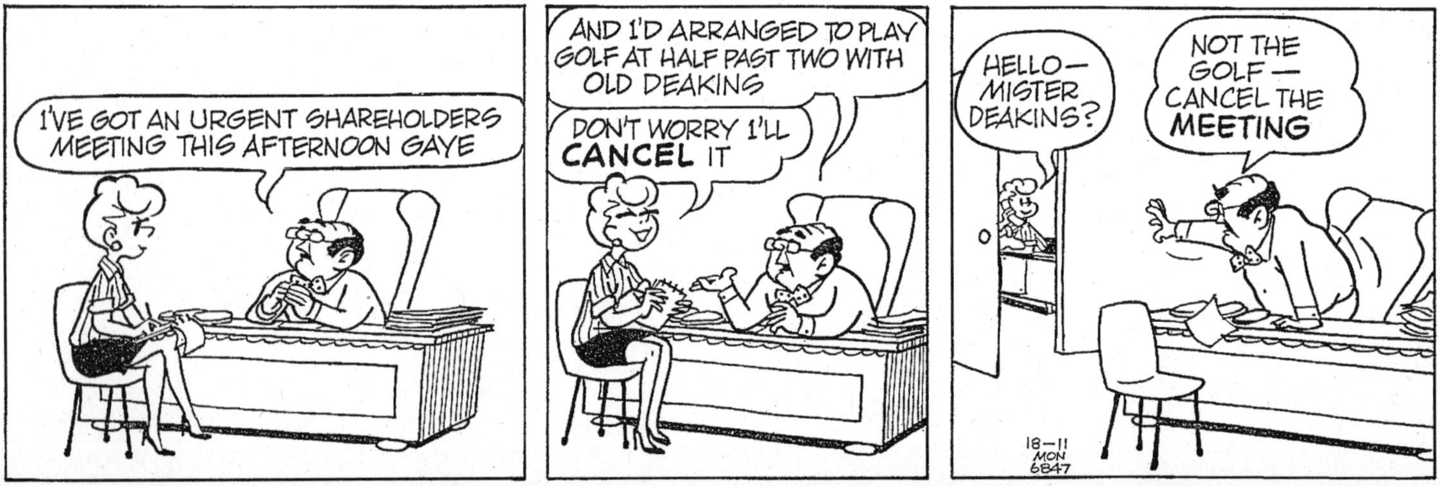
I'VE GOT AN URGENT SHAREHOLDERS MEETING THIS AFTERNOON GAYE
AND I'D ARRANGED TO PLAY GOLF AT HALF PAST TWO WITH OLD DEAKING
DON'T WORRY I'LL CANCEL IT
HELLO— MISTER DEAKINS?
NOT THE GOLF— CANCEL THE MEETING
18—11 MON 6847

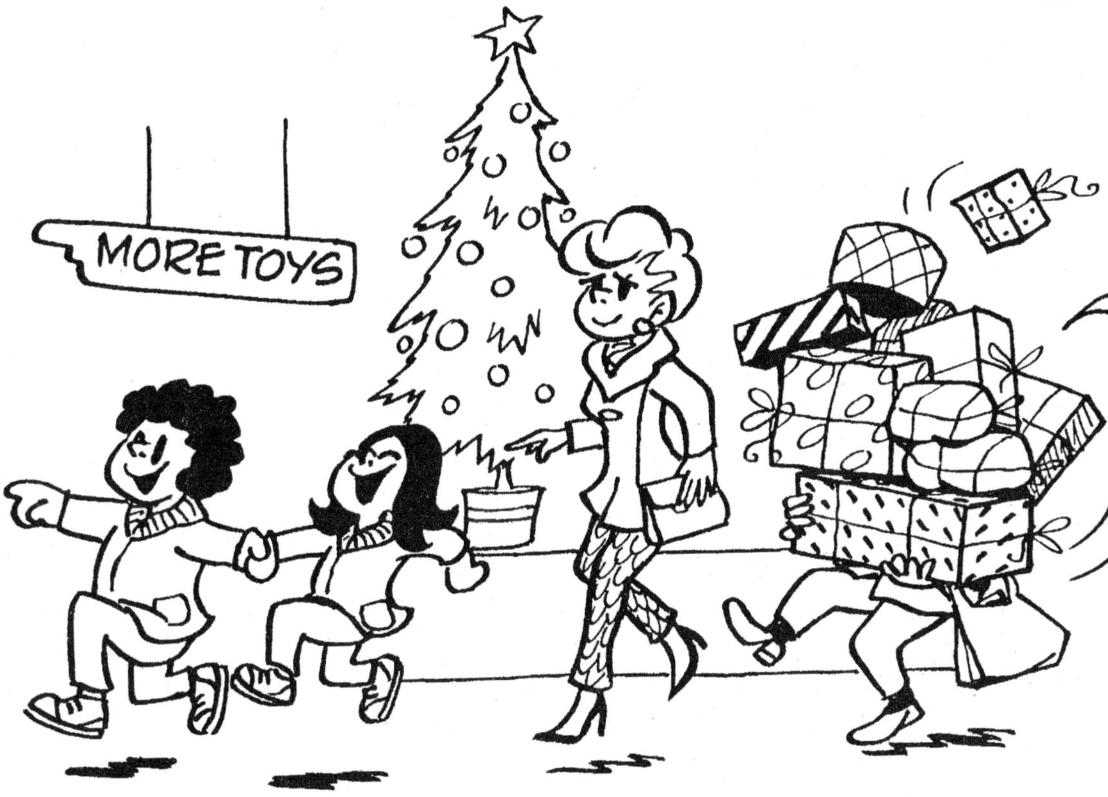
MORE TOYS

CHRISTMAS SHOPPING WITH MIGGY AND FLIVVER TAKES A LITTLE MONEY AND A LOT OF PATIENCE — OR IS IT THE OTHER WAY AROUND?

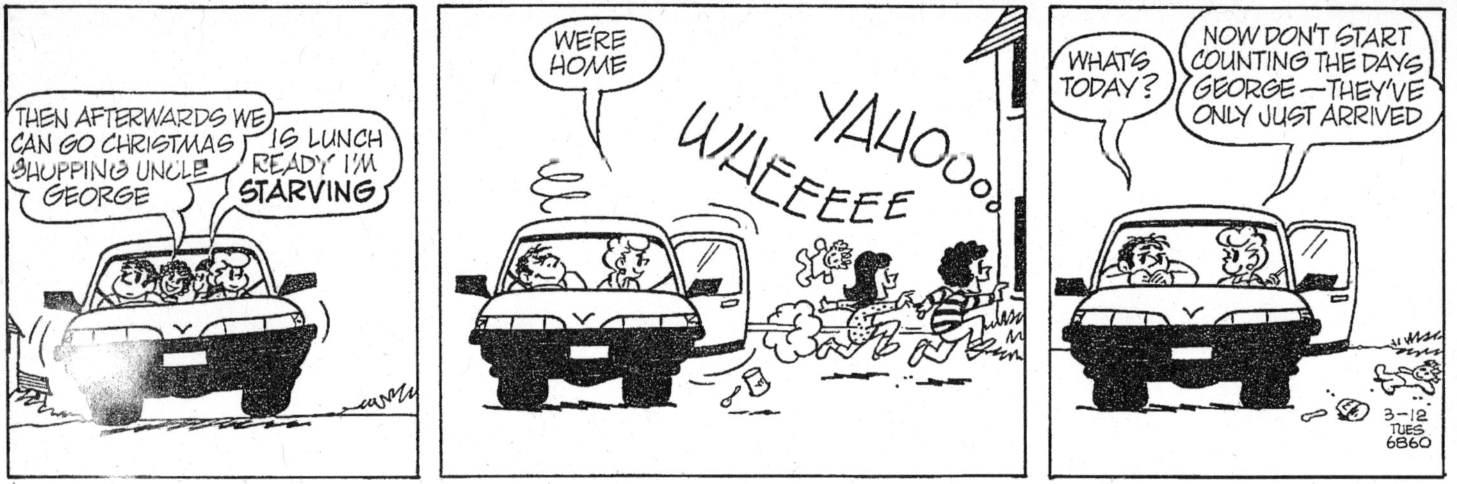
THEN AFTERWARDS WE CAN GO CHRISTMAS SHOPPING UNCLE GEORGE
IS LUNCH READY I'M **STARVING**
WE'RE HOME
YAHOOOOO
WHEEEEEE
WHAT'S TODAY?
NOW DON'T START COUNTING THE DAYS GEORGE—THEY'VE ONLY JUST ARRIVED
3—12 TUES 6860

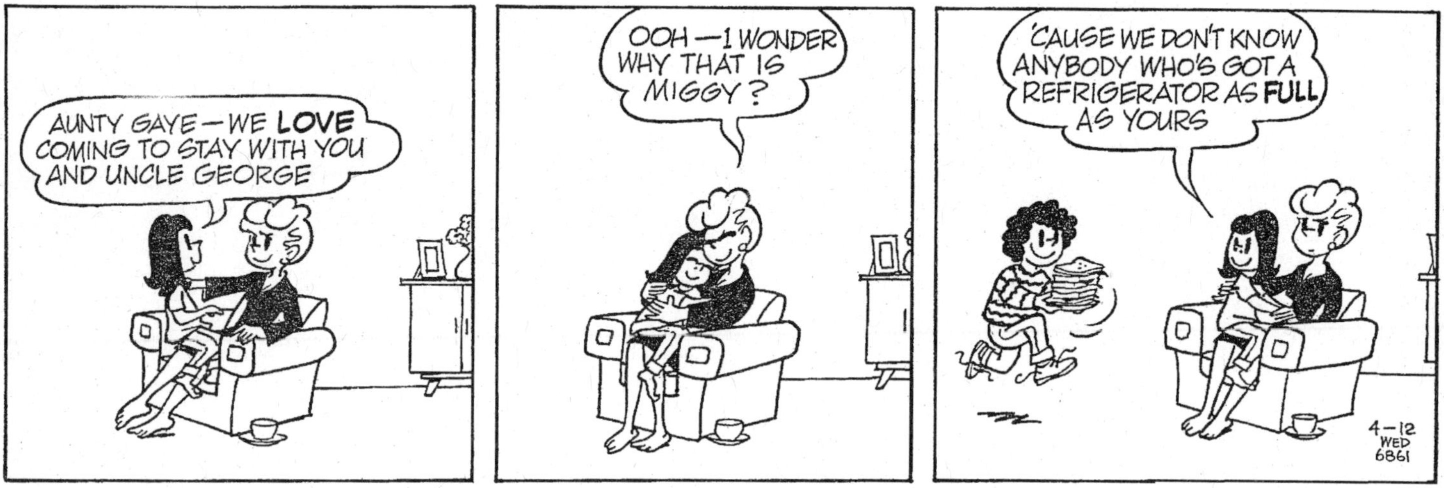
AUNTY GAYE—WE **LOVE** COMING TO STAY WITH YOU AND UNCLE GEORGE
OOH—I WONDER WHY THAT IS MIGGY?
'CAUSE WE DON'T KNOW ANYBODY WHO'S GOT A REFRIGERATOR AS **FULL** AS YOURS
4—12 WED 6861

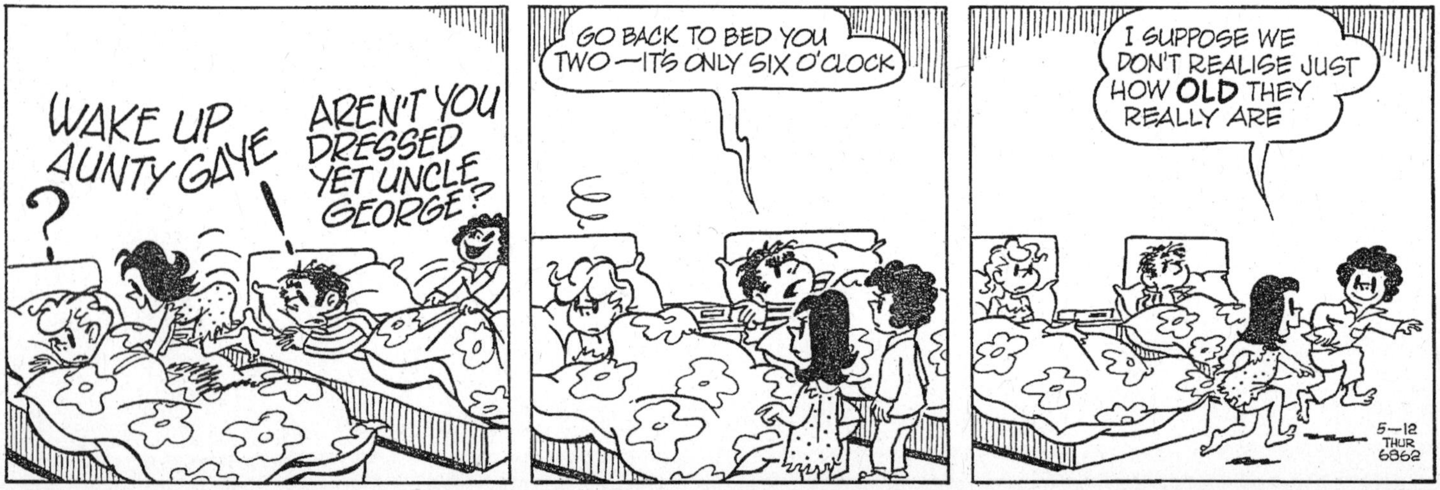
WAKE UP AUNTY GAYE
AREN'T YOU DRESSED YET UNCLE GEORGE?
?
!
GO BACK TO BED YOU TWO—IT'S ONLY SIX O'CLOCK
I SUPPOSE WE DON'T REALISE JUST HOW **OLD** THEY REALLY ARE
5—12 THUR 6862

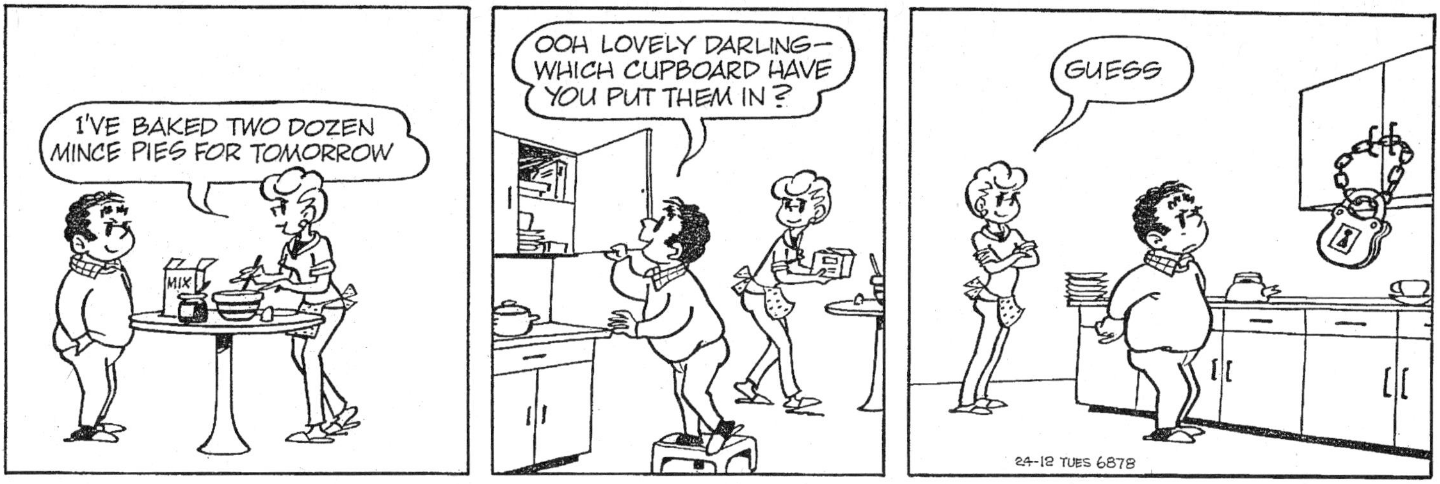
I'VE BAKED TWO DOZEN MINCE PIES FOR TOMORROW
MIX
OOH LOVELY DARLING— WHICH CUPBOARD HAVE YOU PUT THEM IN?
GUESS
24-12 TUES 6878

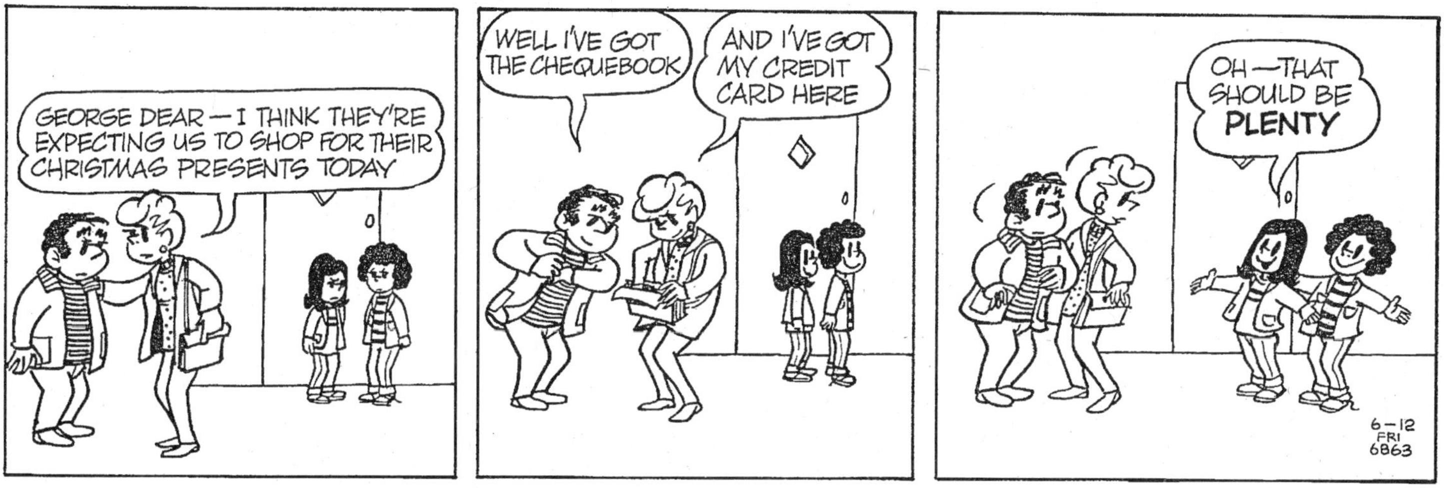
GEORGE DEAR — I THINK THEY'RE EXPECTING US TO SHOP FOR THEIR CHRISTMAS PRESENTS TODAY
WELL I'VE GOT THE CHEQUEBOOK
AND I'VE GOT MY CREDIT CARD HERE
OH —THAT SHOULD BE **PLENTY**
6-12 FRI 6863

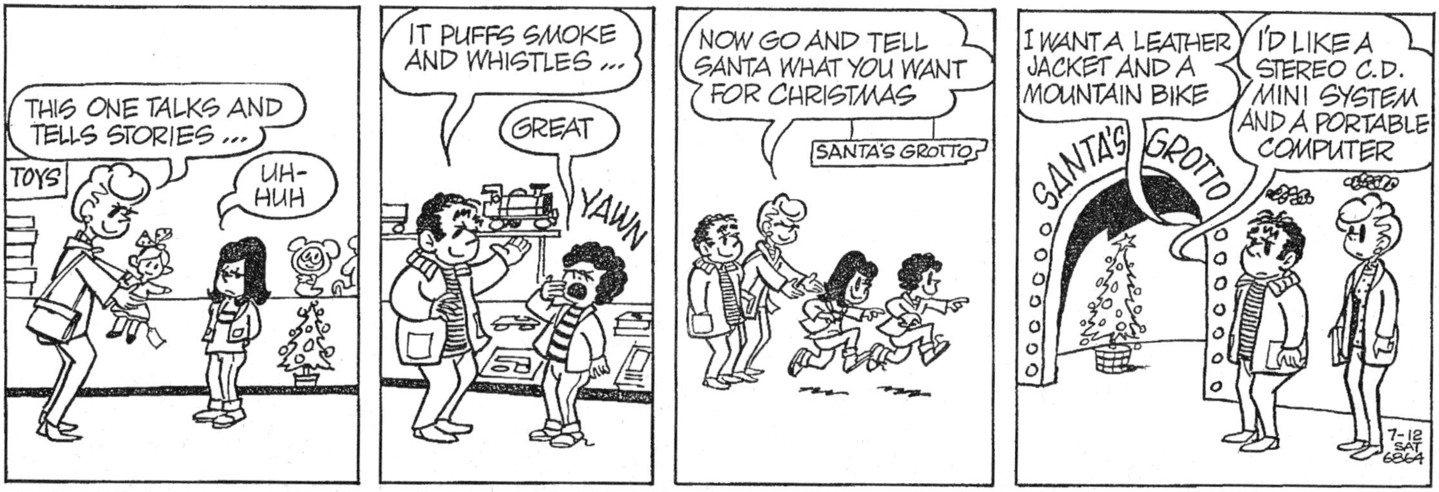
TOYS
THIS ONE TALKS AND TELLS STORIES ...
UH-HUH
IT PUFFS SMOKE AND WHISTLES ...
GREAT
YAWN
NOW GO AND TELL SANTA WHAT YOU WANT FOR CHRISTMAS
SANTA'S GROTTO
I WANT A LEATHER JACKET AND A MOUNTAIN BIKE
I'D LIKE A STEREO C.D. MINI SYSTEM AND A PORTABLE COMPUTER
SANTA'S GROTTO
7-12 SAT 6864

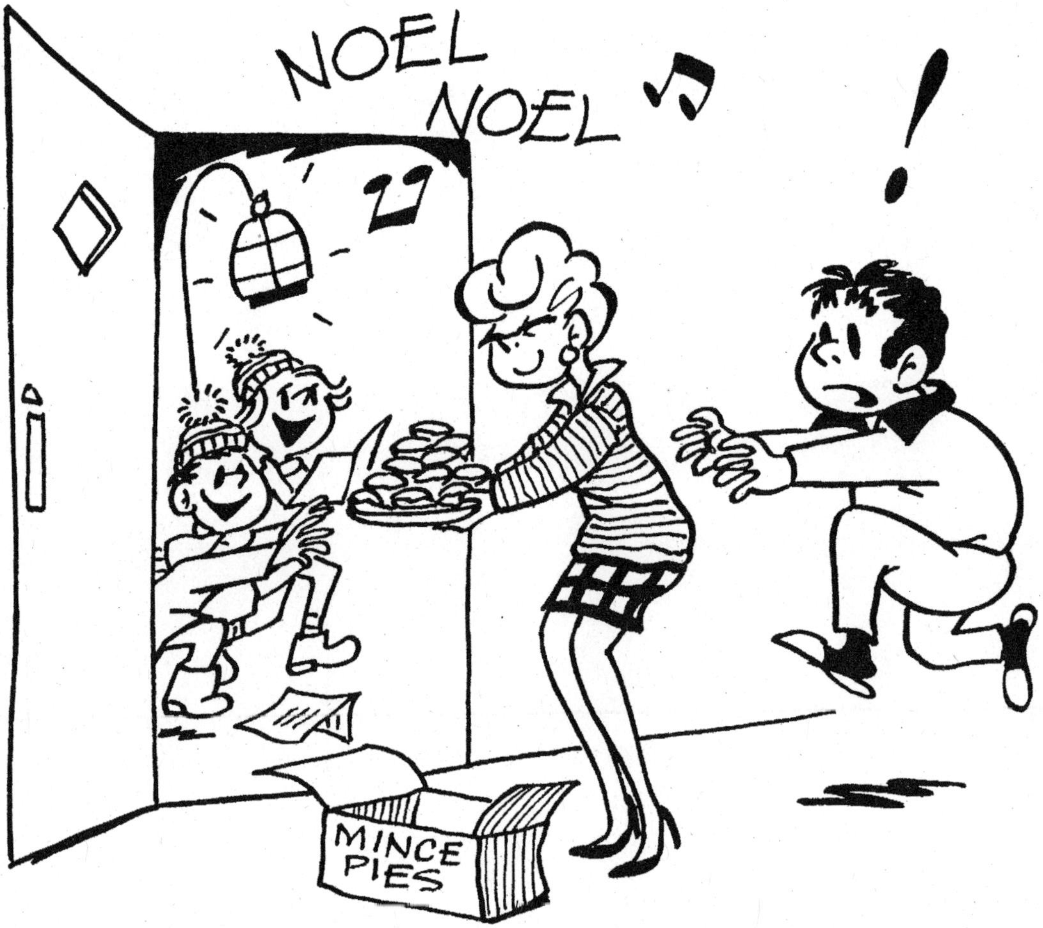
NOEL
NOEL
!
MINCE PIES

CHRISTMAS TIME — THE SEASON OF GOOD-WILL TOWARD MEN AND ACCORDING TO GAYE — ESPECIALLY CAROL SINGERS

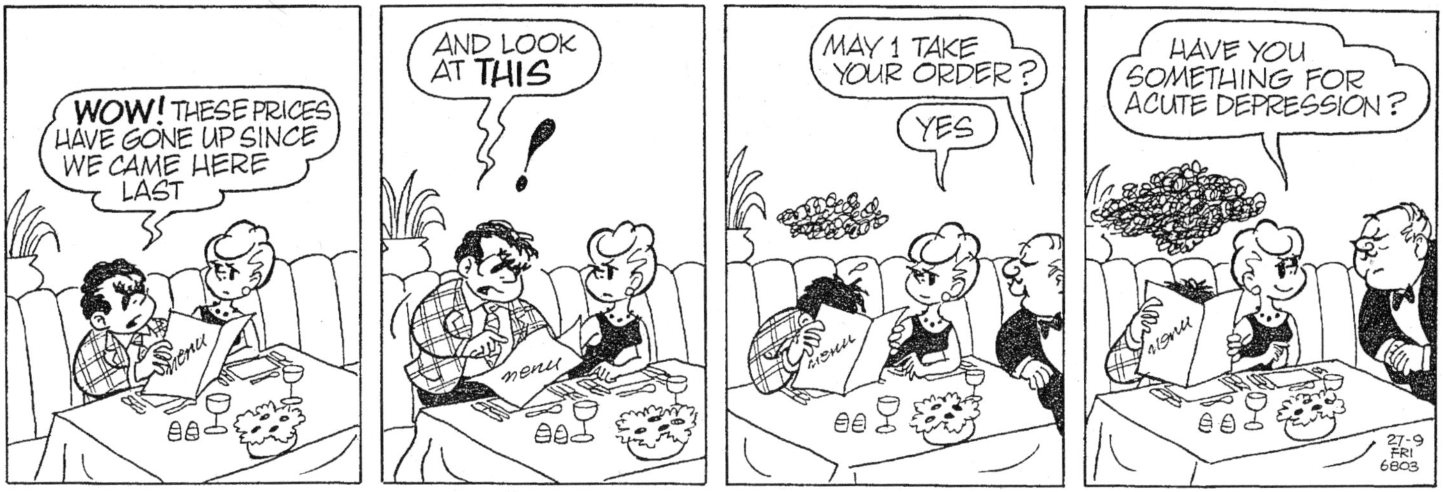
WOW! THESE PRICES HAVE GONE UP SINCE WE CAME HERE LAST
menu
AND LOOK AT THIS
!
menu
MAY I TAKE YOUR ORDER?
YES
menu
HAVE YOU SOMETHING FOR ACUTE DEPRESSION?
menu
27-9 FRI 6803

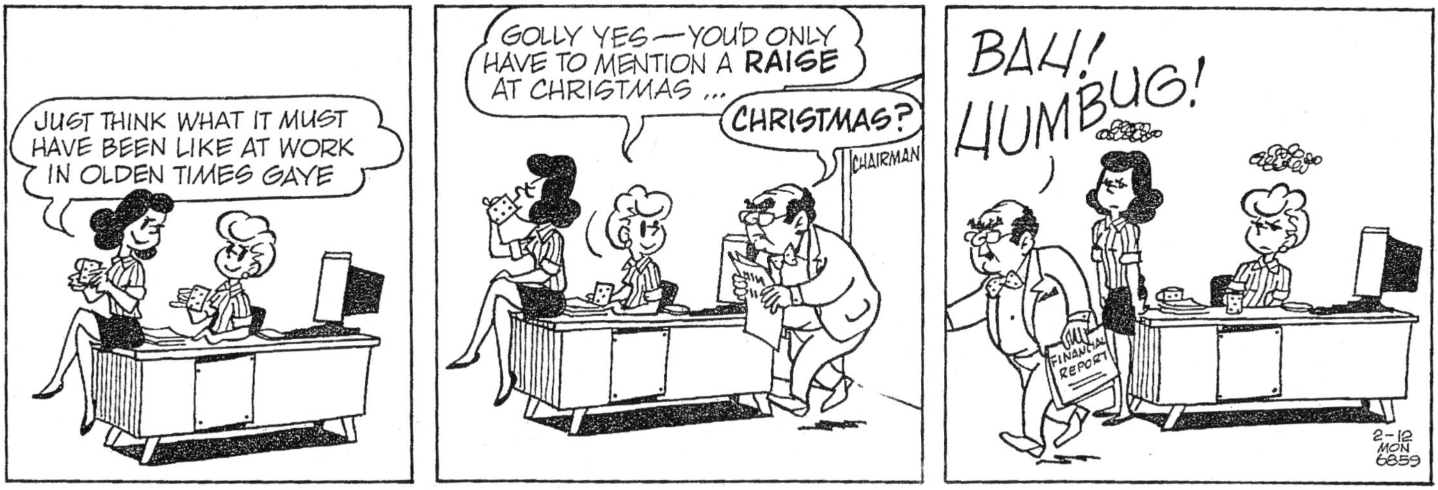
JUST THINK WHAT IT MUST HAVE BEEN LIKE AT WORK IN OLDEN TIMES GAYE
GOLLY YES—YOU'D ONLY HAVE TO MENTION A RAISE AT CHRISTMAS ...
CHRISTMAS?
CHAIRMAN
BAH! HUMBUG!
FINANCIAL REPORT
2-12 MON 6859

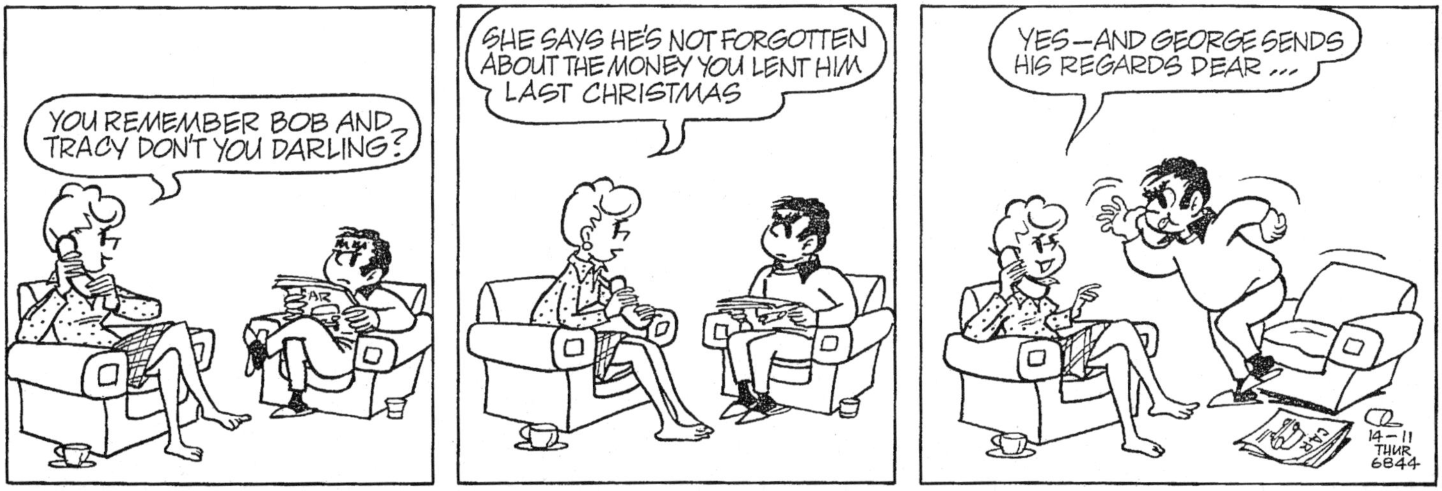
YOU REMEMBER BOB AND TRACY DON'T YOU DARLING?
SHE SAYS HE'S NOT FORGOTTEN ABOUT THE MONEY YOU LENT HIM LAST CHRISTMAS
YES—AND GEORGE SENDS HIS REGARDS DEAR ...
14-11 THUR 6844

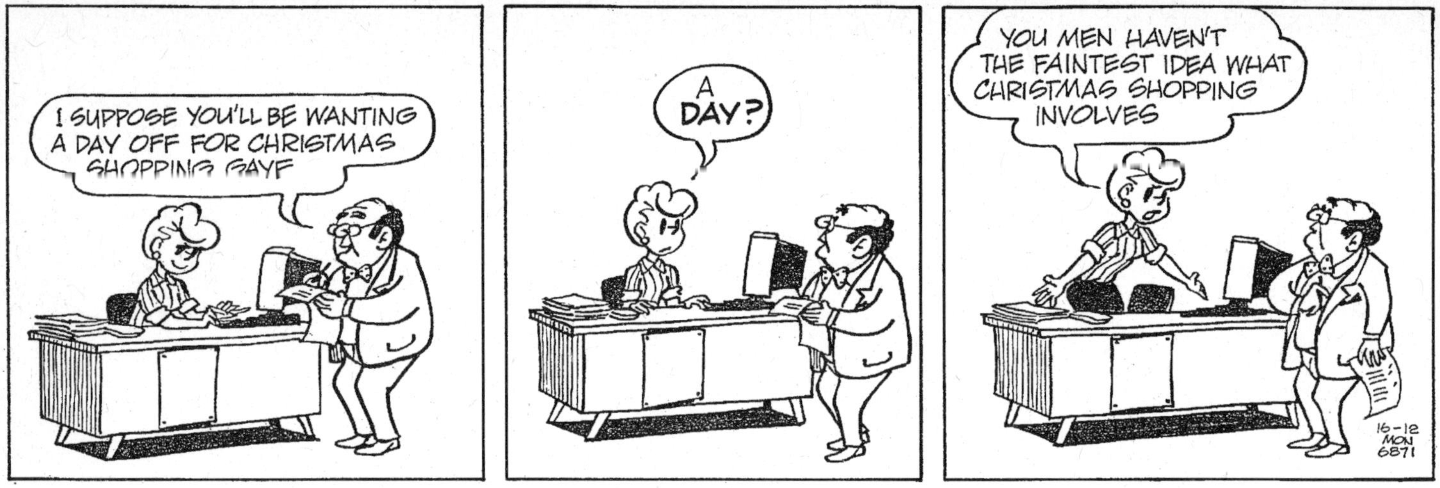
I SUPPOSE YOU'LL BE WANTING A DAY OFF FOR CHRISTMAS SHOPPING GAYE
A DAY?
YOU MEN HAVEN'T THE FAINTEST IDEA WHAT CHRISTMAS SHOPPING INVOLVES
16-12 MON 6871

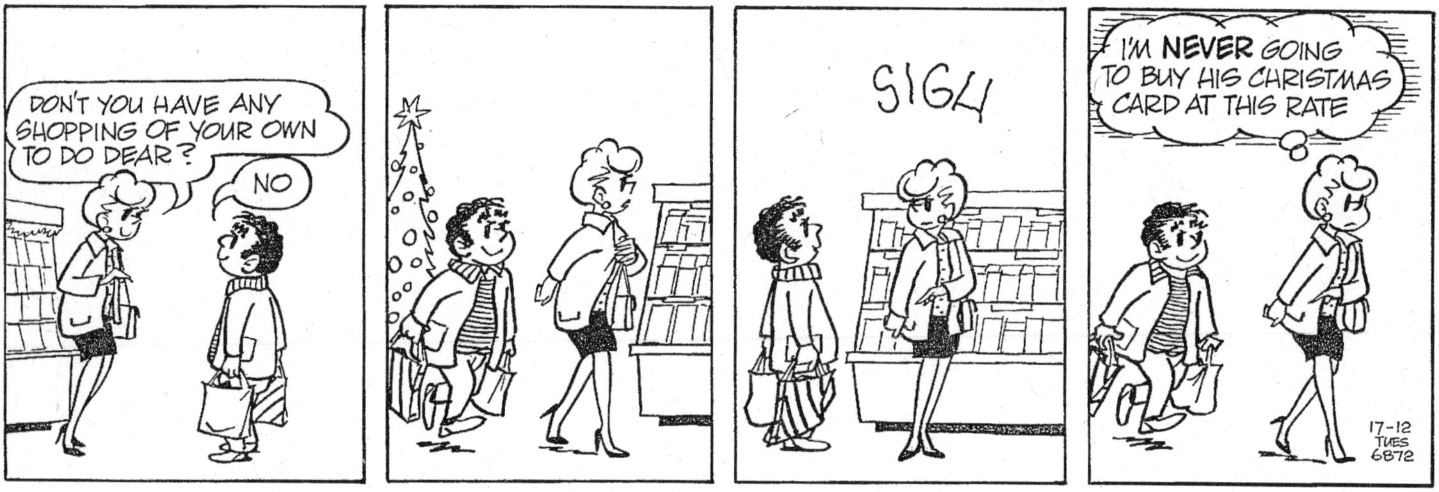
DON'T YOU HAVE ANY SHOPPING OF YOUR OWN TO DO DEAR?
NO
SIGH
I'M NEVER GOING TO BUY HIS CHRISTMAS CARD AT THIS RATE
17-12 TUES 6872

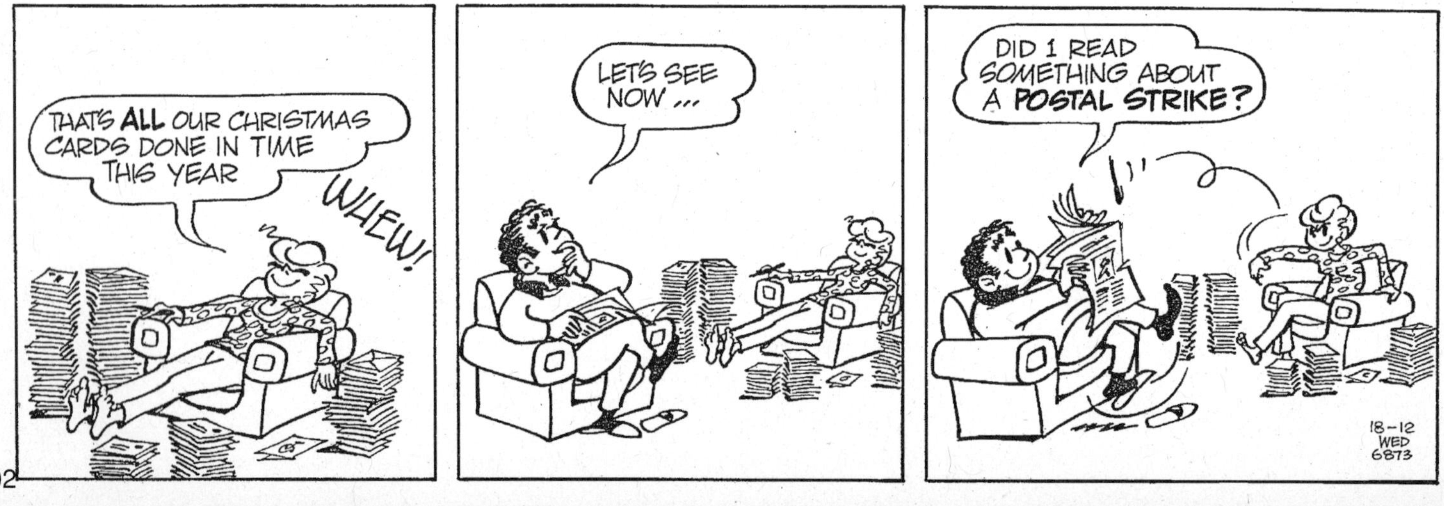
THAT'S ALL OUR CHRISTMAS CARDS DONE IN TIME THIS YEAR
WHEW!
LET'S SEE NOW ...
DID I READ SOMETHING ABOUT A POSTAL STRIKE?
18-12 WED 6873

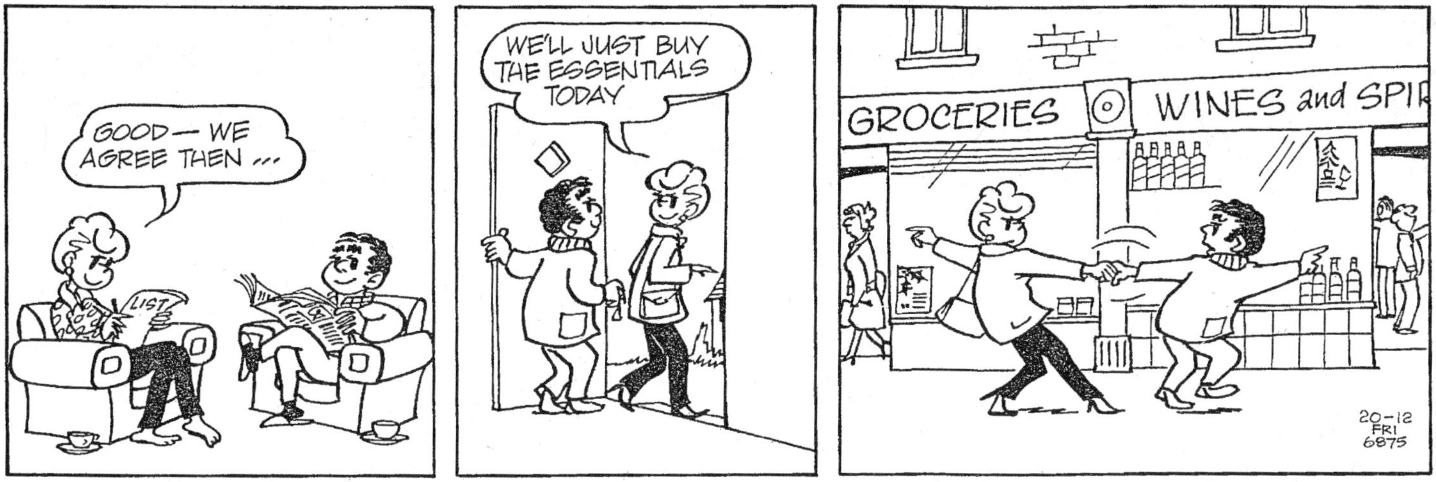
GOOD— WE AGREE THEN ...
LIST
WE'LL JUST BUY THE ESSENTIALS TODAY
GROCERIES
WINES and SPIR
20-12 FRI 6875

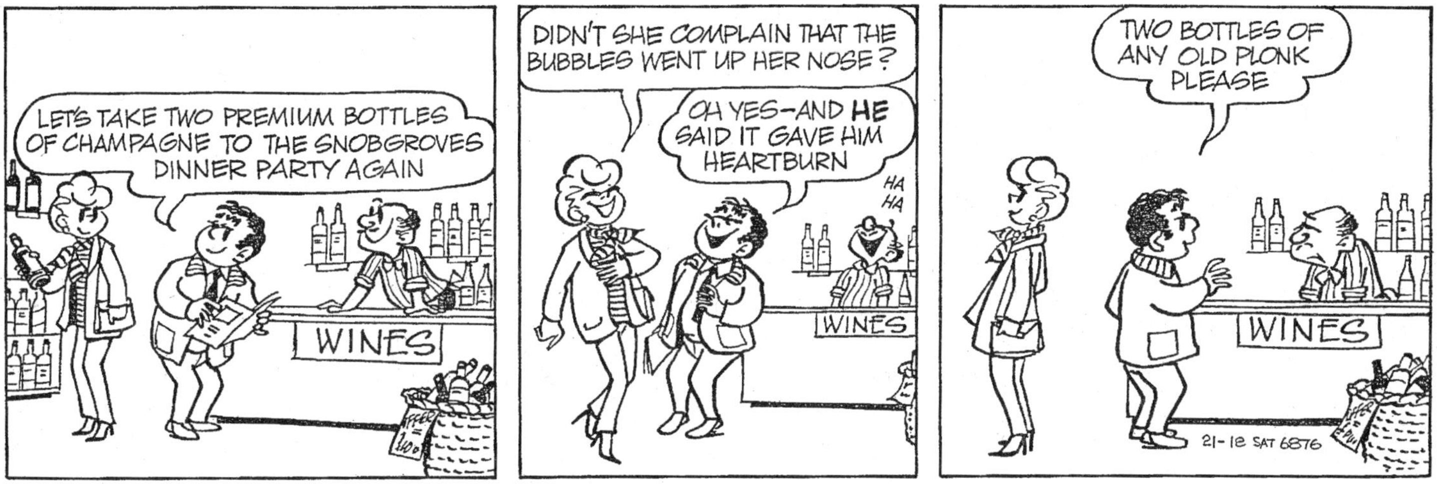
LET'S TAKE TWO PREMIUM BOTTLES OF CHAMPAGNE TO THE SNOBGROVES DINNER PARTY AGAIN
WINES
DIDN'T SHE COMPLAIN THAT THE BUBBLES WENT UP HER NOSE?
OH YES—AND **HE** SAID IT GAVE HIM HEARTBURN
HA HA
WINES
TWO BOTTLES OF ANY OLD PLONK PLEASE
WINES
21-12 SAT 6876

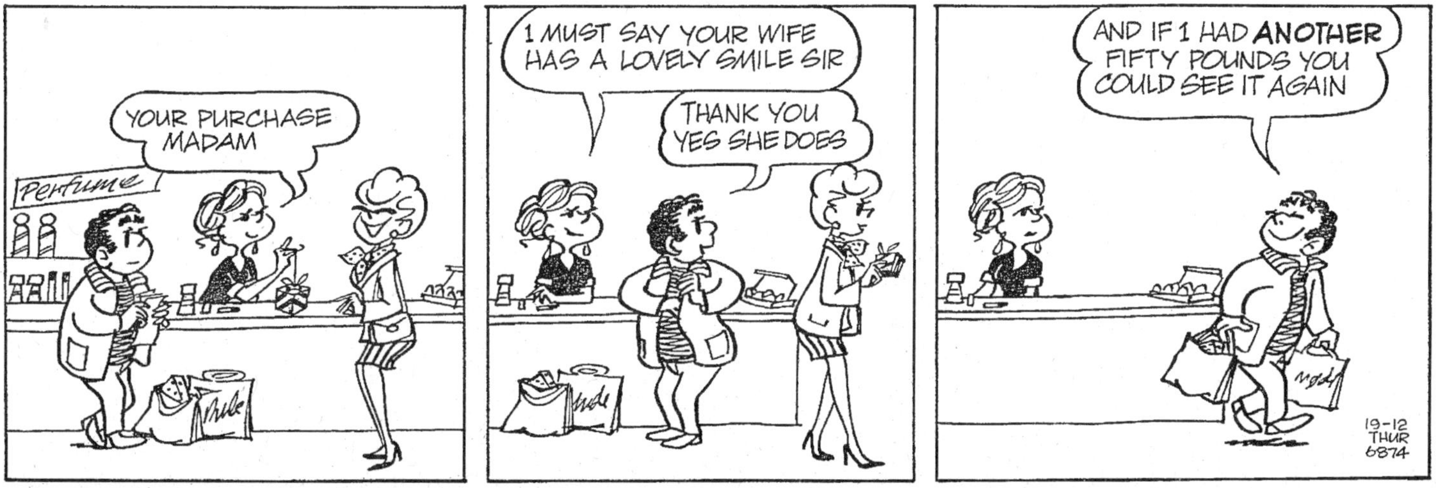
YOUR PURCHASE MADAM
Perfume
I MUST SAY YOUR WIFE HAS A LOVELY SMILE SIR
THANK YOU YES SHE DOES
AND IF I HAD **ANOTHER** FIFTY POUNDS YOU COULD SEE IT AGAIN
19-12 THUR 6874

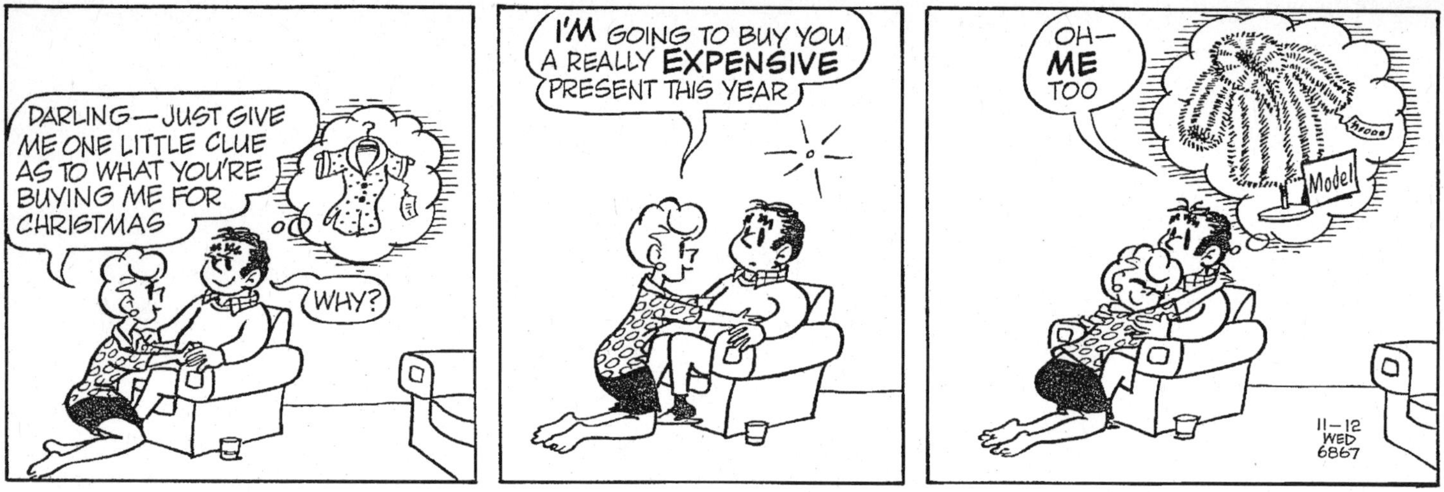
DARLING— JUST GIVE ME ONE LITTLE CLUE AS TO WHAT YOU'RE BUYING ME FOR CHRISTMAS
WHY?
I'M GOING TO BUY YOU A REALLY EXPENSIVE PRESENT THIS YEAR
OH— ME TOO
Model
11—12 WED 6867

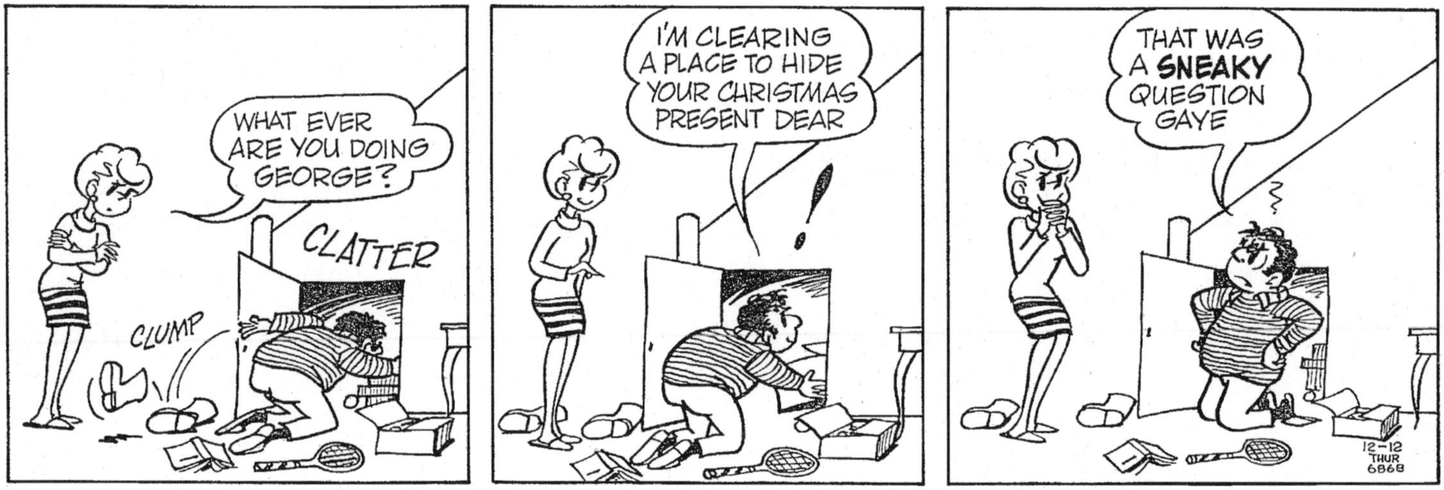
WHAT EVER ARE YOU DOING GEORGE?
CLATTER
CLUMP
I'M CLEARING A PLACE TO HIDE YOUR CHRISTMAS PRESENT DEAR
THAT WAS A SNEAKY QUESTION GAYE
12—12 THUR 6868

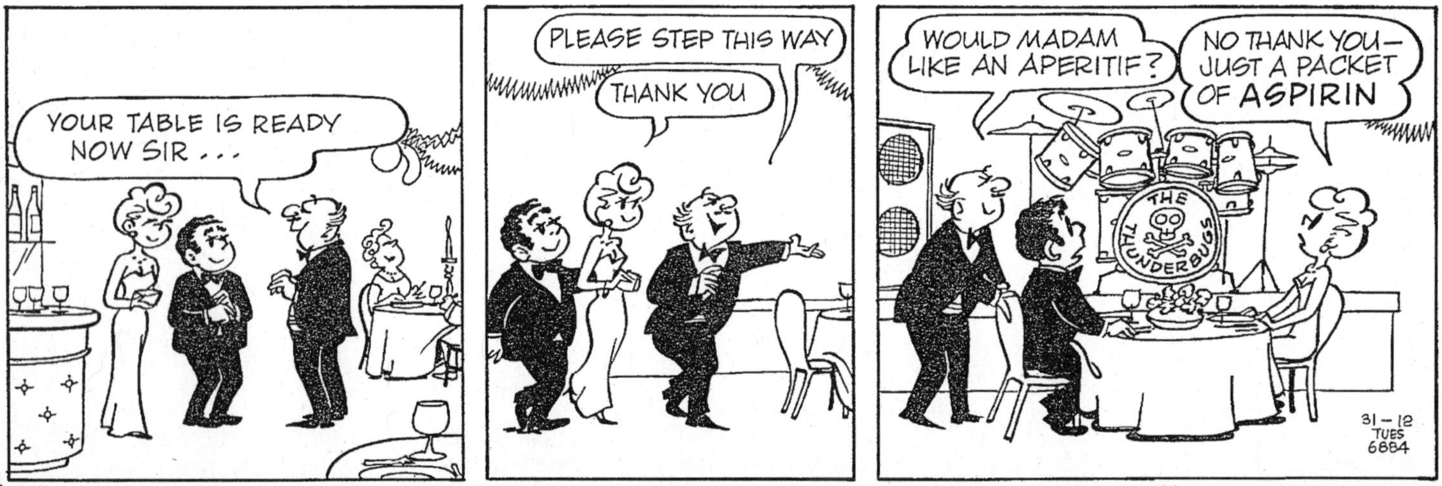
YOUR TABLE IS READY NOW SIR . . .
PLEASE STEP THIS WAY
THANK YOU
WOULD MADAM LIKE AN APERITIF?
NO THANK YOU— JUST A PACKET OF ASPIRIN
THE THUNDERBUGS
31—12 TUES 6884

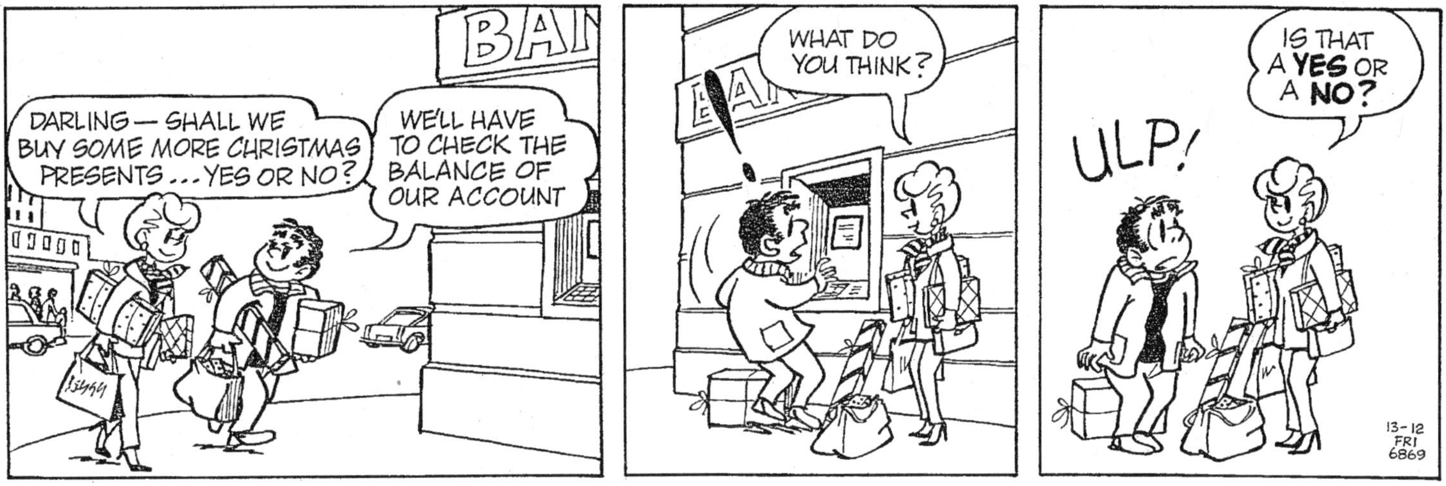
BAN
DARLING — SHALL WE BUY SOME MORE CHRISTMAS PRESENTS ... YES OR NO?
WE'LL HAVE TO CHECK THE BALANCE OF OUR ACCOUNT
WHAT DO YOU THINK?
!
ULP!
IS THAT A **YES** OR A **NO**?
13-12 FRI 6869

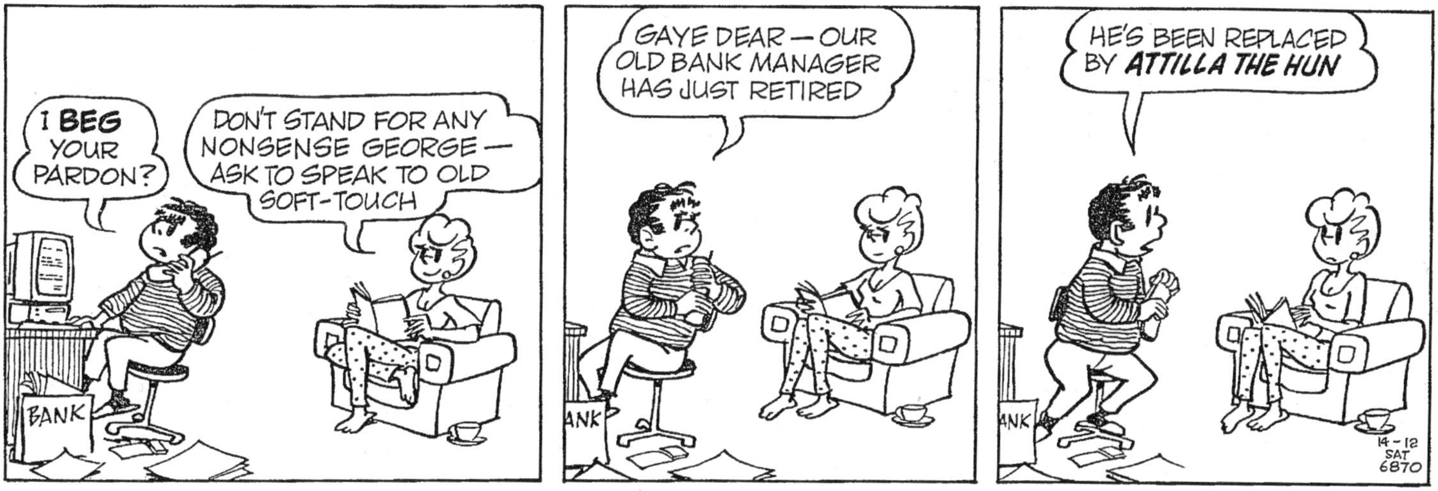
I **BEG** YOUR PARDON?
DON'T STAND FOR ANY NONSENSE GEORGE — ASK TO SPEAK TO OLD SOFT-TOUCH
BANK
GAYE DEAR — OUR OLD BANK MANAGER HAS JUST RETIRED
HE'S BEEN REPLACED BY ***ATTILLA THE HUN***
14-12 SAT 6870

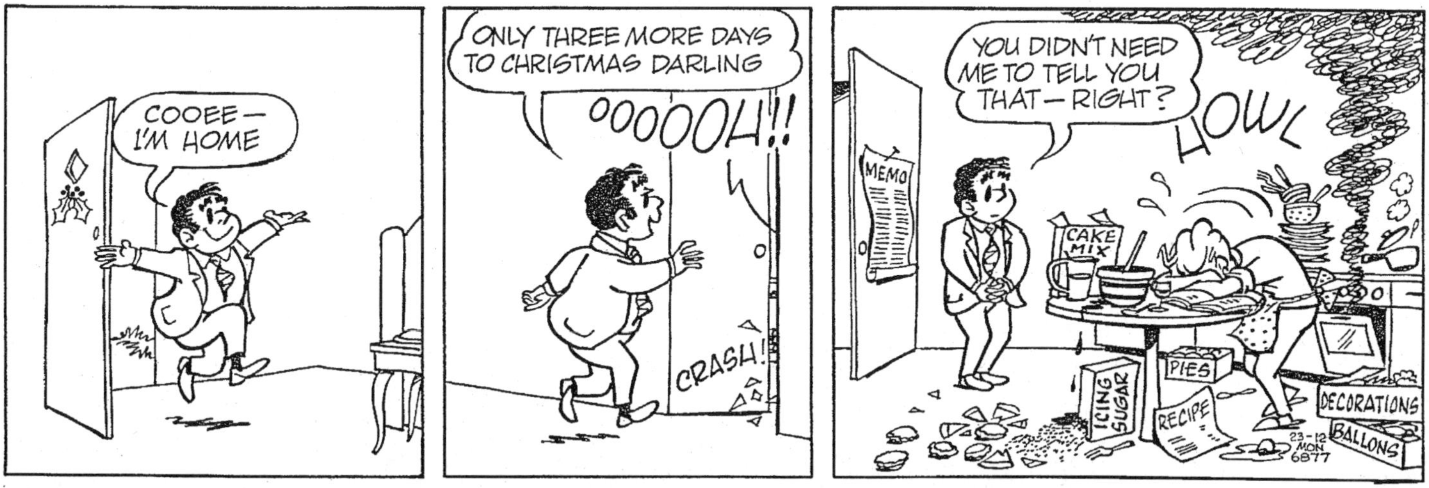
COOEE — I'M HOME
ONLY THREE MORE DAYS TO CHRISTMAS DARLING
OOOOOH!!
CRASH!
YOU DIDN'T NEED ME TO TELL YOU THAT — RIGHT?
HOWL
MEMO
CAKE MIX
PIES
ICING SUGAR
RECIPE
DECORATIONS
BALLONS
23-12 MON 6877

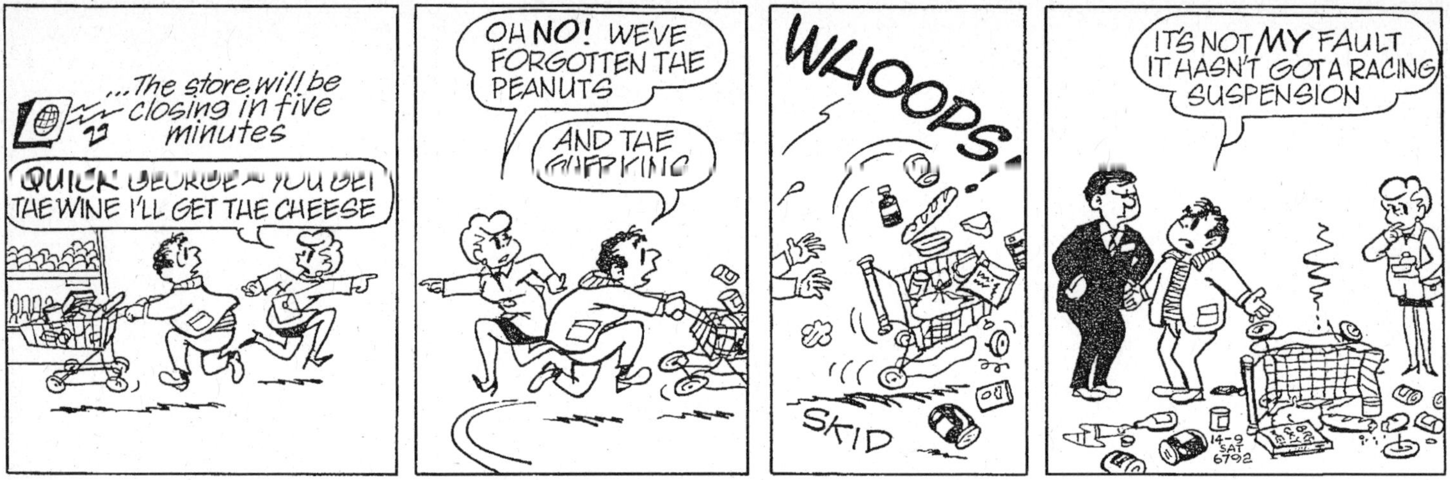
...The store will be closing in five minutes
QUICK GEORGE — YOU GET THE WINE I'LL GET THE CHEESE
OH NO! WE'VE FORGOTTEN THE PEANUTS
AND THE GHERKINS
WHOOPS!
SKID
IT'S NOT MY FAULT IT HASN'T GOT A RACING SUSPENSION
14-9 SAT 6792

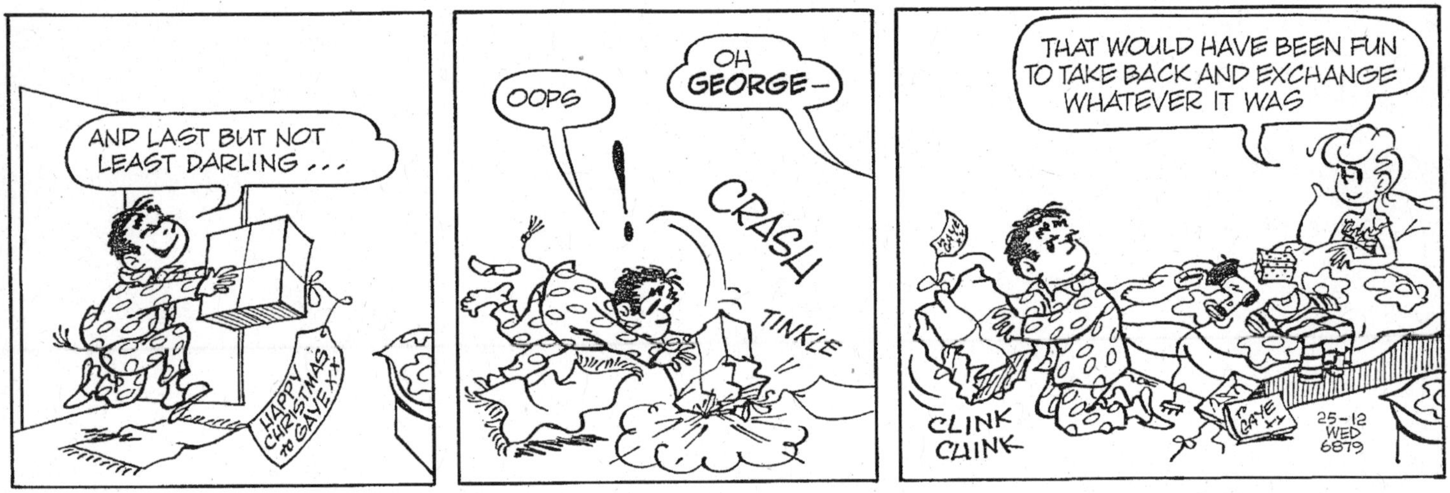
AND LAST BUT NOT LEAST DARLING ...
HAPPY CHRISTMAS to GAYE XX
OOPS
!
OH GEORGE —
CRASH
TINKLE
THAT WOULD HAVE BEEN FUN TO TAKE BACK AND EXCHANGE WHATEVER IT WAS
CLINK CLINK
25-12 WED 6879

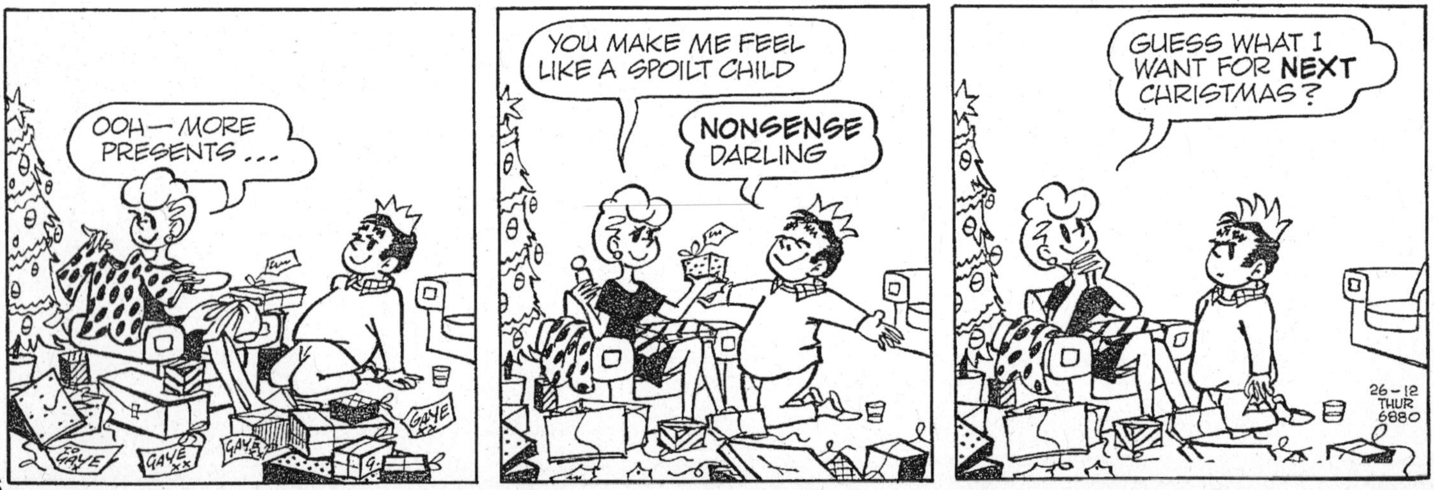
OOH — MORE PRESENTS ...
YOU MAKE ME FEEL LIKE A SPOILT CHILD
NONSENSE DARLING
GUESS WHAT I WANT FOR NEXT CHRISTMAS?
26-12 THUR 6880

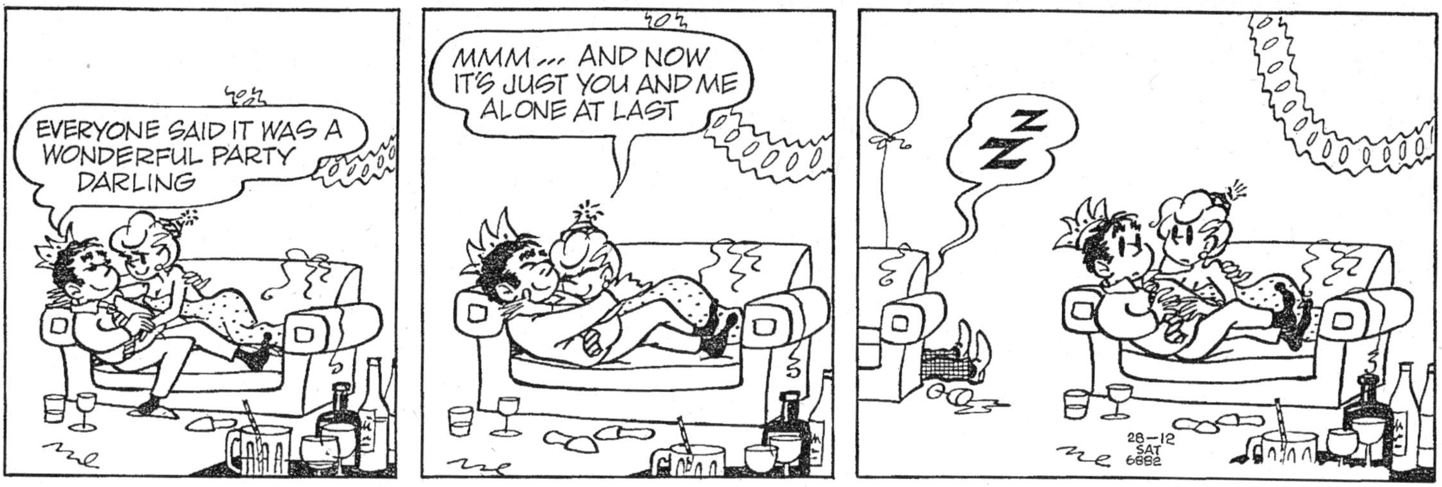
EVERYONE SAID IT WAS A WONDERFUL PARTY DARLING
MMM ... AND NOW IT'S JUST YOU AND ME ALONE AT LAST
Z Z
28—12 SAT 6882

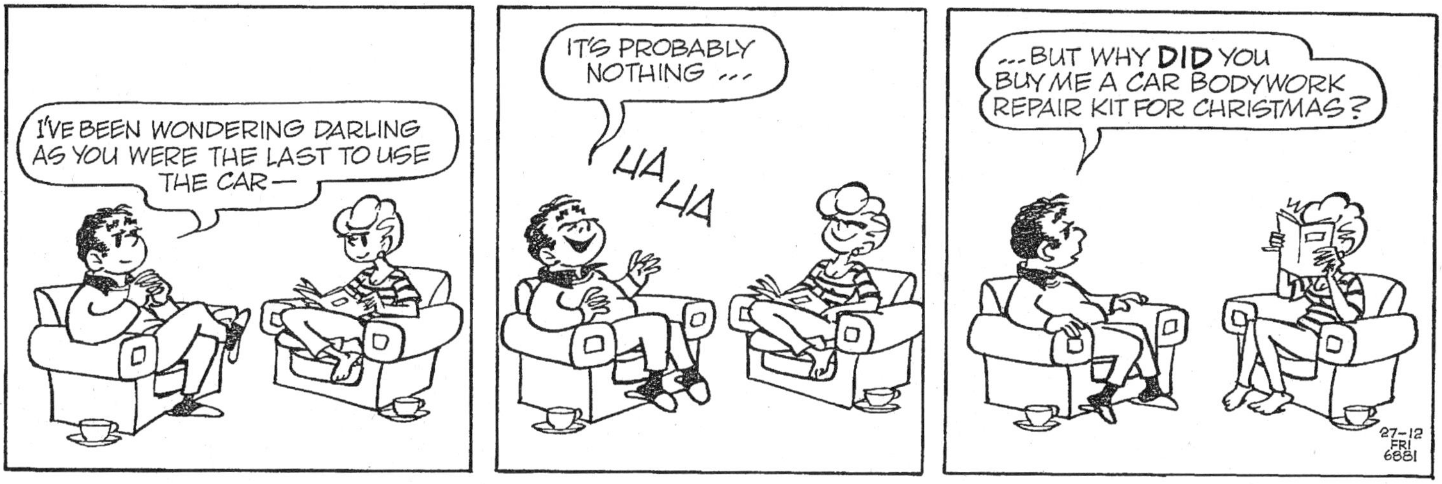
I'VE BEEN WONDERING DARLING AS YOU WERE THE LAST TO USE THE CAR—
IT'S PROBABLY NOTHING ...
HA HA
...BUT WHY **DID** YOU BUY ME A CAR BODYWORK REPAIR KIT FOR CHRISTMAS?
27—12 FRI 6881

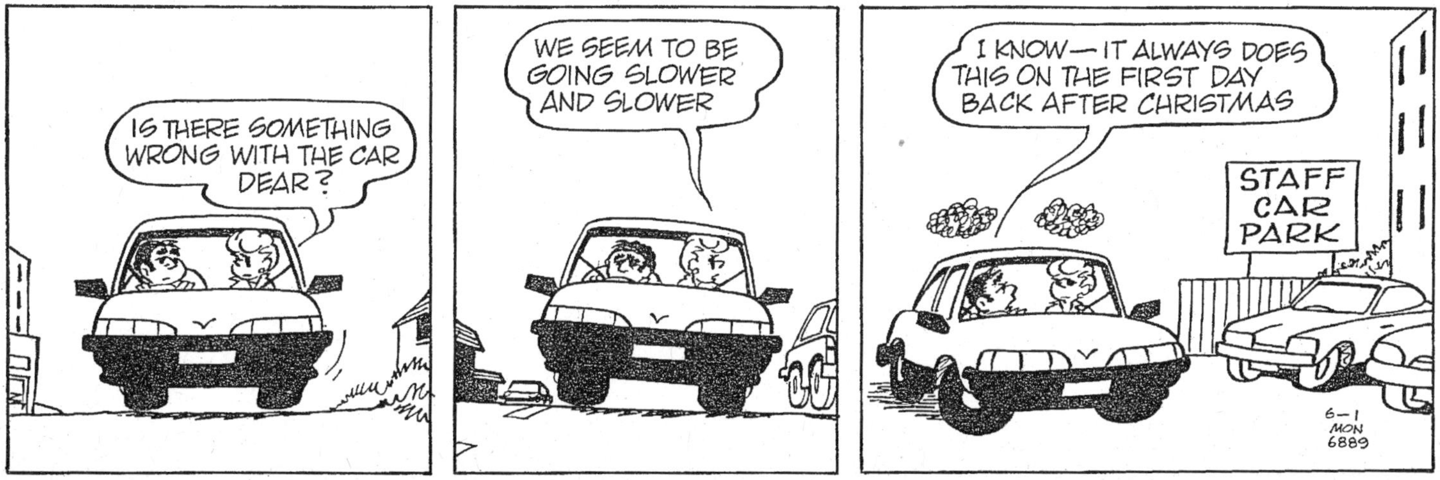
IS THERE SOMETHING WRONG WITH THE CAR DEAR?
WE SEEM TO BE GOING SLOWER AND SLOWER
I KNOW— IT ALWAYS DOES THIS ON THE FIRST DAY BACK AFTER CHRISTMAS
STAFF CAR PARK
6—1 MON 6889

GEORGE SAYS HE CAN NEVER
REMEMBER — AS A CHILD — SNOW
TRICKLING UNCOMFORTABLY DOWN
THE BACK OF HIS NECK

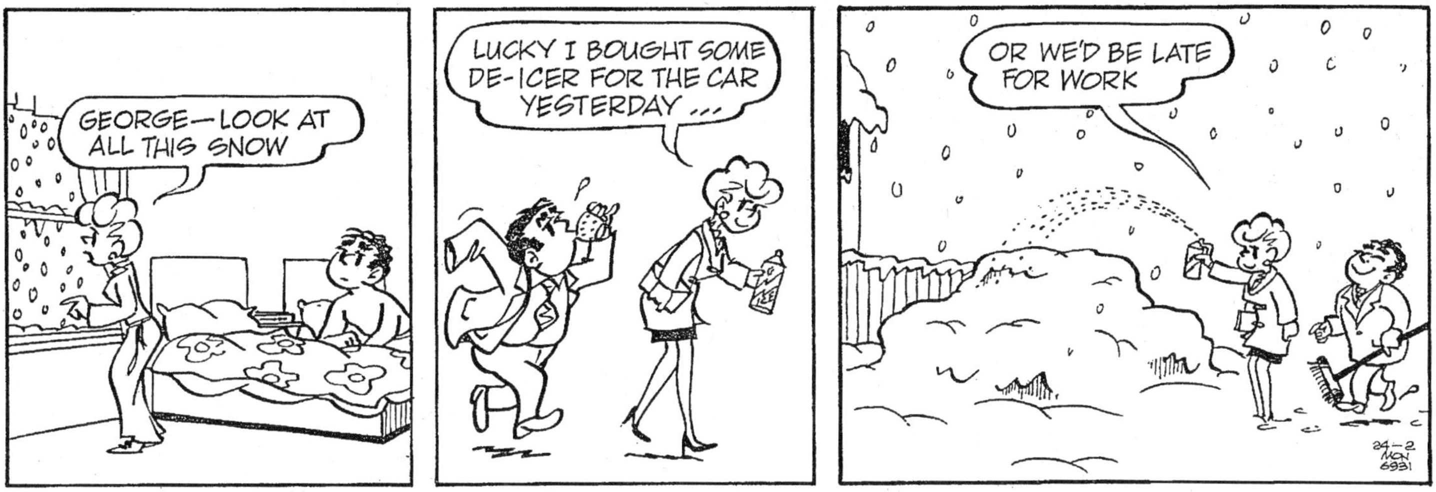
GEORGE—LOOK AT ALL THIS SNOW
LUCKY I BOUGHT SOME DE-ICER FOR THE CAR YESTERDAY ...
OR WE'D BE LATE FOR WORK
24-2 MON 6931

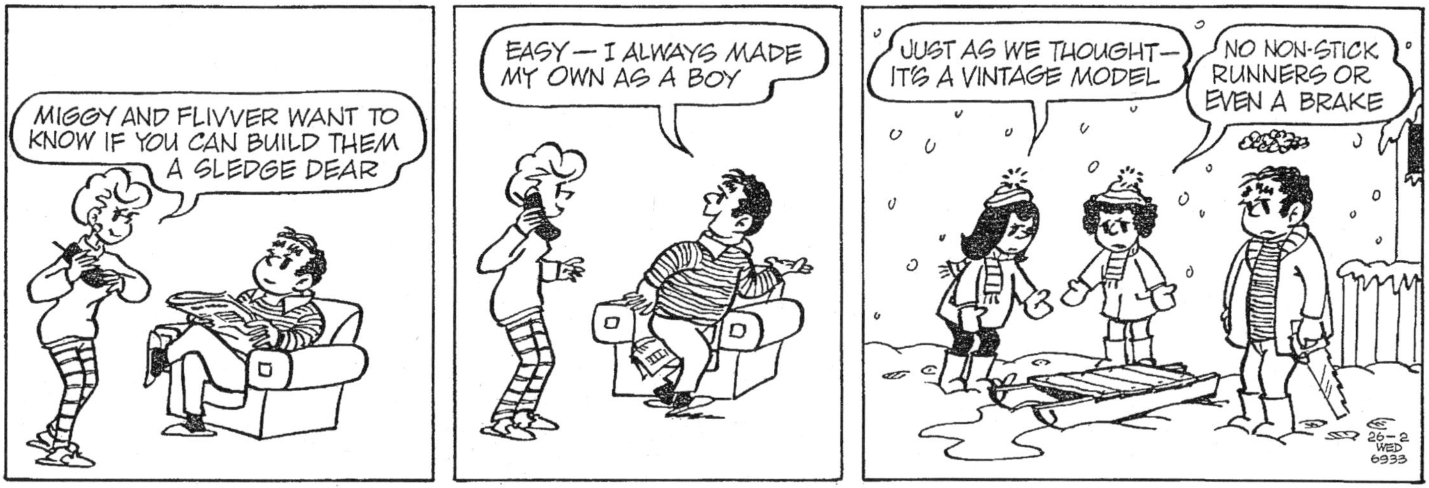
MIGGY AND FLIVVER WANT TO KNOW IF YOU CAN BUILD THEM A SLEDGE DEAR
EASY—I ALWAYS MADE MY OWN AS A BOY
JUST AS WE THOUGHT—IT'S A VINTAGE MODEL
NO NON-STICK RUNNERS OR EVEN A BRAKE
26-2 WED 6933

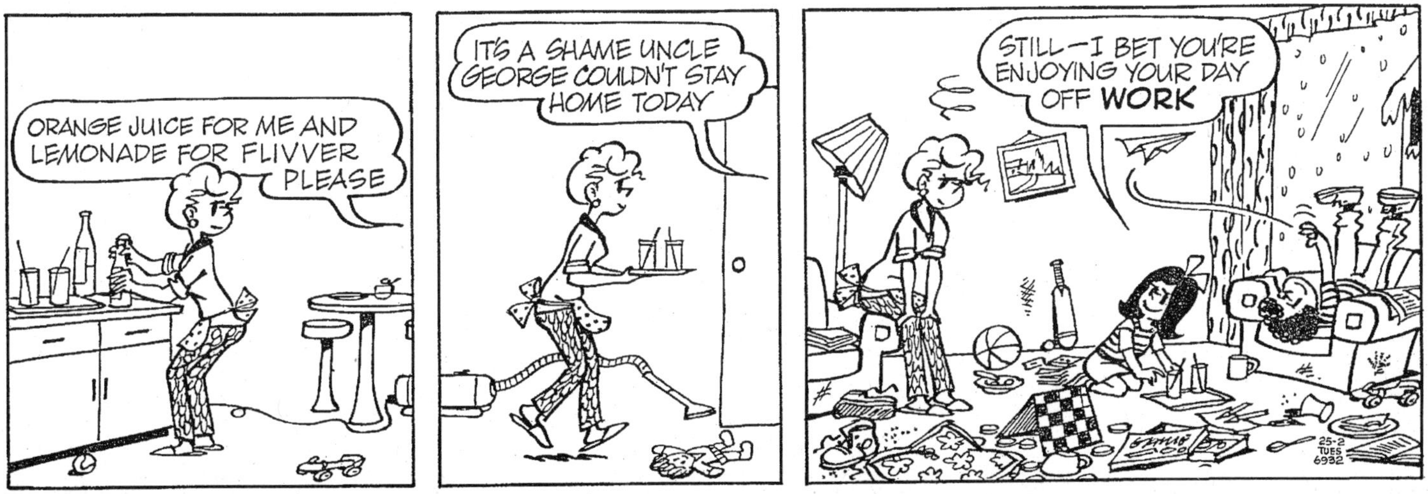
ORANGE JUICE FOR ME AND LEMONADE FOR FLIVVER PLEASE
IT'S A SHAME UNCLE GEORGE COULDN'T STAY HOME TODAY
STILL—I BET YOU'RE ENJOYING YOUR DAY OFF **WORK**
25-2 TUES 6932

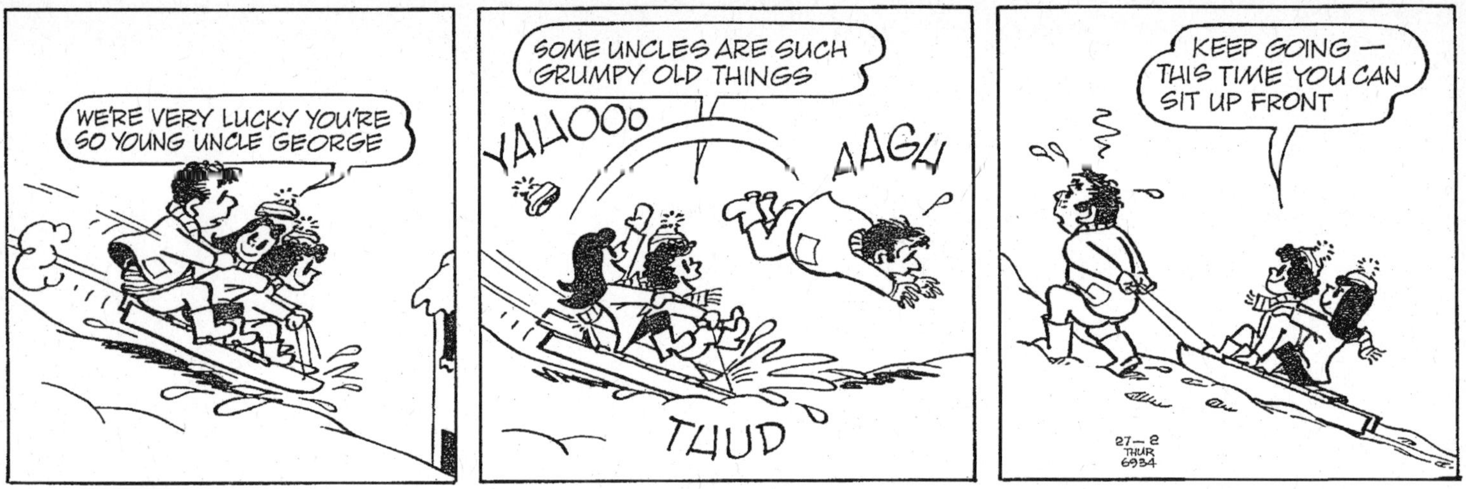
WE'RE VERY LUCKY YOU'RE SO YOUNG UNCLE GEORGE
SOME UNCLES ARE SUCH GRUMPY OLD THINGS
YAHOOO
AAGH
THUD
KEEP GOING — THIS TIME YOU CAN SIT UP FRONT
27—2 THUR 6934

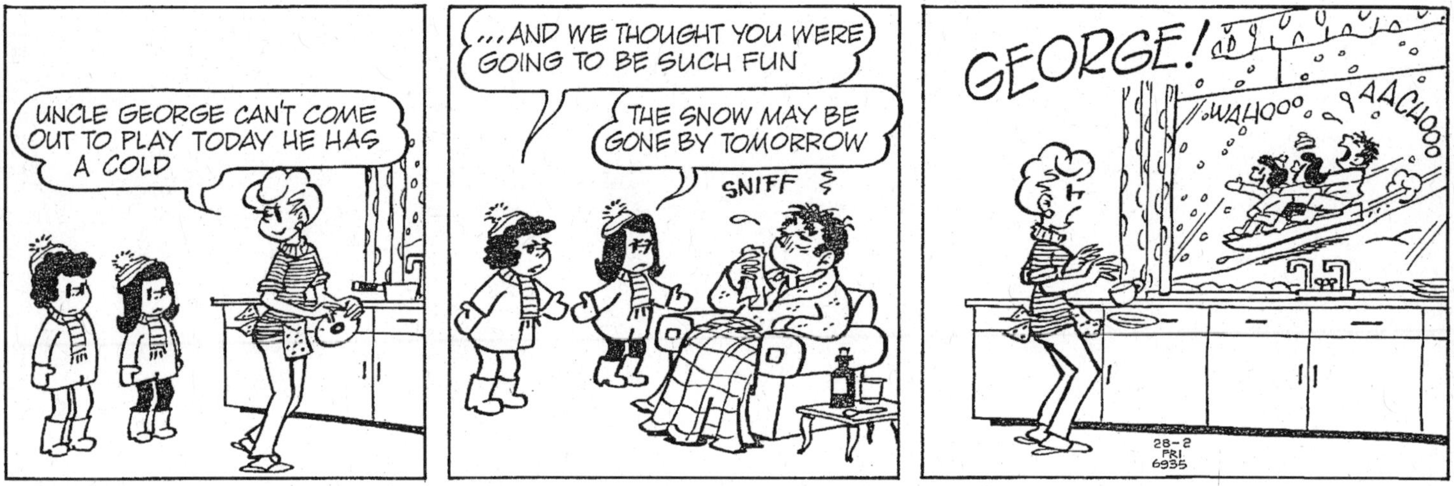
UNCLE GEORGE CAN'T COME OUT TO PLAY TODAY HE HAS A COLD
...AND WE THOUGHT YOU WERE GOING TO BE SUCH FUN
THE SNOW MAY BE GONE BY TOMORROW
SNIFF
GEORGE!
WAHOOO
AACHOOO
28-2 FRI 6935

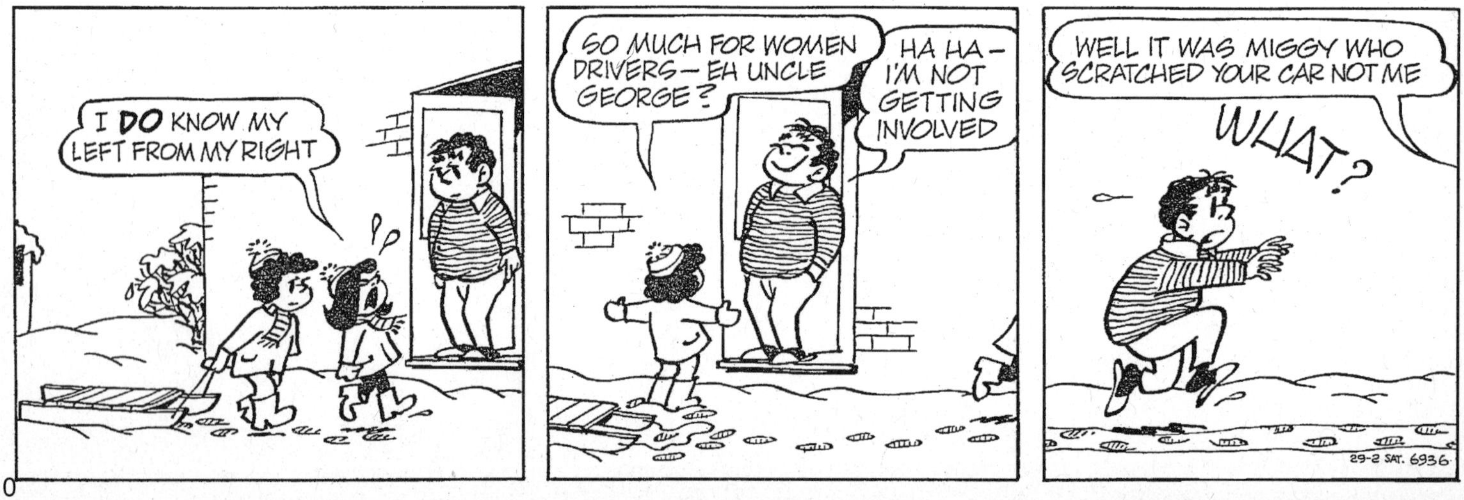
I DO KNOW MY LEFT FROM MY RIGHT
SO MUCH FOR WOMEN DRIVERS— EH UNCLE GEORGE?
HA HA— I'M NOT GETTING INVOLVED
WELL IT WAS MIGGY WHO SCRATCHED YOUR CAR NOT ME
WHAT?
29-2 SAT. 6936

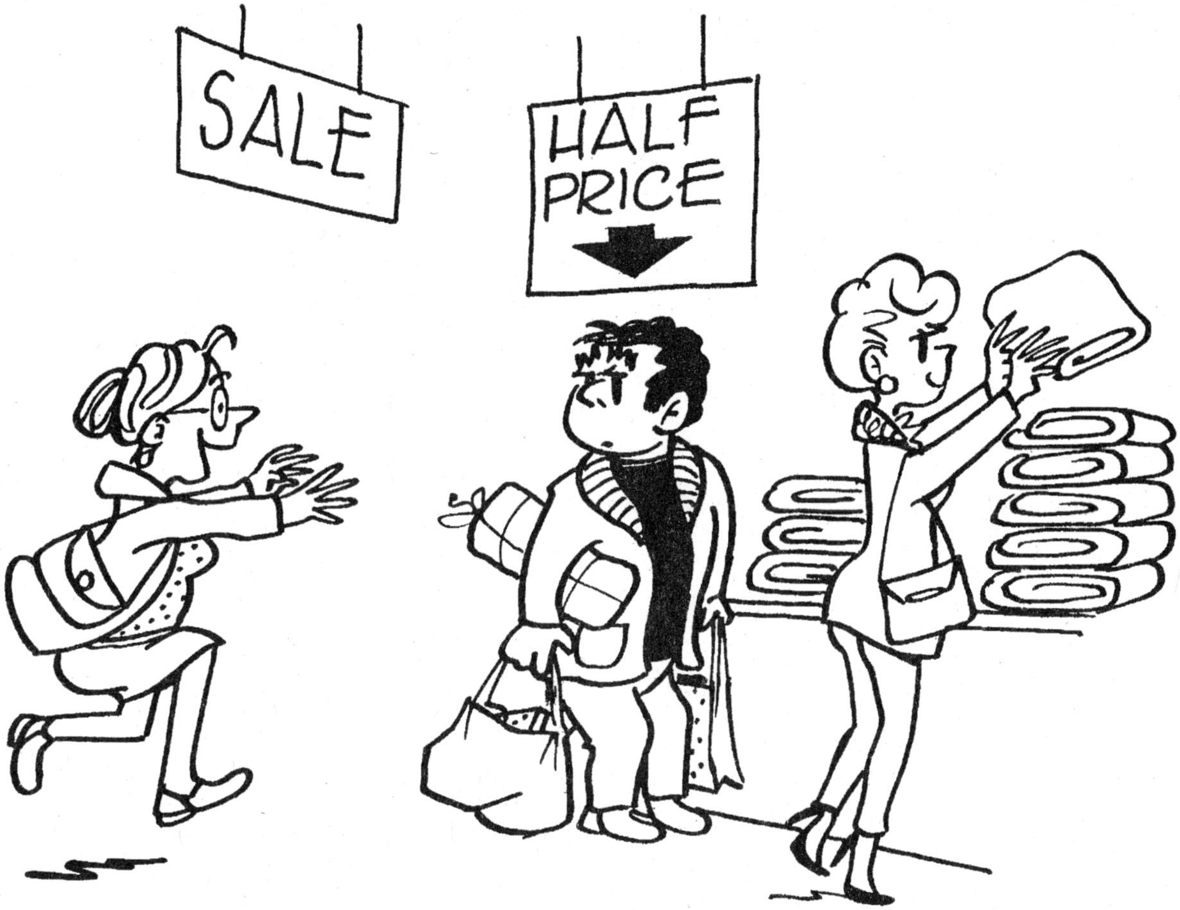
SALE
HALF PRICE

LIKE MANY WOMEN — BARGAIN HUNTING IS ONE OF GAYE'S FAVOURITE PASTIMES

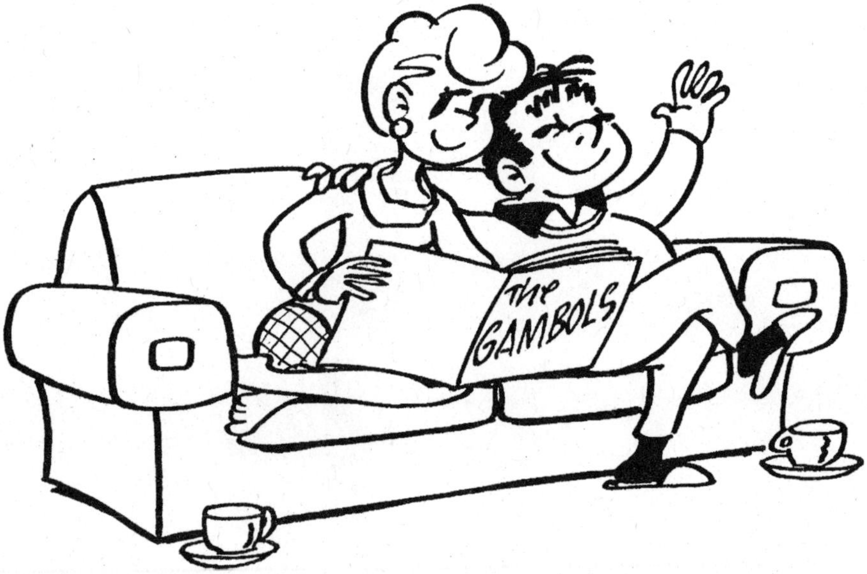
The
GAMBOLS

AND SO WE COME TO THE LAST PAGE OF
OUR UNIQUE GAMBOLS ANNUAL No. 46 —
WE'RE LOOKING FORWARD TO SEEING YOU
AGAIN TOMORROW MORNING IN THE EXPRESS
WHERE YOU CAN FOLLOW THE GAMBOLS
EVERY DAY — TILL THEN KEEP SMILING!